ARISTOTLE'S *Art of Rhetoric*

ARISTOTLE'S
Art of Rhetoric

◉◉◉◉◉◉◉◉◉◉◉◉◉◉◉◉◉◉◉◉◉◉◉◉◉◉

TRANSLATED AND WITH
AN INTERPRETIVE ESSAY
BY ROBERT C. BARTLETT

◉◉◉◉◉◉◉◉◉◉◉◉◉

The University of Chicago Press
CHICAGO AND LONDON

The University of Chicago Press, Chicago 60637
The University of Chicago Press, Ltd., London
© 2019 by The University of Chicago
Published 2019
Paperback edition 2021
Printed in the United States of America

30 29 28 27 26 25 24 23   2 3 4 5

ISBN-13: 978-0-226-59162-9 (cloth)
ISBN-13: 978-0-226-78990-3 (paper)
ISBN-13: 978-0-226-59176-6 (e-book)
DOI: https://doi.org/10.7208/chicago
/9780226591766.001.0001

Library of Congress Cataloging-in-Publication Data

Names: Aristotle, author. | Bartlett, Robert C.,
    1964– translator, writer of added commentary.
Title: Aristotle's art of rhetoric / translated and with
    an interpretive essay by Robert C. Bartlett.
Other titles: Rhetoric. English (Bartlett) | Art of
    rhetoric
Description: Chicago : The University of Chicago
    Press, 2018. | Includes bibliographical references
    and index.
Identifiers: LCCN 2018025296 |
    ISBN 9780226591629 (cloth : alk. paper) |
    ISBN 9780226591766 (e-book)
Subjects: LCSH: Rhetoric—Early works to 1800. |
    Philosophy, Ancient—Early Works to 1800.
Classification: LCC PA3893 .R313 2018 | DDC 808.5—
    dc23
LC record available at https://lccn.loc.gov/2018
    025296

⊚ This paper meets the requirements of ANSI/NISO
Z39.48-1992 (Permanence of Paper).

CONTENTS

PREFACE

The chief purpose of the present volume is to encourage serious study of the art of rhetoric, by way of a return to its origins in Aristotle. The political importance of rhetoric is clear enough: for republican government to function, citizens must be able to stand before their fellows, express themselves clearly, and persuade a sufficient number of them that this policy, that treaty, these laws, should be approved or condemned. Hence the histories of the great republics supply us with impressive examples of political rhetoric—Thucydides' *War of the Peloponnesians and Athenians* above all—just as do the leading republican or democratic statesmen, Pericles, Cicero, Abraham Lincoln, and Winston Churchill among them.

The fate of rhetoric in our time is uncertain. After a long period of seeming neglect or indifference, rhetoric has in recent decades begun to attract attention once again. To track this rise, fall, and revival of rhetoric in any detail would be a great undertaking. Perhaps it will suffice to sketch some of the principal developments. To begin at the very beginning, the art of rhetoric seems to have been born in Greek antiquity.[1] And in the leading philosophical circles there, rhetoric was thought to be a necessary supplement to public life because the truth is of limited political use, every community being a Cave that will remain more or less untouched by the sun's light. It would always fall to persuasive rhetoric, then, to bridge the chasm between impotent truth and potent opinion, wherever brute force did not simply dictate the field. The relatively high status of rhetoric as a subject of study endured, with some inevitable peaks and valleys, in the long period stretching from Greek and Roman antiquity—Isocrates

---

1 · Cicero (*De oratore* 1.20.91 and *Brutus* 46) traces the origin of the art of rhetoric to Corax and Tisias of Syracuse.

and Aristotle, Cicero and Quintilian—through the Middle Ages. As one-third of the "trivium," rhetoric was regarded as a necessary part of a sound liberal education, together with grammar and logic (or dialectic). This high status of rhetoric began to falter with the advent of the modern Enlightenment, when rhetoric came to be regarded, or at any rate presented, as an unnecessary "nuisance" and even a danger.[2] For in the bright light cast by scientific reason, invigorated by its novel method, mere persuasion came to be viewed as the relic of a benighted age.

Crucial to the demotion of rhetoric, and of Aristotelian rhetoric especially, was the assault on the early modern university led most notably by Thomas Hobbes.[3] The university was at its core Scholastic, and Hobbes's attack on it took aim at both elements of Scholasticism—Christianity, of course, but Aristotle too: "And since the authority of Aristotle is only current there [in the university], that study is not properly philosophy... but Aristotelity." "And I believe that scarce anything can be more absurdly said in natural philosophy than that which now is called *Aristotle's Metaphysics*; nor more repugnant to government than much of that he hath said in his *Politics*; nor more ignorantly than a great part of his *Ethics*."[4]

It is true that Hobbes omits from this list of bad books Aristotle's *Rhetoric*,[5] which Hobbes had studied carefully and fruitfully: his account of the passions, central to his political philosophy, is to a considerable de-

---

2 · "What can that large number of debaters contribute to policy with their inept views but a nuisance?" Thomas Hobbes, *De Cive* 10.10. Consider also: "And though they [orators] reason, yet take they not their rise from true principles, but from vulgar received opinions, which for the most part are erroneous. Neither endeavor they so much to fit their speech to the nature of the things they speak of, as to the passions of their minds to whom they speak; when it happens, that opinions are delivered not by right reason, but by a certain violence of mind. Nor is this the fault in the *man*, but in the nature of *eloquence*, whose end, as all the masters of rhetoric teach us, is not truth (except by chance), but victory; and whose property is not to inform, but to allure." *De Cive* 10.11 (emphasis original); consider also Hobbes's contrast between logic and rhetoric at 12.12.

3 · A classic account of the history of rhetoric is George Kennedy, *A New History of Classical Rhetoric* (Princeton: Princeton University Press, 1994), which covers the period before 400 BCE through to Boethius, i.e., the early sixth century CE. Consider also James A. Herrick, *The History and Theory of Rhetoric: An Introduction*, 5th ed. (New York: Routledge, 2013). See also Paul D. Brandes, *A History of Aristotle's "Rhetoric": With a Bibliography of Early Printings* (Metuchen, NJ: Scarecrow Press, 1989).

4 · Thomas Hobbes, *Leviathan* 46.13 and 46.11.

5 · According to John Aubrey, Hobbes judged Aristotle to be "the worst teacher that ever was, the worst polititian and ethick"—with the important qualification that "his

gree indebted to Aristotle's own account in the *Rhetoric*.[6] As the printer of the 1681 edition of Hobbes's *Works* put it, in a preface to Hobbes's painstaking translation or paraphrase of the *Rhetoric* (*A Briefe of the Art of Rhetorique*, 1637), "Mr. Hobbes chose to recommend by his translation the rhetoric of Aristotle, as being the most accomplished work on that subject which the world has yet seen; having been admired in all ages, and in particular highly approved by the father of the Roman eloquence [i.e., Cicero], a very competent judge."[7] Nevertheless, Hobbes declined the opportunity to praise Aristotle's *Art of Rhetoric*, in part because he came to see the need to attack the rhetoric he had inherited. That the very attack on classical rhetoric was not without its own rhetoric does not undo the fact of the attack.[8] With the discovery of an altogether new "moral science" or of a political science finally deserving of that name, it seemed that the need for the troublesome rhetoric of old would eventually fade away, together with the "repugnant" and "ignorant" political philosophy that accompanied it. Not only the foundation of all government, but also the regular conduct of it, would for the first time in human history be guided by the light of reason ("public reason"). A new understanding of popular sovereignty and the consultation of the law or laws of nature, for example, would help dislodge antique rhetoric, which too often gave power to the eloquent as distinguished from the prudent or just—what

---

rhetorique and discourse of animals was rare." John Aubrey, *Brief Lives*, ed. Andrew Clark (Oxford: Clarendon Press, 1898), 1:357.

6 · "It would be difficult to find another classical work whose importance for Hobbes's political philosophy can be compared with that of the *Rhetoric*. The central chapters of Hobbes's anthropology . . . betray in style and contents that their author was a zealous reader, not to say disciple of the *Rhetoric*." Leo Strauss, *The Political Philosophy of Hobbes: Its Basis and Genesis* (Chicago: University of Chicago Press, 1952 [originally published 1936]), 35.

7 · "Preface," in *English Works of Thomas Hobbes*, ed. William Molesworth (London: John Bohn, 1840), 6:422. See also John T. Harwood, ed., *The Rhetorics of Thomas Hobbes and Bernard Lamy* (Carbondale: Southern Illinois University Press, 1986).

8 · On Hobbes's attack on rhetoric, which (to repeat) included the use of a rhetoric all his own, consider Bryan Garsten's indispensable account in *Saving Persuasion: A Defense of Rhetoric and Judgment* (Cambridge, MA: Harvard University Press, 2006), chap. 1; see also David Johnston, *The Rhetoric of "Leviathan": Thomas Hobbes and the Politics of Cultural Transformation* (Princeton: Princeton University Press, 1986); Quentin Skinner, *Reason and Rhetoric in the Philosophy of Hobbes* (Cambridge: Cambridge University Press, 1996); and Ioannis Evrigenis, *Images of Anarchy: The Rhetoric and Science in Hobbes's State of Nature* (Cambridge: Cambridge University Press, 2014).

Hobbes decried as the "aristocracy of orators."[9] If many of the political speeches that survive from the eighteenth and nineteenth centuries dazzle us with their elaborate eloquence and erudition, especially as compared to the utterances, actual or electronic, of our politicians today, it nonetheless seems true that the art of rhetoric fell into some disfavor and desuetude as the Enlightenment advanced.[10]

Only when doubts about the "modern project" began to be widely felt, only when the hopes attending the Enlightenment came at length to be seen as naive or fantastic, did the art of rhetoric begin its return to the scene, in the academy if not in the public square. The postmodern era, in other words, has witnessed the return of rhetoric, not as the necessary supplement to reason, but as its necessary substitute. Stale or moribund programs in rhetoric began to buzz anew. According to Stanley Fish, "deconstructive or poststructuralist thought" is "supremely rhetorical" because it "systematically asserts and demonstrates the mediated, constructed, partial, socially constituted nature of all realities, be they phenomenal, linguistic, or psychological."[11] When there is no text, only interpretation, when there is no objective truth to strive to find, all becomes the hegemony of this or that "discourse," which can be distinguished by its persuasive power but not by its access to the truth. And rhetoric became the academic study of those "discourses." The new interest in rhetoric, then, is just the flip side of the demise of reason in some quarters of the academy. Consider in this regard the prevalence, even in ordinary conversation, of "narrative": every important political event, for example, will be greeted by "competing narratives," that is, explanations, all of which may wish to be regarded as true but which do not seriously regard themselves as true.

This alliance between rhetoric and extreme relativism had an analogue in antiquity. If sophistry and rhetoric are, strictly speaking, separate things, they were with good reason often paired.[12] For sophists were

9 · Thomas Hobbes, *The Elements of Law, Natural and Politic*, ed. Ferdinand Tönnies (London: Frank Cass, 1969) 2.2.

10 · For an analysis of the decline of rhetoric in the modern period, see again Garsten, *Saving Persuasion*.

11 · Stanley Fish, "Rhetoric," in *Rhetoric in an Antifoundational World: Language, Culture, Pedagogy*, ed. Michael Bernard-Donals and Richard R. Glejzer (New Haven: Yale University Press, 1998), 53.

12 · For a statement of both the separation and the pairing, consider Plato, *Gorgias* 465c and context.

admired or condemned for their ability to speak "wisely" or "cleverly," that is, with the skill of a consummate rhetorician. If not all rhetoricians were sophists (consider Plato, *Meno* 95b9–c4), then all sophists could nonetheless be assumed to be rhetoricians. At any rate, the greatest of the ancient sophists, Protagoras, prided himself on the brilliance of his speech, with its ready access to revamped myths, poetry made to serve his own ends, and other "cloaks" or "protective measures"—including in his case a ballyhooed frankness (Plato, *Protagoras* 317b3–c1; 316d6). All of these devices together revealed a remarkable dexterity in speech even as they concealed enough for safety's sake. According to Aristotle, Protagoras went so far as to profess that he could "make the weaker argument the stronger," which amounts to saying that he claimed he could, through clever speech, make the unjust cause triumph over the just. Aristotle adds: "Hence human beings were justly disgusted by what Protagoras professed" (*Art of Rhetoric* 1402a22–27).

It is hardly a surprise, then, that rhetoric had its critics from early on, the most impressive of them being Plato's Socrates. In the *Gorgias*, Plato has Socrates issue a stinging rebuke of rhetoric. There he denies that it is an art at all, a body of knowledge (*technē*), but calls it instead a "knack," born of trial-and-error experience, whose chief purpose is to persuade by way of flattery as distinguished from teaching. Yet this tough criticism must be balanced against the following facts: Socrates was himself a master rhetorician, capable of doing what he liked with all his interlocutors;[13] in the very dialogue in which he excoriates rhetoric, or a kind of rhetoric, he is shown to be eagerly seeking out the company of Gorgias, the most famous teacher of rhetoric, in order to learn from him the "power" of the man's art (*Gorgias* 447c1–2); and Plato's own astonishing powers of persuasion helped transform the reputation of Socrates and therewith of philosophy over the millennia. But above all, it was Plato's Socrates who taught the inadmissibility of the sun's light into the Cave and hence the permanent ground of the need for rhetoric (consider in this regard Plato, *Republic* 498c9–d1 as well as 450a5–6).

Still, Plato or his Socrates was willing to let stand the more visible criticism of rhetoric, which amounts to the charge that the very great power exercised by rhetoric over human beings is too easily separable from decent ends, be they political or philosophic. In this way Plato staked out a middle ground between the sophist's eager embrace of rhetoric, on the

13 · Consider Xenophon, *Memorabilia* 1.2.14.

one hand, and a too simple rejection of rhetoric, on the other. If today
we observe, in the contemporary heirs of Protagoras, a keen interest in a
rhetoric that is shorn of the serious concern for truth or that is dogmati-
cally convinced of the "socially constituted nature of all realities," where
is to be found a sounder rhetoric? Where is to be found a rhetoric that is
both guided by a longing for the truth and elevated by knowledge of "the
noble things and the just things" that politics at its best can accomplish
(*Nicomachean Ethics* 1094b15)?

It is my hope that the present edition of Aristotle's inquiry into rhetoric will help revive in our time a rhetoric both powerful and decent, dedi-
cated in part to the sober governance of democratic republics.

◉   ◉   ◉

This translation of the *Art of Rhetoric* strives to be as literal as English usage allows. The advantages—and the limitations—of literal translation
need not be rehearsed in detail here, for by now they have been set forth
many times, including by the present translator. I hope it will be enough
to say that literal translations permit those without a reading knowledge
of the original language the best possible access to the original text; William of Moerbeke's faithful renderings of Aristotle into Latin can serve
as a model in this regard. I have attempted to render consistently all key
terms by what seemed to me the closest English equivalents, resorting to
explanatory footnotes when the demands of idiom or intelligibility made
such consistency impossible. Readers may therefore be confident that
when *nature* appears in the translation, for example, it is reflecting the
presence of the same Greek word or family of words (*physis, phyō*) in the
original. It should go without saying that the identification of key terms
and the selection of their English counterparts depend in the end on the
translator's interpretation of Aristotle or on an understanding of his intention. The outlines of my understanding of that intention are found in
the interpretive essay, and the choice of key words and their equivalents
are recorded in the list of Greek terms and in the glossary.

The translation is based on the critical edition of the Greek text edited by
Rudolf Kassel: *Aristotelis Ars rhetorica* (Berlin: Walter de Gruyter, 1976).
I have also consulted earlier editions of the Greek, including that of W. D.
Ross (*Aristotelis Ars rhetorica*, Oxford Classical Texts [Oxford: Clarendon
Press, 1959]) and the classic three-volume edition and commentary of
E. M. Cope, originally published in 1877 and completed after Cope's
death by J. E. Sandys (*The Rhetoric of Aristotle with a Commentary*

[Cambridge: Cambridge University Press, 2009]). As readers will see from the notes, I had constant recourse to the masterful, two-volume commentary of William M. A. Grimaldi, S.J.: *Aristotle, Rhetoric I* (New York: Fordham University Press, 1980) and *Aristotle, Rhetoric II* (New York: Fordham University Press, 1988). It is regrettable indeed that Fr. Grimaldi did not live to write on the third and final book of the *Art of Rhetoric*.

Two of the difficulties attending the translation of the *Rhetoric* deserve mention at the outset. First, the well-known terseness or elliptical character of Aristotle's Greek is very much on display here, and this characteristic places a special demand on translators when they attempt to traverse the distance from the Lyceum to the modern classroom. Where the grammar or meaning of the Greek clearly implies a given noun, verb, or phrase, I have supplied it without cluttering the translation with square brackets. I have instead used such brackets to indicate words or phrases that in my view are required for sense but that are to a greater degree open to interpretation; on a few occasions such brackets contain an alternative translation that helps convey the nuance of a term.

Second, it so happens that two Greek words—*logos* and *pistis*—are central to the argument of the *Rhetoric* but impossible to convey by a single English term. *Logos* means in the first place "speech," the articulate sounds that human beings by nature make. It can by extension refer to a speech, an address or oration, as well as an argument, be it sound or unsound, spoken or written. (In specialized contexts, *logos* can also be translated as "definition," "ratio," or, in book 3 of the *Rhetoric*, "fable.") *Pistis* is related to the verb *pisteuein*, meaning "to trust in," "to have faith" (in something or someone, including a god), "to find credible." In the context of a discussion of rhetoric, *pistis* is both the means to prompt such a conviction—a "proof" or (as I prefer to translate it) "mode of persuasion"—*and* the state of mind so prompted—a "conviction" that something is so. Accordingly, in its adjectival form, the word indicates that something is "credible." It hardly needs to be added that what is credible may not always be true, just as what is true may not always be credible (consider *Art of Rhetoric* 1397a17–19).

All dates in the notes are BCE, except of course in references to modern scholarly works.

I am grateful to Matthew Baldwin, Kaishuo Chen, Timothy Mc-Cranor, and William Twomey for their able assistance in the preparation of the manuscript. Bradley Van Uden deserves special thanks for his work on the general index. I take this opportunity to express my thanks also to the Behrakis family, whose dedication to preserving and promoting the legacy of Hellenic culture, and whose philanthropic generosity, have made it possible for me to hold the Behrakis Professorship in Hellenic Political Studies at Boston College. I am grateful to them, and to my colleagues at Boston College.

R. C. B.

OVERVIEW OF THE
ART OF RHETORIC

A. What is rhetoric?
    1.   Rhetoric, dialectic, and politics: 1.1–3
B. The subject matters of rhetoric and its source materials (specific topics)
    1.   Deliberative rhetoric: 1.4–8
    2.   Epideictic rhetoric: 1.9
    3.   Judicial rhetoric: 1.10–15
C. The modes of persuasion (*pisteis*)
    1.   Passion (*pathos*): 2.1–11
    2.   Character (*ēthos*): 2.12–17
    3.   The *logos* and what is common to all rhetoric: 2.18–26
D. Diction: 3.1–12
E. The arrangement of the parts of a speech: 3.13–19

BIBLIOGRAPHY

Editions of the Greek Text and English Translations

Bekker, Immanuel, ed. *Aristotelis Opera.* 5 vols. Berlin: Walter de Gruyter, 1960. Facsimile of the 1831 ed.

Buckley, Theodore, ed. and trans. *Aristotle's Treatise on Rhetoric.* Amherst, NY: Prometheus Books, 1995. Originally published 1906.

Cooper, Lane, ed. and trans. *The Rhetoric of Aristotle.* New York: D. Appleton, 1932.

Cope, E. M., ed. *The Rhetoric of Aristotle with a Commentary.* Rev. and ed. J. E. Sandys. 3 vols. Cambridge: Cambridge University Press, 2009. Originally published 1877.

Dufour, M., ed. and trans. *Aristote, Rhétorique.* 2 vols. Budé. Paris: Les Belles Lettres, 1932–38.

Dufour, M., and André Wartelle, ed. and trans. *Aristote, Rhétorique.* Vol. 3. Budé. Paris: Les Belles Lettres, 1973.

Freese, John Henry, ed. and trans. *Aristotle, The "Art" of Rhetoric.* Loeb Classical Library. Cambridge, MA: Harvard University Press, 1926.

Jebb, R., and J. E. Sandys, eds. *The Rhetoric of Aristotle.* Cambridge: Cambridge University Press, 1909.

Kassel, Rudolf, ed. *Aristotelis Ars rhetorica.* Berlin: Walter de Gruyter, 1976.

Kennedy, George, ed. and trans. *Aristotle, On Rhetoric: A Theory of Civic Discourse.* Oxford: Oxford University Press, 1991.

Lawson-Tancred, H. C., trans. *Aristotle, The Art of Rhetoric.* New York: Penguin, 1991.

Roberts, W. Rhys, ed. and trans. *Aristotle, Rhetoric.* Mineola, NY: Dover, 2004. Originally published 1924.

Roemer, Adolphus, ed. *Aristotelis Ars rhetorica.* 2nd ed. Leipzig: Teubner, 1923.

Ross, W. D., ed. *Aristotelis Ars rhetorica.* Oxford Classical Texts. Oxford: Clarendon Press, 1959.

Sachs, Joe, ed. and trans. *Plato, Gorgias, and Aristotle, Rhetoric.* Newburyport, MA: Focus Publishing, 2009.

Spengel, L., ed. *Aristotelis Ars rhetorica.* 2 vols. Leipzig: Teubner, 1867.

Victorius. *Petri Victorii Commentarii in tres libros Aristotelis De arte dicendi.* Florence, 1548.

Other Works

Arnhart, Larry. *Aristotle on Political Reasoning: A Commentary on the "Rhetoric."*
     Dekalb: Northern Illinois University Press, 1981.
Aubrey, John. *Brief Lives.* Ed. Andrew Clark. Oxford: Clarendon Press, 1898.
Averroes. *Commentaire moyen à la "Rhétorique."* Ed. and trans. Maroun Aouad. 3 vols.
     Paris: J. Vrin, 2002.
———. *Three Short Commentaries on Aristotle's "Topics," "Rhetoric," and "Poetics."* Ed.
     and trans. Charles E. Butterworth. Albany: SUNY Press, 1977.
Bitzer, Lloyd F. "Aristotle's Enthymeme Revisited." *Quarterly Journal of Speech* 45.4
     (1959): 399–408.
Braet, Antoine. "The Enthymeme in Aristotle's *Rhetoric*: From Argumentation The-
     ory to Logic." *Informal Logic* 19.2–3 (1999): 101–17.
Brandes, Paul D. *A History of Aristotle's "Rhetoric": With a Bibliography of Early Print-
     ings.* Metuchen, NJ: Scarecrow Press, 1989.
Conley, Thomas M. "The Enthymeme in Perspective," *Quarterly Journal of Speech* 70.2
     (1984): 168–87.
Cope, E. M. *An Introduction to Aristotle's "Rhetoric."* London: Macmillan, 1867.
———. "On the Sophistical Rhetoric." *Journal of Classical and Sacred Philology* 2.5
     (1855): 129–68.
———. "On the Sophistical Rhetoric." *Journal of Classical and Sacred Philology* 3.9
     (1856): 253–88.
Enos, Richard Leo, and Lois Peters Agnew, eds. *Landmark Essays on Aristotelian Rhet-
     oric.* Mahwah, NJ: Lawrence Erlbaum Associates, 1998.
Evrigenis, Ioannis. *Images of Anarchy: The Rhetoric and Science in Hobbes's State of Na-
     ture.* Cambridge: Cambridge University Press, 2014.
Ezzaher, Lahcen Elyazghi. *Three Arabic Treatises on Aristotle's "Rhetoric": The Com-
     mentaries of al-Farabi, Avicenna, and Averroes.* Carbondale: Southern Illinois Uni-
     versity Press, 2015.
Fish, Stanley. "Rhetoric." In *Rhetoric in an Antifoundational World: Language, Culture,
     Pedagogy.* Ed. Michael Bernard-Donals and Richard R. Glejzer. New Haven: Yale
     University Press, 1998.
Furley, David, and Alexander Nehemas, eds. *Aristotle's "Rhetoric": Philosophical Essays.*
     Princeton: Princeton University Press, 1994.
Garsten, Bryan. *Saving Persuasion: A Defense of Rhetoric and Judgment.* Cambridge,
     MA: Harvard University Press, 2006.
Garver, Eugene. *Aristotle's "Rhetoric": An Art of Character.* Chicago: University of
     Chicago Press, 1995.
Grimaldi, William M. A. *Aristotle, Rhetoric I: A Commentary.* New York: Fordham
     University Press, 1980.
———. *Aristotle, Rhetoric II: A Commentary.* New York: Fordham University Press,
     1988.
———. *Studies in the Philosophy of Aristotle's "Rhetoric."* Wiesbaden: Franz Steiner, 1972.

Gross, Alan G., and Arthur E. Walzer, eds. *Rereading Aristotle's "Rhetoric."* Carbondale: Southern Illinois University Press. 2000.

Habinek, Thomas. *Ancient Rhetoric: From Aristotle to Philostratus.* London: Penguin, 2018.

Harwood, John T., ed. *The Rhetorics of Thomas Hobbes and Bernard Lamy.* Carbondale: Southern Illinois University Press, 1986.

Hegel, G. W. F. *Hegel's Philosophy of Mind: Part Three of the Encyclopedia of the Philosophical Sciences.* Trans. William Wallace. Oxford: Clarendon Press, 1971.

Heidegger, Martin. *Basic Concepts of Aristotelian Philosophy.* Trans. Robert D. Metcalf and Mark B. Tanzer. Bloomington: Indiana University Press, 2009.

———. *Being and Time.* Trans. Joan Stambaugh. Albany: SUNY Press, 2010.

Herrick, James A. *The History and Theory of Rhetoric: An Introduction.* 5th ed. New York: Routledge, 2013.

Hobbes, Thomas. *Aristotle's Treatise on Rhetoric.* Oxford: D.A. Talboys, 1833.

———. *The Elements of Law, Natural and Politic.* Ed. Ferdinand Tönnies. London: Frank Cass, 1969.

———. *English Works of Thomas Hobbes.* Ed. William Molesworth. London: John Bohn, 1840.

———. *On the Citizen [De Cive].* Ed. Richard Tuck and Michael Silverthorne. Cambridge: Cambridge University Press, 1998.

Johnston, David. *The Rhetoric of "Leviathan": Thomas Hobbes and the Politics of Cultural Transformation.* Princeton: Princeton University Press, 1986.

Kassel, Rudolf. *Der Text der Aristotelischen "Rhetorik."* Berlin: Walter de Gruyter, 1971.

Kennedy, George. *A New History of Classical Rhetoric.* Princeton: Princeton University Press, 1994.

Lord, Carnes. "The Intention of Aristotle's 'Rhetoric.'" *Hermes* 109.3 (1981): 326–39.

Perry, Ben Edwin. *Aesopica.* Urbana: University of Illinois Press, 1952.

Plescia, Joseph. *The Oath and Perjury in Ancient Greece.* Tallahassee: Florida State University Press, 1970.

Radt, Stefan L. "Zu Aristoteles *Rhetorik*." *Mnemosyne* 32 (1979): 284–306.

Rainold, John. *John Rainold's Oxford Lectures on Aristotle's "Rhetoric."* Ed. Lawrence D. Green. Newark, DE: University of Delaware Press, 1986.

Raphael, Sally. "Rhetoric, Dialectic, and Syllogistic Argument: Aristotle's Position in *Rhetoric* I–II." *Phronesis* 19.2 (1974): 153–67.

Rapp, Christof. *Aristoteles, Rhetorik.* Translation, introduction, and commentary. 2 vols. Berlin: Akademie Verlag, 2002.

Roberts, W. Rhys. "Notes on Aristotle's 'Rhetoric.'" *American Journal of Philology* 45.4 (1924): 351–61.

Rorty, Amélie Oksenberg, ed. *Essays on Aristotle's "Rhetoric."* Berkeley: University of California Press, 1996.

Ross, W. D. *Aristotle's Prior and Posterior Analytics.* Oxford: Clarendon Press, 1949.

Skinner, Quentin. *Reason and Rhetoric in the Philosophy of Hobbes.* Cambridge: Cambridge University Press, 1996.

Strauss, Leo. "On Natural Law." In *Studies in Platonic Political Philosophy*, 137–46. Chicago: University of Chicago Press, 1983.

———. *The Political Philosophy of Hobbes: Its Basis and Genesis*. Chicago: University of Chicago Press, 1952. Originally published 1936.

Wartelle, André. *Lexique de la "Rhétorique" d'Aristote*. Budé. Paris: Les Belles Lettres, 1982.

ABBREVIATIONS

Bywater   Ingram Bywater. "Aristotelia V." *Journal of Philology* 32 (1913): 107–22.

Burkett   John Walt Burkett. "Aristotle, *Rhetoric* III: A Commentary." PhD diss., Texas Christian University, 2011.

Cope   E. M. Cope, ed. *The Rhetoric of Aristotle with a Commentary*. 3 vols. Cambridge: Cambridge University Press, 2009.

Cope-Sandys   E. M. Cope and J. E. Sandys, eds. *The Rhetoric of Aristotle: A Commentary*. Cambridge: Cambridge University Press, 2009. (Beginning at 3.17, Sandy completes the commentary left unfinished at the time of Cope's death.)

Denniston   J. D. Denniston. *Greek Particles*. 2nd ed. Indianapolis: Hackett, 1996.

DK   Hermann Diels and Walther Kranz. *Die Fragmente der Vorsokratiker*. 6th ed. 3 vols. Berlin: Weidmann, 1961.

Freese   John Henry Freese, ed. and trans. *Aristotle, The "Art" of Rhetoric*. Loeb Classical Library. Cambridge, MA: Harvard University Press, 1926.

Grimaldi   William M. A. Grimaldi, S.J. *Aristotle, Rhetoric: A Commentary*. 2 vols. New York: Fordham University Press, 1980, 1988.

Grimaldi, *Studies*   William M. A. Grimaldi, S.J. *Studies in the Philosophy of Aristotle's "Rhetoric."* Wiesbaden: Franz Steiner, 1972.

Kassel   Rudolf Kassel, ed. *Aristotelis Ars rhetorica*. Berlin: Walter de Gruyter, 1976.

Kennedy   George Kennedy, ed. and trans. *Aristotle, On Rhetoric: A Theory of Civic Discourse*. Oxford: Oxford University Press, 1991.

Kock   Theodor Kock, ed. *Comicorum Atticorum fragmenta*. 3 vols.
                Leipzig: Teubner, 1880–88.

LSJ   *Greek-English Lexicon*. Ed. Henry George Liddell and Robert
                Scott; rev. Henry Stuart Jones. Oxford: Clarendon Press, 1990.

Nauck   August Nauck and Bruno Snell, eds. *Tragicorum Graecorum frag-
                menta*. Hildesheim: G. Olms, 1964.

OCD   *Oxford Classical Dictionary*. Ed. Esther Eidinow. 4th ed. Oxford:
                Oxford University Press, 2012.

Roberts   W. Rhys Roberts, ed. and trans. *Aristotle, Rhetoric*. Mineola: NY:
                Dover, 2004.

Ross   W. D. Ross, ed. *Aristotelis Ars rhetorica*. Oxford Classical Texts.
                Oxford: Clarendon Press, 1959.

Sachs   Joe Sachs, ed. and trans. *Plato, Gorgias, and Aristotle, Rhetoric*.
                Newburyport, MA: Focus Publishing, 2009.

Spengel   L. Spengel, ed. *Aristotelis Ars rhetorica*. 2 vols. Leipzig: Teubner,
                1867.

Thurot   Charles Thurot. "Observations critiques sur la *Rhétorique*
                d'Aristote." *Revue Archéologique*, n.s., 5 (1862): 40–61.

Vahlen   J. Vahlen. "Zur Kritik aristotelischer Schriften (Poetik und
                Rhetorik)." *Sitzungsberichte der Wiener Akademie der Wissen-
                schaften. Phil.-hist. Classe* 38 (1861): 59–148.

Victorius   *Petri Victorii Commentarii in tres libros Aristotelis De arte dicendi*.
                Florence, 1548.

ARISTOTLE'S
Art of Rhetoric

⊙ ⊙

Outline of Book 1

A. What is rhetoric?
  1. Rhetoric, dialectic, and politics: 1.1–3
     a) Rhetoric and dialectic: 1.1
     b) Technical writers and the misuse of rhetoric
     c) Utility of rhetoric
     d) Rhetoric defined: 1.2
     e) Modes of persuasion (*pisteis*)
     f) Rhetoric and politics
     g) Example, enthymeme, and sign, both necessary and non-necessary
  2. Kinds of rhetoric: 1.3
     a) Deliberative
     b) Judicial
     c) Epideictic
B. The subject matters of rhetoric and its source materials (specific topics)
  1. Deliberative rhetoric: 1.4–8
     a) Advice regarding good and bad things: 1.4
     b) The five political subjects
     c) Happiness and its parts: 1.5
     d) The good as the advantageous, both agreed on and disputed: 1.6
     e) The greater good and the more advantageous: 1.7
     f) Regimes and what is advantageous to each: 1.8
  2. Epideictic rhetoric: 1.9
     a) What is noble?
     b) Praise and blame
     c) Praise and advice
     d) Amplification

Book 1

Rhetoric is a counterpart of dialectic.[1] For both rhetoric and dialectic are   1354a1
concerned with those sorts of things that are in a way commonly available
to the cognizance of quite all people and that do not belong to a distinct
science. Hence all people do in a way share in both rhetoric and dialectic,
for everyone to some extent attempts both to scrutinize an argument and   5
to maintain one, and to speak in both self-defense and accusation. Now,
some among the many[2] do these things at random, others through a certain facility stemming from a characteristic habit.[3] But since both ways
are possible, it is clear that it would be possible also to carry out these
things by means of a method. For it is possible to reflect on the cause of   10

---

1 · Aristotle's *Topics* is devoted to analyzing dialectic or the dialectical syllogism. A
syllogism according to Aristotle is "an argument [*logos*] in which certain [premises]
having been posited, something else other than those [premises] necessarily results
through them" (*Topics* 100a25–27; compare *Rhetoric* 1356b15–17), and the dialectical
syllogism is a method of reasoning that (like the rhetorical syllogism) is based on accepted opinions (*ta endoxa*)—that is, from "opinions that seem to be so to all or to most
people or to the wise and, among these latter, either to all or to most of them or to those
who are especially well-known and highly regarded [*endoxois*]" (*Topics* 100a30–b23;
consider also 104a8–11).
2 · Or "the majority." In Greek as in English, the expression (*hoi polloi*) can carry a pejorative connotation.
3 · This phrase attempts to capture the meaning of two abstract nouns: the ability in
question arises through a *sunētheia*—a habit or custom, in particular one that arises
from living together with others—and from a *hexis*—a fixed state or characteristic.
According to Aristotle, moral virtue itself is a *hexis*, one that arises through correct
habituation rather than teaching strictly speaking. As Grimaldi puts it, Aristotle here
points to the "familiarity acquired through the repetition of an action over a long period of time."

the fact that some hit the mark as they do through a certain facility, while others do so by accident, and all would surely agree that such reflection is the task of an art.

As things stand, those who have composed arts of speeches have writ-ten of[4] just a small part of it,[5] for only modes of persuasion[6] are a technical matter (the rest being [merely] supplementary); but about enthymemes,[7] which are in fact the body of a mode of persuasion, they say nothing, whereas they concern themselves to the greatest extent with what is ex-traneous to the matter at hand. For slander and pity and anger, and such passions of the soul, do not pertain to that matter but relate rather to the juror.[8] As a result, if all judgments were rendered as they are now in some cities, at least, and in the well-governed ones especially, [authors of tech-nical treatises] would have nothing whatever to say. For quite all people suppose that the laws should make such declarations, but some even put the laws to use, and so forbid speaking about anything extraneous to the matter at hand, just as in the Areopagus[9]—their belief about this being correct. For one must not warp the juror by inducing anger in him or envy or pity: this would be just as if someone should make crooked the mea-suring stick he is about to use.

Further, it is manifest that it belongs to the litigant to establish only that the matter at issue is or is not so, or did or did not happen. But whether the matter is great or small [in importance], or just or un-

4 · Or, with some MSS, "have provided" (*peporikasin*); Kassel alters the text to read, in translation, "have labored over" (*peponēkasin*).

5 · Some MSS read "have provided no part of it, so to speak."

6 · *Pisteis* (singular *pistis*). A traditional translation is "proof," but the Greek term as used by Aristotle refers to that which prompts one to trust or have faith in or give cre-dence to (*pisteuein*) something or someone. Thus a *pistis* may be, but certainly need not be, logically sound: not just the argument strictly speaking, but the passions of the au-dience and the perceived character of the speaker, too, constitute *pisteis*.

7 · Aristotle did not coin this term—consider, e.g., Sophocles, *Oedipus at Colonus* 292 and 1199 as well as Xenophon, *Anabasis of Cyrus* 6.1.19–22 and *Cynegetikos* 13.9—but he made a new use of it, to refer to "rhetorical syllogisms" as distinguished from "logi-cal (or dialectical) syllogisms."

8 · Or "judge" (*dikastēs*). The modern distinction between judge and juror was un-known in the courts of Aristotle's day: the assembled jurors *were* the judge.

9 · Located northwest of the Acropolis in Athens, the Areopagus (roughly "Rocky Hill of Ares") housed the Council, and although the judicial functions of the Areopa-gus changed over time, it seems to have remained "the court for deliberate homicide, wounding, and arson" (*OCD* s.v.).

just—in all such cases as the legislator did not offer a clear definition, it   30
is surely the case that the juror himself must form a judgment and not
be instructed by the litigants. It is especially appropriate, then, for correctly posited laws to define all those things that admit of being defined
and to leave the fewest possible matters for the judges. This is so, first,
because it is easier to find one person or a few people, rather than many,
who are prudent and able to legislate and adjudicate. Second, acts of leg-   1354b
islation arise from examinations conducted over a long time, whereas
judgments are offered on the spot, and the result of this is that it is difficult for judges to assign what is just and what is advantageous in a noble
manner. But the greatest consideration of all is that the legislator's judg-   5
ment is not partial but instead concerns future events and is universal,
whereas the assemblyman and the juror judge matters that are at hand
right now and are definite. In their cases, friendly feeling and hatred and
private advantage have often intervened, such that it is no longer possible   10
to contemplate what is true in an adequate way. Instead, private pleasure
or pain clouds their judgment. As for the other considerations, just as
we are saying, one should make the judge[10] authoritative over the fewest of them as possible; but as to whether something has happened or
has not happened, or will or will not be, or is or is not so, this is necessarily left to the judges: it is impossible for the legislator to foresee these   15
things.

If, then, these things are so, it is manifest that all those technical writers
who define other matters treat what is extraneous to the subject—for example, what the preface[11] and narration [of a speech] should contain, and
each of the other parts of it, for they do not concern themselves in this   20
with anything other than how to make the judge be of a certain sort—but
about the technical modes of persuasion they establish nothing. Yet it is
from just this that someone could become skilled in enthymemes. It is for
this reason that, although the same method pertains to both speaking in
the public assembly[12] and judicial speech,[13] and although what concerns

10 · The term for "judge" here (*ho kritēs*) is a general one, as distinguished from the
term used previously that clearly signifies a judge or juror (*dikastēs*); the same word in
the plural appears also toward the end of the sentence.

11 · Or "proem" (*prooimion*). See 3.13–19 for Aristotle's account of the parts of a speech
and their proper arrangement, including the preface (3.13).

12 · *Dēmēgorika*: the term suggests speaking before the *demos*, the common people.

13 · *Dikanika*, traditionally translated as "forensic." The term clearly denotes matters
of justice or the judiciary.

25   speaking in the assembly is nobler and more characteristic of a citizen[14]
than what concerns private transactions, about speaking in the public
assembly [the technical writers] say nothing, whereas when it comes to
pleading a case in court, all attempt to write in a technical way. This is so
because, when one speaks in the assembly, it is less to the purpose to speak
about things extraneous to the subject; and speaking in the assembly is
less pernicious than judicial speech because it deals to a greater degree
with common concerns.[15] For in the political assembly the judge judges
30   about his own affairs, so that nothing else is needed than to demonstrate
that what the advisor contends is so. But in judicial matters this is not
sufficient; rather, it *is* to the purpose at hand to win over the listener. For
here the judgment concerns the affairs of others, so that, while they examine them in relation to their own concerns and listen for their own
delight,[16] they give themselves over to the litigants but do not really
1355a   judge. Hence in many places, just as we said before, the law forbids speaking outside the matter in question. But in the assembly the judges themselves keep an adequate watch over this.

Since it is manifest that the technical method is concerned with modes
5   of persuasion; and the mode of persuasion is a demonstration of a sort (for
we give credence to[17] something especially when we suppose it to have
been demonstrated); and a rhetorical demonstration is an enthymeme
(and this is simply authoritative, so to speak, among the modes of persuasion); and the enthymeme is a certain sort of syllogism[18] (it belongs
to dialectic, either to the whole of dialectic or to some part of it, to see
10   what concerns every syllogism alike), it is clear that he who is especially
able to reflect on this—from what things and how a syllogism comes to
be—would also be especially skilled at enthymemes, because he has at
his disposal the sorts of things the enthymeme is concerned with and the
respects in which it differs from logical syllogisms. For it belongs to the

14 · As distinguished from being characteristic of an itinerant orator or sophist, for example. Another translation is possible: "more political."

15 · The last clause is bracketed by Kassel but present (with some variant readings) in
the MSS.

16 · Or, perhaps, "as a favor" (*pros charin*: see LSJ s.v. VI.2.b).

17 · The verb (*pisteuein*) is connected with the term for "mode of persuasion": *pistis*.
See also n. 6 above.

18 · Some scholars suggest that syllogism (or the related verb) should often be rendered
as "deductive argument" or "deductive reasoning," but the more literal rendering has
been used throughout.

same capacity to see both what is true and what resembles the truth; at   15
the same time, human beings have a natural competency when it comes to
what is true, and for the most part they do hit upon the truth. Hence being able to aim at[19] the generally accepted opinions[20] belongs to one who
is similarly skilled also as regards the truth.

That the others, then, write in a technical way about matters extraneous to the subject, and why they have inclined more toward the pleading   20
of judicial cases, is manifest.

But rhetoric is useful because what is true and what is just are by nature
superior to[21] their opposites, such that, if the judgments [rendered in a
given instance] do not accord with what is proper, it is necessarily the case
that they are defeated on account of their opposites [i.e., by falsehood and
injustice].[22] And this is deserving of censure.

Further, in the case of some people, not even if we should have the   25
most precise science[23] would it be an easy thing to persuade them by
speaking on the basis of it. For an argument that accords with science
[amounts to] teaching, but this is impossible [in their case]; it is necessary, rather, to fashion modes of persuasion and speeches through commonly available things, just as we were saying also in the *Topics* concerning engagement with the many.[24]

And, further, one must be able to persuade others of opposites, just as   30
is the case also with syllogisms, not so that we may do both—for one must
not persuade others of base things—but so that it not escape our notice
how the matter stands and how, when someone else uses arguments unjustly, we ourselves may be able to counter them. Now, none of the other
arts forms syllogisms of opposites: dialectic and rhetoric alone do this, for 35
both are similarly concerned with opposites. Yet the underlying subject

19 · The term used (*stochastikōs*) is ambiguous: it may mean "skilled in aiming at or hit-
ting something"—or merely "in guessing at something."

20 · *Ta endoxa*: things that exist in the element of (generally accepted or reputable)
opinion.

21 · Or "stronger than" (*kreittō*). What is naturally stronger than something would
seem bound to prevail over it; what is naturally superior to, i.e., better than, something
need not (consider in this regard the following note).

22 · Commentators divide over the proper reading and interpretation of this clause,
and I follow Grimaldi's reasoning. Others suggest: "that they are defeated on account
of [the advocates] themselves."

23 · Or "knowledge," knowledge strictly understood (*epistēmē*).

24 · The term "engagement" (or "converse": *enteuxis*) appears (in the plural) also at
Topics 101a26–34.

matters are not similar; instead, what is true and what is better by nature are always more readily established by syllogistic reasoning and are more persuasive, to put it simply.

In addition to these considerations, it is strange if it is a shameful thing not to be able to come to one's own aid with one's body but *not* a shameful thing to be unable to do so by means of argument, which is to a greater degree a human being's own than is the use of the body. And if someone using such a capacity of argument should do great harm, this, at least, is common to all good things—except virtue—and especially so in the case of the most useful things, such as strength, health, wealth, [and] generalship. For someone using these things justly would perform the greatest benefits—and unjustly, the greatest harm.

That rhetoric, then, does not belong to some one, definite subject matter, but is in this respect like dialectic, and that it is useful, are manifest. Manifest, too, is the fact that its task is not to persuade but rather to see the persuasive points that are available in each case, just as in all the other arts as well. For it does not belong to medicine to produce health but rather to advance health to the extent that a given case admits of it: even in the case of those unable to attain health, it is nonetheless possible to treat them in a fine manner.

In addition to these points, it is manifest also that it belongs to the same art [i.e., rhetoric] to see both what is persuasive and what appears to be persuasive, just as in the case of dialectic, too, which sees what is a syllogism and what appears to be a syllogism. For sophistry resides not in the capacity but rather in the choice involved [in how one puts that capacity to use]—except that here, [in rhetoric], one orator will act in accord with the science, another in accord with his choice, whereas in dialectic the sophist acts in accord with his choice, [and] the dialectician acts not in accord with his choice but in accord with the capacity in question.[25]

But let us at this point attempt to speak about the method itself, both how and on the basis of what we will be able to attain the objectives proposed. Once we have defined again, as if from the beginning, what it is, let us state the points that remain.

25 · Just as the (true) dialectician follows the dictates of the science or capacity of dialectics, whereas the sophist chooses for his own purposes to misuse it, so the (true) rhetorician follows the dictates of the science or capacity of rhetoric, whereas another sort of rhetorician, without a distinguishing name of his own but corresponding to the sophist, will choose for his own purposes to misuse rhetoric.

CHAPTER 2

Let rhetoric, then, be a capacity to observe what admits of being persuasive in each case, for this is the task of no other art. Each of the others is
an art of teaching and persuading about whatever underlies it—for example, medicine is concerned with the things productive of health and   30
illness; geometry, with the characteristics accruing to magnitudes; arith-
metic, with numbers; and similarly as regards the other arts and sciences.
But rhetoric seems to be the capacity to observe what is persuasive concerning any given matter, so to speak. Hence we assert that its technical
skill is not concerned with any particular, definite class.

Now, of the modes of persuasion, some are non-technical, others tech-   35
nical. I mean by "non-technical" all those modes of persuasion that are
not supplied through us but are instead available beforehand—for example, witnesses, [evidence gained by] torture,[26] contracts, and all such
things; by "technical" I mean all such modes of persuasion as can be supplied by a method and [hence] by us. The former of these, as a result, must
simply be put to use, the latter discovered.   1356a

Of the modes of persuasion supplied by a speech, there are three forms:
some reside in the character of the speaker; some in how the listener is
disposed; and some in the argument itself, by establishing or appearing
to establish something. [Modes of persuasion arise] through one's char-   5
acter, whenever the speech is stated in such a way as to render the speaker
deserving of credence. For to those who are decent we give credence to a
greater degree and more quickly concerning everything in general, but in
those matters that are imprecise and leave room for doubt, we give credence to them even completely. And such credence should arise through
the speech rather than on account of one's prior opinion that the speaker 10
is a fellow of a certain sort. For it is not as some of the technical writers
have it—that in the art of rhetoric the decency of the speaker contributes
indeed nothing to the persuasion. Rather, character wields pretty much
the greatest authority, so to speak, when it comes to persuasion.

[Modes of persuasion arise also] through the listeners, when they are
led by the speech to a given passion, for we do not render similar judg-   15
ments when we are pained and when delighted or when feeling friendly

---

26 · See 1.15 (1376b31–1377a7) for Aristotle's discussion of the use of torture to gain
evidence.

and when feeling hatred. It is with this [appeal to the passions] alone, we
contend, that technical writers at present attempt to concern themselves.
Now, what pertains to these things, each in turn, will be made clear when
we speak about the passions.[27] People also lend credence to something

20   on account of arguments [*logoi*], when we establish what is true or what
appears to be, on the basis of those things that induce persuasion in each
case.

Since modes of persuasion arise through these things, it is manifest
that grasping them belongs to someone capable of forming syllogisms;
and of reflecting on what concerns characters and the virtues; and, third,
[of reflecting on] the passions—both what each of the passions is and
what sort of thing it is, and from what the passions come to be present

25   and how they do so. As a result, it turns out that rhetoric is a sort of offshoot of dialectic and of the concern with characters, and this [latter]
concern can be justly addressed as the political art [or science]. Hence
rhetoric even slips in under the rubric of the political art [or science],
as do those who lay claim to [a knowledge of rhetoric], partly through a

30   lack of education, partly through boasting and other, characteristically
human, causes. For rhetoric is a certain part of dialectic and is similar to
it, just as we said when we began: neither rhetoric nor dialectic is a science concerned with how any particular subject stands, but they are instead certain capacities for supplying arguments. What concerns their ca-

35   pacity, then, and how they stand vis-à-vis one another, have for the most
part been stated adequately.

As for those modes of persuasion that arise through establishing some-

1356b   thing or appearing to establish something, just as in dialectics there is, on
the one hand, induction, and, on the other, the syllogism as well as the apparent syllogism, so too here, similarly, [in rhetoric]: the example is induction, on the one hand, the enthymeme a syllogism, on the other, and the
apparent enthymeme[28] an apparent syllogism. For I call an enthymeme a

5   "rhetorical syllogism," an example "rhetorical induction."[29] And everyone
fashions the modes of persuasion that arise through positively establishing something by stating either examples or enthymemes, and not by any-

27 · See 2.2–11.

28 · For Aristotle's discussion of the apparent enthymeme, see 2.24.

29 · Kassel marks the whole of the paragraph up to this point as a later edition of Aristotle's, but it is present in the MSS (and quoted by Dionysius of Halicarnassus). For
Aristotle's discussion of the example, see 2.20.

thing apart from these. As a result, if in fact it is necessary in general to establish anything whatever either by means of syllogism or by means of induction—and this is clear to us on the basis of the *Analytics*[30]—then each of the former two [that is, enthymeme and example] must neces-   10
sarily be the same as each of the latter two [that is, syllogism and induction]. What the difference is between an example and an enthymeme is manifest on the basis of the *Topics*,[31] for what concerns syllogism and induction was previously spoken of there: establishing that something is so, by reference to many similar instances, is, in dialectic, induction and, in rhetoric, example. But establishing that, certain [premises] being the   15
case, something else results from those [premises] because of them,[32] either universally or for the most part,[33] alongside those premises by virtue of their being so—this in dialectic is called a syllogism, in rhetoric an enthymeme. And it is manifest also that some good belongs to each form of rhetoric,[34] for what was said in the *Methods*[35] holds similarly here as well: 20
some rhetorical displays rely on examples, others on enthymemes, just as some orators rely on examples, others on enthymemes. Now, the speeches that proceed by way of examples are no less persuasive, but those characterized by enthymemes produce greater applause. As for the cause of these

30 · Consider *Prior Analytics* 68b9–14 and *Posterior Analytics* 81a39–b42.

31 · The reference seems to be a general one, for "there is no specific passage [in the *Topics*] which discusses the difference mentioned" (Grimaldi ad loc.); "enthymeme" is mentioned only once in the *Topics*: 164a6. Since syllogism and induction are defined in the *Topics*, one might infer on that basis the comparable difference between the enthymeme and the example in rhetoric. Although Aristotle says here that induction in dialectic is "the same" as induction in rhetoric, the latter being dubbed "example," just as syllogism in dialectic is "the same" as a syllogism in rhetoric, it being dubbed "enthymeme," he defines induction in the *Topics* as "the passage from particulars to universals" (105a13–14), whereas the rhetorical example proceeds from particular to particular. At 2.20 (1393a26) Aristotle says only that the example is "similar" to induction, as also accords with the fact that rhetoric is but a "counterpart" of dialectic.

32 · Kassel deletes, as an intrusive gloss, the words translated as "because of them" (*dia tauta*).

33 · This clause may modify either the premises in question or the conclusion drawn from them.

34 · Grimaldi suggests that this sentence be taken to mean "that indeed the kind of rhetoric that is the correct [*agathon*] kind . . . possesses each of the two inferential methods." I follow Cope's rendering; the two kinds of rhetoric implied by the statement would be that which relies on examples and that which relies on enthymemes.

35 · Aristotle evidently refers to a work of his that is no longer extant.

25   things, and how each should be used, we will speak about them later.³⁶
But for now, let us define more plainly what concerns them.

What is persuasive is persuasive to someone, and either it immediately
supplies in itself the stuff of persuasion and conviction, or it does so by
being held to establish something through things of that sort. Moreover,
since no art examines each individual case—medicine, for example, does

30   not examine what is healthful for Socrates or Callias,³⁷ but rather what is
such for these or those types (for this is characteristic of art, whereas what
pertains to each individual is indefinite and not subject to a science)—
rhetoric, too, will not reflect on the accepted opinion pertaining to each
individual—for example, the accepted opinion belonging to Socrates or
Hippias.³⁸ It will instead reflect on the opinions of these or those sorts of
people, just as is the case also with dialectic. For dialectic does not form

35   syllogisms on the basis of any chance things—for some things appear [to
be the case] even to those who talk nonsense—but rather on the basis of
those matters that require argument, while rhetoric forms them on the

1357a   basis of those that are the customary subjects of deliberation.³⁹

The task or work of rhetoric is concerned with the sorts of things about
which we deliberate and for which we do not possess arts, and among the
sorts of listeners who are unable to take a synoptic view of what proceeds
through many stages or to calculate from afar. And we deliberate about

5   things that appear to admit of being more than one way. For when it
comes to things that cannot have been otherwise, or will not be or are not
otherwise, no one deliberates about them, if he supposes them to be such,
since there is nothing to be gained thereby. It is also possible in some cases
to form syllogisms and to draw conclusions from prior syllogisms, and in
other cases to do so from things that are without a syllogism but in need

10   of one because they are not accepted opinions. The former of these are
necessarily not easy to follow, on account of their length—one supposes
the judge to be a simple fellow—the latter are not persuasive because they

36 · See, in general, 2.18–26.

37 · This may refer to Callias, son of Hipponicus, who features in the writings of Plato
and Xenophon, where he appears as a wealthy patron of the sophists and prominent
citizen of democratic Athens.

38 · This may refer to Hippias of Elis, a famed sophist depicted in two dialogues of
Plato, the *Greater Hippias* and the *Lesser Hippias*.

39 · The last clause of this sentence is disputed. Kassel emends the text such that it
would read, in translation, "while rhetoric forms them on the basis of those things that
appear to be the case to those already accustomed to deliberating."

do not proceed from agreed-on things or from accepted opinions. As a result, both the enthymeme and the example are necessarily concerned with things that for the most part admit of being otherwise, the example being an instance of induction, the enthymeme a syllogism, and one that is based on few things and often on fewer than those on which is based the first syllogism.[40] For if one of these [premises] is known, there is no need to state it, since the listener himself will add it — for example, given that Dorieus[41] has won the contest in which a wreath is at stake, it is sufficient to say that he won an Olympic victory; that a wreath is at stake in the Olympic games, there is no need to add, for all know this.

Now, few of the things on which the rhetorical syllogisms are based are necessary, for most of the matters with which judgments and examinations are concerned admit of being otherwise, since people deliberate about and examine the things they are concerned with when they act, and actions all belong to this class [of things that can be otherwise], and none of these, so to speak, exists of necessity. Moreover, since the things that happen for the most part and are possible are necessarily inferred syllogistically from other things of like sort, whereas necessary things are inferred from necessities — this too is clear to us from the *Analytics*[42] — it is manifest that the premises on the basis of which enthymemes are stated will, some of them, be necessary, but the greatest number of them will be only for the most part so. And enthymemes are based on likelihoods[43] and on signs, the result being that each of these bases is necessarily the same as each [sort of enthymeme, dealing either with what is for the most part so or what is necessary]. For what is likely is what happens for the most part, but not in an unqualified sense as some define it; rather, it is that which is concerned with things that admit of being otherwise, the likely being related to that in regard to which it is likely, as the universal is to the particular.

When it comes to signs, one sort is as a given individual is to the universal, another as a given universal is to the particular. Of these signs, the necessary one is "decisive evidence,"[44] the non-necessary one is without

15

20

25

30

35

1357b

---

40 · Like Cope, Grimaldi suggests that "first syllogism" refers to "the syllogism in its elementary, typical, unchanged form" — presumably a deductive argument with at least two premises.

41 · Thucydides mentions a Dorieus of Rhodes having won a second Olympic victory in the games of 428: *War of the Peloponnesians and Athenians* 3.8.1.

42 · Consider *Prior Analytics* 29b32–35.

43 · Or "probabilities" (*eikota*), here and throughout.

44 · *Tekmērion*: see the glossary under "decisive evidence," as well as 2.25 (1402b12–19).

5   a name to distinguish it. Now, I call "necessary" those from which the
[demonstrative]⁴⁵ syllogism comes to be. Hence a sign of this sort constitutes decisive evidence, for whenever people suppose that a statement does
not admit of being refuted, they then suppose that they are adducing decisive evidence that it has been established and thus concluded. For "deci-
10 sive evidence" and "conclusion" are the same thing in the ancient language.

     There is among the signs one sort that is as a given individual is to the
universal, in the following way: if, for example, somebody should say, as a
sign that the wise as such are just, "Socrates was wise and just." This, then,
is a sign, but a refutable one (even if what is said is true), for it does not
15 take the form of a syllogism. But if someone should say, for example, "he
has a fever" as a sign that he is sick, or "she is lactating" as a sign that she has
given birth, this is a necessary sign; this alone of the signs is decisive evidence, for it alone is, if true, irrefutable. And the sign that is like the universal in relation to the particular is, for example, if someone should say
that, since a person is breathing with difficulty, it is a sign that he has a
20 fever. But this too is refutable, even if true [in a particular case]: it is possible even for someone who is not feverish to have difficulty breathing.

     What the likely is, then, and what a sign and decisive evidence are, and
in what respect they differ, have now been stated. A more manifest definition of these things, and on account of what cause some things do not
25 admit of syllogistic form while others do admit of it, have been stated in
the *Analytics*.⁴⁶

     That an example is [an instance of] induction, and with what sorts of
things induction is concerned, have been stated. But [an example] is neither as part is to whole nor whole to part nor whole to whole, but as part
is to part, or similar to similar; whenever both things [being compared]
30 fall under the same class, the one being more familiar than the other, this
is an example—for instance, that Dionysius is plotting tyranny because
he is requesting a bodyguard. For Peisistratus previously did in fact so
plot and requested a bodyguard, and once he obtained it he became tyrant, and so too Theagenes among the Megarians.⁴⁷ In fact all the oth-

---

45 · Consider *Posterior Analytics* 73a24: "Demonstration [*apodeixis*] is therefore the
syllogism from necessary [premises]."
46 · Consider *Prior Analytics* 70a3–b38.
47 · Peisistratus made himself tyrant of Athens in 561 with a bodyguard selected from
the Athenian *demos* or people. Similarly, Theagenes made himself tyrant of Megara,
sometime between 640 and 620, and Dionysius I (ca. 430–367) became tyrant of Syracuse in 406–405. Consider also Plato, *Republic* 566b-c.

ers whom people know of become an example for the case of Dionysius,   35
about whom they do not yet know if he is making his request for this reason. But all these things fall under the same universal—namely, that he
who requests a bodyguard is plotting tyranny.

On what the modes of persuasion that seem demonstrative rely, then,   1358a
has been stated. But as for enthymemes, a very great difference among
them, which has most escaped the notice of nearly everyone, pertains also
to the dialectical method in syllogisms. For some enthymemes pertain to
rhetoric (just as some syllogisms pertain to the dialectical method), but   5
other enthymemes pertain to other arts and capacities, some of these latter being in existence, others of them not yet firmly established. Hence
[the differences in question] escape the notice of the listeners, and the
more people touch on [their specific subject matter] in the appropriate
way, the more they depart from [dialectic or rhetoric].[48] But what is being
said will be clearer once it has been stated at greater length.   10

For I say that both dialectical and rhetorical syllogisms are concerned
with those things we say are "topics,"[49] and these are the ones that belong
in common to matters of justice and physics as well as to politics and
many things that differ in kind—for example, the topic of the more and
the less. For this topic will not afford a greater basis to form syllogisms or   15
to state an enthymeme about matters of justice than it will to form them
about physics or anything else whatever, even though these subject matters differ in kind. But specific topics, by contrast, are all those that are
derived from premises pertaining to each kind and class of thing. For example, there are premises pertaining to physics from which are derived
neither an enthymeme nor a syllogism concerning ethics[50], and there are   20
other premises about ethics from which there will not be derived [en-
thymemes or syllogisms] concerning physics. And this holds similarly in
all cases. And those topics [in the general sense] will not make one prudent about any class of things, for they are not concerned with any underlying subject matter. But as for these specific topics, insofar as someone is

48 · The text is difficult and has occasioned several emendations. No wonder that Aristotle immediately acknowledges the lack of clarity here.

49 · Literally meaning "place," a *topos* or "topic" in rhetoric is a place to look for something or what is found there: a heading or classification containing rhetorical arguments of the same kind. Aristotle distinguishes general or common topics from specific topics, the former not belonging to any particular subject matter, the latter being
derived from such defined subjects as physics or ethics.

50 · That is, with "matters pertaining to character" (*ta ēthika*), here and throughout.

better at selecting premises, the more he will unawares fashion a science
different from dialectic and rhetoric. For if he hits on its principles [or
starting points], it will no longer be a matter of dialectic or rhetoric but
rather that science whose principles he has. And yet the greatest number
of enthymemes stated are derived from these kinds of topics, which are
particular and specific, whereas fewer are derived from the common topics. Just as in the *Topics*, then, so also here, in the case of enthymemes, one
must distinguish the specific kinds and the [common] topics, from which
enthymemes are derived. I mean by "specific kinds" the particular points
relating to each given class of thing [or subject matter], and by "topics"
those that are equally common for all classes alike.[51]

But let us first grasp the kinds of rhetoric so that, by defining how
many they are, we may grasp separately the elements[52] and the premises
pertaining to them.

CHAPTER 3

Of rhetoric there are three kinds in number, for such is also the number
of those who listen to speeches. Now, the speech is composed of three
things: the speaker; and that about which he speaks; and the person to
whom he speaks. And the goal of the speech is relative to this person
(I mean the listener). It is necessarily the case that the listener is either an
onlooker or a judge, and a judge either of past events or of future ones.
An assemblyman is an example of one who judges about future events,
whereas a juror is an example of one who judges about past events; he
who judges [the speaker's] capacity is simply an onlooker. There would as
a necessary result be three kinds of speeches that are rhetorical: deliberative, judicial,[53] and epideictic.[54]

To the deliberative belong exhortation and dissuasion, for both those

51 · For Aristotle's treatment of the common topics, see 2.18–26. Most commentators
take the "kinds" (*eidē*) mentioned to refer to the specific or particular topics, as distinguished from the common topics.

52 · At 2.22 (1396b21–22) Aristotle will equate the "elements" (*stoicheia*) of enthymemes with their "topics."

53 · The traditional translation is "forensic"; see also n. 13 above.

54 · The first mention of "epideictic" rhetoric, derived from the verb *epideiknumi*,
which means "to show, display, set forth, or point out": a speech marked by epideictic
rhetoric will set forth reasons to praise or blame someone or something.

who advise[55] in private and those who speak out in the common assembly   10
always do one or the other of these. To the judicial speech belong accusation and defense, for litigants necessarily do one or the other of these.
To the epideictic speech belong praise and blame. The times pertaining
to each of these are, in the case of one who advises, the future (for he advises about future events, whether he exhorts or dissuades); in the case of   15
the juror, it is the past (for he who accuses and he who defends are always
concerned with deeds done); and in the case of epideictic rhetoric, the
most authoritative consideration is the present, for all people praise or
blame in reference to the given circumstances, though they often make
additional use also of recollections of past events and of conjectures in   20
anticipation of future ones.

    The goal in each of these is different—in fact there are three goals for
the three [kinds of rhetoric]: to him who advises the goal is the advantageous and the harmful (for he who exhorts is advising something on the
grounds that it is better, he who dissuades does so on the grounds that it
is worse); all else they take as subordinate to this, either that something   25
is just or unjust, or noble or base. For those who speak in courtrooms,
the goal is the just and the unjust, and they take all else as subordinate to
these. For those who praise and blame, the goal is the noble and the base,
and they refer all else to these. There is a sign that what has been stated
is the goal for each of these, for when it comes to the other matters, they   30
sometimes would not dispute them—for example, someone being tried
in court might not dispute that something happened or that he did harm
thereby. But that he committed an injustice he would never agree to, for
in that case there would be no need of a trial. And similarly, those who advise often let drop other matters, but that what they are advising is disad-   35
vantageous, or that what they are dissuading from is advantageous—this
they would not agree to. But that it is not[56] unjust to enslave neighbors
and those who have committed no injustice, they often give no thought
to at all. And similarly, both those who praise and those who blame do
not examine whether someone acted advantageously or harmfully, but   1359a
they often praise him because, in slighting what was profitable for him-

55 · "Deliberative" rhetoric (*sumbouleutikon*) is bound up with the giving of "advice"
(*sumbouleuein*) or the conduct of deliberation, especially in a political assembly, a connection it is difficult to maintain in translation. An alternative translation to "deliberative rhetoric" would be "advisory rhetoric."
56 · Some editors suggest deleting the "not," but it is present in the MSS.

self, he acted because it was noble to do so—for example, they praise
Achilles because he came to the aid of his comrade Patroclus, knowing
that he himself must die, when it was otherwise possible for him to live.[57]
To him, then, such a death was nobler, whereas continuing to live was advantageous.

It is manifest, on the basis of what has been said, that it is necessary in the first place to be in possession of premises [or propositions][58]
about these things. For decisive evidence and likelihoods and [non-
necessary] signs are rhetorical premises. A syllogism is wholly composed of premises [or propositions], and the enthymeme is a syllogism
made up of the premises [or propositions] mentioned. Now, since impossible things can neither be done nor have been done—only possible
things can be—and since what either has not happened or will not happen cannot have been done and will not be done, he who advises, he
who judges, and he who makes epideictic speeches must necessarily
have premises [or propositions] concerning what is possible and impossible, and whether something has or has not happened and whether
it will or will not be. Moreover, all who praise and blame, or exhort and
dissuade, or accuse and defend, attempt not only to establish the points
mentioned, but also that the good or the bad at stake, or the noble or
the base, or the just or the unjust, is either great or small. And this they
do either by speaking of these things in themselves or by comparing
them to one another. [Since all this is so,] it is clear that they must also
be in possession of premises [or propositions] pertaining to greatness
and smallness, and the greater and the lesser, as regards both the universal and a given particular—for example, what is the greater or lesser
good, or the greater or lesser act of injustice, or of justice, and similarly
in the other cases as well.

The things about which one must necessarily have premises [or propo-
sitions], then, have been stated. But after this one must define what concerns each of these in particular—for example, about what things there is

57 · Consider Homer, *Iliad* 18.78–137.

58 · Aristotle uses the term *protasis* to mean either "premise" or "proposition," the latter here referring to a general thought (e.g., what is impossible cannot come to pass)
that would probably not appear as such in a given enthymeme but would rather lie behind a specific premise adapted to the circumstances at hand. Consider Sally Raphael,
"Rhetoric, Dialectic, and Syllogistic Argument: Aristotle's Position in *Rhetoric* I–II,"
Phronesis 19.2 (1974): 165.

advice; about what there are epideictic speeches; and, third, about what there are legal trials.[59]

CHAPTER 4

First, then, one must grasp the sorts of good or bad things the advisor   30
gives advice about, since he is concerned not with *all* of them but only
with so many good and bad things as may or may not come into being.
But as for all those that either are or will be of necessity, or for which it
is impossible that they either be or come to be—about these there will
be no advice. Indeed, the advisor is not even concerned with quite all the
things that admit of coming into being, for there are some goods, among   35
those that may or may not come into being, that are by nature or from
chance, and about these the giving of advice is pointless. But it is clear
that the advisor is concerned with all such things as there is deliberation
about, and these are all such things as can by their nature be traced back
to us, the beginning of whose coming-into-being is up to us. For we in-   1359b
vestigate matters up to that point at which we discover whether they are
possible or impossible for us to carry out.

   As for enumerating in a precise way each particular [subject of delib-
eration] and dividing them into the kinds that people are accustomed
to debating or dealing with, and, further, giving a true definition of each
of them insofar as is possible, there is no need on the present occasion   5
to seek these things out, because this does not belong to the rhetorical
art but rather to an art marked by greater prudence and truth. As things
stand, in fact, many more subjects of study have been given to rhetoric
than are properly its. For what we happen to have said previously[60] is
true—that rhetoric is composed of the science of analytics, on the one   10
hand, and of the political art [or science] concerned with characters, on
the other, and in some respects it is similar to dialectics, but in others to
sophistic arguments. Insofar as someone attempts to fashion either dialectic or this [art of rhetoric], not into capacities but sciences, he will unawares obscure their nature by effecting the change, reconstructing them   15
as sciences of the given underlying subject matters rather than of arguments or speeches alone. But, nevertheless, let us speak at present about

59 · *Dikai* (singular *dikē*): a legal adjudication, a suit or trial, as well as the punishment
meted out as a result of it.
60 · Consider 1356a25–31.

all those things it is relevant to define, things that also leave to the political science their examination.

As for the things all people deliberate about, and the things advisors
20   speak about in public, the most important of them happen to be five in number. These are what concerns revenues; and war and peace; and, further, what concerns the guarding of the territory; and imports and exports; and legislation. As a result, he who is going to give advice about
25   revenues must know what and how many are the city's sources of income so that, if something is deficient, it may be added to, and if it has fallen short, it may be increased. Further, he must know quite all of the city's expenses, so that if any is superfluous, it may be removed, and if any is too great, it may be reduced. For it is not only by adding to what is available
30   to them that people become wealthier, but also by removing expenses. It is possible to gain a synoptic view of these things, not only from one's experience dealing with private affairs, but, with a view to giving advice about them, one must necessarily also be a skilled inquirer into the discoveries made by others.

As for what concerns war and peace, one must know the city's power,
35   both how much is already available to it and how much can be made available; both what the character of the available power is and what can be added to it; and, further, what wars it has waged and how it waged them. It is necessary to know these things, not only in the case of one's own city, but also in that of the bordering ones, against whom the city is likely to wage war, so that it may maintain peaceful relations with those who are
1360a   stronger and so that it may be up to them themselves whether they wage war against those who are weaker. They must know also the powers [of their neighbors], whether they are similar or dissimilar [to their own], for it is possible in this to gain the upper hand over them or to get the worst of it at their hands. It is also necessary, in addition to these considerations,
5   to have reflected on not only one's own wars but also how those of others have turned out. For from like things, like things by nature arise.

Further, concerning the guarding of the territory, one must not overlook how it is guarded. Rather, one must know both the size of the guard and its character as well as the locations of the guard posts—this is im-
10   possible for someone who is without experience of the territory—so that if the guard is too small it may be added to, and if it is superfluous somewhere it may be removed, and in this way a closer watch can be kept over the appropriate locations.

Further, concerning sustenance, one must know how much expenditure[61] is sufficient for the city and what sort of sustenance is produced at home and what imported, and what exports they require and what imports, so that contracts and agreements may be made with importers and   15
exporters respectively. For it is necessary to maintain a careful watch so that the citizens be blameless in relation to two groups: those who are stronger than they and those who are useful to them in these matters.

With a view to [the city's] safety, [the rhetorician] must necessarily be able to reflect on quite all the relevant matters, but not least he must understand what concerns legislation. For it is in the laws that the city's sal-   20
vation lies, such that it is necessary for him to know how many kinds of regime there are, and what sorts of things are advantageous to each, and by what things the regime is naturally corrupted, including both what is the regime's own and what is in opposition to it. I mean by "corrupted by what is its own" that—apart from the best regime—all the other regimes are corrupted both by being relaxed and by being tightened: democracy,   25
for example, becomes weaker not only when it is relaxed, such that it will end in oligarchy, but also when it is excessively tightened, just as is the case also with the hook nose and the snub nose. Not only does either the hook nose or the snub arrive at the mean when it is relaxed, but when it becomes either excessively hooked or snubbed, it is so arranged as not   30
even to seem to be a nose. But it is useful, with a view to legislative acts, for someone considering the matter not only to understand what regime is advantageous on the basis of past events, but also to know the regimes present among other peoples and what sorts of regimes harmonize with what sorts of peoples. It is clear as a result that, for legislation, accounts of traveling the earth are useful—for in these it is possible to grasp the laws [or customs] of nations—and for instances of political[62] advice, the inquiries of those who write about human actions are useful. But quite all of these are the task of politics, not of rhetoric. Such, then, are the most important matters of which someone who is going to give advice must have a grasp.

But as for those things on the basis of which one must exhort or dissuade concerning these matters and the rest, let us speak of them again.   1360b

61 · Both Ross and Kassel delete the word translated as "expenditure" (*dapanē*), but it is present in the MSS and defended by Grimaldi.
62 · The reading of most MSS; Kassel, following a Latin translation that is itself based on a medieval Arabic translation, reads "military" or "martial" (*polemikas*).

CHAPTER 5

There is a certain target for pretty much all people, both each in private
and all in common, by aiming at which they both choose and avoid certain things. And this target is, to speak summarily, happiness together
with its parts. As a result, let us grasp, by way of a paradigm,[63] what happiness is, simply speaking, and from what things its parts are constituted,
since it is with happiness, and with the things that are either conducive
to it or contrary to it, that all exhortation and dissuasion are concerned.
For the things that supply happiness or some part of it, or make it greater
rather than less, one must do, whereas those that ruin or impede happiness, or produce what opposes it, one must not do. So let happiness be a
faring well that is accompanied by virtue; or self-sufficiency of life; or the
life that is most pleasant and accompanied by security; or an abundance
of possessions and bodies[64] accompanied by the capacity to guard these
and to carry out the actions connected with them. For quite all agree that
happiness is pretty much one or more of these things.

If, then, happiness is something of this sort, it is necessarily the case
that its parts are good birth; abundance of friends; fine[65] friends; wealth;
good children; abundance of children; a good old age; and, further, the
virtues of the body—for example, health, beauty, strength, size, athletic
power; reputation; honor; good luck; [and] virtue or its parts: prudence,
courage, moderation, justice.[66] For in this way one would be most self-
sufficient, if he should have available to himself goods both internal and
external, for there are no other goods beyond these: internal to him are
those pertaining to soul and those in the body, external are good birth
and friends and money and honor. Further, we suppose it to be fitting to
have available to one also certain powers as well as luck, for in this way
life would be most secure.

So let us grasp, in similar fashion, also what each of these is. Good
birth, then, for a nation and a city, is being autochthonous or ancient and
for the first inhabitants to have been distinguished leaders and many of
those descended from them to be distinguished by their qualities that

63 · Or "example," as the term is elsewhere translated.
64 · The term may mean "slaves," although this is not certain; a similar formulation appears also at 1383b1–3.
65 · The term (*chrēstos*) can also mean "useful," "good of its kind," "serviceable."
66 · The clause beginning "or its parts: . . ." is missing from some MSS and generally
omitted by modern editors.

elicit emulation. But for a private person good birth is derived either from
the men's side or from the women's, and the legitimacy of birth on both   35
sides, and (just as in the case of a city) from the fact that the first ancestors are known either for virtue or wealth or some other of the honorable
things, and that many of those in one's familial line—men and women,
youths and elders—are distinguished.

It is not unclear what having good children and an abundance of chil-   1361a
dren is. In the case of what is held in common, it is youths who are numerous and good, and good in bodily virtue—for example, size, beauty,
strength, athletic power. The virtues of a youth's soul are moderation and
courage. For a private individual, having good children and an abundance   5
of children consists in having many such children of one's own, both female and male. The virtue of the female body is beauty and size, that of
the soul, moderation and a love of work free of illiberality. And in like
fashion, both privately and in common, as regards both men and women,   10
one must seek to have each of these sorts of things. For all those whose affairs pertaining to women are in a poor condition, as is the case with the
Lacedaemonians,[67] are more or less half unhappy.

The parts of wealth are abundance of money, land, possession of properties distinguished by their number and size and excellence, and, further,
possession of furniture and slaves and cattle distinguished by their number and excellence—and all of these being secure and liberal and useful.   15
Things that bear fruit are more useful, those that look to enjoyment are
liberal. I mean by "things that bear fruit" those from which income is derived, whereas things characterized by enjoyment are those from which
nothing worth mentioning arises apart from their use. A defining indication of "security" is possessing things in such a place and in such a way that   20
their use is up to one; and an indication of whether things are one's own
or not is when it is up to oneself to alienate them (and I mean by "alienate
them" giving them away or selling them). In general, being wealthy consists more in the use involved than in the possession, for in fact the activity bound up with such things, and their use, is wealth.

Good reputation is being supposed by all to be serious or to have the   25
sort of thing that all—or the many or the good or the prudent—aim at.
Honor is a sign of a reputation for doing good deeds, and it is especially
those who do good deeds who are justly honored, not but that someone

---

67 · That is, the Spartans. For Aristotle's view of the Spartan regime in general and their
treatment of their women in particular, consider *Politics* 2.9.

30   who is capable of doing good is honored as well. Doing good deeds pertains either to preservation and all the causes of existing, or to wealth, or
to some other of the goods whose possession is not easy, either in general
or at a given place or time. For many attain honor on account of things
that [otherwise] seem small, but the locations[68] involved, and the crucial
moments, are responsible [for this bestowal of honor]. The parts of honor
35   are sacrifices, memorials in verse and in prose, prizes, land grants, front
row seats,[69] burial markers, likenesses made, sustenance at the public ex-
pense, characteristically barbarian honors (such as lying prostrate before
one and stepping aside in deference), [and] gifts that are honored among
each people. For the gift is a giving of one's property and a sign of honor.
Hence both those who love money and the ambitious[70] aim at receiving
1361b   gifts, since gifts supply what both types are in need of: a gift is a possession, which lovers of money aim at, and it is an honor, which the ambitious aim at.

A virtue of body is health, and this in such a way that, when using their
5   bodies, people are free of illness. For many are healthy as Herodicus[71] is
said to be, people whom nobody would deem happy in point of health
because they abstain from all the characteristically human things, or from
the greatest number of them. Beauty differs according to each time of life.
The beauty of youth consists in having a body useful for exertions when it
comes to both the running track and the use of force [in general], it being
10   pleasant to see this just for the enjoyment of it. Hence the pentathletes[72]
are most beautiful because they are naturally fitted for bodily force together with speed. The beauty of someone in his bloom relates to the exertions of war, and its being pleasant [to see] seems to go together with its
being fearsome. The beauty of an elder relates to his being competent for

68 · Here Aristotle uses the term *topoi* evidently in its literal sense; some MSS read
"characters" or "ways" (*tropoi*).
69 · In Plato's *Laws*, the Athenian Stranger suggests that a resident alien or foreigner
who comes across someone beating his mother or father and aids the person being at-
tacked is to be rewarded with a front row seat at the public contests or games: *Laws*
881b6 (see also 947a1).
70 · Literally, "those who love honor," here and throughout.
71 · A famous physician hailing from Thrace. In Plato's *Republic* (406a–b), Socrates
says that Herodicus mixed gymnastic or physical training with medicine and, being
sickly himself, subsequently "worried himself to death, then many others afterward."
72 · Pentathletes in antiquity competed in running, discus, javelin, long jump, and
wrestling.

the necessary exertions and free of pain,[73] through his being without any
of the disfigurements that mar old age. Strength is the capacity to move   15
another as one wishes, and one necessarily moves another either by pulling or pushing, or by lifting up, or by squeezing or compressing, such that
the strong person is strong either in all of these or in some of them. Virtue
of size consists in superiority over the majority in height and depth and
width to such a degree that one's motions are not as a result made slower   20
by the excess. And the virtue of body in athletic contests consists of size
and strength and speed, for speed is a sort of strength. He who is capable
of throwing his legs in a certain way and moving them quickly and for a
considerable distance is a skilled runner; he who is capable of pressing
and holding down another is a skilled wrestler; he who is capable of re-   25
pelling someone with a blow, a skilled boxer; he who can do so with both
of these latter is a skilled pancratist;[74] he who is capable in all of these is
a pentathlete.

   A good old age is aging slowly without pain. For it is not to enjoy
a good old age if one ages quickly, nor if one ages slowly but painfully.
A good old age arises from the virtues of the body and from luck, for
someone who is not free of illness nor strong will not be free of suffer-   30
ing, and without luck he would not survive free of pain and for a long
time. There is also a certain other capacity for being long-lived separate
from strength and health, for many who are without the bodily virtues are
long-lived [nonetheless]. But the precise account concerning these things
is not at all useful for what concerns us at present.   35

   It is not unclear what having an abundance of friends and having fine
friends are, once a friend has been defined: the friend is the sort of person
who is apt to act so as to bring about the things he supposes to be good for
another, for that other's sake. And so he who has many of this description
has an abundance of friends, and he who has also decent men [as friends]
has fine friends.

   Good luck is the coming into being and having at one's disposal either   1362a
all or the greatest number or the most important sorts of goods whose
cause is luck. Now, luck is a cause of some things of which there are arts,
but also of many things for which there is no art—for example, of all such
things as nature is the cause (but chance also admits of being contrary to

73 · Or, perhaps, "and causing no pain [to others]."
74 · One who practices the all-out sport combining (as Aristotle here indicates) wrestling and boxing.

5   nature): art is a cause of health, but nature is a cause of beauty and size. In
general, the sorts of goods that stem from luck are those for which people
are envied. Luck is also a cause of those goods that are contrary to reasonable expectation—for example, if the other brothers are ugly but this one
is handsome; or the others did not see the treasure but this fellow did
discover it; or the arrow happened to hit the fellow next to him but not

10 him himself; or if someone who frequents a place is the only one not to
go there, while the others who went there just once were destroyed. For
all such things are held to be instances of good luck.

But as for virtue, since it is in fact the topic most closely akin to praise,
it must be defined when we give an account of praise.[75]

CHAPTER 6

15 What things one must aim at, then, when fashioning an exhortation,
and what when dissuading someone (be they future things or already at
hand), are manifest, for these latter are the opposites of the former.

Now, since it has been posited that the target for someone giving advice is the advantageous (and people do not deliberate about the end but
rather about the things conducive to the end, and these are things ad-

20 vantageous for actions), and since the advantageous is a good, it must be
grasped what the elements of the good and advantageous in an unqualified sense would be.

So let a good be that which is choiceworthy[76] for its own sake, and that
for the sake of which we choose something other than it, and that which
all things, or all things that have sense perception or intellect, aim at (or
would aim at, should they gain intellect). And all that intellect would as-

25 sign to each, and all that intellect does assign to each individually—this
is what is good for each; and that which, when it is present, renders each
in a good condition and possessed of self-sufficiency; the good is also the
self-sufficient and that which is productive or protective of such things,
and that on which such sorts of things follow and that prevent or destroy

30 their opposites. And things follow in a twofold sense: they do so either simultaneously or subsequently. For example, understanding is subsequent
to learning, but being alive is simultaneous with being healthy. Things
are productive in a threefold way: some things are productive as being

---

75 · See 1.9 for Aristotle's account of praise.
76 · Or, simply, "chosen" (as a matter of fact), here and throughout.

healthy is productive of health; others as food is productive of health; and still others as exercising is, because it for the most part produces health. These things being posited, it is necessary that gaining goods is good, as is also casting off bad things. For in the latter [the good] follows simultaneously with not having what is bad, and in the former it follows subsequently the possession of what is good. So also gaining a greater good in place of a lesser one, and a lesser bad in place of a greater one. For to the extent that the greater exceeds the lesser, [the good involved] is gaining the one and casting off the other.

The virtues, too, are necessarily good, for it is in reference to the virtues that those possessed of them are in a good condition; and the virtues are productive of goods and prompt actions accordingly. But about each virtue—both what and of what sort they are—this must be spoken of separately.[77] Pleasure, too, is a good, for all animals aim at it by nature. As a result, both pleasant things and the noble are necessarily good, for the former are productive of pleasure, and, of things noble, some are pleasant, others choiceworthy for their own sake.

To speak of it point by point, the following are necessarily good: happiness, for it is both choiceworthy for its own sake and self-sufficient, and we choose all else for its sake; justice; courage; moderation; greatness of soul; magnificence; and the other characteristics of this sort, for they are virtues of soul; also health and beauty and the like, for they are virtues of body and productive of many things. For example, health is productive of both pleasure and being alive. Hence health is held to be the best thing, since it is a cause of two of the most honored things in the eyes of the many: pleasure and being alive. Wealth: for it is a virtue of possession and productive of many [goods]. A friend and friendship: for a friend is both choiceworthy in himself and productive of many [goods]. Honor, reputation: for these are pleasant and productive of many [goods], and it is for the most part the case that the things for which people are honored follow upon these. A capacity to speak and to act, for everything of that sort is productive of goods; further, having a good nature, a good memory, ease of learning, shrewdness, [and] all things of that sort: these are capacities productive of goods. Similarly, too, all the sciences and the arts; and being alive, for even if no other good should attend it, it is choiceworthy in itself. Also what is just, for it is something advantageous in common.

These, then, are the goods that are pretty much agreed on. But in the

35

1362b

5

10

15

20

25

77 · Consider 1.9.

30   case of those goods subject to dispute, the [rhetorical] syllogisms are
based on the following. That is good, whose opposite is bad; and it is the
opposite of what is advantageous to enemies. For example, if our being
cowards is especially advantageous to our enemies, it is clear that courage would be especially advantageous to the citizens. And in general, that
which is the opposite of what our enemies wish for or delight in appears
35   advantageous. Hence it has been well said:

>   Verily Priam would rejoice.[78]

This is not always so, but it is so for the most part. For nothing prevents
the same thing from sometimes being advantageous to one's opponents
too. Hence it is said that bad things draw human beings together, when
the same thing is harmful to both sides.

1363a   That of which there is no excess is good,[79] but that which is greater
than it should be is bad. And that for the sake of which much labor has
been expended or cost incurred, for it has already appeared to be a good,
and such a thing is supposed to be an end [or goal], and an end of many
5   things. But the end is good. Hence these words were uttered:

>   And for Priam to boast of[80]

and

>   It is a shameful thing to wait so long.[81]

And, as the proverb has it, "the pitcher at the doors."[82] And that which
many people aim at and what is manifestly fought over, for that which all

---

78 · Homer, *Iliad* 1.255. Here Nestor urges Achilles and Agamemnon to put aside their
angry quarrel, which would bring much delight to Priam and all the Trojans, were they
to learn of it.

79 · Some editors emend the text here to read "That which is not an excess is good"; but
both Ross and Kassel, as also Grimaldi, abide by the reading of the MSS.

80 · Homer, *Iliad* 2.160. The complete line from which Aristotle's brief quotation is
taken is "And they [i.e., the Greeks] would leave Argive Helen for Priam to boast of."
Here Hera begs Athena to prevent the Greeks from leaving Troy—and so from leaving Helen behind.

81 · Homer, *Iliad* 2.298. Here Odysseus exhorts his fellow soldiers not to withdraw
from Troy but to hold on, for to withdraw now, empty-handed after nine long years,
would be shameful.

82 · Aristotle's quotation is compressed: "To break the pitcher at the doors," as the
original proverb probably ran, means "to labor in vain."

people aim at is, as we saw,[83] good, and "many" people appears to be tantamount to "all." It is also what is praised, for nobody praises what is not   10
good, and that which even enemies, including the base among them,[84]
praise. For it is just as if all already agree about what it is, even those who
have suffered badly because of it; it is on account of the good's being manifest that they would agree about it, just as those whom one's friends blame
and whom one's enemies do not blame are indeed base. Hence the Corin-   15
thians supposed that they had been reviled by Simonides when he wrote:

> With Corinthians, Troy finds no fault.[85]

And what anyone who is prudent or good, man or woman, is inclined
to prefer—for example, Athena, [who was inclined to prefer] Odysseus;
Theseus, Helen;[86] the goddesses, Alexander;[87] and Homer, Achilles.

And, in general, what is choiceworthy [is good]. And people choose   20
to do both the previously mentioned things and those that are bad for
their enemies and good for their friends, and things that are possible.
And these latter are twofold: those that might come to pass, and those
that easily come to pass. Easy are all those that come to pass without pain
or in a short time, for "difficult" is defined either by pain or by a considerable length of time. [It is choiceworthy and hence good] also if some-   25
thing happens as people wish it to, and they wish either for nothing bad
or for a lesser amount of it than of the relevant good; and this will be the
case if the penalty exacted is either unnoticed or small. And those things

---

83 · See 1362a21–24.

84 · All modern editors except Ross bracket the words translated as "including the base
among them" (*kai hoi phauloi*), but they are present in the MSS. A literal rendering is
"that which enemies and the base praise." Grimaldi defends the phrase and suggests
taking it as modifying "enemies": not just enemies, but the *phauloi* among them—even
they—are compelled to approve of what is good.

85 · The original context of this line of Simonides (ca. 556–468) is lost, but whatever
Simonides's intention, the Corinthians, who had fought together with the Achaeans
(Homer, *Iliad* 2.570), evidently were offended at the thought that the Trojans, the en-
emy, found nothing to criticize in them.

86 · Theseus, together with his friend Pirithous, is said to have abducted Helen because
he desired to marry a daughter of Zeus.

87 · Aristotle here alludes to the "judgment of Paris" (or Alexander): after Eris (Strife)
was barred from entering the wedding of Peleus and Thetis, she cast a golden apple among the goddesses, intending it for the one deemed the most beautiful. Hera,
Aphrodite, and Athena contended for that title and accepted Alexander (Paris) as
judge of their beauty. See also 2.23 (1399a3) below.

that are peculiarly one's own and possessed by no one else and are extraordinary, for in this way the honor involved is greater. And the things
that are fitting for them, such as those appropriate given their familial
30   line and power. [Choiceworthy, too,] are the things people suppose they
lack, even if they are small, for they choose to act on these things nonetheless. And things that are readily brought about, for these are possible,
given that they are easy; and those things are readily brought about that
all people, or the many, or one's peers or inferiors, have already accomplished. And those things that will delight friends or vex enemies. And all
35   such things as those whom people admire choose to do. And the things
for which they have a good nature or at which they are experienced, for
they suppose they will more easily accomplish them. And things that no
paltry fellow chooses, for these are praised to a greater degree. And things
for which people happen to have a desire, for these things appear not only
1363b pleasant but also better. And above all, each person chooses relative to the
things he is fond of—for example, lovers of victory [choose a given thing
or deed], if there will be a victory involved, the lovers of honor, if there
will be honor at stake, lovers of money, if there will be money, and so on
with the rest.

From these things, then, one must grasp the modes of persuasion concerning the good and the advantageous.

CHAPTER 7

5   But since people often agree that both of two things are advantageous,
while disagreeing about which one is more so, it would be necessary to
speak next about the greater good and the more advantageous. So let
one thing exceed another when it is as much as and still more than it,
whereas that which is contained in something else is exceeded by it. And
10   let "greater" and "more" always be in relation to "lesser," but "great" and
"small" and "much" and "little" relate to the size of most things; and let
"great" be what exceeds, and what falls short be "small," and similarly with
"much" and "little."

Now we say that that which is choiceworthy for its own sake, and not
for the sake of something else, is good; and good, too, is that at which
all things aim, and that which something possessed of intellect and pru-
15   dence would choose, and that which is productive and protective [of a
good], or what follows on such things. Moreover, the end is that for the
sake of which [one acts], and the end is that for the sake of which all else is

done; and what is good for someone himself is what has these characteristics in relation to him. [Since all this is so,] it is necessarily the case that
the greater number [of goods] is better than one or than fewer of them,
when that one good or those fewer goods are numbered among them, for   20
it exceeds them, whereas what is contained in something is exceeded by
it. And if the greatest thing exceeds another greatest thing, the former
exceeds the latter; and in the case of all such things as exceed others, the
greatest of the former will exceed the greatest of the latter. For example, if
the biggest man is bigger than the biggest woman, then in general men are
bigger than women. And if men generally are bigger than women, then   25
the biggest man will be bigger than the biggest woman. For there is a proportion between the superiority of one class to another and the greatest
[or biggest] things within them.

And when *this* follows on *that*, but not *that* on *this* (and "follows on"
is either simultaneously or subsequently or potentially) [then the *that* is
greater], for the use of that which follows is contained already in that of   30
what precedes: to be alive follows simultaneously on being healthy, but
being healthy does not follow on being alive; and understanding follows
subsequently on learning; and robbing follows potentially on desecrating
a temple, for someone who has desecrated a temple might also rob one.
And things that exceed the same thing by a greater amount [than something else] are greater, for they must necessarily exceed even that greater
amount.[88] And things productive of a greater good are themselves greater,   35
for, as we saw, this is what it is to be productive of the greater; and similarly in the case of that which is produced by something greater, for if
something healthful is more choiceworthy than something pleasant and
is a greater good, then health is greater than pleasure. And that which   1364a
is more choiceworthy[89] in itself [is greater] than that which is not so in
itself—for example, strength is greater than the healthful, for the latter is
not for its own sake whereas the former is, since that is in fact, as we saw,
the good.

And if one thing is an end, the other not an end, for the latter is for the

88 · "This is to say that any A which surpasses a B, *which B itself is greater than C*, is
greater" (Grimaldi; emphasis original). Or, as Freese (ad loc.) puts it, "Eight is greater
than 2 by 6, which itself is greater than 2." This difficult sentence has occasioned emendation and considerable commentary. I follow in the main Grimaldi's reading and
translation.

89 · The reading of the MSS; modern editors except Ross and Grimaldi alter the text to
read "And that which is choiceworthy."

sake of something else, the former for its own sake. For example, exercising is for the sake of having a body in good condition. And that which
has a lesser additional need of another thing or of others, for it is more
self-sufficient (and "having lesser need" is needing fewer things or things
easier to attain). And when *this* is not or cannot come to be without *that*,
but *that* can be without *this*, that which has no such need is more self-
sufficient and as a result appears to be a greater good. And if one thing
is a starting point,[90] the other not a starting point; and if one is a cause,
the other not a cause, for the same reason: without a cause and a starting point, it is impossible for anything to be or to come to be. And in the
case of two starting points, what stems from the greater starting point is
greater, and in the case of two causes, what stems from the greater cause
is greater; and, conversely, where there are two starting points, the starting point of what is greater is greater, and where there are two causes, the
cause of what is greater is greater.

It is clear, then, on the basis of what has been said, that something
can appear greater in two ways: if something is a starting point but the
other is not, the former will seem to be greater; and if something is not
a starting point [but an end] and the other *is* a starting point, [the former but not the latter will seem to be greater,] for the end, not the starting point, is greater, just as Leodamas,[91] in leveling his accusation against
Callistratus,[92] asserted that he who deliberated about the matter is more
unjust than is the fellow who actually carried it out, for it would not have
been done if someone had not deliberated about it. But then again, when
accusing Chabrias,[93] [Leodamas said that] he who carried it out is more
unjust than he who [merely] deliberated about it, for it would not have
happened were there not someone who actually did it. And it is for this
reason that people devise plots—so they may carry them out.

What is scarcer is also [a greater good] than what is plentiful—for example, gold is a greater good than iron, despite being less useful. For the
possession of gold is a greater thing because it is more difficult to attain.

90 · Or "principle" (*archē*), here and throughout.
91 · Leodamas was a well-known Athenian orator, a younger contemporary of Demosthenes and Aeschines.
92 · Callistratus was a prominent Athenian orator and politician, most influential in
Athens ca. 377–361.
93 · Chabrias (ca. 420–357) was a celebrated Athenian general; he and Callistratus
were prosecuted by Leodamas in 366 for their involvement in the loss to the Thebans
of a town near Athenian territory.

But in another way what is plentiful is a greater good than what is rare, because the use of it exceeds [the use of what is rarer]: "often" exceeds "rarely." Hence it is said, "Best is water."[94] And in general the more difficult [is greater] than the easier, for it is rarer. But in another way the easier is a greater good than the more difficult, for it is as we wish it to be. And that whose contrary is greater, or the deprivation of which is greater, [is greater]. And virtue is greater than non-virtue, vice of non-vice, for the former in both cases are ends, the latter not.[95] And those things whose products are nobler or more shameful are themselves greater; and the products of those things whose virtues and vices are greater will be greater too, since as causes and starting points are to the results, so the results are to the causes and starting points. And those things the excess of which is more choiceworthy or nobler—for example, seeing precisely is more choiceworthy than smelling precisely, for sight is more choiceworthy than sense of smell, and putting love of a comrade over love of money is nobler, the result being that loving a comrade is more choiceworthy than loving money. And correspondingly, the excesses of better things are better, those of nobler things, nobler. And the things for which the desires are nobler or better [are greater], for the longings for greater things are greater; and the desires for nobler or better things are better or nobler for the same reason. And the subject matters whose sciences are nobler and more serious are themselves nobler or more serious, for as a given science is, so also is the truth [of concern to it]: each science exercises command over what is its own. And the sciences of the more serious and nobler things are proportionate to those things for the same reasons.

That which the prudent—or all people or the many or most people or the most excellent—would judge or have judged to be good or greater[96] is necessarily so, either simply or insofar as they judged in accord with prudence. This is a point common to other cases as well: what something is, and its quantity and quality, are what the relevant science and pru-

30

35

1364b

5

10

15

---

94 · Pindar, *Olympian* 1.1: "Best is water, but gold, like a blazing fire, stands out in the night, supreme of lordly wealth."

95 · Some commentators suggest emending the reading of the MSS here because they balk at the thought that vice can be an end, a *telos*, according to Aristotle. But Cope (ad loc.) suggests: "Positive virtue and positive vice, which can be ends or objects to aim at, are in so far superior to mere negatives which can not."

96 · The reading of the MSS, defended by Grimaldi among others. Ross and Kassel offer emendations, the text of the latter giving this translation: "would judge or have judged to be a greater good."

dence would say they are. But it is about goods that we have spoken, for "good" was defined[97] as that which things possessed of prudence would choose in each case. It is clear, then, that that which prudence affirms to a greater degree is a greater [good]. And that which is available to better people, either simply or insofar as they are better—for example, courage is better than strength. And what the better person would choose, either simply or insofar as he is better—for example, it is better to suffer injustice than to inflict it, for this is what the more just person would choose.

Also the more pleasant than the less pleasant, for all things seek pleasure; and people long to feel pleasure for its own sake, and it is in reference to these that the good and the end were defined. The more pleasant pleasure is what is both freer from pain and longer-lasting. And the nobler than the less noble, for the noble is either what is pleasant or choiceworthy in itself. And all those things that people wish to be the causes of—they themselves either for themselves or for their friends—are greater goods, and all those things that they least of all wish to be the cause of are greater ills. Longer-lasting things are greater than the less long-lasting, and the more stable than the less stable. For the use of the more stable exceeds in point of time, the use of the longer-lasting exceeds as regards our wish: whenever people wish for something, the use of what is stable is available to them to a greater degree [than is that of the less stable].

Just as certain consequences would follow from words that are linguistic coordinates and have similar grammatical inflections,[98] so there are other [such consequences] as well: for example, if "courageously" is nobler and more choiceworthy than "moderately," then "courage" is also more choiceworthy than "moderation," as is "being courageous" than "being moderate." And that which all choose [is greater] than that which not all choose; and that which most choose rather than what fewer choose. For "good" is, as we saw,[99] that at which all aim, such that that at which more people aim is greater. And what even one's opponents or enemies aim at, or what certain judges or those whom these judges judge [to be competent] aim at—for in the former case it is as if all would assert that it is so; in the latter, the authorities and the knowers. And sometimes that which all share in is greater—for not so to share is a mark of dishonor—but sometimes that which no one or few share in—for it is rarer. So also

97 · Consider 1363b14–15.
98 · See also 2.23 (1397a20–22).
99 · Consider 1362a21–24.

the more praiseworthy things, since these are nobler. And, similarly, those things for which the honors are greater, for honor is like a certain mark of deserving; and those things for which the penalties are greater [are greater]. Also things that are greater than those that are agreed to be great or appear to be.

And the same things divided up into parts appear greater, since a greater number of things appears to exceed [a lesser]. So it is too that the poet[100] contends that the following persuaded Meleager to stand up [and fight]:

> So many evils come to human beings whose city has been seized:
> People perish, and fire levels a city with the dust,
> And others lead off children.

And putting points together and building one on top of another, as Epicharmus[101] did, both because this is the same as division (for such putting together shows the excess involved to be great) and because it appears to be a starting point and cause of great things. And since that which is more difficult and rarer is greater, the crucial moments and relevant ages and places and times and capacities produce great things. For if the actions carried out are beyond one's capacity and age and peers, and if they are done in a given way or at a given place or time, they will be possessed of a certain greatness among things noble, good, or just (or their opposites). Hence also the epigram concerning the Olympic champion:

> Previously I held on my shoulders a rough basket,
> Carrying fish from Argos to Tegea.[102]

And Iphicrates[103] used to praise himself by stating the things from which he got his start. And what stems from one's own nature is greater than

---

100 · Homer, *Iliad* 9.592–94. The words are spoken by Meleager's wife, Cleopatra (as reported by Phoenix), and prove sufficient to prompt Meleager to act against the Curetes besieging the city.

101 · Epicharmus was a comic writer and playwright from Sicily, active in the first quarter of the fifth century. Aristotle speaks of him also in the *Poetics* (1448a32 and context); see also 1410b4–5 below.

102 · The same quotation appears again, more briefly, at 1367b18–19.

103 · Presumably the distinguished Athenian general here mentioned (ca. 415–353) was of humble origins; a partial quotation or paraphrase of his remark is given below at 1367b18. He later became a mercenary commander in Thrace.

30   what is acquired, for it is more difficult. Hence also the poet contends,
"Self-taught am I."[104]

And the greatest part of what is great: for example, Pericles, when he
says in his funeral oration that the youths having been taken away from
the city is just as if the spring should be taken away from the year.[105] And
things that are useful where the need is greater [are themselves greater]—
for example, things useful in old age and illnesses. And where there are

35   two [useful things], the one nearer the end [or goal] is greater. And what
is such for a particular person himself is greater than that which is such
without qualification. And what is possible rather than impossible, since
the former is useful to oneself, the latter not. Also things bound up with
the end [or goal] of life, for ends are more important than things condu-

1365b cive to the end. And those that relate to the truth are greater than those
that relate to opinion, and the defining mark of what relates to opinion is that which one would not choose if it were going to go unnoticed.
Hence to receive a benefaction would, in the element of opinion, be more
choiceworthy than to perform a benefaction, for the former will be chosen even if it goes unnoticed, but it does not seem that one would choose

5   to benefit another if doing so goes unnoticed. And all those things that
people wish to be rather than to seem to be, for these are more related to
the truth. Hence people assert that even justice is a small thing, because it
is more choiceworthy to seem to be just than to be it—but not so in the
case of being healthy.

And that which is useful for many things—for example, what is useful

10   for living and living well and pleasure and performing noble acts. Hence
wealth and health are held to be very great things, since they can be put
to quite all of these uses. And what is freer of pain and what is accompanied by pleasure [are choiceworthy], for there is more than one [good at
issue], such that it is a good thing for both pleasure and the freedom from
pain to be present. And of two goods, the greater is that which, when it
is added to the same thing, makes the whole greater. And those things
whose presence does not go unnoticed [are greater] than those that do

15   go unnoticed, for these tend in the direction of the truth. Hence being

104 · It is not certain which poet Aristotle has in mind. Phemius (Homer, *Odyssey*
22.347) says that he is "self-taught" (*autodidaktos*) in poetry. Cope (ad loc.) refers to
Pindar, *Olympian* 2.86–88 and 9.100–102, as well as *Nemean* 3.40–41, where the poet
stresses the goodness of being born with genius.
105 · This phrase does not appear in the funeral oration of Pericles as recorded by
Thucydides.

wealthy would appear to be a greater good than seeming to be it. And that which one cherishes, in some cases by those who have it by itself, in other cases by those who have it together with other things. Hence there is not an equal penalty involved if somebody puts out the eye of a one-eyed man or that of a man having two, for in the former case he removes what is cherished.

On the basis of what things, then, one must adduce modes of persuasion, when exhorting and dissuading, has for the most part been stated.   20

CHAPTER 8

But with a view to being able to persuade and advise in a fine manner, the greatest and most authoritative consideration of quite all is to grasp *all* the regimes and to distinguish the habits of each, their legal customs, and what is advantageous to each. For indeed everyone is persuaded by what   25 is advantageous, and that which preserves the regime is to its advantage. And, further, the declaration of the authoritative body is authoritative, but the authoritative bodies have been distinguished in reference to the regimes: there are as many authoritative bodies as there are regimes. And there are four regimes: democracy, oligarchy, aristocracy, [and] monar-   30 chy. As a result, that which is authoritative and judges is always some part of these, or the whole. And democracy is a regime in which they distribute offices among themselves by lot, oligarchy that in which the distribution is done on the basis of property assessments, aristocracy that in which they do so according to education (and I mean by "education" the one established by law), for those who have remained within the legal   35 customs rule in an aristocracy, and these necessarily appear best—hence it has its name.[106] Monarchy, as its name indicates, is the regime in which   1366a one person is authoritative over quite all things; and of these monarchies, the one that rules in accord with a certain ordered arrangement is kingship, the one that is unlimited is tyranny.

So one must not overlook the end of each regime, for people choose things conducive to the end. In democracy the end is freedom; in oligar-   5 chy, wealth; in aristocracy, matters pertaining to education and the legal customs; in tyranny, the protection [of the tyranny itself]. It is clear, then, that one must distinguish the habits bearing on the end of each regime, as well as the lawful conventions and advantageous things, if in fact

106 · The word "best" (*aristoi*) forms the root of "aristocracy"—the rule of the best.

it is in reference to this end that people make their choices. Now, since modes of persuasion arise not only through demonstrative argument but
10   also through speech pertaining to matters of character[107] (for we trust the speaker because he appears to be of a certain sort, and this is so if he appears to be good or well intentioned or both), we must grasp the characters belonging to each of the regimes. For it is necessarily the case that the character belonging to each regime is most persuasive to each. And these will be grasped through the same considerations: the characters are
15   manifest in reference to the choice involved, and one's choice refers to the end [one aims at].

Those things, then, future or present, that must be aimed at when formulating exhortations; and on the basis of what one must grasp the modes of persuasion pertaining to the advantageous; and, further, what
20   concerns the characters and lawful customs relating to the regimes, and through what and in what manner we will have ready access to them—these matters have been stated to the extent commensurate with the present occasion. For what concerns them has been stated precisely in the *Politics*.

CHAPTER 9

After this, let us speak about virtue and vice, and noble and base, since
25   these are the concerns targeted by anyone who praises and blames. In speaking about these we will as a result also make clear at the same time those considerations on the basis of which we will be taken to be people of a certain sort of character, which was the second[108] sort of a mode of persuasion. For from these same considerations we will also render both us ourselves and another person trustworthy in point of virtue. But since
30   it happens that people often praise—seriously or not—not only a human being or a god but also inanimate things and any chance animal, one must in the same way also grasp the premises pertaining to these. Let us as a result speak also about them, at least insofar as they serve as an example.

What is noble, then, is what is choiceworthy for its own sake, and

107 · That is, what is "ethical" (*ēthikos*).
108 · At 1.2 (1356a1–3), Aristotle had listed modes of persuasion connected with the speaker's character first; but just above, at 1.8 (1366a9–10), Aristotle had spoken of modes of persuasion that arise "not only through a demonstrative argument but also through speech pertaining to matters of character," which could suggest that demonstrative modes of persuasion or proofs are first simply, if not first in rhetoric.

praiseworthy accordingly, or it is that which is good, it being pleasant because it is good. So if this is the noble, virtue is necessarily noble, 35
since virtue, being good, is praised. And virtue, as it seems, is a capacity
to provide and protect good things, and a capacity to effect many great
benefactions—even all benefactions pertaining to everything. And the 1366b
parts of virtue are justice, courage, moderation, magnificence, greatness
of soul, liberality, gentleness, prudence, [and] wisdom. The greatest virtues are necessarily the ones of most use for others, if in fact virtue is a capacity for benefaction. For this reason people honor especially those who 5
are just and courageous: the latter in war and the former also in peace are
useful for others. Then there is liberality, for [the liberal] give freely and
do not quarrel over money, which is what others aim at especially. Justice
is a virtue through which each attains the things that are one's own, and 10
as the law [indicates], injustice being that through which one attains what
belongs to others and not as the law indicates. Courage is that through
which people are skilled in carrying out noble deeds amid dangers, and
as the law commands, and as servants of the law; cowardice is the opposite. Moderation is a virtue through which people are disposed toward
the bodily pleasures as the law commands; licentiousness is the opposite. 15
Liberality is characterized by beneficence pertaining to money; stinginess
is the opposite. Greatness of soul is a virtue productive of great benefactions, smallness of soul its opposite,[109] magnificence a virtue productive
of great things in expenditures. Smallness of soul and parsimony are the 20
opposite. Prudence is a virtue of understanding, in reference to which
people are able to deliberate well about the good and bad things said to
bear on happiness.

What concerns virtue and vice in general, then, and their parts, has been
stated sufficiently for the present occasion, and as for what concerns the
rest, it is not difficult to see. For it is manifest that the things productive 25
of virtue are necessarily noble (since they look to virtue), as are also the
things that arise from virtue, and such things are both signs of virtue and
its deeds. And since these signs are noble, as are also the deeds characteristic of a good person or the things he suffers or undergoes, it is necessarily the case that all the deeds of courage, or the signs of courage, or the 30
actions carried out courageously, are noble, and so too just things and
deeds done justly (but not just sufferings [or punishments], for in this

---

109 · This clause pertaining to smallness of soul is bracketed by most modern editors as
a gloss, although it appears in all but one of the principal MSS.

alone of the virtues it is not always noble to suffer justly; rather, being punished justly is more shameful than undergoing it unjustly), and similarly in the case of the other virtues.

35   All those things for which honor is the reward are noble, and all those that are done for honor rather than money. And all those virtuous actions someone carries out not for his own sake. So too all those things that are good unqualifiedly that someone does on behalf of the fatherland, while overlooking his own [good]. And the things good by nature, and which

1367a   are good not for him himself, [are noble,] for [natural goods] of that sort would be for his own sake [and hence not noble]. And all such things as admit of being present to someone who has died rather than the living, for things possessed by somebody living have to a greater degree the character of being for his own sake. And all such deeds as are for the sake of others, since they are less for one's own sake. And all such actions as ben-

5   efit others, but not oneself, and as benefit benefactors—for that is just. And beneficent deeds, for they do not pertain to oneself. And the opposite of those things that prompt people to feel shame, since they feel ashamed at saying and doing or being about to do ugly things, just as when Alcaeus says,

10   And I wish to say something, but a sense of shame[110] prevents me,

so Sappho wrote [in response],

> If you had a longing for fine or noble things
> And your tongue were not stirred to say something bad,
> Shame would not have hold of your eyes
> But you would speak about what is just.

15   And those things are noble for which people contend, while not feeling fear, for they have this experience concerning those goods that bear on reputation.

        And the virtues of those who are by nature more serious are nobler, as are their deeds, as, for example, those of a man rather than a woman. And those virtues characterized by the enjoyment they bring others, rather than oneself. Hence what is just, and justice [itself], are noble. And being

20   avenged on one's enemies and not being reconciled with them, for payback is just and justice is noble, and it belongs to a courageous man not to get the worst of it, and victory and honor are among the noble things. For

---

110 · "Sense of shame" here translates *aidōs*, which can also mean "respect" or "awe."

these are choiceworthy even when they bear no fruit, and they make clear an excess of [or preeminence in] virtue. And things deserving of remembrance, the more deserving being nobler. And those things that attend someone who is not alive—things that honor attends[111]—are nobler, as are extraordinary things and those that are available to a single person only, for they are more readily remembered. And possessions that bear no fruit, for these are more liberal. And things peculiar to each [people or city] in turn are noble, and all such signs of what is praised among them—for example, in Lacedaemon to have long hair is noble, for that is a sign of a free man, since it is not at all easy to perform a menial task with long hair. And undertaking no vulgar art, for it belongs to a free man not to live with a view to another person.

One must, for the purposes of praise and blame, take things that closely resemble given qualities as being the same as they—for example, that the cautious person is "cool and calculating" and the simpleton, "upstanding," or that the unfeeling is "gentle"; and each is always referred to by what is the best among the qualities that follow closely together—for example, the angry and the manic are "frank," the stubborn, "magnificent" and "august"; and [one must speak of] those characterized by the excesses as though they are characterized by the corresponding virtues—for example, the reckless man is "courageous" and the spendthrift, "liberal." For this will be the opinion of the many, and, at the same time, fallacious reasoning derives from the cause in question: if someone is apt to run risks where it is not necessary to do so, all the more would he be held to be such where it *is* noble to run them, and if someone is lavish with any chance persons, he will be such also with friends. For the excess of virtue is to benefit everyone.

But one must examine also those among whom the praise is given, for, just as Socrates used to say, it is not difficult to praise Athenians among Athenians.[112] But one must speak of whatever is honored among each [people] as though it were present to hand—for example, among Scythians or Laconians[113] or philosophers. And in general, one must lead what

25

30

35

1367b

5

10

111 · The clause is excised by Kassel, although most editors, in accord with the MSS, read it.

112 · See Plato, *Menexenus* 235d. Aristotle refers to the same remark again at 3.14 (1415b30–31).

113 · Scythians were regarded as warlike barbarians, and Laconians are Spartans. So great, then, can be the range in the character of one's audience, from Scythians to philosophers.

is honored in the direction of the noble, since it is held, at least, to be its near neighbor. And all such deeds as accord with what is fitting—for example, if they are worthy of someone's ancestors and his own prior deeds, for acquiring additional honor is held to be a mark of happiness and noble. And if something goes beyond what is fitting but tends in the direction of what is better and what is nobler than that—for example, if someone while enjoying good fortune is measured, but is great-souled amid misfortune, or someone who, in becoming greater, becomes also better and more given to reconciliation. Of such a character is the re-mark of Iphicrates, "from such things to such things," and [the remark] of the Olympic victor, "previously on my shoulders a rough . . . ,"[114] and the remark of Simonides, "she being of a father, a husband, and brothers—tyrants one and all."[115] Since praise is derived from a person's actions, and since it is especially the mark of a serious person that his action accords with his choice, one must attempt to show that he acts in accord with choice, and it is useful [to show] that he appears to have so acted many times. Hence things that have happened by accident and chance must be taken as residing in his choice, since if many similar things are adduced, they will be held to be a sign of his virtue and choice.

Praise is speech that indicates the greatness of someone's virtue. One must, then, point out that the actions in question are of such a [virtu-ous] character; and an encomium is praise of a person's deeds. Attendant circumstances—for example, good birth and education—are conducive to persuasion [or credibility], for it is likely that good human beings arise from those who are good, and one who has thus been reared is such him-self. Hence we offer encomiums of those who have carried out certain ac-tions. Deeds are a sign of one's characteristic state [of soul], since we would praise even someone who has performed no action, if we should trust that he is of such a character. Deeming someone blessed and deeming some-one happy are in themselves the same thing, but these are not the same as praise and an encomium; rather, just as happiness encompasses virtue, so also deeming someone happy encompasses praise and an encomium.[116]

Praise and advice have a common form, for the points you might pro-pose by way of offering advice become an encomium when their phras-

114 · See 1365a26–27 for a more complete citation of the same line.
115 · See Thucydides, *War of the Peloponnesians and Athenians* 6.59.3 for a fuller version of the Simonides quotation. The woman in question is Archedike, daughter of Hippias, tyrant of Athens.
116 · On happiness, praise, and an encomium, consider *Nicomachean Ethics* 1.12.

ing[117] is altered. When, then, we grasp the things one must do and the sort of person one should be, in stating these as proposals, one should change their phrasing and turn them around—for example, that one should not pride oneself on what is due to luck but rather on what is due to oneself. When stated this way, it amounts to a proposal, but in the following way it is praise: "He prides himself not on the things that are his due to luck, but rather on things that are due to him himself." As a result, whenever you wish to praise someone, see what it is that you might propose [as advice]; and whenever you wish to propose something [as advice], see what it is that you might praise. The phrasing will of necessity be opposite, when what is a prohibition [in the giving of advice] undergoes a change and becomes [in the case of praise] not a prohibition.[118]

One must also make use of many kinds of amplification—for example, if someone acts alone or first or with few others, or if he above all has done something, for quite all of these are noble. And matters deriving from the time involved or the crucial moments, if these go beyond what can be expected. And if someone has successfully done the same thing many times, for that is a great thing and would be held to stem, not from chance, but from him himself. If incentives and honors have been invented or established on his account, and if he was the first for whom a given encomium was made—as in the case of Hippolochus,[119] for example, or as in the statues erected in the marketplace for Harmodius and Aristogeiton.[120] This applies similarly in the case of opposites too. Even if you are without sufficient resources as regards the person himself, set him alongside others by way of comparison. This is in fact what Isocrates used to do, on account of his not[121] being habituated to speaking in courtrooms. And

---

117 · Or "diction," as the term (*lexis*) is translated in book 3.

118 · This sentence has prompted considerable commentary, and Grimaldi is dissatisfied with all suggested interpretations, including his own (which I follow). Cope suggests: "The expression must be contradictory . . . when the prohibitive and the non-prohibitive are interchanged."

119 · Nothing is known of Hippolochus.

120 · The lovers Harmodius and Aristogeiton are credited (wrongly, according to Thucydides: *War of the Peloponnesians and Athenians* 6.53–59 as well as 1.20) with assassinating the Athenian tyrant Hippias: see also 2.23 (1398a18–22) below, as well as Aristotle, *Athenian Regime* 18.

121 · The reading of one MS and most editors (although not Kassel); other MSS read "his being habituated to speaking in courtrooms." Grimaldi defends the reading adopted in our text on the grounds that Isocrates "explicitly remarks" that he "had decided early in his career to devote his life to works of larger significance than petty legal

one must compare the person in question to those held in high regard, for doing so serves the purpose of amplification, and it is noble if he is better than serious persons. Amplification reasonably falls among kinds of praise, since it is bound up with excess [or preeminence], and such excess [or preeminence] belongs to what is noble. Hence even if there is no need to compare him to those held in high regard, one must nonetheless compare him to the many,[122] since excess [or preeminence] is held to reveal virtue.

25

In general, of the classes of things common to quite all [the kinds of rhetorical] speeches, amplification is most suited to epideictic ones, which take up actions that are agreed on, it remaining, as a result, just to bestow greatness and nobility on them. Examples are most suited to deliberative speeches, for we judge future events by divining on the basis of past ones. Enthymemes are most suited to judicial speeches, for what has happened in the past, on account of its lack of clarity, especially admits of [arguments concerning] cause and demonstration.

30

These things, then, form the basis of almost all statements of praise and blame; they are the sorts of things people must look to in uttering praise and blame; and they are that from which encomiums and reproaches come to be. Given these, their opposites are manifest, for blame arises from the opposite considerations.

35

CHAPTER 10

1368b   Next would be to speak about what concerns accusation and defense—from how many and what sorts of things the syllogisms should be formed. Now, one must grasp three things: first, for the sake of what, and for how many things, people commit injustice; second, how they themselves are disposed when they do so; and third, the sorts of people who are treated unjustly and what their condition is. Once we have defined what doing injustice is, let us then speak of the points that follow.

5

So let doing injustice be doing harm voluntarily contrary to the law. And "law" is both particular law and general[123] law. I mean by "partic-

cases." Isocrates (436–338) was a leading orator or rhetorician in Athens; see also, e.g., 2.23 below (1399a2–6).

122 · The text here is uncertain, and another rendering is possible: "Hence even if one does not compare him to those held in high regard, one must nonetheless compare him to others."

123 · *Koinos*: a law that is shared, general, or common.

ular" the law that has been written down in accord with which people govern themselves, whereas by "general" I mean all those unwritten laws that seem to be agreed on by everyone. And people carry out voluntarily   10 all such things as they know [they are doing] and are not compelled to do. Things that people do voluntarily are not in all cases objects of their choice,[124] but things they do choose are, all of them, done knowingly, for nobody chooses what he is ignorant of.

People choose to do harm and to perform base acts contrary to the law on account of vice and a lack of self-restraint. If certain people have a moral defect,[125] either one or more than one, then they are unjust also in   15 connection with that defect they happen to have. For example, one person is illiberal concerning money; another is licentious concerning the bodily pleasures; another, soft when it comes to taking the easy way; another, a coward concerning dangers, for on account of their fear, people abandon those who run risks with them; another is ambitious on account   20 of honor; another sharp-tempered on account of his anger; another is rivalrous for victory;[126] another bitter on account of vengeance; another a fool because he is deceived about just and unjust; another shameless because he thinks little of reputation—and similarly in the case of each of the others with their underlying [defects] respectively. But what concerns these is clear—some points on the basis of what has been said about the   25 virtues, others on the basis of what will be said about the passions.

But it remains to state for the sake of what people commit injustice and what their state is when they do commit it, and against whom they so act. First, then, let us define what things they long for and what sorts of things they avoid when they undertake to commit injustice. For it is clear that the accuser must examine how many and which of these things characterize the accused, things that all who commit injustice against their neighbors aim at, just as it is clear that he who is defending himself must   30

---

124 · In *Magna moralia* 1189a31–36, Aristotle indicates that "the voluntary is not the chosen. For we do many things voluntarily before having thought and deliberated about them—for example, we sit down and stand up and do many other things of this sort voluntarily without thinking, but things by choice are, as we saw, all accompanied by thought." Consider also *Nicomachean Ethics* 3.2 (1111b6–10): "Now, choice appears to be something voluntary, but not the same thing as it; rather, what is voluntary is wider in scope. For both children and animals share in what is voluntary but not in choice, and we say that sudden actions are voluntary but do not stem from choice."

125 · The term is *mochthēria*, elsewhere translated as "depravity" (see, e.g., 1403b35).

126 · Or, more literally, "fond of victory" (*philonikos*).

examine which of these things, and how many of them, do *not* characterize him.

Now, all actions that everyone performs are, some of them, not due
to them themselves, while others are due to them. Of those actions that
are not due to themselves, some they do through chance, others of neces-
35   sity; and of those traceable to necessity, some occur through force, others by nature. As a result, of all those things they do that are not traceable
to them themselves, some arise from luck, others from nature, still others through force. As for all those things due to themselves and for which
1369a   they themselves are the cause, some arise through habit, others through
longing; and of these latter, some arise through a rational longing, others
through a non-rational one. There is also wishing, which is a longing for
what is good (for nobody wishes for anything except when he supposes it
5   to be good); and non-rational longings are anger and desire. As a result,
all that people do is necessarily traceable to seven causes: chance, nature,
force, habit, calculation, spiritedness, [and] desire.

Making further distinctions among the actions by reference to one's
age or characteristics or certain other things is superfluous. For if it has
10   happened that the young are given to anger or desires, it is not on account
of their youth that they do such things but rather on account of their anger and desire. And neither is it through wealth and poverty, although it
has turned out that the poor, on account of their need, desire money, the
wealthy on account of superfluity desire unnecessary pleasures. But these
15   too will act not on account of wealth and poverty but rather desire. And
similarly, too, both the just and the unjust, and the others who are said
to act according to their respective characteristics, will act on account of
these: either on account of calculation or passion, although it is through
fine characters and passions that [the just or virtuous] act, the contrary
[characters and passions] in the case of the others. It does turn out, to be
20   sure, that this or that sort of action follows this or that sort of characteristic. For it is perhaps the case that fine opinions and desires pertaining to
the pleasures will from the outset attend the moderate person, on account
of his being moderate, just as the opposite desires and opinions pertaining to these same pleasures will attend the licentious.

25   Hence one must leave aside such distinctions and examine instead
what sorts of things usually follow on what sorts of things. For if someone
is light or dark or large or small, nothing has been ordained so as to follow from such things, but if someone is young or older or just or unjust,
this already makes a difference. And in general, all such things as produce

a difference in the characters of human beings—for example, the opinion
someone has that he is wealthy or poor will make a difference, and that he
is lucky or unlucky. We will speak about these things later,[127] but for now   30
let us speak first about the points that remain.

The sorts of things that arise from chance are all those whose cause
is indeterminate and that do not arise for the sake of something and are
neither always nor for the most part nor regularly so. What concerns
these things is clear from the definition of chance.[128] As for all the sorts   35
of things that arise by nature, their cause is in themselves and regular, for   1369b
they either always or for the most part turn out in a similar way. As for
those things that are contrary to nature, there is no need to render a precise account of them, as to whether they occur in accord with a certain nature or another cause—but chance would seem to be the cause in fact of
such things. What occurs through force is all that is done by people them-   5
selves but contrary to their desire or calculations. What occurs through
habit is all that people do because they have done it many times before.
What occurs through calculation is held to be advantageous, on the basis of the goods mentioned, either as an end or as being conducive to the
end, when such things are done for the advantage in question—for even   10
licentious people do some advantageous things, but they do them not
on account of the advantage involved but rather the pleasure. [Actions]
marked by the spirit of vengeance are done through spiritedness and anger. But there is a difference between vengeance and punishment: punishment is for the sake of the person suffering it, vengeance for that of the
person inflicting it, so that he may gain satisfaction thereby. Now, what
anger is will be clear in what concerns the passions,[129] but all that is done   15
through desire appears pleasant. And both the customary and the habitual reside among the pleasures, for there are many things that, though
they are by nature not pleasant, produce pleasure when people become
habituated to them.

To speak in a summary way, quite all the things that people do on their
own account either are good or appear good, or are pleasant or appear   20
pleasant. And since all that people do on their own account they do voluntarily, but involuntarily all that they do not do on their own account,
all that people do voluntarily would be such things as either are good or

127 · Consider 2.15–17.
128 · Consider 1.5 above (1361b39–1362a12); Aristotle may also have in mind his discussion of chance as a cause in the *Physics* (195b31–198a13).
129 · Consider 2.2.

appear good or are pleasant or appear pleasant. For I set down as being among goods the removal of things that are bad or appear to be bad, or
25   the exchange of a greater ill for a lesser one (for these are in a way choice-worthy), and similarly I set down among pleasures the removal of pains or of apparent ones, or the exchange of lesser pains in place of greater ones. One must therefore grasp what the advantageous and pleasant things are, both how many they are and of what sort. As for what concerns the ad-
30   vantageous in deliberative speeches, that was spoken of before,[130] but let us speak now about what concerns the pleasant. And one must regard the definitions as sufficient, if they are in each case neither unclear nor [overly] precise.

CHAPTER 11

Let our hypothesis be that pleasure is a certain motion of the soul and a concentrated, perceptible settling into the soul's underlying natural con-
35   dition, whereas pain is the opposite. So if pleasure is such, it is clear that
1370a   the pleasant is that which is productive of the disposition stated, and that which is destructive of it (or productive of the opposed settling) is painful. It is necessary, then, that entering into the natural state is for the most
5   part pleasant, and especially when what happens in accord with nature has recovered its own natural state. And so too with habits, for the habitual happens just as if it is already by nature: habit bears some similarity to nature, since what happens often is close to what happens always, and while nature is a matter of "always," habit is a matter of "often." Pleasant, too, is what is not compulsory [or forced], since compulsion is contrary
10   to nature. Hence the necessities are painful,[131] and it has been correctly said that "every necessity is naturally a grievous thing."[132] The cares we take, our serious concerns, and our intense efforts are painful, for these are marked by necessity and compulsion, unless they become habitual, and in this way habit makes them pleasant. And the opposites of these things are pleasant. Hence things characterized by what is easygoing, the
15   freedom from toil, the absence of care, play and recreation, fall among things pleasant. For none of these relates to necessity.

130 · Consider 1.6.

131 · Most editors, with some manuscript support, read here "necessity is painful."

132 · Aristotle cites this line again at *Eudemian Ethics* 1223a30–33 and there attributes it to Evanus of Paros (consider, e.g., Plato, *Apology of Socrates* 20b8 and context); see also *Metaphysics* 1015a29–30.

And quite everything the desire for which is present in us, is pleasant, for desire is a longing for the pleasant. Of the desires, some are non-
rational, some accompanied by reason [or speech]. I mean by "non-
rational" all those desires that people have but not on the basis of some   20
supposition they have formed. And such are all those said to be by nature, just as are the desires present on account of the body—for example,
thirst and hunger for nourishment and the desire relating to each kind
of nourishment; and those desires connected with taste and sex and, in
general, objects of touch; and desires connected with smell[133] and hearing and sight. But desires accompanied by reason [or speech] are those   25
things people have a desire for as the result of undergoing some persuasion. For people desire both to behold and to possess many things because of what they have heard and been persuaded of. And since to feel
pleasure is to perceive some experience, and imagination is a sort of weak
perception, a certain imagination of what one remembers or hopes for
will attend the person remembering or hoping. And if this is so, it is clear   30
that pleasures, too, will simultaneously attend those who remember and
those who hope, since in fact perception, too, [is present]. It is necessarily
the case, then, that all the pleasant things are either present now, in being
perceived, or are in the past, in being remembered, or lie in the future, in
being hoped for, since people perceive the things now present, remember
past events, and hope for the things that will be in the future.   35

Memories are pleasant, then, and not just memories of all those   1370b
[events] that were pleasant when they were happening, but even of some
that were not in fact pleasant at the time—if what followed them was
subsequently noble and good. Hence this too has been said:

But sweet it is to remember toils, for someone who has been saved.[134]

And   5

For afterward even in pains does a man take delight as he remembers them,
He who suffers many things and accomplishes many things.[135]

And a cause of this is that not having something bad is pleasant too. And
as for what resides in hope, they are all those things that seem to delight or

133 · All the editors bracket as a gloss a word (*euōdias*) that appears here in the MSS; it
could be rendered as "pleasant aromas."
134 · Euripides, *Andromeda* (= Nauck fr. 131).
135 · Homer, *Odyssey* 15.400–401. The second line as it has come down to us in the
texts of Homer differs from Aristotle's quotation.

benefit greatly when they are present, and to benefit someone painlessly. In general, people both hope for and remember all such things as, when
10   they are present, for the most part bring delight. Hence even being angry is pleasant, just as Homer, too, wrote about spirited anger:

> which is sweeter by far than honey dripping down.[136]

For nobody feels anger at someone who manifestly cannot be the target of vengeance, nor at those much above them in power, with whom they either are not angry or are less angry.
15   And a certain pleasure follows most desires, for either by remembering how they attained [the object of their desire] or by hoping that they will attain it, people enjoy a certain pleasure—for example, those in the grip of fever take delight in their thirst, when they remember how they used to drink and when they hope they will drink again,[137] and lovers al-
20   ways delight when they converse and write about, and do[138] something pertaining to, the beloved. For in quite all such things, by calling up memories of the sort of person he is, people suppose that they are perceiving their beloved. And this becomes the starting point of love for everyone—whenever they take delight not only in the presence of the beloved but also in remembering him in his absence. Indeed, people are in love when-
25   ever they also feel pain by virtue of the beloved's absence. So too, similarly, in instances of mourning and lamentation a certain pleasure subsequently arises. For pain attends the fact that the person is not present, but there is pleasure in remembering and seeing him, in a way, both the things he used to do and the sort of person he was. So it is that this too was reasonably said:

> Thus he spoke, and in all he roused a desire to weep.[139]

30   And being avenged is pleasant, for whatever one fails to attain is painful, attaining it, pleasant. And those who are angry feel pain to an unsurpass-

136 · Homer, *Iliad* 18.109; see also 2.2 below (1378b6–7).

137 · Another interpretation of the text is possible: "for example, those gripped by thirst, in their fever, take delight when they remember"—although Grimaldi recommends taking the Greek in the manner reflected in the translation.

138 · Or, as Cope suggests, "write some poetry [*poiountes ti*] concerning their beloved."

139 · Homer, *Iliad* 23.108 and *Odyssey* 4.183. Achilles is referred to in the first quotation, just after he has been visited by the shade of Patroclus; Menelaus, in the second, has just called to mind his absent friend Odysseus, to an audience that includes Telemachus, son of Odysseus.

able degree when they are not avenged but feel delight when they hope to be so. And being victorious is pleasant—not just for those who love victory but for all. For there is an imagining of preeminence, for which all have a desire, to a greater or lesser degree. Given that being victorious 35 is pleasant, playful activities that are combative or competitive[140] are necessarily pleasant as well, since being victorious often arises in these, and 1371a so too games of knucklebones and ball playing and dicing and draughts. Similar too is what pertains to games of a more serious character: some such games become pleasant, if one is practiced in them, but others are 5 pleasant immediately—for example, the chase and all manner of hunting. For wherever there is rivalry, there too is victory. Hence both the judicial and the eristic [arts] are pleasant to those accustomed to them and capable of them.

Both honor and good reputation are among the most pleasant things, because each person comes thereby to imagine himself to be such as the serious person is, and all the more so whenever this is asserted by those 10 whom he supposes to be telling the truth. Such are those who are nearby rather than distant; one's usual associates and fellow citizens rather than those far removed; those who exist now rather than those who will be in the future; the prudent rather than the foolish; and many rather than few. For it is more likely that those mentioned, rather than their opposites, are telling the truth, since it is a matter of no concern to someone to gain honor or reputation from those for whom he feels much contempt, 15 as in the case of children or beasts,[141] at least not for the sake of the reputation itself; but if in fact that is of some concern to him, it is for some other reason.

The friend, too, is something pleasant, for feeling friendly love is pleasant (nobody is a wine-lover[142] who does not delight in wine) and being loved as a friend is pleasant. For here too there is an imagining of his possessing the good that all who perceive it desire. And to be loved as a friend 20 is to be cherished for one's own sake. And being admired is pleasant because it is the same thing as being honored. Being flattered, too, and the flatterer are pleasant, for the flatterer appears to be an admirer and ap-

140 · Literally, "eristic," which probably refers in this context to any contentious amusement, but it can refer also to a specific kind of contentious disputing or (false) syllogistic reasoning whose sole purpose is to get the better of an opponent; see just below at 1371a7, as well as 2.24 (1402a4).

141 · Grimaldi suggests taking "beasts" in a metaphorical sense: "brutish men."

142 · That is, a *philoinos*, a "friend" to wine.

25   pears to be a friend. And doing the same things frequently is pleasant, for
      what is customary is, as we saw,[143] pleasant. And change is pleasant, since
      change is a return to what is natural: what is always the same creates an
      excess in the established condition. Hence it was said:

          Change in all things is sweet.[144]

      For this reason, things that occur only occasionally are pleasant, when it
      comes to both human beings and affairs, for these are a change from the
30   present and are at the same time rare because occasional.
          Both learning and wondering are for the most part pleasant, for in
      wonder there is desire to learn[145] such that the object of wonder is an ob-
      ject of desire, and in learning there is a coming into one's natural state.
35   Both benefiting others and being benefited oneself are among the pleas-
1371b ant things, for being benefited is attaining the things people desire, and
      bestowing benefits is [a sign of] the power or capacity to do so and hence
      a mark of one's superiority,[146] both of which people aim at. And because
      what is productive of benefit is pleasant, it is pleasant also for human be-
      ings to restore their neighbors [to their former condition] and to make
      up for the things they lack. Since both learning and wondering are pleas-
5   ant, so too the following sorts of things are necessarily pleasant: the imita-
      tive, like painting and sculpture and poetry, and everything that is a good
      imitation, even if the thing imitated is itself not pleasant. For it is not in
      this that one takes delight; instead, there is an inference drawn[147] that
10   *this* thing here is *that* there, such that one learns something as a result. So
      too sudden turns of events and being barely saved from dangers, for all of
      these evoke wonder.
          Since what accords with nature is pleasant, and things that are akin are
      related to one another in accord with nature, all that is akin and similar is
      for the most part pleasant, such as human being to human being, horse to

143 · Consider 1369b16–18.
144 · Euripides, *Orestes* 234; consider also *Nicomachean Ethics* 1154b28–29 and context.
145 · Most of the MSS here read the infinitive "to learn" (*mathein*), as does Kassel, but
Grimaldi argues that it must be omitted. Omitting it would produce this translation:
"for in wonder there is desire such that the object of wonder is an object of desire." Aristotle here may wish to connect being filled with wonder (*thaumadzein*) with learning,
just as Socrates once connected it with philosophy: Plato, *Theaetetus* 155d2–3.
146 · Following the suggestion of Grimaldi. But some take the Greek in such a way as
to give this translation: "and bestowing benefits is [a mark of] possession and in fact
of preeminence."
147 · Literally, "a syllogism."

horse, and youth to youth. Hence also as the proverbs have it, that "age-   15
mate to age-mate is delightful" and "always the similar one" and "beast
knows beast" and "for jackdaw alongside jackdaw," and all else of that
sort. But since quite everything similar and akin is pleasant to itself, and
since each has himself undergone this experience above all in relation to
himself, all are necessarily self-lovers to a greater or lesser degree. For all   20
such things apply to oneself especially. And since all are self-lovers, it is
necessarily the case that everyone finds his own things pleasant—for example, his own deeds and speeches. Hence also people are fond of flattery, for the most part, and of those who love them, of honor, and of their
children, for children are their own works. And bringing to completion   25
what lacks something is pleasant, for that then becomes their own work.

     And since ruling is very pleasant, it is pleasant also to be held to be
wise, for being prudent is the mark of a ruler, and wisdom is knowledge of
many wondrous things. Further, since people are for the most part lovers
of honor, it is necessarily pleasant also to censure[148] their neighbors, and   30
to rule over them, and to spend one's time in that at which one is held to
be at one's best, just as also the poet contends:

> And to this each one presses on, allotting to the greatest part of the day
> Whatever he himself happens to be best at.[149]

And similarly, since play is among the pleasant things, so too is all relaxation; and laughter is among the pleasant things, so what prompts laugh-   35
ter is necessarily pleasant as well, both human beings and speeches as well   1372a
as deeds. But what concerns laughable things was defined separately in
the [writings] concerning poetics.[150]

     As for what concerns pleasant things, then, let these points be stated,
whereas the painful things are manifest on the basis of their opposites.

CHAPTER 12

These, then, are the things for the sake of which people commit injustice.
But how they are disposed [when they commit injustice], and against   5
whom they commit it—let us now speak of these. They commit injustice
whenever they suppose that it is possible for the matter in question to

---

148 · The verb "to censure" (*epitimaō*) has the same root as the word for "honor" (*timē*).
149 · Euripides, *Antiope* (= Nauck fr. 183); see also Plato, *Gorgias* 484e5.
150 · The text of the *Poetics* as it has come down to us is missing the treatment of comedy (see also 3.18 [1419b6–7] below).

be carried out, and possible for them themselves, whether in carrying it out they would go undetected or, in failing to go undetected, they would pay no penalty or, in paying a penalty, the punishment they would suffer would be less than the profit they would gain for themselves or for those they care about. As for the sorts of things that appear to be possible and those that appear impossible, these will be spoken of in what comes later (for these are common to all speeches).[151]

But those who are capable speakers, and those skilled in action and experienced in many contests, suppose that they are especially capable of committing injustice without suffering punishment, if they have many friends to boot, and if they are wealthy. And they suppose that they are capable of injustice especially if they themselves fall among the classes stated, but, failing that, if they have friends of that sort available to them, or servants or partners. It is for these reasons that they are capable of both acting and going undetected and not paying a penalty. So too if they are the friends of those treated unjustly or of the judges. For friends, on the one hand, are not on guard against suffering injustice and, in addition, reconcile before taking the matter to court; and judges, on the other, gratify those who are their friends and either let them off altogether or impose small punishments.

Apt to go undetected are those who stand in contrast to the accusations leveled—for example, a weak person accused in a matter of assault and one who is poor and ugly in a matter of adultery. Apt to go undetected, too, are those acts that are altogether manifest and done in plain sight, for these are unguarded against because no one would suppose them [to be at all possible], and those acts that are so great and of such a character that not even a single person would suppose them to be possible, since these acts, too, go unguarded against. For all are on guard against what they are accustomed to, as in the case of diseases, and so too in the case of injustices, but nobody takes proper precautions against a disease from which no one has yet suffered. So too those who have no enemies or many enemies: the former because they suppose that they will get off, since no one is on guard against them; the latter go undetected because opinion has it that they would not undertake something against those on their guard, and because they have at their disposal the defense that they would not undertake any such thing. And those who avail themselves of devices and hiding places for concealment, or have

---

151 · Consider 2.19 (1392a8–b14).

ready means to dispose of [stolen goods]; and in the case of those who fail to go undetected, there is either avoiding the trial or its lengthy postponement, or corrupting the judges.

In the case of those who do incur a penalty, there is avoiding the full   35
payment of it or a lengthy postponement in doing so or, on account of his lack of resources, the person in question will have nothing whatever to lose. And there are those for whom the profits are manifest or great or immediate, the penalties small or immanifest or distant. And the person   1372b
for whom the punishment is not equal to the advantage involved, as is held to be the case with tyranny. And those for whom the injustices committed are gains, the only penalty involved being reproach. And there are those for whom, by contrast, the injustices lead to a certain praise—for example, if it turns out simultaneously that someone also avenges his father or mother, as in the case of Zeno,[152] whereas the penalties are exacted   5
in the form of money or exile or some such thing. For both reasons, then, people commit injustice and do so while being in either state, and yet they are not the same but rather are opposed in point of character.

And those who have often gone either undetected or unpunished; and those who have often failed, for in such things, just as in warfare, there   10
are some who keep returning to the fray. And those for whom the pleasure involved is immediate, the pain subsequent, or the profit immediate, the penalty subsequent. For such are those who lack self-restraint, and lack of self-restraint is concerned with all that people long for.[153] And those, by contrast, for whom the pain or the penalty is immediately at hand, whereas what is pleasant and advantageous is subsequent and longer lasting, for those who are self-restrained and more prudent pursue   15
such things. And those for whom it is possible to seem to act through chance or necessity or nature or habit and, in general, to be held to make a mistake but not to commit an injustice. And those for whom it may be possible to attain an equitable consideration.[154] And all those who are in need—and people are in need in two ways: either because they are in   20
need of what is necessary (as are the poor) or because they are in need of what is superfluous (as are the rich). Both those who are exceedingly well thought of and those who are exceedingly ill thought of [commit injus-

---

152 · It is unknown to whom, or to what incident, this refers.

153 · Aristotle discusses "self-restraint" (*engkrateia*) and its opposite at length in the *Nicomachean Ethics* 7.1–10.

154 · Aristotle thus alludes to "equity" (*to epieikes*) in its relation to justice: see also 1.13 (1374a26–b23) below.

tice], the former because they will not be reputed [to have done it], the latter because their reputation will be no worse off.

People undertake [to commit injustice] when they are so disposed, then, and they commit injustice against the following sorts of people and commit the following sorts of injustices: against those who have what they themselves are in need of, as regards either the necessities or superfluities or enjoyment. And against both those who are distant and those close at hand, for from the latter the taking is swift, from the former the revenge is slow—for example, those who plunder the Carthaginians.[155] And against those who do not take precautions and are not likely to be on guard but instead to be trusting, since it is easy for anyone to escape their notice. And against the easygoing, since it belongs to a painstaking man to prosecute a case. And those who are sensitive to shame, for they are not apt to do battle over gain; and those who have been done injustice by many and not prosecuted them, since these are, as the proverb has it, "Mysian booty."[156] And against those who have never yet been the victim of injustice and those who often are: both are off their guard, the former on the grounds that it would never happen to them, the latter on the grounds that it could not happen yet again. And against those who have been slandered or are easily slandered, for such people either choose not [to prosecute], out of fear of the judges, or are unable to persuade them, since they are hated and the object of grudges. And against those in relation to whom they have the pretext that they treated badly either their ancestors or them themselves or their friends, or were going to treat badly either them themselves or their ancestors or those in their care. For, as the proverb has it, "wickedness needs only a pretext." And against enemies and friends, for the latter case is easy, the former pleasant. Also against the friendless. And against those who do not speak or act cleverly, for either they do not undertake a prosecution or are reconciled or bring nothing to a successful conclusion. And against those—such as foreigners and the self-employed—for whom there is no profit in wasting time while keeping an eye on either a lawsuit or a settlement, for they settle the matter for a small sum, and they readily put an end to it.

[People commit injustices] also against those who have committed many injustices or the kinds of injustices such as are now being inflicted on them: it is held to be close to doing no injustice, whenever somebody

155 · Carthage was a prosperous city on the coast of North Africa and hence quite distant from Greece.
156 · That is, "easy pickings."

is done some such injustice as he, too, is accustomed to committing—
I mean, for example, if someone should assault a person who is accustomed to acting insolently.[157] And against those who have done some
harm or wanted to do it or want to do or will do some harm, for [this sort
of injustice] has something both pleasant and noble about it, and it ap-   15
pears to be close to doing no injustice at all. And against those [by whose
suffering] the perpetrators will gratify either friends or those they admire or beloveds or those in positions of authority or, in general, those
in dependence on whom they live. And against those in regard to whom
there is a possibility of attaining equitable treatment or consideration.
And against those with whom they have previously leveled an accusation or had a prior break, as Callippus did in the Dion affair,[158] for such   20
things also appear close to doing no injustice. And [people commit in-
justice] against those who are about to be done injustice by others, if they
themselves do not do it first, on the grounds that in that case deliberation is no longer possible, just as it is said that Aenesidemus sent the cottabus [prize] to Gelon, who had enslaved a city, because he beat him to
the punch in doing what in fact he himself was going to do.[159] They also
commit injustice against some because, having done so, they will be able
to do many just deeds, on the grounds that they will easily cure the harm   25
done—just as Jason the Thessalian said that he had to commit some injustices so that he would also be able to do much that is just.[160]

[People also commit those injustices] that all or many are accustomed
to committing, for they suppose that they will attain forgiveness. And
[they steal] things that are easily hidden, and all such sorts of things as
are quickly used up—edible goods, for example—or things that are eas-   30
ily altered in shape or color or composition, and things for which there
is a ready supply of hiding places; and the sorts of things that are easily
carried and can be made to disappear even in small places; and those that

157 · That is, "hubristically," with hubristic arrogance.
158 · See Plutarch, *Life of Dion* 981e–983b, although Plutarch does not state how it is
that Callippus defended himself after having murdered his friend Dion; presumably he
claimed that Dion or his relatives were about to kill him.
159 · Nothing is known of the incident Aristotle here speaks of, although mention is
made of an Aenesidemus in Herodotus (7.154 and 165). Gelon (ca. 540–478) was tyrant
first at Gela and later at Syracuse. Cottabus was a game usually played at drinking parties; the reward or prize for winning was eggs, cake, and sweetmeats.
160 · Jason the Thessalian was tyrant of Pherae (ca. 385–370); according to Plutarch,
"when [Jason] outraged or molested anyone [he] always used to say that those who
will act justly in great matters must be unjust in small ones" (cited by Grimaldi ad loc.).

are indistinguishable from or similar to the many such things already in the possession of the unjust person. And [they commit such injustices] as those treated unjustly are ashamed to speak of—for example, insolent
35   treatment of the women in their household or against them themselves or their sons. And those things that someone, in bringing them to court, might be held to be merely litigious—such are small matters and those for which there is forgiveness.

These, then, are pretty much the states that those who commit injustice are in, and the sorts of injustices they commit, and against what sorts of people, and why.

CHAPTER 13

1373b   Let us go through all the unjust acts, as well as the acts of justice, beginning from here first: things just and unjust have been defined in relation to two laws as well as to the persons involved, also in a twofold sense. I mean, in the case of law, particular law, on the one hand, and general law,
5   on the other,[161] the particular being defined by each group in relation to themselves, and this being in one case unwritten law, in another, written. As for general law, it is the law that accords with nature. For there is something that all people divine, a general [or shared] justice and injustice by nature, even if there is no community in relation to one another and no compact, such as Sophocles's Antigone, too, manifestly means when she
10   says that it is a just thing, though prohibited, to bury Polyneices, on the grounds that this is just by nature:

For not as something of today, indeed, or tomorrow, but as everlasting
This lives, and no one knows whence it appears.[162]

15   And as Empedocles says about not killing what is animate, since doing so is not a just thing for some people but unjust for others:

But rather [not killing what is animate] is lawful for all, extended unbroken throughout both wide-ruling aether
And boundless earth in turn.[163]

161 · See 1.10 (1368b6–11).
162 · Sophocles, Antigone 456–57. In the second line of the quotation, Aristotle changes Sophocles's "these things" (tauta) to "this" (touto).
163 · = DK B 135. Empedocles was among the most important of the pre-Socratic philosophers or scientists (ca. 493–433). Editors divide on the proper reading of the second line; some suggest, instead of "earth in turn" (au gēs), "sunlight" or "sunbeams" (augēs).

And what Alcidamas says in his *Messeniacus*.[164]

As for persons, there is a twofold division, since the things one must do and must not do have been defined in relation to the common [good] or in relation to a particular person among those in the community. Hence   20
it is possible to commit unjust acts and to perform just acts in a twofold sense: either in relation to a single, defined person or in relation to the community. For he who commits adultery and strikes another commits injustice against some definite person, whereas he who fails to march on campaign commits it against the community.

Now, since all the unjust acts have been distinguished, with some of   25
them being in relation to the community, some in relation to another person or persons, let us take up what it is to be treated unjustly and speak about that. To be treated unjustly, then, is to suffer unjust acts at the hands of one who acts voluntarily, for acting unjustly was defined previously[165] as being voluntary. Now, since it is necessary for the victim of injustice to   30
be harmed, and to be harmed involuntarily, the harms suffered are manifest on the basis of points made previously. For the good and bad things in themselves were stated before, and so too what is voluntary, to the effect that voluntary things are all that people do knowingly.[166] It is as a result necessary that all accusations pertain either to the community or to what is private, and are leveled either against someone who acted in ignorance   35
and involuntarily or against one who did so voluntarily and knowingly; and, in the latter case, some accusations are leveled against one who has made the relevant choice, others against somebody who acts on account of his passion. Now, as for spiritedness, it will be spoken of in what bears on the passions,[167] but the sorts of things people choose and how they are disposed [when they choose] were stated previously.[168]

But people, while often agreeing that a given act was done, do not   1374a
agree either with the legal charge or with what the charge concerns—for

---

164 · Alcidamas was a fourth-century rhetorician, a student of Gorgias. The speech referred to is said to have been in support of the Messenians in their bid for freedom from their constant oppressors, the Spartans. No quotation appears in Aristotle's text as we have it, but the scholiast supplies what appears to be the relevant remark: "Free did god send forth all; nature made no one a slave." This work is cited again at 2.23 (1397a11).

165 · Consider 1.10 (1368b6–12 and context).

166 · Consider 1.6, on good and bad; and 1.10 (1368b9–14 and context), on the voluntary.

167 · Consider 2.2.

168 · Consider 1.11–12.

example, someone did take something but did not steal it; and he struck the first blow but acted without insolence; and he engaged in intercourse but committed no adultery; or he stole but did not rob a temple (for what
5   was stolen did not belong to a god); or he did trespass, but not on public land; or he did hold talks with enemies but committed no treason. For these reasons, definitions should be established about these matters—what theft is, what insolence, what adultery—so that, should we wish to show that injustice does or does not pertain in a given case, we would be
10 able to make plain where the just course lies. And all such things as bear on someone's being unjust and base, or not unjust, constitute the point of dispute, for it is in the person's choice that wickedness and the commission of injustice are found, and names of this sort already convey the choice—for example, "insolence" and "theft." For if someone struck another, it is not always the case that he thereby acted with insolence, but [only] if he struck him for the sake of a given [insolent] purpose—for ex-
15 ample, for the sake of dishonoring him or feeling pleasure himself. And it is not always the case that, if someone took something in stealth, he thereby committed theft, but only if he did so with harm in mind and for his own use and advantage. And what holds in these cases holds similarly in the rest as well.

      Now, there are, as we saw, two kinds of just and unjust things (for some
20 are written, others unwritten), and those about which the laws make pronouncements have been stated. But of the unwritten, there are in turn two kinds. They are, on the one hand, those that refer to a certain preeminence in [or excess of] virtue and vice, to which reproach and praise, as well as dishonor and honor, and privileges attach—for example, being grateful to a benefactor and benefiting one's benefactor in return and be-
25 ing apt to assist one's friends, and other things of that sort. There are also, on the other hand, those just things missing from the particular and written law. For equity[169] is held to be just, and equity is what is just, but beyond the written law. This happens in some cases voluntarily and in other
30 cases involuntarily on the part of legislators—involuntarily whenever the omission escapes their notice, voluntarily whenever they are unable to give a precise definition, and yet it is necessary to speak universally, but it is not possible to do so but only to speak about what is for the most part the case. Also all those things that are not easy to define precisely, through

169 · Aristotle discusses equity at length also in the *Nicomachean Ethics*: 5.10.

lack of the relevant experience—for example, how large and what sort of an iron instrument is used in "wounding"—since a lifetime would be insufficient to enumerate such things. If then the matter is beyond precise definition, but legislating is nonetheless needed, it is necessary to speak in an unqualified way such that, if somebody raises his hand or delivers a 35 blow while wearing a ring, then, according to the written law, he will be liable and in fact commits an injustice, but in truth [in a given case] he 1374b commits no injustice—and this is what is equitable.

If, then, equity is what has been stated, it is manifest what sorts of things are and are not equitable and what sorts of human beings are not equitable. Matters characterized by equity are those for which there should be some forgiveness, and it is an act of equity not to deem worthy 5 of equal treatment mistakes made and injustices committed, nor indeed misfortunes: misfortunes are all those things that are beyond reasonable expectation and do not proceed from wickedness; mistakes are all those things that are not beyond reasonable expectation and do not proceed from baseness; injustices all those that are also not beyond reasonable expectation but do proceed from baseness.

It also belongs to equity to show forgiveness in human affairs and to 10 examine, not the law, but the legislator, and not the legislator's statement but his understanding, and not the action but the choice involved in it, and not the part but the whole, and not the sort of person the fellow is 15 now but the sort of person he always or for the most part was. It belongs to equity, too, to remember the good things one has undergone, rather than the bad, and the good things one has undergone more than those that one has done [for another]. So too to tolerate it when being treated unjustly. And to be willing to have things decided by speech [or reason] rather than by deed. And to be willing to proceed to arbitration rather than to a 20 legal suit, for the arbitrator sees what is equitable, whereas the juror sees [only] the law, and the arbitrator was invented for this reason—so that equity would hold sway.

Let what concerns matters of equity, then, be defined in this way.

CHAPTER 14

An unjust act is greater, the greater the injustice from which it stems. Hence 25 the least things may be the greatest injustices—as, for example, what Callistratus accused Melanopus of, namely, of defrauding the temple administrators of three consecrated half-obols[170]—whereas when it comes to justice the opposite holds. These things are so as a result of the potential that lies within [the perpetrator]: he who stole three consecrated half-

30   obols might commit any injustice whatsoever. So the greater injustice is sometimes judged in this way, but sometimes from the actual harm that results. And [an injustice] for which there is no vengeance equal [to the harm done], but every act of vengeance instead proves insufficient, [is a greater injustice than one for which such vengeance can be exacted], as well as that injustice for which there is no remedy, for it is a difficult—in fact an impossible—thing [to avenge]. And that injustice for which the sufferer can attain no legal trial, for then it is without remedy: a legal trial is both a punishment and a remedy. And the injustice involved is greater if the very person who has suffered and been done an injustice has inflicted

35   on himself a great punishment, for then he who has done the injustice deserves to be punished by a still greater penalty. For example, Sophocles,

1375a   when pleading on behalf of Euctemon, who had slit his own throat after having been insolently treated, said that he (Sophocles) assessed as a penalty nothing less than what the sufferer had assessed in his own case.

And that unjust act is greater which one has committed alone or first or together with few others; and to err time and again is a great matter. And that unjust act is greater for which preventative and punitive mea-

5   sures are sought out and invented—as in Argos, for example, where they punish the person on whose account a law is passed, as well as those on whose account a prison is built. And the more bestial the unjust act, the greater it is, and so too the more it proceeds from forethought. And that which fosters, in those who hear of it, greater fear than pity. And the devices of the rhetorical art are of such a character, [to the effect] that someone has destroyed or transgressed many just obligations (for ex-

10   ample, oaths, pledges, sureties,[171] marriage vows), since this constitutes an excess made up of many particular injustices.[172] And [an act of injustice is

170 · Nothing is known of this incident, although three half-obols is a small sum. Xenophon states that Melanopus was an ambassador to Thebes, together with Callistratus (*Hellenica* 6.3.2–3). See also Plutarch, *Demosthenes* 13, where Melanopus is said to be a rival of Callistratus.

171 · The same word (*pisteis*) is usually translated as "modes of persuasion."

172 · It is a matter of some controversy what Aristotle means here by "the devices of the rhetorical art" (*ta rhētorika*), but, as Grimaldi suggests, he seems to have in mind the use of "amplification" to heighten a sense of fear (as distinguished from pity) in the audience.

greater when it is committed] in the very place where the unjust are punished, which is in fact what those who bear false witness do: where would
they *not* commit injustice, if they would do it even in a courtroom? And
involving matters to which shame especially attaches. And if the injustice
is perpetrated against him by whom the perpetrator had been benefited:
the perpetrator commits a greater number of unjust acts both because   15
he does harm and because he performs no benefaction [in return]. And
that which goes against the dictates of unwritten justice, since it belongs
to a better person to be just absent the necessity to be it. The written dictates of justice, then, are marked by necessity, the unwritten not. But in
another way, the injustice is greater if it goes against what is written, for
he who commits injustice when the acts are frightening to him because
he is subject to a penalty, would also commit injustices that are not subject to a penalty.   20

    What concerns the greater unjust act and the lesser, then, has been
stated.

CHAPTER 15

It follows next, after the points stated, to run through what concerns
those modes of persuasion called "non-technical,"[173] for these belong particularly to judicial speeches. They are five in number: laws, witnesses,
contracts, [evidence gained by] torture, [and] oaths. Let us speak first,   25
then, about laws—how they ought to be used when exhorting and dissuading, and how when accusing and defending.

    For it is manifest that, if the written law is contrary to the matter at
hand, then one must make use of the general law and matters of equity,
on the grounds that these are the more just and that this constitutes us-   30
ing one's "best judgment,"[174] namely, not using in every instance the written laws. It is manifest, too, that the equitable always remains and never
changes—the general law does not change either, since it accords with
nature—whereas the written laws often do change. Hence what was
said in Sophocles's *Antigone*: she defends herself because she buried [her
brother] in violation of Creon's law but not in violation of the unwrit-   35
ten one:

173 · See 1.2 (1355b35 and context).
174 · Aristotle here refers to a part of the oath taken by a juror, namely, that he is bound
to use his best judgment in deciding a case. See, e.g., Joseph Plescia, *The Oath and Perjury in Ancient Greece* (Tallahassee: Florida State University Press, 1970).

1375b   For not as something of today, indeed, or tomorrow, but as everlasting . . .
          For these things, then, I was not, [because I feared the pride] of any man,
               going to . . .¹⁷⁵

   And [one should say] that the just is something true and advantageous,
5 but what is [merely] held to be just is not, such that the written law is not
   true and advantageous either, since it does not carry out the proper work
   of law. And that the judge is like the assayer of silver in that he distinguishes the counterfeit justice from the true. Also that it belongs to a better man to make use of and abide by the unwritten rather than the written laws. And [it must be stated by the speaker] if somewhere a given law
   is contrary to a law held in high regard—or even that it contradicts itself.
10 For example, sometimes one law commands that whatever has been contracted is authoritative, whereas another law prohibits forming contracts
   that are contrary to the law. And if the law is ambiguous, then one must as
   a result turn it around and see which of its two meanings will harmonize
   with either what is just or what is advantageous, and then put that meaning to use. And if the matters with a view to which the law was originally
15 set down no longer remain, whereas the law does remain, then one must
   try to make this clear and contend in this way against the law.
       But if the written law favors the affair at hand, then it must be stated
   that the "by one's best judgment" clause¹⁷⁶ is not for the sake of adjudicat-
   ing contrary to the law but so that, if somebody is ignorant of what the
   law means, he does not perjure himself. And [one should say] that nobody
   chooses what is good unqualifiedly [for the community as a whole] but instead what is good for himself [, whereas the law does look to what is good
20 unqualifiedly for the community as a whole, and so must be obeyed]. And
   that there is no difference at all between a law's not having been set down
   and its not being used. And that, in the other arts, there is no profit in being "smarter than the doctor," for the doctor's error does not do as much
   harm as does being habituated to disobey the authority; and that seeking
25 to be wiser than the laws is just the thing that is prohibited in the laws that
   are praised. Let what concerns laws, then, be defined in this way.

175 · Aristotle's quotation of the second line here (*Antigone* 458) differs slightly from
the reading of the texts of the play as we have them. The original reads, in translation,
"For these things I was not—because I feared the pride of any man—going to pay the
penalty among the gods" (*Antigone* 458–60). See also 1.13 above for Aristotle's earlier
use of *Antigone*.
176 · See n. 174 above.

As for what concerns witnesses, witnesses are twofold: the ancients and the recent, and among these latter there are those who share in the risk at hand and those who stand apart from it. I mean by "ancients" both the poets and all those notables whose judgments are manifest. For example, the Athenians made use of Homer as a witness concerning Salamis and, just recently, the Tenedians made use of Periander the Corinthian concerning the Sigeans.[177] And Cleophon used the elegiacs of Solon against Critias, saying that from long ago his household was outrageous, since otherwise Solon would never have written,

Say to red-haired Critias for me to listen to his father.[178]   35

Now, witnesses of these sorts are concerned with past events, but about   1376a
future events it is the interpreters of divine signs[179]—just as Themistocles said that there must be a naval battle, citing the wooden wall.[180] Further, proverbs, too, are witnesses, as was said.[181] For example, if somebody should advise one not to make friends with an old man, the proverb "Never do good to an old man" bears witness to this, or if he advises someone to do away with the sons whose fathers he has also done away with: "A fool is he who, having killed the father, leaves the sons untouched."[182]

Recent witnesses are all those notables who have rendered a judgment about something, for their judgments are useful to those engaged in disputes about the same things. For example, Euboulus, in courtroom proceedings against Chares, made use of what Plato said against Archebius—   10
that people's admitting they are wicked was making real headway in the

---

177 · It is said that the Athenian statesman-poet Solon acted in favor of Athens' claim to the island of Salamis by referring to Homer, *Iliad* 2.557–58 ("Ajax led from Salamis twelve ships / And stationed them where the phalanxes of Athenians stood"). Periander was the tyrant of Corinth (ca. 625–585) whose arbitration of a dispute between Athens and Mytilene over Sigeum was evidently appealed to later by the people of Tenedos.
178 · The Critias criticized by Cleophon is the sometime associate of Socrates and a member of the Thirty Tyrants in Athens; the Critias mentioned by Solon is the son of Dropides (see Plato, *Charmides* 157e) and a nephew of Solon.
179 · Or "soothsayers" (*chrēsmologoi*); see also 3.5 (1407b4).
180 · In the summer of 480, Themistocles convinced the Athenians to withdraw from Athens to Salamis, Aegina, and Troezen; the "wooden wall" refers to the mass of (wooden) ships.
181 · Since Aristotle has not in fact said this before, although he has certainly cited proverbs, editors have proposed various emendations.
182 · See also 2.21 (1395a15–17).

city.[183] Also those who share in the risk [of the trial, together with the accused,] if they are held to be lying. Such sorts of persons, then, are witnesses only of these things—whether something happened or not, whether it is or is not so—but they are not witnesses about what sort of a thing is in question—for example, whether it is just or unjust, or advantageous or disadvantageous. But witnesses at some remove from the case are most trustworthy even about these sorts of things, and the ancients are most trustworthy, since they cannot be corrupted.

For someone without witnesses, confirmation of his testimonies consists in saying that one must judge on the basis of likelihoods, and that this *is* "by one's best judgment,"[184] and that it is not possible for likelihoods to deceive for a sum of money, and that likelihoods do not get convicted of bearing false witness. But in the case of someone who does have witnesses against one who does not, the former should say that likelihoods cannot be examined at trial and that there would be no need at all of witnesses if it were sufficient to theorize on the basis of arguments.

Some testimonies concern the person himself, others the adversary, and some the matter at hand, others the person's character. It is manifest, as a result, that it is not possible ever to be at a loss for useful testimony. For if there is no such testimony bearing on the matter at hand, either in agreement with oneself or against the opponent, there is nonetheless testimony concerning either one's own equitable character or the baseness of the opponent. As for the other matters pertaining to a witness—whether friend or foe or in between these, whether he is well thought of or not well thought of or in between these, and all other such distinctions—one must speak of them on the basis of the same topics as those that form the basis of the enthymemes we state.

As for what concerns contracts, the use of arguments extends to amplifying them or pruning them back, or rendering them credible or not credible: if the contracts support one, then they are credible and authoritative, but if they redound to the benefit of the opponent, then they are the opposite. As for making contracts credible or not credible, this is no

183 · Euboulus (ca. 405–335) was an important Athenian statesman and financier, responsible for improving Athens' financial health. Chares (ca. 400–325) was a famous Athenian general; Isocrates's *On the Peace* is directed at him in particular (see below 3.17 [1418a32]). Since we do not know who Archebius was, we cannot identify the Plato here mentioned: some maintain it is Plato the philosopher, others the comic poet of the same name.

184 · Aristotle again refers to the oath sworn by jurors (see n. 174 above).

different from what concerns witnesses, since contracts are credible in light of the character of their signatories or guarantors. And when the contract is agreed to exist, and it supports one's own position, then one must amplify its scope, for the contract is a private and particular law, and although contracts do not render the law authoritative, the laws do render authoritative the contracts that accord with law; and in general the law itself is a certain contract such that whoever distrusts or destroys the contract destroys the laws as well. Further, the majority of transactions, and especially voluntary ones, refer to contracts such that, if contracts are stripped of their authority, the use that human beings make of one another is undone. And all such other things as are fitting [to say] can be seen at a glance.

But if the contract is opposed to one and favors the opponents' side, then, first, the very things that someone might use to combat a law that is opposed to one are fitting here too. For it would be absurd if we suppose that we must not obey laws that were incorrectly set down and that the people who set them down erred in doing so, whereas we suppose it necessary to obey contracts. Next [one should say] that the juror is an arbiter of the just; it is not this thing [i.e., the contract], then, that must be examined, but rather what has greater justice to it. And the just cannot be twisted either by deception or by necessity (for it is by nature), whereas contracts do arise when people have been deceived or are under the press of necessity. In addition to these points, one must examine whether the contract is opposed to something in either the written or the general laws and, in the case of the written laws, whether it is opposed to the laws of one's own [city] or to foreign ones, and then whether it is opposed to other contracts that are subsequent or prior [to the contract at issue]. For the subsequent contracts are authoritative, or the prior ones are correct and the subsequent ones deceptive—whichever way may be useful. Further, one must see where the advantage lies, if somewhere the contract is in opposition to the advantage of the judges, and all other things of that sort, for these too are in like fashion readily observable.

But [evidence gained by] torture is a sort of testimony, and it is held to have something trustworthy about it because there is present in it a certain necessity. It is not difficult to see the possibilities concerning this too, which can be amplified, if that supports one's own case, to the effect that [evidence so gained] alone constitutes true testimony.

And if [the evidence gained by torture] is in opposition to one's own case and favors the opponent, one might resolve the difficulty by stating

1377a

the truth about the whole class of torture. For those under the press of necessity state falsehoods no less than the truth, both those who endure
5   it to the end and so do not tell the truth and those who readily make false accusations so they may put a stop to it more quickly. And one must refer to examples of the sorts of things that have happened, examples that are known to the judges.[185] One must also say that [the evidence gained by] torture is not true, for many tough-minded and thick-skinned people, and those whose souls are capable, endure necessities nobly, whereas cowards and the cautious are bold until they see before them the necessities at work—with the result that there is nothing credible in [evidence gained by] torture.

In what concerns oaths, it is possible to make a fourfold division. For either one administers and takes an oath; or one does neither; or the one but not the other; and, in this latter case, either somebody administers an
10   oath but does not take one or he takes an oath but does not administer one. Further, and in a manner different from these, [one may consider] whether a given oath has been sworn either by oneself or by the other party. If, then, one does not administer an oath, [one should say that it is] because people easily swear false oaths and because someone who has sworn an oath still does not make restitution, on the one hand, while, on the other, the [jurors] will, one supposes, convict anybody who does not swear an oath; and that this risk, which lies in the hands of the jurors, is
15   the superior one to take, since he trusts in them but not in his opponent.

But someone who does not take the oath himself [should say] that an oath is taken in exchange for money and that, if he were base, he would have taken it, since it is superior to be base for the sake of something than for the sake of nothing: by swearing the oath, then, he will gain; by not swearing it, he will not. Thus one's not swearing an oath would arise through virtue and not through [fear of] committing perjury. And the re-
20   mark of Xenophanes is fitting, that "a legal challenge made to a pious man by an impious one is not fair."[186] Rather, it is as if a strong man should invite a weak one to strike him or to be struck. But if someone does take the

185 · At this point most modern editors bracket the lines of text that run to the end of this paragraph, Ross's Oxford text being the principal exception. Though absent from most MSS, the lines do appear in one important MS.
186 · As Grimaldi notes, another translation of the same line, whose context has not survived, is possible: "a legal challenge made to a pious man is not itself equal to one made to an impious man."

oath, [he should say] that it is because he trusts in himself and not in the other fellow; and, turning the remark of Xenophanes around, one must assert that it would be fair in this way—for the impious man to administer the oath and for the pious man to swear it. And it would be a terrible thing for someone to be unwilling to do so himself when it comes to matters about which he thinks it right for those who adjudicate them to swear an oath. And if one does administer an oath, [one should say] that being willing to turn it over to the gods is a pious thing and that there should be no need whatever for the opponent to require other judges [than himself], since one is putting the decision in the hands of [the opponent] himself.[187] [One should also say] that it is absurd [for the opponent] to be unwilling to swear an oath in matters in which he deems it right for others [i.e., the jurors] so to swear.

Now, since it is clear how one ought to speak in each case, it is clear also how one should speak when they are paired—for example, if a person is himself willing to take an oath but not to administer one; and if he administers an oath but is unwilling to take one; and if he is willing both to take an oath and to administer one; or if he is willing to do neither of these. The pairs being necessarily composed of the points already stated, the relevant arguments, too, are composed of those same points as a result. And if an oath has already been sworn by someone and yet stands in opposition [to the present oath], he must say that this is not perjury. For committing injustice is a voluntary thing, and committing perjury is to commit injustice, whereas what arises through force and what through being deceived are involuntary. Here then one must conclude, in the case of committing perjury, that it is caused by the thought in mind and not by the mouth alone. But if, on the other hand, an oath has indeed already been sworn by the opponent that is contrary [to his present oath, then one should say] that he who does not abide by the things to which he has sworn an oath subverts everything. It is for this reason that people make use of the laws [only] after having sworn an oath: "They think it right for you[188] to abide by your oaths, if you are sitting in judgment, whereas they themselves do not abide by them." And all the other things someone might say by way of amplification.

187 · Here the MSS differ, and it is uncertain whether Aristotle says that the matter is being handed over to the opponent himself or to the judges themselves (as William of Moerbeke's Latin translation takes it).
188 · The plural "you."

Outline of Book 2

A. The modes of persuasion (*pisteis*)
  1. Passion (*pathos*): 2.1–11
     a) Anger: 2.2
     b) Gentleness: 2.3
     c) Friendliness; enmity and hatred: 2.4
     d) Fear; confidence: 2.5
     e) Shame; shamelessness: 2.6
     f) Graciousness (*charis*); lack of graciousness: 2.7
     g) Pity: 2.8
     h) Righteous indignation (*nemesis*): 2.9
     i) Envy: 2.10
     j) Emulation; contempt: 2.11
  2. Character (*ēthos*): 2.12–17
     a) The young: 2.12
     b) The old: 2.13
     c) Those in their prime: 2.14
     d) Goods from chance and their effect on character: 2.15–17
        (1) Good birth: 2.15
        (2) Wealth: 2.16
        (3) Power: 2.17
        (4) Good fortune in general
  3. The *logos* and what is common to all rhetoric: 2.18–26
     a) Points common to all rhetoric: 2.18–19
        (1) Possible and impossible
        (2) Questions of fact
        (3) Future events
        (4) Greatness and smallness; greater and smaller

b) Common modes of persuasion: example and enthymeme: 2.20–21
  (1) Example: 2.20
    (a) Factual
    (b) Made-up: comparison or fables
  (2) Maxims: 2.21
c) Common topics belonging to enthymemes: 2.22–23
  (1) Opposites
  (2) Similar grammatical inflections
  (3) Mutual relations
  (4) More and less
  (5) Time
  (6) Turning statements used against you against the other
  (7) Definition
  (8) Ways a given term can be used
  (9) Division
  (10) Induction
  (11) Judgments of others
  (12) Parts
  (13) Consequent
  (14) Opposites properly speaking
  (15) Use of opposites to form paradoxes
  (16) Proportionality
  (17) Same cause must give rise to same effect
  (18) Change in what people choose
  (19) Possible reason *is* the reason
  (20) Motives
  (21) Hard to credit or unlikely
  (22) Inconsistencies
  (23) Cause of the prejudice involved
  (24) No cause, no effect
  (25) Some better way
  (26) What is contrary to what has been done in the past
  (27) Accusation or defense on the basis of errors committed
  (28) Proper names
d) Common topics belonging to apparent enthymemes: 2.24
  (1) Matters of diction
    (a) "Therefore"
    (b) Key points of any syllogism
    (c) Homonymy

Book 2

1377b These, then, are the things on the basis of which one must both exhort and dissuade; and praise and blame; and accuse and defend; and these are the sorts of opinions and premises that are useful with a view to the modes of persuasion in these cases. For enthymemes are concerned with
20 these matters and are based on them, as appropriate for each kind of speechmaking. And since rhetoric is for the sake of a judgment—people judge advice given, and a legal trial *is* a judgment—it is necessary [for the speaker] to look not only to the speech in question, as to how it will be demonstrative and credible, but also to establishing that he himself is a
25 certain sort of person and to rendering the judge of a certain sort. For this makes a great difference in point of credibility, especially when it comes to matters of advice, and then also in legal proceedings—the fact that the speaker appears to be of a certain sort and that [the listeners or judges] suppose him to be disposed toward them in a certain way, and, in addition to these, that they themselves happen to be disposed in a certain way.
30 Now, it is more useful for the speaker to appear to be of a certain sort when giving advice, whereas the listener's being disposed in a certain way is more useful in judicial matters. For the same things do not appear to be the case to those who are friendly and to those who hate, or to those who
1378a are angry and to those of a gentle disposition; rather, they appear to be either entirely different or different in magnitude. It seems to the friend that the friend about whom he renders a judgment either does no injustice or commits a petty injustice, whereas to the person who hates him, the opposite seems to be the case. And to someone who desires something
5 and is hopeful about it, if what is to come is pleasant, then it appears that it will come to be and will be good; but to someone apathetic or indeed annoyed by the prospect, the opposite appears.

Now, there are three causes of the speakers themselves being credible, for such is the number of the reasons (apart from demonstrations) we give credence to someone. And these are prudence and virtue and goodwill. For people speak falsely about the matters they state or in the advice they give either for all of these reasons together or for some one of them. That is, either on account of a lack of prudence [the speakers] do not opine correctly; or, though they do opine correctly, on account of their malice they do not state their opinions; or, though they are prudent and fair-minded,[1] they are without goodwill. Hence it can be that, though they know what is best, they do not advise it. And there is no other cause at work apart from these. It is necessarily the case, therefore, that he who seems to possess all three of these is credible in the eyes of his audience. As for what would make people appear prudent and serious, this must be grasped from the distinctions made concerning the virtues, for it is on the basis of these same things that a given person would establish that either another or he himself is of a certain sort. As for what concerns goodwill and friendliness, this must be spoken about in what pertains to the passions.[2]

The passions are all those things on account of which people, undergoing a change, differ in the judgments they make, things that pain and pleasure accompany—for example, anger,[3] pity, fear, and the other things of that sort, as well as their opposites. But what pertains to each must be divided in three. I mean, for example, in what concerns anger: how the angry are disposed, and with whom they are accustomed to being angry, and at what sorts of things. For if we should grasp one or two of these, but not all of them together, it would be impossible to foster anger in another, and similarly in the case of the other [passions]. Just as we wrote up propositions in what was stated previously, so let us do the same concerning these too and go through them in the manner stated.

CHAPTER 2

So let anger be a longing, accompanied by pain, for manifest vengeance on account of a manifest slight that was carried out against oneself or

---

1 · Or, perhaps, "equitable" (*epieikeis*).

2 · Consider 2.4, where Aristotle treats friendliness or friendly affection (*philia*).

3 · The term Aristotle uses (*orgē*) can also have the more general meaning "temperament," "disposition," "mood," but it often also means simply "anger."

those in one's circle, on the part of those for whom such a slight is inappropriate.[4]

    If, then, this is anger, the angry person is necessarily always angry at a
35   particular individual—for example, at Cleon but not at "human being"
1378b as such, and because he did or was about to do something against oneself
or somebody in one's circle; it is necessary, too, that a certain pleasure attend every instance of anger, namely, the pleasure that stems from the
hope of being avenged. For it is pleasant to suppose that one will attain
what one is aiming at; nobody aims at things that are manifestly impos-
5   sible for himself, and the angry person aims at things possible for himself.
Hence it was beautifully said of spiritedness:

> Which is sweeter by far than honey dripping down,
> In the breast of men it spreads.[5]

For in fact a certain pleasure attends it both for this reason and because
the angry while away their time thinking about exacting revenge; the
10   imagination of it that then arises fosters pleasure, just as in dreams.

    Now, slighting is an actualization of an opinion about something
that appears to be worth nothing—for we suppose that both bad things
and good ones are worth taking seriously, as is whatever is conducive to
them—whereas all such things as amount to nothing at all, or are petty,
we suppose to be worth nothing. And there are three forms of slights: con-
15   tempt as well as spitefulness and insolence. For he who feels contempt,
slights—all those things people suppose to be worth nothing they feel
contempt for, and they slight things worth nothing—and so too does the
spiteful person.[6] For spitefulness is an impediment to someone [else's]
wishes, not so that the spiteful person himself may gain something but so
that the other fellow may not. And since he is not concerned that he him-
20   self gain, he slights the fellow. For he clearly does not suppose either that
the person will harm him—in that case he would fear him and not slight

4 · "Manifest" in each instance could also be "apparent." Editors have suggested various
emendations of this sentence, and I render Kassel's text. Grimaldi suggests a reading
that could be translated as follows: "a manifest slight on the part of one who is unfit to
slight anything concerning oneself or those in one's circle."

5 · Homer, *Iliad* 18.109–10. See also 1.11 above (1370b11–15), where the first line is
quoted.

6 · The reading of all the modern editors. The principal MSS read "and the spiteful person appears to feel contempt."

him—or that the person will do him any benefit worth mentioning—for in that case he would reflect on how to be his friend.

And he who is insolent to someone also slights him, for insolence is doing and saying[7] such things as are a source of shame to the person suffering them, not so that some other advantage may accrue to the insolent person or because something happened to him, but so that he may gain pleasure thereby: those who retaliate are not insolent but instead exact revenge. And a cause of the pleasure the insolent feel is their supposing that, by inflicting harm, they themselves are to a greater degree superior. Hence the young and the wealthy are insolent, for they suppose that, by being insolent, they are superior. Dishonor belongs to insolence, and he who dishonors, slights. For that which is worth nothing is without any honor, be it as something good or bad. Hence Achilles in his anger says:

He dishonored [me], for, having seized the prize, he himself keeps it,[8]

and

As if I were some vagabond without honor,[9]

[thus speaking] as one angered for these reasons.

And people suppose that it is fitting for them to be thought much of by those who are their inferiors in familial line, power, virtue, and, in general, in whatever respect he himself is much superior—for example, when it comes to money the wealthy man is superior to the poor man; in speaking, the skilled rhetorician to one unable to speak; and ruler to ruled, as well as somebody who supposes he deserves to rule over one deserving to be ruled. Hence it was said:

Great is the spiritedness of kings fostered by Zeus,[10]

and

But even afterward he holds a grudge,[11]

7 · Some MSS read, in place of "doing and saying" (*prattein kai legein*), "harming and hurting" (*blaptein kai lupein*).
8 · Homer, *Iliad* 1.356.
9 · Homer, *Iliad* 9.648.
10 · Homer, *Iliad* 2.196.
11 · Homer, *Iliad* 1.82. Here the prophet Calchas speaks to Achilles about Agamemnon.

since they are indignant[12] on account of their superiority. Further, [someone becomes angry at] those by whom he supposes that he ought to be well treated, namely, those whom he has treated or is treating well—either he himself or someone on his account or someone in his circle—or whom he wishes or wished to treat well.

10   It is manifest by now, on the basis of these points, how the angry themselves are disposed and at whom they are angry and for what sorts of reasons. For they themselves are angry when they are pained, since he who is feeling pain aims at something.

    And if someone places a direct obstacle before another in anything—for example, before a thirsty man in drinking—and even if someone does not do this directly, he appears to be doing what amounts to the same thing; or if somebody acts against him or fails to act in concert

15 with him; or if somebody annoys someone in this condition in any other respect—he is angry with them all. Hence those who are ailing, poor, in love, [or] thirsty—in general those who are in the grip of some desire and who do not succeed [in satisfying it]—are given to anger and readily roused to it, especially against those who slight their present circumstance: for example, an ailing person is readily roused to anger against those who slight illness, a poor person against those who slight poverty, a

20 warrior against those who slight war, a lover against those who slight love, and similarly in the other cases as well.[13] For each has the path already paved for his own anger by the underlying passion in question. And, further, if someone happens to expect the opposite [of what comes to pass], for what is much contrary to expectation causes greater pain, just as what

25 is much contrary to expectation also brings delight if what comes to pass is something the person wants.

    Hence it is manifest from these considerations what sorts of seasons and times and dispositions and ages are such as to prompt people to anger, and where and when they do so. Manifest, too, is the fact that, when people are to a greater degree in these conditions, they are all the more readily prompted to anger. Those who are so disposed, then, are themselves readily prompted to anger; and they are angry at those who ridi-

30 cule and scoff at and mock them, for those who do so are insolent. [They

---

12 · Not the word elsewhere translated as "indignation" (*nemesis* and the related verb: see 2.9) but *aganakteō*—"to be vexed or indignantly angry."

13 · Although it is without a counterpart in the MSS as we have them, the Latin translation of William of Moerbeke adds here: "And if this is not the case, [he is angry] even if somebody slights anything else whatever."

get angry also] at those who do harm in such things as constitute signs of
insolence, and these are necessarily such as are neither payback for something nor profitable to those who do them, since it is then that such acts
seem to be done through insolence. [People also become angry] at those
who speak badly of and feel contempt for things they themselves take especially seriously—for example, those who are ambitious in philosophy,
if somebody [speaks badly of] philosophy, and those who take seriously   35
their looks, if somebody [speaks badly of] their looks, and similarly in the
other cases. And people become much angrier at these things if they suspect that they themselves do not possess them, either at all or to any great
degree, or are held not to possess them, for whenever they are of the firm   1379b
conviction that they are superior in the respects in which they are being
mocked, they pay it no mind. And [people are angrier] at friends than at
those who are not friends, for they suppose that it is more appropriate to
be treated well by them than not to be. And at those who are accustomed
to honoring them or paying heed to them, if to the contrary they do not   5
now deal with them in this way, for in fact they suppose that they are being treated contemptuously by them: otherwise they would do the same
as they did before. And at those who do not confer benefits in return for
benefits done them or at those who do not pay them back equally, and at
those who act to oppose them, if they are inferior to them. For all such
people appear contemptuous, the latter [because they act] as though they
are opposing inferiors, the former as though the benefits in question were   10
bestowed by inferiors. And people get angrier at those who are of no account, if they slight them in something, for it was posited[14] that the anger connected to slights is directed against those for whom such slighting
is inappropriate, and it is appropriate for those in inferior positions not
to slight someone. And at friends, if the friends do not speak well of or
benefit them, and even more so if they say or do the contrary; and if the
friends fail to perceive that they are in need, just as Antiphon's Plexippus   15
was angry at Meleager, since failing to perceive this need is the sign of a
slight: the needs of those whom we give thought to, do not escape our notice.[15] And at those who delight in one's misfortunes and are in general
cheerful amid one's misfortunes, for this is a sign that they are either an

14 · Consider 1378a31–33 and 1378b10–13.
15 · For the story probably here alluded to, see Diodorus Siculus 4.34.1–6 and Ovid,
Metamorphoses 8.420–44. Plexippus, the uncle of Meleager, criticized him for giving
to his beloved, Atalanta, the skin of the Calydonian boar he had killed: Meleager evidently overlooked his uncle's claim to honor in favor of Atalanta.

enemy or treating one slightingly. And people become angry at those who
20   pay it no mind if they cause them pain. Hence they are angry also at those
who announce bad news, and at those who either listen to their faults
[being spoken of] or look on those faults [without doing anything about
them], for they are thus similar to those who slight them, or to enemies.
For friends share our pain, and all feel pain when they look on faults that
are [in a sense] their own.

Further, they get angry at those who slight them in the presence of five
25   kinds of people: in the presence of those who are their rivals in honor;
those whom they admire; those by whom they wish to be admired; [and]
either those before whom they feel shame or among those who feel shame
before them. If someone slights them in these circumstances, their anger
is greater. And they become angry at those who slight people whom it
would be shameful for them not to aid—for example, parents, offspring,
30   wives, the ruled. And at those who lack gratitude, for the slight involved
is contrary to what is fitting. They also get angry at those who are ironic to
them when they are being serious, irony being a mark of contempt. And
at those who bestow benefactions on others but not on them themselves,
for this too is a mark of contempt, namely, not deeming one to be deserving of the things that all others deserve. Forgetfulness, too, is productive
35   of anger—for example, forgetting names, though it is a petty matter. For
even forgetting is held to be a sign of a slight: forgetting arises through
neglect, and neglect is a sort of slight.

1380a   Those at whom people get angry, then, and what state they are in when
angry, and through what sorts of causes, have been spoken of together. It
is also clear that [the speaker] must, by his speech, affect [the listeners]
such that they are actually in an angry state and that his opponents are
responsible for such things as prompt people to anger, and that his opponents are just the sort of persons at whom people get angry.

CHAPTER 3

5   Now, since being angry is the opposite of being gentle, and anger of gentleness, one must grasp how the gentle are disposed and toward whom
they are gentle, and through what causes they are such.

So let gentleness be the settling down and quieting of anger. If, then,
people are angry at those who slight them, and slighting is voluntary, it is
10   manifest that people are gentle with those who do none of these things
or with those who do them involuntarily or appear to be that sort of per-

son. And with those who wish to do the opposite of what they did in fact. And with all those who are [with others] such as they are also with themselves, for nobody is held to slight himself. And with those who admit to and regret what they have done: people then cease being angry on the grounds that they gain just recompense in the pain the others feel   15 because of what they have done. A sign of this is found in the punishment of household servants. For we punish more those who talk back and defend themselves, whereas with those who agree that they are being justly punished, our spiritedness ceases. A cause of this is that defending oneself against what is manifest constitutes a lack of respect,[16] and lack of respect is itself a slight and a mark of contempt. At any rate, we do   20 not respect those for whom we feel much contempt. And [people are gentle] with those who humble themselves before them and who do not talk back, since they appear to agree that they are inferior; those who are inferior are afraid, and nobody who is afraid of someone slights him. And the fact that anger ceases before those who humble themselves is made clear by dogs, who do not bite those who assume a submissive posture.[17]   25 And with those who are serious when they themselves are being serious, since it seems to them that they are being taken seriously and not being treated contemptuously. And with those who have done them some greater favor. And with those who beg a favor and entreat them, for they are thus humbler. And with those who are not insolent or mocking or do not slight anyone, or not anyone who is a fine person or the sort of person   30 they themselves in fact are.

In general one must examine the things that produce gentleness on the basis of their opposites, and [people do not get angry] at those whom they fear or those whom they respect, for while they are in that state, they are not angry: it is impossible to feel fear and anger simultaneously. And with those who have acted in anger they are not angry or are less angry,   35 for they do not appear to act in a slighting way. And nobody who is angry at someone slights him, for slighting is painless, whereas anger is ac-   1380b companied by pain. And [people are gentle] with those who are respectful toward them.

It is also clear that the gentle are in a state opposite to that of being angry—as when [enjoying] playfulness, laughter, feasting, contentedness, an accomplishment, gratification, and, in general, [when enjoying]

16 · Or "shamelessness" (*anaischuntia*).
17 · Literally, "those who sit down."

5   painlessness and a pleasure that is not insolent and a hope that is reasonable.[18] Further, when they have been angry for some time already and
not just recently so, for time brings an end to anger. And vengeance exacted against one person first brings to an end even a greater anger at another. Hence Philocrates put it well, when someone said to him, while the
people were angry, "Why don't you defend yourself?"

"Not yet."

"But when?"

10   "When I see that they have falsely accused somebody else."[19] For
people become gentle when they use up their anger on another, as happened in the case of Ergophilus. For although they were more harshly
disposed to him than to Callisthenes, they let him go because they had
passed a death sentence on Callisthenes the day before.[20] And if people

15   feel pity[21] [they are gentle]; and so too if others have suffered a greater ill
than those who are angry at them would have inflicted on them, for then
the angry suppose that it is just as if they themselves had exacted revenge.
And if they suppose that they themselves are unjust and hence justly suffer: anger does not arise in relation to[22] what is just. For they no longer
believe that they are suffering contrary to what is fitting, and this, as we
saw, is what anger is. Hence one must punish first by means of speech:

20   then even slaves are less indignant[23] when being punished. And [people
are gentler or calmer] if they suppose that someone punished will not perceive that he is suffering through their doing, in payback for what they
suffered at his hands, for anger has to do with the individual, as is clear
from its definition. Hence it was correctly written,

Say that it was Odysseus, sacker of cities,[24]

18 · Or, perhaps, "equitable," "decent" (*epieikei*).

19 · Philocrates was a well-known statesman and orator, responsible for initiating
peace negotiations with Philip II of Macedon in 348. He was later (in 343) accused of
corruption in the peace negotiations and was condemned to death in absentia.

20 · Ergophilus was an Athenian general active in the Hellespont in 363–362. He was
removed from command, according to Demosthenes (*Against Aristocrates* 104), and,
after his subsequent trial at Athens, was fined (Demosthenes, *On the False Embassy* 180).

21 · Reading the correction (*eleousin*) of one MS and with the texts of Grimaldi, Spengel, and Cope. The MSS read "if they convict" (*helōsin*).

22 · Or "against."

23 · Not the word elsewhere translated as "indignation" (*nemesis* and the related verb:
see 2.9) but *aganakteō*—"to be vexed or indignantly angry"; see also 1379a6.

24 · Homer, *Odyssey* 9.504.

on the grounds that he would not have been avenged if it had gone unperceived who had done the deed and in return for what. As a result, people are not angry either at those who do not perceive it or again at those who have died, on the grounds that the dead have suffered the ultimate and will not feel pain or perceive anything, which is what the angry aim at. Hence, in the case of Hector, the poet said it well when [Apollo] wished to put an end to Achilles's anger at the dead man:

> For it is indeed dumb earth that he in his wrath outrages.[25]

It is clear, then, that those who wish to effect a softening must speak on the basis of these topics, thus rendering their listeners in such a condition; and by depicting those at whom they are angry as frightening or deserving of respect or as having done them a gracious favor or as having acted involuntarily or as being much pained by what they have done.

CHAPTER 4

As for those whom people have friendly affection for[26] and those whom they hate, and why, let us speak of these once we have defined friendship and friendly affection. So let feeling such affection be wishing for someone the things one supposes to be good, for that person's sake and not one's own, and being apt to bring these about to the extent possible. A friend is one who feels this affection and has it returned, and those who suppose that they are so disposed toward one another suppose that they are friends.

Given these hypotheses, it is necessarily the case that a friend is one who shares in the other fellow's pleasure at the good things and his pain at what is grievous, for no other reason than that fellow's sake. For all people delight when what they wish for comes to pass and are pained when the opposite occurs, such that pleasures and pains are a sign of what it is one is wishing for. [Friends are also] those for whom the same things are good and bad and who share the same friends and enemies. For they must necessarily wish for the same things, such that he who wishes the same things for both himself and the other fellow comes into sight as that fellow's friend. And people have affection for those who have performed

25 · Homer, *Iliad* 24.54.
26 · This phrase translates the verb *phileō*, referring to friendly (as distinguished from erotic) love; henceforth it will be rendered chiefly by "to have friendly affection for" or simply "affection for."

some benefaction, either for them themselves or for those whom they care about, whether it be a great benefaction, or eagerly done, or at such crucial moments as the sorts [of benefactions just mentioned imply], and done for the sake of the friends. Or those whom they suppose wish to per-
15   form some such benefit. And [people have affection for] the friends of friends and those who are held in affection by the people they themselves have affection for. And they have affection for those who share their enemies and who hate the people they hate, and they have affection for those who are hated by the people they themselves hate. For the same things as appear good to all of these appear as such also to the friends themselves,
20   the result being that they wish the good things for them—which, as we saw, is the mark of a friend.

Further, people have affection for those who are apt to be beneficial when it comes to money and one's preservation. Hence they honor the liberal and courageous. So too the just; and they assume that those who do not live off others are of this description.[27] Such also are those who live from their own labor, including among these farmers and, above all the rest, those who work with their own hands. They also have affection
25   for the prudent because they are not unjust, as well as those who are not meddling busybodies, for the same reason.

We also feel affection for those with whom we wish to be friends, if they manifestly wish to be ours. And such are those who are good in point of virtue and are well thought of, either among everyone altogether or among the best or among those whom we admire or among those who admire us.

30   Further, people have affection for those whom it is pleasant to spend time with and live with day to day. Such are those who are agreeable and not given to being censorious about one's mistakes and who are neither contentious nor quarrelsome. For all people of that sort are combative, and the combative appear to wish for what is contrary [to the wishes of others]. And [people have affection for] those who are skilled at cracking jokes and at putting up with others doing the same, for each has the
35   same purpose in view as his neighbor, namely, being able to take a joke and to make one in good humor. And [people have affection for] those who praise the goods they have, and especially those goods they fear they
1381b lack. Also those who are respectable in appearance, in their dress, in their

---

27 · I follow the punctuation of Kassel. Differently punctuated, the passage would read "Hence they honor the liberal and courageous and just; and they assume that those who do not live off others are of this description."

whole way of life. [People have affection also for] someone who does not criticize mistakes made or benefactions done, for both are marks of being censorious. And those who do not cling to past wrongs and do not nurse grievances, but instead are easily reconciled, since people suppose that they will be toward them as they are toward others. And [people have affection for] someone who does not speak badly of others or even know the bad things about his neighbors or them, but [knows] instead the good things, for this is what a good person does. And those who do not offer opposition to them when they are angry or being serious about something, for such would be combative types. And those who are in some way seriously disposed toward them—for example, by admiring them and supposing them to be serious human beings and by taking delight in them, particularly when they have had these feelings elicited by qualities they themselves especially wish to be admired for or in reference to which they wish to seem to be serious or pleasing. And [people have affection for] those who are similar to them and undertake the same pursuits, if they are not too annoying and their livelihood does not derive from the same source, for then "potter [envies] potter"[28] comes to pass. And those who desire the same things that admit of being shared by them simultaneously—otherwise, the same thing results here too.

[People have friendly affection also for] those before whom they are so disposed as not to be ashamed of their own deeds that run contrary to [mere] opinion—provided they feel no contempt for them; [they have affection also for] those before whom they *are* ashamed of their own deeds that do run contrary to what matters in truth [as distinguished from mere opinion]. And those who are their rivals in honor and those by whom they wish to be emulated but not envied: these they either have affection for or wish to befriend. And those whom they join in accomplishing good things, provided they not gain greater ills as a result. And those who have a like affection for both friends who are absent and friends who are present. Hence all have affection for those who are disposed in this way to friends who have died. And in general, [people have affection for] those who are intensely fond of friendship and do not leave their friends in the lurch: they have most affection for those among the good who are good at being friends. And [people have affection for] someone who does not

28 · See Hesiod, *Works and Days* 25–26, as well as 2.10 below. The relevant lines read "And potter envies potter and carpenter, carpenter / And beggar envies beggar and singer a singer." The context suggests that such "Strife" (Eris) as this is advantageous for human beings, since it prompts them to work hard.

refashion himself with a view to them; such also are those who even speak
30   of their own faults, since it was stated that we are not ashamed before our
friends in matters that run contrary to [mere] opinion.[29] If, then, someone who does feel shame at such things is not a friend, he who does not
feel such shame is likely a friend. And [people have affection for] those
who are not frightening and before whom we feel confidence, for nobody
is a friend to someone whom he fears. Forms of friendship are compan-
35   ionship, kinship, blood ties, and the like. Things apt to produce friendship are gracious favors,[30] and doing them for someone when he has not
asked for a favor, and not advertising the fact, for in this way it appears to
be for his own sake and not for some other reason.

1382a   It is manifest that what concerns enmity and feeling hatred can be observed on the basis of the opposite points. Things apt to produce enmity
are anger, spitefulness, [and] slander. Anger, then, arises from things done
against oneself, whereas enmity arises even without anything being done
against oneself: if we suppose that a fellow is such and such, we hate him.
5   And anger always concerns particulars—for example, against Callias or
Socrates—but hatred is also directed against classes—for *everyone* hates
the thief and the sycophant as such.[31] Anger is curable with time, hatred
incurable; the former aims at [inflicting] pain, the latter, harm. For the
angry person wishes to perceive [the object of his anger in some pain],[32]
10   but to one who hates, it makes no difference at all. All painful things
are subject to sense perception, but particularly harmful things are least
subject to perception—[for example,] injustice and foolishness—for the
presence of vice causes no pain [in the vicious themselves]. In addition,
the one state is accompanied by pain, the other is not: he who is angry is
pained thereby, but he who hates is not. The one might also come to feel
pity, under many circumstances, the other under no circumstance, for he
15   who is angry wants the person at whom he is angry to suffer proportion-

29 · See just above, at 1381b19–21.

30 · That is, benefactions performed without thought for oneself or from "graciousness" (*charis*), which is treated below at 2.7; see also n. 52 below.

31 · A "sycophant" was a shakedown artist who threatened the rich with frivolous lawsuits unless they paid up. Callias (ca. 450–370) was a wealthy Athenian noted for the
money he spent on sophists; the conversations recorded in Plato's *Protagoras* and Xenophon's *Symposium* are set in his home.

32 · The phrase is ambiguous and may refer instead to the angry person's wish to have
the object of his anger perceive it.

ately in return, whereas he who hates wants the object of his hatred to cease to exist.

It is manifest, then, on the basis of these considerations, that it is possible both to demonstrate who are enemies or friends and to make enemies or friends of those who are not such; and to undo the claims of those who say they are enemies or friends; and to lead those who are one's opponents, on account of their anger or enmity, in whichever of the two directions[33] one might choose.

But as for the sorts of things people fear, and whom they fear, and how   20
they are disposed when they fear—these will be manifest in what follows.

CHAPTER 5

So let fear be a certain pain and perturbation arising from an imagining of an impending ill[34] that is destructive or painful. For people do not fear all bad things—for example, [nobody is afraid that] he will be unjust or slow-witted—but they fear instead all those things that amount to great pains or destruction, and these only if they do not appear far-off but so   25
close as to be about to happen. For people do not fear things that are very far-off: all know that they will die, but because it is not close at hand, they give it no thought.

So if this is what fear is, frightening things are necessarily all those that appear to have a great capacity to bring about destruction or such harm as tends to issue in great pain. Hence even the signs of such things   30
are frightening, for they appear to be close to the frightening thing itself, since this is what is dangerous, namely, the drawing near of what is frightening. Such signs include the enmity and anger of those capable of effecting something, for it is clear that they wish to do so, the result being that they are close to doing it. And injustice [is a frightening sign], when it is equipped with power, for the unjust person is unjust by dint   35
of the choice he makes. And virtue that has been treated insolently [is a   1382b
frightening sign], when it is equipped with power, since it is clear that virtue always chooses [to act] when it is treated with insolence, and now it has the power to do so. And the fear belonging to those who are able to effect

33 · That is, if the opponent is angry, one can lead him either to (greater) anger or to gentleness; if the opponent feels enmity or hatred, one can lead him either to (greater) enmity or to friendliness.
34 · Or "bad thing" (*kakos*).

something [is itself frightening], for such a person is necessarily in a state of readiness [to act].

5   Now, since the many are inferior and too weak to resist gaining a profit and are cowards amid dangers, it is for the most part a frightening thing for someone to be subject to another. As a result, someone who has done something terrible is frightened by his accomplices because they are likely either to denounce him or to leave him in the lurch. And those capable of committing injustice [are feared] by those capable of suffering injustice, on the grounds that for the most part human beings commit injustice 10   whenever they have the ability to do so. And those who have been done injustice or believe that they have been done injustice are frightening, since they are always keeping a careful watch for the right moment [to retaliate]. And those who have committed injustice [are frightening], if they are equipped with power, since they fear suffering retaliation; and such was set down as being what "frightening" is. And those who are rivals for the same things, insofar as it is impossible for those things to be available to both sides at the same time: it is with such sorts as these that 15   people are always at war. And those who are a source of fear to people more powerful than a given person [are frightening to that person], for if they should be capable of harming the stronger, all the more would they be capable of harming him. And those whom people stronger than a given person fear [are frightening to that person], for the same reason. And those who have done away with others stronger than oneself; and those who are attacking people weaker than oneself, for either they are already frightening or they will be once they have thus grown in strength.

20   Among those who have suffered injustice or are enemies or rivals, it is not the hot-tempered and outspoken [who are frightening], but rather those who are gentle and ironic and cunning, since it is unclear if these latter are close to acting, and the result of this is that it is never manifest if they are far from doing so. And all that is frightening that is caused by those who have erred and that does not admit of being set right is more frightening, whether such frightening things are altogether impossible 25   to set right or doing so is not up to them but rather their opponents; and in those cases where assistance does not exist or is not easy to attain. To speak simply, frightening things are all those that elicit pity, when they happen to others or are about to happen. The most frightening things, so to say, and the things people fear, are pretty much these.

But as for how people themselves are disposed when they are afraid, let

us now speak of that. So if fear goes together with a certain expectation   30
of suffering something destructive, it is manifest that nobody is afraid
who supposes that he would not suffer anything at all. And neither do
people fear those things they suppose they would not suffer, nor do they
fear those at whose hands they do not suppose they would suffer, nor do
they experience fear during the time when they do not suppose it. It is
necessary, then, that those who do suppose they might suffer something
are afraid—both those at whose hands they might suffer it and the things   35
in question, and at the relevant time. And those who are enjoying great
good fortune and are of the opinion that they are enjoying it do not sup-   1383a
pose they might suffer something—hence they are insolent and slighting
and confident—and what makes people such is wealth, strength, abundance of friends, [and] power. And neither do those who have already
suffered what they hold to be all manner of terrible things, and so have
grown coldly indifferent to the future, like those in the course of being   5
cudgeled to death. Rather, [if there is to be fear,] some hope of salvation
must endure concerning the matter over which they anxiously contend.
And there is a sign of this. For fear renders people apt to deliberate, yet
no one deliberates about hopeless things.

As a result, one must render [the audience] such, whenever it is better to instill fear in them, to the effect that they are just such as to suffer
something, for even others, greater than they, have suffered it. One must   10
also point out people similar to them who are suffering or have in fact suffered, and at the hands of those whom they did not suppose would inflict
it, and the things they did not suppose they would suffer and the time
when they did not suppose it.

Now, since it is manifest what fear is, and also what the frightening
things are and what state each is in when he is afraid, it is manifest also,
on the basis of these points, what feeling confident is and what sorts of   15
things people feel confident about and how the confident are themselves
disposed. For confidence is the contrary of fear, and what inspires confidence is the contrary of the frightening.[35] As a result confidence is hope
accompanied by an imagining that the things that bring salvation are
nearby and that the frightening things either do not exist or are far-off.
Things that inspire confidence are the remoteness of the terrible and the

35 · The principal MSS read "for confidence is the contrary of the frightening"; but all
modern editors accept the supplement, reproduced in the translation, that is found in
the 1536 edition of Francisco Trincavelli.

20   proximity of the confidence-inspiring.[36] And if there are ways of setting
things right and means of assistance that are numerous or great or both,
[then people feel confident]; if they have neither suffered nor committed
injustice; if there are no rivals at all, or if the rivals have no power, or, if
they do have power, they are friends, or they have performed some benefaction for them or been done one by them; or if those whose interests
25   are the same as theirs are more numerous or stronger or both [than those
whose interests are at odds with them].

And people are themselves confident when they are disposed in this
way: if they suppose they have brought many things to a successful conclusion and not suffered in so doing, or if they have faced terrible things
many times and managed to escape. For human beings are without the
passion [of fear] in a twofold sense: either by virtue of not having been
30   tested[37] or by having the means to come to one's own aid—just as, amid
dangers at sea, those who have not been tested by a storm are confident
about what will happen, as are also those who, on account of their experience, have the means to come to their own aid [in such a circumstance].
And [people feel confident] whenever something is not frightening to
their peers, or to their inferiors, or to those whose superiors they suppose
they are. And people suppose they are superior to those over whom they
have prevailed, either over them themselves or their superiors or their
35   peers. And if they suppose that they have available to themselves more
1383b   and greater things, being preeminent in which things they are frightening to others. And these things are a powerful abundance of money, and
bodies, and friends, and land, and the provisions for war—either all of
these or the greatest of them. And if they have not committed injustice
against anyone, or not against many, or not against those they are afraid
5   of. And, in general, if their affairs pertaining to gods are in a fine state, as
regards signs and oracles and the rest. For anger inspires confidence, and
it is not committing injustice but rather suffering it that is productive of
anger; and the divine is thought to come to the assistance of the victims
of injustice. And [people feel confident] whenever, in undertaking something, they suppose that they would not likely suffer anything now or in
10   the future, or they suppose that they will be successful.

36 · Several editors offer emendations of the text at this point, since Aristotle seems to
use in the definition the thing to be defined. But Grimaldi defends the MSS.
37 · The verb "to have been tested" (*pepeirasthai*) is linked to the word for "experience"
(*empeiria*) that appears near the end of the sentence: to be tested is to gain experience.

What concerns both the frightening and the confidence-inspiring has been stated.

CHAPTER 6

The sorts of things that prompt people to feel ashamed or to be shameless, and before whom and how they are disposed when feeling it, are clear on the basis of the following points. So let shame be a certain pain and per- turbation pertaining to those bad things (present or past or future) that 15 appear to bring disrepute, and let shamelessness be a certain slighting of and apathetic indifference to these same things.

If, then, shame is as defined, one necessarily feels shame at such bad deeds as are held to be ugly,[38] either by the person himself or by those to whom he gives thought. And such are all those deeds that stem from vice—for example, throwing away one's shield or running away, for these 20 stem from cowardice. And making off with deposits entrusted to one, for this stems from injustice. And having sexual relations with those with whom one should not, or where one should not, or when one should not, for this stems from licentiousness. And profiting from petty or ugly things or from the powerless—for example, from the poor or the dead 25 (hence also the proverb, "gaining even from a corpse")—for this stems from shameful profiteering and illiberality. And not assisting someone with money when one is capable of doing so, or assisting him less than one could. And being assisted by those who are less well-off. And borrowing money when it will seem to be asking for a favor, and asking for a favor when that will seem to be asking to get back something owed you, and asking to get back something owed when that will seem to be asking for a favor; and praising somebody so that one will be held to be asking him for 30 a favor, and, although one has failed to attain anything, to ask nonethe- less.[39] For all these are signs of illiberality.

And praising someone in his presence is a sign of flattery; also over- praising someone's good qualities while whitewashing his defects; exces- sively grieving when in the presence of someone grieving; and all other

38 · The word "ugly" here (*aischra*) refers to the opposite of what is noble or beautiful (*kalos*) and shares the root of the word for "shamelessness" (*anaischuntia*).
39 · Both the precise meaning and the subjects of the verbs in this sentence are am- biguous and have prompted various readings. I follow Grimaldi's reading of it for the most part.

35   such things, for they are signs of flattery. And not enduring the labors that
1384a   are endured by elders or the pampered or those in positions of greater au-
         thority or those who are in general less capable, for all these are signs of
         softness. And being benefited by another, and often, and criticizing the
         benefaction the fellow performed, since all these are signs of a small soul
5   and being in a humbled state. Saying anything and everything about one-
         self and broadcasting this,[40] and claiming as one's own what are [the ac-
         complishments] of others, for these smack of bragging. It holds similarly
         with the deeds and the signs, and comparable things, that stem from each
         of the other vices of character, for they are ugly and shameful.[41]

         And, in addition to these, not sharing in the noble things that all share
10   in, or those things that all who are similar to one, or the greatest number,
         share in. I mean by "similar" those of the same nation, fellow citizens, age-
         mates, kin, and, in general, those who are of an equal station. For in this
         case it is a shameful thing not to have a share—for example, not to share
         in education to the same extent, and in other things similarly. All these
         are more shameful if they appear on account of one's own doing, for in
15   that case they then appear to stem to a greater degree from one's vice,[42] if
         the person himself is responsible for the attributes that are his, past, pres-
         ent, or future. And in suffering or having suffered or being about to suffer
         such things as bring dishonor and reproach, people are ashamed; these in-
         clude acts of subservience involving either one's body or ugly deeds done
20   to one, among which is to be treated with insolence (and some acts of li-
         centiousness, both voluntary and involuntary, are shameful; but others,
         when bound up with force, are involuntary). Tolerating such things and
         failing to defend oneself stem from a lack of manliness or from cowardice.
         These things, then, and others of this sort, prompt people to feel shame.

         Now, since shame is an imagining pertaining to disrepute and is felt
25   for the sake of that very disrepute and not the consequences involved;
         and since nobody gives thought to an opinion bearing on one's reputa-
         tion[43] except on account of those who form that opinion, it is necessarily
         the case that people feel shame before those whom they hold in esteem.

40 · The MSS differ here, and another translation is possible: "Speaking about oneself
and broadcasting this."

41 · One MS reads "shameless" (*anaischunta*).

42 · Or "badness" (*kakia*).

43 · This phrase attempts to capture the ambiguity of the Greek: the word for "opinion"
(*doxa*) can also mean "reputation"; hence also "disrepute" (*adoxia*) or the loss of one's
reputation in the element of opinion (*doxa*).

There is esteem for those who admire one and those whom one admires; and for those by whom one wishes to be admired; and for those whose rival in honor one is; and for those for whose opinion one does not feel contempt.

Now, people wish to be admired by, and they themselves admire, all those in possession of some honorable good, or those who, having authority over something they desperately need, grant it to them—for example, as lovers [admire their beloveds and wish to be admired by them]. And people feel rivalry in honor with those who are similar to them. They pay heed to the prudent on the grounds that they speak the truth, and both elders and the educated are of this description. And things that are before all eyes and out in the open bring more shame; hence also the proverb "Shame[44] resides in the eyes." For this reason people feel more shame before those who will always be present and those who are concerned with them—because in both cases they are "in the eyes" [of the others]. And [people feel more shame before] those who are not liable to the same charges, for clearly those people are of the opinion that the contrary things are best. And before those who are not sympathetic to people who appear to err, for it is said that nobody feels indignation[45] at his neighbors for doing the things that he himself does, the result being that someone clearly is indignant at those things he himself does not do.

And [people feel shame] before those apt to broadcast things to many people, for [to people of that sort] there is no difference at all between not forming an opinion about something and not broadcasting it publicly. Apt to so broadcast things are those who have been treated unjustly, because they maintain a keen watch for opportunities to do so, as well as slanderers, since if in fact they will slander those who have committed no error, all the more will they in the case of those who *have* erred. And [people feel shame before] those who spend their time preoccupied with the errors of their neighbors—for example, those given to mockery, and comic poets, for these are in their way slanderers and apt to broadcast faults publicly. [People feel shame] also in the presence of those whom

44 · Not the word usually translated in this context by "shame" (*aischunē*), but *aidōs*, which can also mean "awe," "respect," "reverence."

45 · The verb is *nemesaō*, related to the noun *nemesis* (and to the goddess so named)—indignation or angry resentment at the unmerited or unjust prosperity of others. Nemesis became the divine embodiment of the desire for (divine) retribution; see e.g., Hesiod, *Works and Days* 200 and 741. See also 2.9 below for Aristotle's extended treatment of indignation (*nemesis*).

they have never failed, since among them they are in a position to be admired. Hence people feel shame before those who have asked them for something for the first time, on the grounds that they are not yet held in any disrepute by them. Such also are those who have just conceived the
15   wish to be friends, for they have observed only what is best about one—hence Euripides's reply to the Syracusans holds good[46]—and those among one's acquaintances of long standing who are aware of nothing untoward about one.

But people are ashamed not only of the things mentioned, which are themselves productive of shame, but also of the signs associated with them—for example, not only being engaged in sex but also the signs
20   thereof. And [people feel shame] not only by doing ugly things, but also by speaking of them. Similarly, [they feel shame] not only before the persons stated, but also before those, such as their servants and their friends, who will make clear [their faults] to those persons.

In general, they are not ashamed before those whose reputation for telling the truth[47] they have much contempt for—nobody is ashamed
25   before a child or a beast.[48] Neither are they ashamed of the same things before both those they are on familiar terms with and those with whom they are not on such terms. Instead, they feel shame before their familiars when it comes to things that seem shameful and truly are such, whereas [they feel shame] before those at a greater remove from themselves when it comes to things that seem shameful according to [mere] convention.

And those disposed as follows would themselves feel shame: first, if there should be certain others before whom people are inclined to feel shame, as we contended, who stand in that relation to them (and these
30   were either people admired by them or who admire them or those by whom they wish to be admired, or those from whom they need some

46 · It is uncertain to what Aristotle here refers. According to the scholiast, Euripides was sent on a diplomatic mission to Syracuse, in the course of the Peloponnesian War, and after his offer of peace and friendship was rebuffed, he is said to have said: "Men of Syracuse, you should respect [or feel shame before: *aischunesthai*] us, if for no other reason than that of our recent request made of you, as your admirers" (cited by Cope ad loc.) But many commentators, including Grimaldi, are dissatisfied with this explanation.

47 · Or, perhaps, "whose opinion about speaking the truth." Grimaldi suggests: "whose views (judgments) on speaking the truth they deeply despise."

48 · The same phrase appears also at 1371a13–17, where Grimaldi suggests taking "beast" in a metaphorical sense: "brutish men."

service that they will not attain if they are held in disrepute); and these whether they are onlookers—just as Cydias[49] said in the assembly concerning the land allotment in Samos, for he judged it right that the Athenians assume the Greeks to be standing around them in a circle, as onlookers and not just as those who would hear later of the votes they might   35 cast—or whether they are such as to be nearby, or those who will perceive what goes on. Hence those who fail in something do not wish even to be seen by those who once emulated them, for those who emulate also admire. And [people are ashamed] whenever they bring shame on deeds or   1385a affairs—whether their own or those of ancestors or of certain others with whom they have some close kinship. And in general [we feel shame] on behalf of those before whom we ourselves feel shame; these are the people mentioned as well as those to whom we ourselves defer, those who have   5 been our teachers or advisors, and if there are others like us with whom we are rivals in honor. For we do, and refrain from doing, many things because of the shame we feel on account of people such as these.[50] And those who are going to be seen and go about in public with those who know full well [what they have done] are more given to shame. Hence Antiphon the poet, when he was on the point of being cudgeled to death by   10 order of Dionysius, said, on seeing those about to die with him covering themselves as they proceeded through the gates, "Why do you cover yourselves? Surely it's not because somebody here may see you tomorrow?"[51]

This, then, about shame. But as for what concerns shamelessness, it is clear that we will have ready access to it on the basis of the opposite considerations.   15

CHAPTER 7

Toward whom people have gracious feelings and for what reasons and how they themselves are then disposed will be clear to those who have de-

49 · An Athenian orator who argued against the establishment of cleruchies (colonies) in Samos, which violated the spirit, at least, of the Second Athenian League, around 365.

50 · For clarity's sake, the third-person plurals of the original in this sentence and the preceding one have been changed to first-person plurals.

51 · The episode is uncertain. Grimaldi notes that according to [Plutarch?] *Lives of the Ten Orators: Antiphon* (833b-c) the orator Antiphon—not the poet of the same name—was put to death for criticizing the tragedies of Dionysius.

fined graciousness.[52] Let graciousness, then, be that in reference to which someone is said to be gracious, namely, a service performed for someone in need and not in return for something nor so that the person performing the service may gain something himself, but rather so that the other fellow may do so. And the service[53] involved will be great if the person is seriously in need, or needs great and difficult things, or if he is in need at critical moments that are great or difficult, or if someone is the only one to perform the service or the first to do so or does it to the greatest degree.

Needs are longings, and especially those longings that are accompanied by pain when one fails to possess something. Desires are of this character—for example, erotic love; so too the desires bound up with bodily suffering and with dangers, for both someone in danger and someone in pain desire something. Hence those who stand by someone in poverty or exile, even if the service they perform is small, have acted with graciousness on account of the greatness of the need involved and the critical character of the occasion, as, for example, the person who gave someone a mat in the Lyceum.[54] It is necessary, then, that the service pertain especially to these sorts of things but, if not, to things of an equal or greater importance. Since it is as a result manifest who[55] is treated graciously and under what circumstances, and how [the gracious are themselves] disposed, it is clear that [arguments] must be supplied on the basis of these considerations, pointing out that some either are or were in such pain and need and that others have performed or are performing some such service to them in such a state of neediness.

It is manifest, too, how it is possible for graciousness to be done away with and to render people ungracious. For either they perform or once performed a service for their own sakes (for this, as we saw, is not graciousness), or because that service happened just by chance, or because

52 · The Greek word *charis*—often rendered as "grace" or "gratitude" or "favor"—has no single English equivalent. As Cope puts it, *charis* "represents the tendency or inclination to benevolence, to do a grace, favour, or service, spontaneous and disinterested ... to another, or to our fellow-man. It also includes the feeling of gratitude, the instinctive inclination to *return* favours received" (emphasis original). Grimaldi contends (emphasis original) that "*in itself charis* means: (a) kindliness, benevolence, (b) gratitude, (c) a favor conferred," although he adopts the translation "kindliness."
53 · Or, perhaps, "graciousness": the noun is not expressed.
54 · The reference is unknown. The Lyceum was the name of Aristotle's school—although Cope suggests that we "do not even know whether it [Lyceum] is the name of a man or a place: it might also be the title of a play or a speech."
55 · One MS here reads "when" (*hote*) graciousness arises.

they were forced to act as they did, or because they gave something back they owed, whether they knew it or not, but did not simply give it: in both cases it is done in return for something, such that there would thus be no graciousness involved at all. And one must examine what concerns 5 quite all the categories,[56] for graciousness is what it is because it involves this thing here, or this amount, or is of this character, or involves this time or that place. And it is a sign [of lacking graciousness] if people have failed to perform a lesser service for us, and if they performed this same service for our enemies (or one equal to or greater than it), for it is clear that these are not done for our sakes at all. Or if someone knowingly performed a service that is paltry or trifling, since no one admits that he is in need of 10 paltry or trifling things.

What concerns being gracious and ungracious has been stated.

CHAPTER 8

As for the sorts of things that elicit pity and those whom people pity, and how they themselves who feel pity are disposed—let us speak of these. So let pity be a certain pain at what is manifestly bad, and destructive or painful, and befalls someone who does not deserve it, which one might expect to suffer oneself (or somebody in one's circle might do so), and this 15 when it appears close at hand. For it is clear that someone who is going to feel pity must necessarily suppose that he is in fact the sort of person who could suffer something bad—either he himself or someone in his circle—and suffer the sort of bad thing as was stated in the definition (or something similar to it or closely comparable). Hence neither those who have been altogether ruined feel pity—since they suppose they could suf- 20 fer nothing further, given what they have already suffered—nor do those who suppose themselves to be exceedingly happy. They are instead inso-lent, for if they suppose that quite all good things are theirs, they clearly suppose also that suffering anything bad at all is impossible, since this lat-ter, too, belongs among the good things.

But the sorts of people who believe they *can* suffer are those who have already suffered and managed to make it through; and those who 25 are older, on account of both their prudence and their experience; and the weak; and those who are rather cowardly; and the educated, for they

56 · That is, the ten categories or predicates that can be said of any being, the other five not mentioned in the text above being relation, position, condition, action, and passion.

are given to calculating well. Also those who have relatives or offspring or wives, for these are one's own and can suffer the sorts of things men-
30 tioned. And those not in the grip of a manly passion—in that of anger, for example, or confident boldness, for these passions least of all calculate what will be—nor disposed toward insolence, for those who are so disposed are also least given to calculating what they will suffer, whereas those in between these can feel pity.[57] Nor, in turn, do those who are exceedingly frightened: those who utterly terrified do not feel pity because of their preoccupation with their own passion. And [some may feel
35 pity] if they suppose that some people, at least, are decent, for one who supposes nobody to be decent will suppose that all are deserving of some-
1386a thing bad. And so, in general, [someone will feel pity] whenever he is in such a state as to remember that these sorts of things have befallen either him himself or those in his circle, or whenever he is in such a state as to expect that they could happen either to him or to those in his circle.

The state people are in, then, when they feel pity, has been spoken of; and the things for which they feel pity are clear on the basis of the defini-
5 tion. For all painful and distressing things that are destructive are productive of pity, as well as those that are ruinous, and all bad things of some magnitude of which chance is a cause. Things distressing and destructive are deaths and assaults and bodily sufferings and old age and illnesses and lack of sustenance. As for those bad things of which chance is a cause,
10 these include lack of friends, few friends—hence being torn away from friends and associates is pitiable—ugliness, weakness, [and] lameness. [It is productive of pity also] if something bad happens when it was only to be expected that something good would occur, in particular when this sort of thing happens often. And when something good happens only after one has suffered—as, for example, when gifts from the King were
15 sent down to Diopeithes only after he had died.[58] And when either nothing good has happened, or it does happen but there is no enjoyment of it. These, then, and those like them, are the sorts of things for which people feel pity.

57 · The reading of the MSS. Kassel, however, moves the clause beginning with "whereas" to the end of the next sentence. He thus has Aristotle suggest that those "between" a manly passion, on the one hand, and terrifying fear, on the other, may still feel pity. This may make for better sense but is without manuscript authority.
58 · The Diopeithes in question may have been a general, ca. 343–342, who led a mission to the Thracian Chersonese. If this is so, then "the King" would be Artaxerxes III of Persia.

But people feel pity also for their acquaintances, unless they are exceedingly close in point of kinship; as for these latter, it is just as if they themselves are going to suffer. Hence Amasis did not cry at his son's being led off to die, as they say, but he did cry at the sight of his friend begging,[59]   20
since this latter is pitiable, the former terrifying. For the terrifying is different from the pitiable; in fact it drives out pity and is often useful to one's opponent.[60] For people no longer[61] pity when what is terrifying is close to them. And people pity those who are like them in age, character,   25
[moral] habits,[62] merit, [and] familial line. For in all these cases, it appears more likely that the same things may befall oneself too. In general, and here too,[63] one must grasp the fact that all the things people fear in their own cases, they feel pity for when they happen to others. And since the sufferings that appear close at hand are pitiable, and since people neither remember events that happened ten thousand years ago nor anticipate those that will happen ten thousand years from now, they generally do   30
not feel pity because of them, or not in the same way; it is necessarily the case that those who contribute to the effect by their bearing and voice and clothing[64] and, in general, by their dramatic display are more pitiable.[65]
For they make the bad thing in question appear closer by setting it before one's eyes, either as being about to happen or as having happened. As for   1386b
things that have just now happened or are just about to, they rouse greater pity on account of their proximity in time. For this reason, too, the relevant signs and the actions involved [also elicit pity]: for example, the clothing of those who have suffered, and everything of that sort, together with the speeches and all else of those who are actually suffering—for ex-

59 · Amasis was king of Egypt: consider Herodotus 3.14, where the anecdote concerns not Amasis but his son Psammenitus.
60 · Following the suggestion of Stefan L. Radt, "Zu Aristoteles *Rhetorik*," *Mnemosyne* 32 (1979): 284–306. The Greek might also mean "useful for the opposite [of pity]."
61 · I follow the text as emended by Vahlen and accepted by most modern editors. The MSS read "people still pity when what is terrifying [*to deinou*] is close to them," which would seem to contradict Aristotle's point in the passage.
62 · Or "characteristic states" or "characters" (*hexeis*), the general class under which the moral virtues fall according to Aristotle.
63 · Consider 2.5 (1382b26–27) for the same thought.
64 · The MSS divide: some read, instead of "clothing" (*esthēsi*), "perception" (*aisthēsi*), which Grimaldi (who rejects it) suggests could be translated as "by a display of feeling."
65 · I follow the general suggestion of Grimaldi. In question is the meaning of the participle (*sunapergadzomenous*) that serves as the subject of the sentence, and of the final adjective (*eleeinoterous*).

5   ample, those in the very act of dying. For quite all of these foster greater
pity because they appear close at hand. Especially pitiable in such moments of crisis are those who are serious [human beings], on the grounds
both that the suffering is undeserved and that it is coming to sight before
our very eyes.

CHAPTER 9

On the one hand, the antithesis of feeling pity is above all what people
10 call righteous indignation,[66] for being pained at someone's faring *badly*
undeservedly is in a certain manner the antithesis of, and stems from the
same character as, being pained at someone's faring *well* undeservedly.
Both passions belong to a fine character, for one should grieve with, and
feel pity for, those who fare badly undeservedly, and one should be indig-
15 nant at those who fare well undeservedly: what comes to pass contrary to
desert is unjust, and so it is that we attribute the feeling of such indignation even to the gods.

On the other hand, envy, too, would seem in the same manner to be
the antithesis of feeling pity, on the grounds that it is closely akin to and
even the same thing as feeling indignation—but in fact envy is different from indignation. For although envy, too, is a perturbing pain at another's faring well, it is not directed at someone who does not deserve it
20 but rather at someone who is one's equal and peer. Not the thought that
something untoward will happen to oneself, but rather the thought that
something is happening to one's neighbor, must be similarly present in
each and every instance [of indignation and envy].[67] For it will cease to
be envy, in the one instance, and indignation, in the other—there will be
fear instead—if the pain and perturbation are present in a person because
he himself will come to have something bad[68] as a result of the other fellow's faring well.
25 It is also manifest that opposite passions will follow on these. For he
who is pained at those who fare badly undeservedly will be pleased by (or

66 · *Nemesaō*, to which the noun *nemesis* is related; see also n. 45 above. "Angry resentment" or "retribution"—i.e., the desire that the undeservedly high and mighty get
what's coming to them—is another possible translation.
67 · I follow the reading suggested by Grimaldi. The word translated as "in each and every
instance" (*hapasin*) could mean "to quite all [human beings who feel resentment or envy]."
68 · Not the usual term translated as "bad" (*kakos*) but *phaulos*: what is paltry, low, or
base.

not pained at) those who fare badly in the opposite way—for example, no fine person would be pained whenever parricides and murderers attain their just deserts. One should delight in those who so fare—just as, in the   30 same way, one should delight in those who fare well deservedly. For both cases are just and prompt a decent person to take delight: the decent person necessarily hopes that what has happened to someone like him could happen also to him himself. And quite all these passions belong to the same character, their opposites to the opposite character, for the same person is spiteful[69] and envious: that by the acquisition and possession   1387a of which someone is pained, by its removal and destruction he must of necessity be delighted. Hence all these things are apt to prevent pity, but they differ on account of the causes mentioned. As a result, they are, all of   5 them, similarly useful in preventing pity from arising.

First, then, let us speak about feeling indignation—at whom people feel it and for what reasons and how they themselves are disposed when filled with such indignation—and then, after this, let us speak about the other [passions]. In fact it is manifest on the basis of what has been said. For if feeling indignation is being pained at someone's faring well when   10 it is manifestly undeserved, it is clear, first, that it is not possible to feel such indignation at all things good: if someone is just or courageous, or if he will attain virtue, no one will be indignant at him for this (for neither do people feel pity at the opposites of these) but rather for his wealth and power and things of that sort—for all those things, to put it simply, that those who are good, and those who are possessed of things good by na-   15 ture[70] (like good birth and beauty and all else of that sort) deserve to have.

Since what is ancient appears to be closely akin to what is by nature, it is necessarily the case that, when people possess the same good, if those among them who have attained it just recently and on that account are faring well, they are then the objects of greater indignation. For the newly rich cause more pain than do those of long-established and inherited wealth.   20 The case is similar with those who rule and are powerful and have many

69 · Or, more or less literally, "one who delights in the bad things [that befall another)]" (*epichairekakos*).

70 · Cope objects to the clause, present in the MSS, "and those who are possessed of things good by nature" on the grounds that, like the (morally) good, such people are here said to be deserving of additional goods like wealth and power: "Birth and beauty certainly have no claim *per se* to any other advantages." Yet Aristotle may here simply reproduce the *endoxon* that the nobly born or good-looking, for example, *do* deserve still more goods (consider Grimaldi ad loc.).

friends and good children and anything else of that sort, especially if, on account of these goods, some other good comes to be theirs. For here, too, the newly rich cause more pain, when they come to hold office on account of their wealth, than do those whose wealth is of long standing, and simi-

25   larly in other cases. A cause of this is that the latter are held to have what is theirs, the former not: what always appears as it now is, is held to be true, such that the others are held to possess what does not belong to them.

And since each good is not the proper desert of just any chance person, but a certain proportion and appropriateness are involved—for example, fine weapons are appropriate not for the just man but for the courageous one, and distinguished marriages are appropriate not for the newly rich

30   but for the wellborn—if, then, someone attains what is not appropriate for him, good though he may be, this fosters indignation. So too when the inferior disputes with the superior, especially when they are engaged in the same affair. Hence this was said:

With Ajax, son of Telamon, he avoided battle.[71]

35   For Zeus would be indignant at him, should he do battle with a better mortal.[72]

1387b   So too even if [the two are not engaged in the same affair] and an infe-rior disputes with a superior in anything whatsoever—for example, if a skilled musician disputes with a just man, for justice is better than musi-cal skill. It is clear, then, on the basis of these points, at whom people feel indignant and for what reason: they are these [sorts of people] and those like them.

But people are themselves prone to feeling indignation if they happen

5   to deserve, and to possess, the greatest goods. For it is unjust to be judged deserving of goods similar to those that people dissimilar [to you] de-serve; and, second, [people are prone to indignation] if they happen to be good and serious, for as such they both judge well and hate injustices. And if they are ambitious and long for certain concerns or affairs, espe-

10   cially when they are ambitious for those that others attain who are unde-serving of them.[73] And, in general, when they deem themselves deserving

71 · Homer, *Iliad* 11.542. The subject of the line is Hector.

72 · This second line does not appear in the extant texts of Homer, but is found in Plu-tarch, *How to Study Poetry* 36a.

73 · Another translation is possible: "especially when they are ambitious for those things of which others happen to be undeserving." "Concerns or affairs" translates *prag-mata*, a general term for the objects of our concerns; political office may be implied here.

of things that they deem others not to deserve, they are apt to feel indignation at these people and over the things in question. Hence in fact slavish and paltry types, and the unambitious, are not prone to indignation, for there is nothing they deem themselves to deserve.

It is also manifest, on the basis of these points, what the sorts of people are whose misfortunes and ill faring, or failures, one should delight in or at any rate not be pained by, for on the basis of the points mentioned the   15
opposite sorts are clear. If, as a result, one's speech puts the judges into such dispositions [as to delight in or not be pained by the circumstances of those they are to judge], and if it points out that those who deem themselves deserving of pity (and the reasons why they deserve it) do not deserve to attain it but rather deserve not to attain it—it would as a result   20
be impossible for the judges to pity them.

CHAPTER 10

It is also clear what things people envy and whom they envy and how they are disposed when envying, if in fact envy is a certain pain at those similar to oneself who are manifestly faring well in the aforementioned goods, not so that the envious person himself may gain something but because the others have done so. The sorts of people who will feel envy are those to whom certain others are, or appear to be, similar. And by "similar"   25
I mean in familial line, kinship, age, characteristic states,[74] reputation,[75] [or] possessions. So too those who are just shy of having everything in their possession. Hence those who carry out great deeds and who enjoy good fortune are envious because they suppose that all are making off with what belongs to them. And those who are honored for something   30
to a distinguished degree, and especially for their wisdom or happiness.[76] And those who are ambitious are more filled with envy than are the unambitious. So too with those who lay claim to wisdom, for they are ambitious when it comes to wisdom. And, in general, those who are fond of having a reputation for some given thing are envious concerning it. And the small-souled, too, for everything seems great to them.

As for the things people envy, these are the goods mentioned. For the   35
deeds or possessions of concern to those who are fond of reputation, to   1388a

74 · Or, perhaps, "[moral] habits" (*hexeis*); see also 2.8 (1386a25) and n. 62.
75 · Or simply "opinion."
76 · The term for "happiness" (*eudaimonia*) is sometimes a euphemism for (material) prosperity.

the ambitious, and to those longing for renown, as well as all that comes
from good fortune—these are in pretty much all cases subject to envy.
This is especially so when people themselves either long for those goods
or suppose that they should have them, or when they possess the goods
that will give them either a slight preeminence or but a slight shortfall.[77]

It is manifest also whom people envy, for this was stated at the same
time: they envy those close to them in time and place and age and reputation (hence it was said: "for kinship, too, knows how to envy") and those
in relation to whom they are rivals in honor, for they are such rivals in relation to those just mentioned. For no one is a rival in honor of those who
lived ten thousand years ago or of those who will one day come to be or of
the dead, nor of those who live at the Columns of Heracles.[78] And neither
are they rivals of those supposed either by them themselves or by others
to be much inferior to them or much superior. In the same way, they *are*
rivals of those engaged in the same sort of things.[79] Since people do feel a
rivalry with their competitors, including competitors in love, and, in general, those who aim at the same things as they, it is necessarily the case that
it is especially these they envy. So in fact it was said,

And potter [envies] potter.[80]

And people are envious of those whose past acquisitions or present suc-
cesses constitute a reproach to them, and these are people close to them
and like them. For it is clearly down to them that they fail to attain the
good in question, the result being that this failure, which is painful, causes
them to feel envy. And [we envy] those who have or have acquired those

77 · As Grimaldi suggests, this last clause means "goods whose possession while not
conferring distinction still confer substantial honor." Cope adds this: "A very great superiority or inferiority places a man beyond the reach of envy. It is when the competition is close . . . that the apparent value of the good competed for is greatly enhanced,
and the envy excited by the success of the opponent proportionately strong."
78 · The expression, which appears also in Aristotle's *Meteorologica* (2.1.10), refers to
the outer limits of the known world, in this case the extreme boundary of the Medi-
terranean Sea.
79 · The meaning of this sentence is uncertain and has occasioned emendation, based
partly on differing MSS and varying punctuation. If one takes this sentence as part of
the previous one, it might be translated (as Grimaldi notes): "And neither are they rivals of those supposed either by them themselves or by others to be much inferior to
them or much superior; so, too, they are not rivals of others in like instances."
80 · Hesiod, *Works and Days* 25. See also 2.4 above (1381b16–17), where the same line
is quoted.

things that it is fitting for us to have or that we possessed at one time.[81]   20
Hence older men are envious of younger ones. And those who spent a
great deal envy those who spent little for the same thing; and those who
attained something with difficulty, or failed to do so at all, envy those
who attained it quickly.

It is clear what things such envious people delight in, and in whom
they delight, and how they are disposed when doing so, since the condition in which they are pained is the same one in which they will, at   25
the opposite things, feel pleasure. As a result, if [the judges] are themselves brought into some such state [of envy], and if those who deem
themselves deserving of pity or of attaining some good [from the judges]
are such as the enviable have been described as being, then they clearly
will not attain any pity from those in authority.

CHAPTER 11

How those who feel emulation are disposed, and by what sorts of things
they are prompted to feel it and in relation to whom, are clear from the   30
following. For if emulation is a certain pain at the manifest presence of
honorable goods that the person himself is capable of attaining, in the
possession of persons similar to him by nature, not because those goods
belong to another but because they do not belong also to him—(hence
emulation both is a decent thing and belongs to decent people, whereas
envy is base and belongs to base people, for the one fellow, on account of
emulation, readies himself to attain good things, whereas the other, on ac-   35
count of his envy, [wishes] that his neighbor not have them); [if all this is
so,] then those who deem themselves deserving of good things but do not   1388b
have them are necessarily apt to feel emulation, for nobody deems himself
worthy of manifestly impossible things. Hence the young and the great-
souled are such. Emulous, too, are those who have the sorts of goods that
are worthy of being possessed by honorable men, and these are wealth and   5
abundance of friends and ruling offices and all such things. For on the
grounds that it is only fitting for them to be good men, they feel emulation when it comes to such goods as are fitting for the good to have. And
they are emulous of those whom others deem deserving [of such goods];
and when it comes to those goods that are held in honor and belong to

81 · For clarity's sake, the third-person-plural verbs or pronouns in this sentence have
been changed to first-person plurals.

one's ancestors or kin or family or nation or city, [the good] are apt to be emulous concerning them, for they suppose that such goods are properly theirs and that they deserve them. And if honorable goods are objects of emulation, the virtues are necessarily such objects, as well as all that is productive of advantage and benefit for others, since people honor those who are beneficent and those who are good. So too all those goods that supply enjoyment to one's neighbors—for example, one's wealth and beauty, rather than one's health.

It is manifest, too, who the objects of emulation are, for those who possess these things (and things of that sort) are objects of emulation; and these are the things mentioned—for example, courage, wisdom, [or] rule. For rulers are capable of benefiting many—[as are also] generals, orators, [and] all those capable of such things. And those whom many wish to be similar to, or whom many wish to have as acquaintances or as friends.[82] Or those whom many admire, or those whom they themselves admire. And those about whom praise and encomiums are given either by poets or speechwriters.

People also feel contempt for the opposite things, since contempt is opposed to emulation, feeling emulation to feeling contempt. Those so disposed as to be emulous of certain persons or to be the object of the emulation of others are necessarily apt to feel contempt for those who possess the bad qualities opposed to the good ones that elicit the emulation, and because of those bad qualities. Hence people often feel contempt for those who are lucky, whenever they enjoy luck that is not accompanied by goods held in honor.

On account of what, then, the passions arise and are dissolved, and on what the modes of persuasion pertaining to them are based, have been stated.

CHAPTER 12

Let us go through next what sorts of characters there are in relation to the passions and the characteristic states[83] and ages and instances of luck. I mean by "passions" anger, desire, and things of that sort, about which

---

82 · The Greek admits of another translation: "And those whom many wish to be similar to, or those who have many acquaintances or many friends."

83 · Or "[moral] habits" (*hexeis*).

we have spoken before;[84] and by "characteristic states," virtues and vices.[85]
What concerns these too was spoken of before, as well as what concerns   35
the sorts of things each person in turn chooses and is apt to carry out.[86]
"Ages" are youth; and one's prime; and old age. By "luck" I mean good   1389a
birth and wealth and powers, and the opposites of these; and, in general,
good luck and bad.

Now, the characters of the young are marked by desire, and they are
such as to do the things they desire. Of the bodily desires, they are especially apt to follow the one for sex,[87] and in this they lack self-restraint.   5
When it comes to desires, the young are easily changeable and fickle, and
although they desire intensely, they cease [to desire] rapidly. For their
wishes are keen but not great, like the thirst and hunger of the sickly.
[The young] are characterized also by spiritedness and a sharp temper,
and they are such as to follow impulse; they also succumb to spiritedness,   10
for on account of a love of honor,[88] they do not tolerate being slighted but
are indignant,[89] if they suppose they have been done an injustice. And although they do love honor, they love victory more, for youth desires superiority, and victory is a kind of superiority. And they love both of these
more than they love money; they are lovers of money least of all, because   15
they have not yet experienced want, as the saying of Pittacus has it concerning Amphiaraus.[90] They have, not a cynical[91] character, but a naïve

84 · See the immediately preceding section, 2.2–11.

85 · For Aristotle's identification of virtues and vices as "characteristic states" (*hexeis*),
as distinguished from either passions or capacities, see *Nicomachean Ethics* 2.5.

86 · Consider 1.6.

87 · The Greek is rather more graceful: "matters pertaining to Aphrodite" (*ta aphro-
disia*).

88 · Or "ambition."

89 · Not the word elsewhere translated as "indignation" (*nemesis*: see 2.9) but
aganakteō—"to be vexed or indignantly angry."

90 · The remark in question has not survived. Pittacus of Mytilene (ca. 650–570) was
one of the seven wise men of Greece and governed Mytilene for a time. Amphiaraus
was an early Greek hero.

91 · "Cynical" here does not of course refer to the philosophical school of the Cynics:
it renders instead *kakoētheis*—literally, "having a bad character"—just as "naïve" here
translates *euētheis*—literally, "having a good character." But as the latter came to mean
having a character that was a little too good—hence simple or naïve—so the former
came to mean having a character a little too bad and, in particular, suspecting everyone's motive. See also 1389b20–21, where Aristotle offers a definition of such "cynicism."

one, because they have not yet observed many wicked things. They are also
readily trusting because they have not yet suffered many deceptions. They
are hopeful, too, because, like those who are drunk, the young are by na-
20   ture hot-blooded, and, at the same time, they have not yet suffered many
failures. In fact they live for the most part on hope, since hope belongs
to the future, memory to times gone by, and for the young the future is
vast, the past brief. On the first day, so to speak, one can remember noth-
25   ing, but hope for anything. They are also readily deceived for the reason
mentioned, since they easily form hopes. They are also rather courageous,
since they are characterized by spiritedness and hopefulness, the former
prompting them not to be afraid, the latter to be confident. Nobody in
the grip of anger is afraid, and hoping for something good inspires confidence. They are also sensitive to shame because, having been educated
30   by the law alone, they do not yet suppose that any other things are noble.
They are also great-souled,[92] for they have not yet been humbled by life—
they are instead without experience of the necessities—and greatness of
soul consists in deeming oneself deserving of great things, which hopefulness brings about.
35   They also choose to do what is noble over what is advantageous, since
they live more by their character than by calculation, and calculation aims
at the advantageous, virtue at the noble. They are also fond of friendship
and comradeship to a greater degree than are the other ages, because they
1389b   delight in living together, and they do not yet judge anything with a view
to advantage, the result being that they do not make friends for that reason either. And quite all the mistakes they make tend in the direction of
excess and vehemence, in violation of the saying of Chilon,[93] for they do
all things excessively: they feel friendly affection to excess and hatred to
5   excess, and all else similarly. They also suppose that they know *everything*
and emphatically affirm it, since this is a cause of doing everything to excess. The injustices they commit are traceable to insolence, not to malice. They are also given to pitying, because they suppose that all are fine
people and better [than they are in fact]. For they take their measure of
10   their neighbors by their own lack of vice, such that they suppose their
neighbors to be suffering undeservedly. They also are fond of laughter

92 · Or "magnanimous."
93 · A Spartan ephor (fl. 560–556) who is credited with the saying "Nothing in excess" (see Diogenes Laertius, *Life of Thales* 1.1.40–41). Even the Spartans—no lovers of
speech or reason (*philologoi*)—honored him (see 1398b13).

and hence are witty, for wittiness is educated insolence. Such, then, is the character of the young.

CHAPTER 13

Those who are older and pretty much past their prime have characters that are in most respects the opposites of these. Because they have lived for many years and been deceived more, and made more mistakes, and because the greater part of affairs turns out poorly, not only do they affirm nothing with assurance, but they affirm everything with far less assurance than they should.[94] They *suppose* things but *know* nothing; and because they waiver, they also always add a "perhaps" and a "maybe," and state everything in this way but nothing unreservedly. They are cynical as well, for cynicism consists in assuming the worst about everything.[95]

Further, they are suspicious of others on account of their distrust, and they are distrustful on account of their experience. They also do not have intense feelings of either friendly affection or hatred for these reasons, but, as the counsel of Bias has it, they love as though they will one day hate and hate as though they will one day love.[96] They are also small-souled because they have been humbled by life: they desire nothing great or extraordinary but only what is conducive to [mere] life.[97] They are also illiberal, since property is one of the necessities, and, at the same time, they know through experience that possessing it is difficult and losing it, easy. They are both cowardly and afraid of everything before the fact, for they are disposed in a way contrary to that of the young. They have become chilled, whereas the young are heated, such that old age paves the way for cowardice, since fear, too, is a certain chill. They are also fond of life, even more so on the final day, so to speak, since desire is for what is absent, and

94 · The text is suspect here and has been emended in various ways. Kassel deletes one word (*agan*) that appears in the MSS, to give this sense in translation: "Not only do they affirm nothing with assurance, but they affirm everything with less assurance than they should."

95 · On "cynicism" here, see n. 91 above.

96 · Bias of Priene was one of the traditional wise men of Greece; for a close approximation of this saying, which seems to have been widely known, consider Plutarch, *Life of Bias* 1.82–88. See also 2.21 (1395a24–26). The term for "love" in both instances here is related to friendship (*philia*), not erotic love.

97 · Or, perhaps, "to their livelihood" (*bios*).

35   people desire above all what they lack. They are also self-lovers more than
they ought to be, for this too is an indication of having a small soul. They
live more than they should with a view to advantage, rather than to what
1390a   is noble, because they are self-lovers: the advantageous is what is good
for oneself, whereas the noble is what is good simply. And they are more
without shame than sensitive to it. Because they do not give thought to
the noble in the same way as they do to the advantageous, they slight their
reputation. They are also of little hope on account of their experience (for
5   the greater part of things turns out poorly; at any rate, for the most part
things turn out worse [than expected]) and, further, on account of their
cowardice.

They also live more by memory than by hope, for what remains of life
for them is small, time gone by, vast; and hope belongs to the future, mem-
10   ory to things past. This is in fact a cause of their garrulity, for they spend
their time speaking of past events, the recollection of which is pleasing
to them. Their outbursts of spiritedness are sharp but weak, and as for
their desires, some [of the elderly] have abandoned them, others have only
weak ones, such that they are neither characterized by desire nor apt to act
according to their desires, but rather as gain dictates. Hence those of this
15   age appear moderate. Their desires have slackened, and they are enslaved
to gain. They also live more according to calculation than to character,
since calculation goes together with what is advantageous, character with
virtue. And the acts of injustice they commit are traceable to malice, not
to insolence. The elderly are also prone to pitying, but not for the same
20   reasons as are the young: the latter are such from their love of human beings, the former from weakness. For the elderly suppose that any and all
sufferings are just around the corner for them, and this is, as we saw, productive of pity. Hence they are querulous and neither witty nor fond of
laughter, since querulousness is the opposite of being fond of laughter.

25   Such, then, are the characters of the young and of the older. As a
result—since all people accept speeches spoken in a way that accords
with their own character, and accept those who are like them—it is not
unclear how, by employing speeches, both the speakers themselves and
their speeches may appear to be of a given sort.

CHAPTER 14

It is manifest that those in their prime will be, as regards their character,
30   in between these, since they remove the excess from each of the other two

and are neither exceedingly confident (for such is rashness) nor overly fearful. Rather, they are nobly disposed toward both [extremes], neither trusting nor distrusting everyone but instead judging to a greater degree according to what is true, living neither with a view to the noble alone nor to the advantageous but with a view to both, and with a view neither to frugality nor to extravagance but to what is fitting. The case is similar with spiritedness and desire. Their moderation is attended by courage, their courage by moderation, for in the case of the young and the old, these have been separated: the young are courageous and licentious, the older moderate and cowardly.

1390b

5

To speak generally, all the beneficial things that youth and old age have separated between them are each possessed by those in their prime, and all that in the other two ages is excessive or deficient is possessed by them in a measured and fitting manner. The body is at its prime from the ages of thirty to thirty-five, the soul at about fifty minus one.

10

As for youth and old age and the prime of life, then, and what sorts of character belong to each, let this much be said.

CHAPTER 15

As regards the goods that arise from chance—at any rate, all those chance goods through which certain character traits also accrue to human beings—let us speak about these next in order. A character trait that belongs to good birth is that he who possesses it is more a lover of honor [or more ambitious than is someone without good birth]. For quite all human beings, when they have something available to them, are accustomed to heaping more on top of it, and good birth is a mark of honor bestowed by one's ancestors; and such good birth is prone to feeling contempt even for those [here and now] who are similar to one's ancestors. This is so because the same things that happen far-off rather than nearby are held in greater honor and lend themselves more to boasting. Now, while "good birth" refers to the virtue of the familial line, "nobility"[98] refers to not degenerating from its nature, which for the most part fails to happen in the case of the wellborn, the majority of whom are paltry types. For there is a certain fruit in the familial lines of men just as there is also in lands, and sometimes if the line is good, extraordinary men arise in it

15

20

25

98 · Not the term usually translated by "nobility" (*to kalon*) but rather *gennaion*, whose root suggests a connection to one's birth.

for a certain time and then it deteriorates once again. Familial lines of a
good nature degenerate into crazier characters—for example, those de-
30   scended from Alcibiades and from Dionysius the elder—stable ones into
stupidity and sluggishness—for example, those descended from Cimon
and Pericles and Socrates.[99]

CHAPTER 16

As for the character traits that accompany wealth, these are plain for
quite all to see. For the wealthy are insolent and arrogant, being affected
in some way by the possession of wealth; they are disposed as are those
1391a   who possess all good things together. For wealth is like a criterion of the
worth of other things, and so all else seems to be purchasable by means
of it. They are also given to self-indulgence[100] and pretentiousness, being self-indulgent on account of luxury and the open display of their
5   prosperity,[101] pretentious and vulgar because they all[102] are accustomed
to spending their time concerned with what is loved and admired by
them, and because they suppose that others strive after[103] the very things
they themselves do. At the same time, it is only to be expected that they
have this experience, for there are many people who do in fact need what
they have. Hence also the remark of Simonides was made about the wise
10   and the wealthy, in response to the question posed by Hiero's wife as to
whether it is superior to be wealthy or wise. He said "wealthy"—for he
contended that he sees the wise spending their time at the doors of the
wealthy.[104] And they suppose that they deserve to rule, for they suppose

99 · The elder Dionysius (ca. 430–367) was tyrant of Syracuse (see also 1.2 [1357b31]).
Cimon was an Athenian statesman and general (ca. 510–450), son of the famed general
Miltiades; he is said to have had three sons, Lacedaemonius (see Thucydides 1.45.2),
Eleus, and Thessalus, though little is known about them. In Plato's *Alcibiades I*, the
two sons of Pericles, Xanthippus and Paralus, are said to be "foolish" (118e5–6), as are
the sons of Socrates in Plutarch's *Life of Cato the Elder* (20.2).
100 · The term (*trupheroi*) suggests also a softness or effeminacy stemming from excessive luxury.
101 · The same term (*eudaimonia*) is usually rendered "happiness." See also n. 76 above.
102 · Commentators here divide on whether Aristotle is referring to all the rich or to
all human beings.
103 · Or "emulate."
104 · Simonides was a lyric and elegiac poet (ca. 556–468) born at Iulis in Ceos. See also
1.6 (1363a15 and context) and 1.9 (1367b19–20). Xenophon recounts Simonides's conversation with Hiero in *Hiero, or Tyrannicus*.

that they possess what renders one deserving of rule. And, in sum, the character trait belonging to wealth is that of a happy[105] fool.

But there is a difference between the characters of those who have re-   15
cently come to possess wealth and those who have had it for a long time, in that the newly rich have all the ills involved, but more of them and in a worse form, since being newly rich is akin to being uneducated in wealth. And the unjust acts they commit are not signs of malice but rather of insolence, in some cases, and, in others, of a lack of self-restraint—for example, in cases of assault and adultery.

CHAPTER 17

And similarly, as for what concerns power, the character traits involved are   20
for the most part manifest. For in some respects power has the same features as does wealth, but in other respects [traits associated with power] are better. For when it comes to their characters, the powerful love honor more and are more manly than the wealthy because they aim at all such deeds as they have the resources to carry out on account of their power.   25
They are also marked by greater seriousness because of the care they exercise, being compelled to examine whatever pertains to their power. They are also more dignified than excessively grave, for their rank renders them more conspicuous,[106] and hence they observe due measure, and being dignified is a softened and attractive form of gravity. And if they commit injustice, theirs is not petty but on a grand scale.   30

Good fortune, in its various parts, contains the character traits of those just mentioned, for the instances of good fortune that are held to be greatest tend toward these; and, further, good fortune provides an advantage when it comes to having good children and the bodily goods. On the one hand, people are more arrogant and more thoughtless on account of good   1391b
fortune, but, on the other, a very good character trait attends good fortune, namely, that [the fortunate] are god-loving[107] and stand in a certain relation to the divine, believing in[108] it on account of the good things that have arisen from chance.

What concerns the character traits that refer to age and luck, then, has   5

105 · Or "prosperous"; see n. 101 above.
106 · Some modern editors, following one MS, read here "more dignified."
107 · "God-loving" (*philotheoi*) can also mean "dear to the gods."
108 · Or "trusting in" (*pisteuontes*), related to the word translated as "mode of persuasion" (*pistis*).

been stated.[109] For the opposites of the things mentioned are manifest
on the basis of the opposite considerations—for example, the character
traits belonging to poverty and misfortune and lack of power.

CHAPTER 18

Now, the use of persuasive speeches is directed toward a judgment to be
rendered, for there is no longer any need of a speech about those things
10   we know and have already judged. Moreover, there is a judgment involved
even if someone uses a speech to exhort or dissuade a single individual,
just as do those who admonish or persuade somebody (for a single person
is no less a judge for all that, since the person who must be persuaded is, to
speak simply, a judge). This is so whether one speaks against an actual litigant or against a proposed subject, for it is necessary to use speech and to
15   do away with the opposing points, against which the speech is directed
as though against a litigant. The same holds also in epideictic speeches,
for the speech is composed for the onlooker as if he were a judge. Nonetheless, the only judge in an unqualified sense is he who judges the points
under investigation in political contests, for what is being investigated
20   [in a courtroom] is the status of the disputed points and [in an assembly]
the matters about which people are deliberating.[110] As for what concerns
the regimes in reference to the relevant character traits, this was spoken
about previously in the matters pertaining to deliberative rhetoric.[111] As
a result, how and through what means one should make speeches bound
up with matters of character[112] would be defined.

Now, since, as we saw, the end pertaining to each kind of speech is dif-
25   ferent, and since the opinions and premises concerning quite all of them
have been grasped, from which people derive the modes of persuasion
they use when they advise and demonstrate and dispute, and from which,
furthermore, it is possible to fashion speeches bound up with matters of
character; and since what concerns these too has been defined, it remains
for us to go through the points common [to the various ends of rhetoric].

109 · Consider 2.12–14 and 15–17.
110 · Kassel brackets everything from the beginning of this chapter to this point. The
text is difficult, and editors have suggested either that the lines belong elsewhere or that
a lacuna must be posited; see Grimaldi (ad loc.) for an extensive account.
111 · Consider 1.8.
112 · In other words, "ethical speeches," where "ethical" carries its literal meaning of
"concerned with character" and not necessarily that of being morally upright.

For all must of necessity make use in their speeches also of what pertains to the possible and the impossible, and some speakers must try to point out that something will be, others that something has already happened. And, further, a common point belonging to quite all speeches concerns greatness [or the importance of something], since all make use of downplaying and amplifying when they advise or dissuade, and praise or blame, and accuse or defend.

Once these points have been defined, let us attempt to speak also about enthymemes in general terms, insofar as we can, and about examples, so that, once we have added the points that remain, we may supply what was proposed at the outset.[113]

Now, of the common points, amplification is most at home in epideictic speeches, as was said;[114] what has happened or taken place, in judicial speeches (for the judgment involved pertains to this); what is possible and what will be in the future, in deliberative speeches.

CHAPTER 19

Let us speak first, then, about possible and impossible. So if it is possible for one of two opposites to be or to come to be, then it would seem to be possible also for the other one to do so—for example, if it is possible for a human being to be made healthy, it is possible also for him to be made sick. For the same capacity[115] belongs to opposites in the respect in which they are opposites. And if it is possible for one of two like things [to be or to come to be], then so also is it possible for the other. And if it is possible for the more difficult, it is possible also for the easier. And if it is possible for something to become serious and beautiful [or noble], then it is possible also for it to come to be in a general sense, for it is more difficult for a beautiful house to exist than for a house in general. And if it is possible for the beginning of something to come into being, so too can its end, for nothing impossible comes to be or even begins to do so—for example, the diameter would neither begin to become, nor indeed become, commensurate [with the side of a square]. And that whose end is possible has a beginning that is possible too, for quite everything comes to be from a beginning. And if it is possible for that which is subsequent

113 · See 2.18–26.
114 · Consider 1.9 (1368a26–30).
115 · The term for "capacity" (or "power," "potentiality") is *dunamis*, which has the same root as the terms for "possible" (*dunatos*) and "impossible" (*adunatos*).

in being or in coming-to-be to come into being, then so too is it for what is prior—for example, if it is possible for a man to come to be, it is possible also for a boy (for the boy comes to be before); and if it is possible for a boy to come to be, so also a man (for that is the beginning). And those things for which there is an erotic love or a desire by nature [are possible], 25 for nobody loves or desires what is impossible, for the most part. And it is possible for those things of which there are sciences and arts both to be and to come to be. And all those things [are possible] the beginning of whose coming-into-being lies with things we could compel or persuade; and these are the things or people over which we enjoy superiority or exercise authority or whose friends we are. And when it is possible for given 30 parts to come to be, so also can the given whole; and when it is possible for a given whole to come to be, so also can its parts, for the most part. For if it is possible for the split down the front, the toe cap, and the uppers to come to be, then it is possible also for shoes to come to be, and if shoes, so also the split down the front and the toe cap. And if it is possible for the 1392b genus as a whole to come to be, so also can the species; and if the species, so also the genus—for example, if it is possible for a sailing ship to come to be, so also a trireme;[116] and if a trireme, so also a sailing ship. And if it is possible for one of two things naturally related to one another to come 5 to be, so also for the other—for example, if double, then also half, and if half, then double. And if it is possible for something to come to be without art and preparation, it is all the more possible with art and due care. Hence it was said by Agathon too,[117]

And moreover some things one must accomplish by art,[118] but others
10   Are present to us by necessity and chance.

And if something is possible for the worse and weaker and more foolish, it is all the more so for their opposites, just as Isocrates said—that it is a terrible thing if he himself will be unable to figure out something, when Euthynus learned it.[119] As for the impossible, it is clear that there is [for

116 · A trireme is a warship and hence a particular kind of sailing ship.

117 · An Athenian tragic poet who appears most notably in Plato's *Symposium*.

118 · Some MSS read "chance" (*tuchē*) here instead of "art" (*technē*), but Kassel defends the reading here adopted, first suggested by Grotius, and supported to some extent by *Nicomachean Ethics* 1140a18–20, where Aristotle cites a different line of Agathon's that also stresses the difference between art and chance.

119 · The remark is not found in the extant writings of Isocrates, although he is thought to have composed a speech entitled *Against Euthynus*; some MSS read "Euthymus" instead of "Euthynus."

the speaker] a ready supply [of arguments] based on the opposites of the points stated.

One must examine whether something has or has not happened on the basis of the following points. First, if something that is less inclined by nature to come to be, does come to be, then that which is more inclined to do so would also have come to be. And if what is accustomed to coming into being has subsequently come to be, then that which precedes it has also come to be—for example, if someone has forgotten something, then he also learned this very thing at some point. And if it was possible for someone to do something and he wished to do it, then he did it; whenever the thing that people wish to do is possible for them, they all do it, since there are no impediments thereto. Further, if he wished to do something and there was nothing external preventing him; if it was possible for him and he was angered; and if it was possible for him and he desired to do it. For the most part, the things that people long for they act on—if it is possible to do so—base types through their lack of self-restraint, the decent because they desire decent things. And if something was about to come to pass and if someone was about to do something, for it is likely that someone about to do something does it. And if all those things that are by nature prior to or for the sake of something have happened, [then that thing has happened too]—for example, if there was lightning, there was also thunder, and if someone undertook to do something, he also carried it out. And if all those things that are by nature subsequent to something, or that for the sake of which something happens, have happened, then both the prior thing and that for the sake of which something is, have happened as well—for example, if there was thunder, there was lightning too, and if he carried something out, he also undertook to do it. Of all these cases together, some arise from necessity, others are as they are [only] for the most part. As for what concerns not coming into being, it is manifest on the basis of the points opposite to those stated.

What will be in the future, too, is clear on the basis of the same things. For what is in one's power[120] and wished for will be; and those things will be for which there is the relevant desire or anger or calculation, together with the requisite power, and so too will all those things that are a part of the impetus of action or are about to act.[121] For in most cases the

120 · The term translated throughout this section as "power" (*dunamis*) is related to the term for "the possible" (*dunaton*); see also n. 115 above.
121 · The Greek is disputed here. For the most part I follow the reading of one MS, most modern editors, and Grimaldi.

5   things that are about to happen come to pass much more than do those
     not about to happen. And if all such things as naturally happen prior to
     something else have themselves happened, [then the something else in
     question naturally happens too]—for example, if it is overcast, it is likely
     to rain. And if that which is for the sake of something else has come to
     be, then it is likely that this something, too, comes to be—for example, if
     there is a foundation, there will be a house as well.

         Concerning the greatness and smallness of things, as well as the greater
10   and the lesser and, in general, great and small, it is manifest on the basis
     of points previously stated by us. For what concerns both the greatness of
     goods and the greater and lesser simply was stated in the matters pertain-
     ing to deliberative speeches.[122] As a result, since the end set forth in each
     kind of speech is a good—for example, the advantageous or the noble
15   or the just—it is manifest that all must grasp the means of amplification
     available by recourse to those ends. But to make a further inquiry, beyond
     these points, into greatness and excess in an unqualified sense is to engage
     in vain speech: with a view to their use, individual matters carry greater
     authority than do universals.

         About the possible and impossible, then, and whether something has
20   come to be or not come to be and will be or will not be; and, further, con-
     cerning the greatness and smallness of things—let these points be stated.

     CHAPTER 20

     It remains to speak of what concerns the modes of persuasion common
     to all [the kinds of rhetorical speeches], since what concerns the particu-
     lar modes of persuasion was stated.[123] Now, the common modes of per-
     suasion are of two kinds: example and enthymeme (for a maxim[124] is a
25   part of an enthymeme). Let us speak first, then, about example, since an
     example is similar to induction, and induction is a starting point [or prin-
     ciple].

     122 · Consider 1.7.
     123 · Since the "particular modes of persuasion" are those (technical) modes of persua-
     sion stemming from matters of passion, character, and the speech itself—consider 1.2
     (1356a1–4)—Aristotle here refers to 2.1–19.
     124 · The term (*gnomē*) means simply "judgment," but it came to mean also "generally
     held judgments" and hence (wise or reputable) "maxims"; consider, e.g., Xenophon,
     Memorabilia 4.2.9 as well as 2.21 below.

Of examples there are two forms: one form of example consists in stating things that have happened previously, the other in making them up oneself. Of this latter, one form is comparison, the other fables[125]—for example, those of Aesop and the Libyan ones.[126] Stating matters of fact is some such thing as the following: if someone should say that one must make preparations against the King [of Persia] and not allow him to subdue Egypt, for Darius previously did not cross over [to Greece] before first taking Egypt, but once he had taken it, he did cross over, and, again, Xerxes did not attack [Greece] before he took it too, but, once he had taken it, he did cross over. As a result, if the [present] King, too, takes Egypt, he will cross over [to Greece]. Hence it must not be permitted.

Comparison is characteristic of Socratic speeches. For example, if someone should say that those who hold office ought not to be chosen by lot, for maintaining that is similar to somebody's saying that one should appoint as athletes, not those who are capable of competing, but those whom the lot determines, or that one should appoint by lot anyone at all among the sailors to pilot the ship, on the grounds that the one on whom the lot falls, but not the person possessed of the requisite knowledge, must pilot.

As for fables, there is Stesichorus's concerning Phalaris,[127] as well as Aesop's on behalf of the demagogue. For when the people of Himera elected Phalaris general with autocratic powers and were about to grant him a bodyguard, Stesichorus, after discussing other matters with them, told them this fable: a horse once had lone possession of a field, and when a stag came and destroyed the pasture, the horse, in his wish to get his revenge on the stag, asked a certain human being if he could exact revenge together with him. The human being said yes, if the horse would accept a bit and if he himself could mount him, equipped with javelins. The horse agreed and the human mounted, but the horse, instead of getting his revenge, was himself enslaved to the human being. "And so you, too," Stesichorus said, "see that you not suffer the same thing as did the horse, in

30

1393b

5

10

15

125 · *Logoi*: simply "accounts" or "speeches."

126 · Quintilian (*Institutes of Oratory* 5.11.20) mentions the Libyan fables, which, like Aesop's, were didactic tales involving animals.

127 · Stesichorus was a Greek poet (born ca. 632) whose work survives only in fragments; consider, e.g., Plato, *Phaedrus* 243a-b and context. Phalaris was tyrant of Acragas in Sicily ca. 570–554, known for his savagery (consider, e.g., *Nicomachean Ethics* 1148b24 and 1149b3 and b28).

20   your wish to get revenge on your enemies. For you already have the bit,
since you have elected him as general with autocratic powers. And if you
grant him a bodyguard and allow him to mount, you will by then already
be enslaved to Phalaris."[128]

And Aesop, when serving in Samos as advocate for a demagogue who
25   was on trial for his life, said: "A fox, while crossing a river, was driven
back into a crevice of the riverbank and, being unable to get free, suffered badly for a long time, with many dog-ticks clinging to her. A hedge-
hog, in his wanderings, felt compassion when he saw her and asked if he
could remove the dog-ticks from her. But the fox did not allow him to do
30   so and, when asked why, replied: 'These ticks are already full of me, and
so draw little blood. If you remove them, others will come along who, in
their hunger, will drain from me the blood that remains.' But, men of Samos," Aesop said, "this fellow here will do no further harm to you (for he
1394a is now rich), and if you kill him, others who are poor will come along to
steal your public funds and spend them."[129]

These fables are characteristic of the public assembly, and they have
this that is good about them, namely, that while it is difficult to discover
past events similar to the matters now at hand, it is easier to find fables.
5   For one must make them up just as one does comparisons, if one is capable of seeing the point of similarity in question, which is in fact easier to
do on the basis of philosophy. It is easier, then, to supply oneself with examples from fables, but for the purpose of deliberation, those that involve
factual matters are more useful, since for the most part the things that will
happen in the future are similar to those that have happened in the past.
10   Someone who is without enthymemes must make use of examples
by way of demonstration (for the persuasion arises through these [two
only]), but when one does have enthymemes one must make use of examples [only] as a kind of testimony, employing them as a follow-up[130]
to the enthymemes. When one puts examples first, this resembles induction, but induction is not suitable to matters of rhetoric, except in a few
cases; when one uses examples as follow-ups [to the enthymemes used],
they resemble witness testimony, and the witness is everywhere persua-

128 · See Ben Edwin Perry, *Aesopica* (Urbana: University of Illinois Press, 1952), 1:
#269a. On the people's granting a request for a bodyguard as a fateful step toward tyr-
anny, see Plato, *Republic* 566b-c.
129 · See Perry, *Aesopica*, 1: #427.
130 · Literally, an "epilogue," that which follows the *logos*.

sive. Hence it is necessary for someone putting examples before an en-   15
thymeme to state many of them, whereas for him who uses them as a follow-up to the enthymeme, even one example is sufficient, since even one
credible[131] witness is sufficient.

How many forms of examples there are, then, and how and when one
ought to use them, have been stated.

CHAPTER 21

As for speeches involving maxims, once it has been stated what a maxim
is, it would then be altogether manifest what sorts of maxims and which   20
ones it is fitting to use in such speeches, and when to use them. A maxim,
then, is a declaration—not, however, pertaining to individual cases (for
example, Iphicrates[132] is this or that sort of person) but rather to a universal. And maxims do not concern all universals—for example, that the
straight is the opposite of the crooked—but concern rather all such things
as actions deal with and are to be either chosen or avoided in relation to   25
action. As a result, since enthymemes are, generally speaking, syllogisms
about such matters, maxims are the conclusions of the enthymemes and
their premises, once the syllogism is removed. For example:

> And never ought any man who is by nature sensible,
> Have his children taught so as to be extraordinarily wise.[133]   30

This, then, is a maxim. But when the cause in question is added, or the
reason why it is so, it is, taken altogether, an enthymeme:

> For apart from any other idleness they have,
> They incur the ill-willed envy of the townsmen.[134]

And   1394b

> There is no man who is happy in all respects,[135]

and

131 · One MS reads, for "credible" (*pistos*), "useful" (*chrēstos*).

132 · On Iphicrates (ca. 415–353), an Athenian general and mercenary commander, see also 1.7 (1365a28) and 1.9 (1367b19).

133 · Euripides, *Medea* 294–95.

134 · Euripides, *Medea* 295–97.

135 · A fragment from Euripides' lost *Stheneboea* (= Nauck fr. 661).

There is no one among men who is free.[136]

5   This is a maxim, but when what comes next is added, it is an enthymeme:

For either to money or to chance he is a slave.

So if what has been stated is a maxim, there are necessarily four forms of maxim, for they will be either accompanied by an explanatory follow-up or not accompanied by such a follow-up. Now, those maxims that need a
10   demonstration are all the ones that say something contrary to opinion or are controversial, but those that do not say anything contrary to opinion are without an explanatory follow-up; and of these latter, it is necessarily the case that some have no need of a follow-up because they are known in advance—for example,

For a man it is best to be healthy, as it seems to me at least,

(since that appears to the many to be the case)—while others are clear as
15   soon as they are stated, to those who take a look at them—for example,

Nobody is a lover who does not always feel affection.[137]

Of those maxims that *are* accompanied by an explanatory follow-up, some are a part of an enthymeme (just as in "And never ought any man who is sensible . . ."), but some have the character of enthymemes yet are
20   not part of one, which are the most highly regarded maxims. And these are the ones in which the cause of what is being said is apparent—for example, "Do not maintain an immortal anger, mortal that you are." For the assertion that "one should not maintain . . ." is a maxim; the "mortal that you are" that is added is the reason why. And similarly, "one who is mortal must think of mortal things / it is not for the mortal to think of immortal things."[138]

25   It is manifest, then, on the basis of what has been said, how many forms of maxim there are and for what sort of thing each is suitable. When it comes to the maxims that are controversial or contrary to opinion, it is not suitable for them to be without a follow-up, but it is suitable either

136 · Euripides, *Hecuba* 864, although the MSS read "mortals" (*thnētōn*) where Aristotle reads "men" (*andrōn*).

137 · Euripides, *Trojan Women* 1051 (although the text of Euripides differs slightly from Aristotle's quotation). Two kinds of love—erotic and friendly—are present in the quotation, *erōs* (in the form of the "lover") and *philia* (in the form of "affection").

138 · For Aristotle's own view of this thought, consider *Nicomachean Ethics* 1177b31–1178a2.

to use the conclusion as a maxim and set out the explanatory "follow-up" first—for example, if someone should say, "As for me, since one should be neither envied nor idle, I deny that one ought to be educated"—or to state this latter part first and say the prior parts after it. As for maxims that are not contrary to opinion, what pertains to them is not unclear, namely, that it is fitting to add the reason why very concisely. Fitting in such uncontroversial cases, too, are the Laconic apothegms and riddling remarks, just as if someone should say what in fact Stesichorus said among the Locrians, that they should not be insolent lest their cicadas sing from the ground.[139]

It is fitting for someone more advanced in age to speak in maxims, and about things he has experience of, since it is inappropriate for someone not of that age to speak in maxims, just as it is also to tell myths, and to do so about things he is inexperienced in, this being a mark of foolishness and lack of education. There is a sufficient sign of this: country bumpkins are the ones most given to uttering maxims, and they declare them with ease. Speaking in a universal way about what is not universal is especially fitting in bitter denunciation and in painting the worst possible picture of something,[140] and in these when one is just beginning [the speech] or after one has made a demonstration. And one should make use of even well-worn maxims that are commonly held, if they are useful. For because they are common, as if all agree to them, they are held to be correct. For example, this is useful to somebody exhorting those whose sacrifices have not been favorable[141] to face up to danger:

A single bird-omen is best: to defend the fatherland,[142]

and to face the danger though they are outnumbered:

139 · The thinly veiled threat suggests that if the Locrians' territory were razed, the cicadas would have no trees from which to sing. The line is quoted again at 3.11 (1412a22–23).
140 · This phrase attempts to capture the nuance of *deinōsis*, whose root is what is "terrible" (*deinos*). As Grimaldi puts it, "The meaning . . . is not quite clear." He suggests "indignation," modeled on the Latin translation of the term (*indignatio*), but he notes that "exaggeration," too, is possible. See also 1401b3, 1417a13, and 1419b25 for the other appearances of the term.
141 · Or, perhaps, "who have not performed the sacrifices."
142 · Homer, *Iliad* 12.243. Hector here addresses Polydamas before they attack the wall of the Achaeans. Polydamas sought to call off the attack because of the unfavorable sign of the eagle and the snake.

15   Impartial is Enyalus,[143]

and to annihilate the enemies' offspring, even though they have committed no injustice:

> Foolish is he who, having killed the father, leaves the sons untouched.[144]

Further, certain proverbs are also maxims—for example, the proverb "An Attic neighbor next door."[145] And one should state maxims
even when they go against sayings that have become public property
20   (I mean by "public property" ones like "Know thyself" and "Nothing in
excess"),[146] whenever doing so will make the speaker's character appear
better or when it will appear passionately stated. A maxim passionately
stated is, for example, when someone angrily contends that it is false that
one has to "know oneself": "For this fellow, at least, if he had known himself, would never have deemed himself worthy of being a general!"[147] And
25   one's character would appear better [if one should assert] that we must
not, as people contend, love as though we will one day hate, but rather
hate as though we will one day love.[148] And one should make clear one's
choice [and hence one's character] by means of the diction of the speech
or, failing that, explain subsequently the cause involved—by saying, for
example: "One should love, not as people contend, but as though one will
30   always love, for doing the other is the mark of a traitor." Or in this way:
"The saying is dissatisfying to me, for the genuine friend loves as though
he will love always."[149] And "Neither is 'nothing in excess' [satisfying to
me]. For one must hate to excess at least those who are evil."

143 · An epithet of Ares, god of war. For the quotation, see Homer, *Iliad* 18.309, where
Hector attempts to persuade Polydamas not to leave the battle now that Achilles has
returned to it: one cannot know whom the god of war will favor.
144 · Aristotle quoted the same line also at 1.15 (1376a7).
145 · The proverb has long been taken to be a criticism of imperial Athens, ever restless
and expanding and hence a difficult neighbor.
146 · Two famous exhortations, the first associated with the oracle at Delphi, the second with the Spartan ephor Chilon (see n. 93 above). Socrates took over as his own the
Delphic maxim "Know thyself."
147 · The import of the remark is a matter of controversy. Grimaldi, like Victorius, suggests that the "fellow" in question is Iphicrates. Had he "known himself" in the sense
of keeping in mind his humble origins, he would never have risen to become general.
148 · See 2.13 above (1389b23–24) for a statement reminiscent of this one, there attributed to the Greek sage Bias.
149 · The verbs in this section translated as "love" are all *philein*: to love as a friend or
to show friendly affection.

Maxims make one great contribution to speeches, on account of the   1395b
vulgarity of the listeners. For they are delighted if someone, when speaking in a general way, hits on the opinions they [already] have in a particular case. What I mean will be clear from the following, as will, at the
same time, how one should hunt for maxims. For the maxim is, as was   5
said, a universal declaration, and people are delighted when something
that they happen to have already assumed in a particular case is stated
by someone in a universal way. If, for example, someone happens to have
bad neighbors or children, he would accept it if the speaker says, "There
is nothing more difficult than a neighbor!" or "There is nothing more
foolish than having children!" As a result, one must hazard a guess as to   10
the character of the prior assumptions they happen to have, and then
speak accordingly about them in a universal way.[150] So this is one use for
speaking in maxims, and another such use is even superior to it: doing
so makes the speeches reflect one's character. And those speeches convey a person's character in which the choice [that guides the speaker] is
clear. All maxims do this because the person stating the maxim thereby   15
makes a general declaration of his choices [or intentions], such that the
maxims are fine and cause the speaker to come to sight as having a fine
character.

About the maxim, then—what it is and how many forms of it there
are and how one ought to make use of it and what advantage it has—this
much has been stated.

CHAPTER 22

But let us speak in a general way about enthymemes, as to the manner in   20
which one ought to seek them out; and, after this, their topics, for each
of these topics is different in kind. Now, that the enthymeme is a sort of
syllogism has been stated previously, as well as how it is a syllogism and in
what respect it differs from dialectical syllogisms.[151] For one should not
draw the conclusion at issue either from steps that go far back or from all   25
the steps involved: the one is unclear on account of its length, the other
amounts to idle talk because it states points that are obvious. This is also
the cause of the fact that the uneducated are more persuasive in crowds

150 · The MSS differ somewhat here, and another translation is possible: "One must
hazard a guess as to the sorts of prior assumptions they happen to have and how it is
that they come to have them, and then speak universally about them."
151 · Consider 1.1–2 above.

than are the educated, just as the poets[152] contend that the uneducated speak "more musically" to a crowd than do the educated. For the edu-
30 cated state general or universal points, whereas the uneducated speak on the basis of the things they know and that are near to hand. As a result, one should speak, not on the basis of just any opinion held, but rather on the basis of those opinions that have been marked off in some way, ei-
1396a ther by the judges in question or by those whose authority they accept. And the fact that this is the way it appears to be, either to everyone or to the greatest number, must be clear [to the speaker]. And he should draw conclusions, not only from necessities, but also from things that are for the most part so.

First, then, one must grasp that, when it comes to the subject matter to be spoken of and reasoned about syllogistically, whether in a political syl-
5 logism or any sort whatever, it is necessary to be in possession of the facts pertaining to it, either all or some of them. For you could draw no con-clusion were you in possession of none of them. I mean, for example, how could we advise the Athenians as to whether or not they must go to war without having a grasp of what their power is, be it naval or infantry or
10 both; and what the size of that power is; and what their sources of revenue are; and who their friends and enemies are; and, further, what enemies they have waged war against and how they did so; and the other things of that sort? Or how could we offer praise, if we did not have a grasp of the naval battle at Salamis or the battle of Marathon or the actions un-dertaken on behalf of the Heraclidae, or something else of that sort?[153]
15 For all people praise others on the basis of the relevant facts that are or are held to be noble. And, similarly, they also blame others on the basis of the contrary considerations, examining what sort [of deed] is or is held to be theirs—for example, that [the Athenians essentially] reduced the Greeks to a state of slavery, and that they [actually] enslaved the Aeginetans and

152 · See, e.g., Euripides, *Hippolytus* 988–89. The word translated as "more musically" (*mousikōterous*) suggests a greater facility with the things of the Muses and so "grace-fully."

153 · All three episodes cast Athens in a very favorable light and would be known im-mediately to any Greek audience. The Greek (but especially Athenian) naval victory at the battle of Salamis in 480 spelled the end of Persian naval supremacy and the foun-dation of the Athenian naval empire; the land battle at Marathon against the Persians (490), also led by Athens, succeeded in repulsing the aggressive threat of King Dar-ius I; and, shortly after the Trojan War, Athens is said to have come to the aid of Hyl-lus, son of Heracles, and his followers, who had sought refuge from the Argives in the Temple of Zeus.

Potidaeans,[154] who had joined them in fighting against the barbarian and   20
excelled in doing so, and all else of that sort, and if they have some other
such failing. And so, in the very same way, both those who level accusations and those who make defense speeches do so by examining the relevant facts; but in this it makes no difference at all whether the subject
is Athenians or Lacedaemonians or a human being or a god: it amounts
to the same thing. For in advising Achilles, or praising and blaming him,   25
or accusing and defending him, one must grasp the things that are or are
held to be his so that we may speak on this basis, praising or blaming him
if something noble or base characterizes him, and accusing or defending him if something just or unjust pertains to him, and advising him as   30
to whether something is advantageous or harmful. What pertains to any
other matter whatsoever is similar to these: for example, concerning justice, one must grasp whether it is good or is not good on the basis of the
attributes that belong to justice and to the good.

Since in fact all people manifestly demonstrate things in this way,
whether they reason syllogistically in a more precise or a less exacting   1396b
way (people basing their arguments not on anything or everything taken
together but rather on those considerations that pertain in a given case);
and since it is clear, through reason, that it is impossible to demonstrate in
any other way, it is manifestly necessary as a result (just as in the *Topics*)[155]
that, first, one be in possession of selected statements concerning what   5
admits of happening and what is most suitable in each case. And as for
those circumstances that arise on the spot, one must search out the relevant premises in the same manner, by looking not to indefinite propositions but rather to the facts at hand pertaining to the subject matter of
the speech and specifying the greatest number of points that are as close
as possible to that subject. For the greater number of facts one has, the   10
easier it is to establish something, and the closer they are to the matter at
hand, the more immediately relevant and less general they will be. I mean
by "general," praising Achilles because he is a human being and because
he is among the demigods and because he went on campaign to Troy. For
these things characterize many others, too, such that somebody given to   15

154 · The island of Aegina was long at odds with Athens and, in 431, the Athenians ex-
pelled the population and subsequently occupied the entire island. In 433, war broke
out between Athens and Potidaea, originally a Corinthian colony, and, after a long and
costly siege, Potidaea was taken by Athens.
155 · Consider, e.g., *Topics* 1.4–18 and, for a summary statement, 105b12–18. Cope suggests that Aristotle has the whole work in mind.

saying these things no more praises Achilles thereby than he does Diomedes. But by "particular" I mean all those things that belong to nobody
else other than Achilles—for example, that he killed Hector, best of the
Trojans, as well as Cygnus (who, being invulnerable, prevented them all
from disembarking) and because Achilles went on campaign, though he
was very young and under no sworn obligation to do so, and all else of
20   that sort.[156]

This, then, is one manner of the selection [of statements], and the
first one, namely, the topical; and let us speak about the elements of enthymemes. (I mean the same thing by the "element" of an enthymeme and
its "topic.") But let us speak first about the things it is necessary to speak
25   of first. For there are two forms of enthymemes: those that establish that
something is or is not so, and those that are refutative; and the two differ
just as, in matters of dialectic, refutation differs from syllogism. The enthymeme that establishes something draws conclusions from agreed-on
points, whereas the refutative enthymeme draws conclusions that are not
agreed to [by one's opponents].

The topics pertaining to each of the kinds [of rhetoric] that are useful
30   and necessary,[157] then, are pretty much in our possession, since the premises concerning each have been selected such that the topics, on which the
enthymemes should be based—topics concerning good or bad, noble or
base, or just or unjust—are available to us, as are also the topics concerning characters, passions, and characteristic states that have been grasped
by us previously.

1397a   But, in addition, let us grasp [topics] in another manner, in a universal
way, and as they pertain to all [the kinds of rhetoric];[158] and as we speak
of them let us take note of those [topics] that are refutative and those

156 · For the story of Cygnus (or Cycnus), son of Poseidon, see Ovid, *Metamorphoses* 12.64–168. The suggestion in the text is that Achilles went to Troy, not because he
was bound by the oath sworn to King Tyndareus, but as a gracious favor to the sons of
Atreus, Agamemnon and Menelaus (see, e.g., Pausanias 3.24.11).

157 · This clause has been taken in various ways. In the main I follow Grimaldi, but
Cope suggests that the kinds of things "useful and necessary" here are (specific) topics,
whereas *topoi* means "general heads or classes"—a reading Grimaldi finds "difficult to
understand": "Now of the general heads or classes of the specific topics that are useful
or necessary we may be said to be pretty nearly in possession" (Cope).

158 · The Greek does not state what is to be grasped or what the "all" is to which the
subject in question pertains: "Let us now lay hold of certain facts about the whole subject" (Roberts trans.). I follow Grimaldi's suggestion, however, that Aristotle is here
preparing the turn to the discussion of (general or universal) topics.

that are demonstrative, and those that belong to apparent enthymemes, which are not really enthymemes, since in fact they are not even syllogisms. Once these have become clear, let us define what pertains to refutations[159] and objections, and the sources from which one ought to bring them to bear on enthymemes.

CHAPTER 23

There is one topic, belonging to [those enthymemes] that establish something, that is based on opposites. For it must be examined whether the one opposite [in a given pair of terms] belongs to [or can be predicated of] the other opposite [in the other pair], confuting [the argument], if it cannot, and establishing it, if it can—for example, that it is good to be moderate, since being licentious is harmful. Or as in the *Messeniacus*: "For if the war is a cause of the present evils, then with peace one must set things aright."[160]

> For if in fact it is not just to become angry
> At those who've done harm involuntarily,
> Neither would it be fitting to feel a debt of gratitude
> To someone compelled to treat another well.[161]

> But if in fact it is possible among mortals
> To make false pronouncements persuasively,
> You ought to believe the opposite, too,
> That mortals are often not persuaded by truths.[162]

Another [topic] is based on similar grammatical inflections.[163] For [the same inflected form] must be similarly present or not present [in the subject]—for example, that the just is not altogether good, for in that case "justly" would be [the same as "well" or "advantageously"]. But as things stand, dying justly is not choiceworthy.

Another [topic] is based on things mutually related to one another. For if doing something nobly or justly belongs to the one thing, then hav-

159 · Or "solutions," that which undoes or dissolves something (*luseōn*), which should be distinguished from the word just translated as "refutations" or "refutative" (*elengktikous*: 1397a2). 2.25 is devoted to an analysis of "refutation" (*lusis*).

160 · Aristotle also cites this work, by Alcidamas, at 1.13 (1373b18).

161 · The authorship of these lines is unknown.

162 · Euripides, *Thyestes* (= Nauck fr. 396).

163 · On "grammatical inflections," see also 1.7 (1364b34–35).

25   ing been so treated belongs to the other, and if [it is noble or just] to give
a command, so also is it to have complied with it—for example, as Diom-
edon the tax-farmer [said] about the taxes, "For if it is not at all shameful
for you to sell them, then neither is it for us to buy them." And if "nobly"
or "justly" belongs to someone who has been so treated, so also does it
belong to him who treated the fellow that way. But there is in this some-
30   thing that can go contrary to reason. For if one person suffered something justly, then he did suffer justly[164]—but perhaps not at your hands.
Hence one must examine separately whether he who suffers deserves to
1397b   suffer and whether he who inflicts it deserves to do so, and then one must
make use [of the argument] in whichever of the two ways is applicable.
For sometimes there is a dispute in such a case, and nothing prevents [one
from saying], as in the *Alcmeon* of Theodectes: "And as for your mother,
5   did no mortal abhor her?" to which [Alcmeon] says in reply: "One ought
to examine it by making a distinction." And when Alphesiboea asks how
so, he says in response: "They judged that she is to die, but not that I am to
kill her."[165] And, for example, there is the trial of Demosthenes and those
who killed Nicanor, for since they were judged to have killed [him] justly,
it was held that he died justly.[166] And there is the case of the man who died
10   in Thebes, where [the accused] bade [the judges] to render a decision as to
whether the fellow died justly, on the grounds that it was not unjust for a
man who died justly to be killed.[167]

Another [topic] is based on more and less—for example, "If not even
gods know all things, much less could human beings." That is, if something is not present where it is more inclined to be present, it is clear
15   that it would not be present where it is less inclined to be. And that he
who strikes even his father strikes also his neighbors follows from [the
premise] that if the less likely is present, the more likely will be too,[168] for

164 · The phrase translated as "then he did suffer justly" is bracketed by Kassel on the
authority of Sauppe but is present in the MSS.
165 · The play is not extant. Theodectes (ca. 375–334) wrote tragedies as well as verse,
and treatises on rhetorical subjects.
166 · Nothing is known of this trial, and the identity of the Demosthenes mentioned
is uncertain.
167 · Either the authenticity or placement of these last two sentences of the paragraph
is questioned by some editors, although the lines and their placement are defended by
Grimaldi.
168 · Here Kassel, Thurot, and others delete a phrase that reappears in almost the same
form a few lines later.

people are less inclined to strike their fathers than they are their neighbors. Either [one can] indeed [speak] in this way, or [one could say that] "if that which is more likely to be present is not . . . ," or "if that which is less likely to be is present . . ."—in accord with whichever of the two one must establish, either that something is present or that it is not.

There is, further, the case of what is neither more nor less. Hence it was said: "Your father, too, is pitiable, having lost his children / But Oeneus is not, he who lost his illustrious offspring?"[169] And [one could say] that   20
if Theseus committed no injustice, then neither did Alexander;[170] and if the sons of Tyndareus did not, then neither did Alexander;[171] and if Hector committed no injustice against Patroclus, then neither did Alexander against Achilles.[172] If none of the others who possess a technical craft are base, then neither are philosophers; and if generals are not base because they are often condemned to die,[173] then neither are sophists. And [one   25
could say] that "if a private person ought to care about the reputation of you all, then you all ought to care about the reputation of the Greeks."

There is another [topic] based on examining the time involved—as Iphicrates did, for example, in the [suit] against Harmodius, saying that "if I had judged that I deserved to have a statue before I did it, you would have granted it; but you won't grant it to me now that I have done it?   30
Don't make a promise in anticipation and then break it in the event."[174] And again, as regards the Thebans allowing Philip to pass through into   1398a Attica, [Philip's emissaries said] that if he had thought it justified [to ask]

169 · The lines are said to come from Antiphon's lost *Meleager*. According to the scholiast, these lines are spoken by Oeneus to a woman (Althaea) who expresses sorrow for her father as he grieves for the loss of his son (and her brother), a man killed, in turn, by (the now-dead) Meleager.

170 · Theseus, it is said (Plutarch, *Theseus* 31), carried off the young Helen, as did Alexander (Paris) later (see also Isocrates, *Helen* 18–20).

171 · The twins Castor and Pollux (or Polydeuces), sons of Tyndareus and Leda and hence brothers to Helen, carried off Aethra as well as their cousins Phoebe and Hilaera.

172 · Hector was of course responsible for the death of Patroclus, as Alexander (Paris) was indirectly responsible for the subsequent death of Achilles.

173 · Cope alone reads here "are often defeated," without apparent warrant from the MSS.

174 · According to Dionysius of Halicarnassus (*Lysias* 12), the Athenian general Iphicrates was granted the honor of having a statute erected of him in recognition of his defeat of a Spartan *mora* or division in 392. Only after retirement did he claim his statue, which claim was opposed by Harmodius.

before coming to their aid in Phocis, they would have granted it. It is absurd, then, if they will not allow him to pass through now, since he gave up [the opportunity to do so before] and trusted in them.[175]

Another [topic] derives from turning statements made against oneself on the person who said them. This manner of speech varies[176]—
5   for example, in *Teucer*;[177] and the way Iphicrates made use of it against Aristophon: when Iphicrates asked him if he would betray the fleet for money, and when he claimed that he would not, Iphicrates said: "Well then, if you, being Aristophon, would not betray it, would I, being Iphicrates?"[178] The [victim of the retort] must seem to be more inclined to commit injustice; otherwise it would appear laughable, if somebody
10   said this against an Aristides,[179] when he brings a charge. [One should not proceed in this way], but rather with a view to fostering the untrustworthiness of the accuser, for in general the accuser claims to be better than the defendant. This claim, then, must be refuted. It is generally absurd when somebody criticizes in others the things that he himself does or would do, or urges them to do things that he himself does not do or would
15   not do.

Another [topic] is based on definition. For example, what is a *daemonion*? Is it a god or the work of a god? Yet whoever supposes that it is a work of a god must necessarily suppose also that gods exist.[180] And as

175 · Two events are alluded to here. In 347, Thebes called in the aid of Philip II of Macedon against Phocis in the Sacred War of 356–346. After a peace was struck in 346 between Macedon and Athens, Philip decided to attack Phocis and so end the war altogether: if he had asked the Thebans' permission to march through their territory toward Athens then, they would have granted it, but in the event he sacked Phocis and returned home. Later, in 339, Philip was aiding certain Greek cities in the Amphissean War and requested the aid (or at least the neutrality) of Thebes, but Athenian envoys persuaded Thebes to ally with Athens instead.

176 · The verb (*diapherei*) can also mean "excels" or "surpasses," and several emendations of the text have been suggested to account for this ambiguity. Among the possibilities is this: "This manner of speech is superior, as, for example, in *Teucer*. Iphicrates made use of it." At stake is the question whether Aristotle is bringing out the various ways the tactic may be used or giving two examples of its excellence.

177 · Probably the lost play of Sophocles.

178 · For Iphicrates the Athenian general, see nn. 132 and 174 above. The same episode is related by Quintilian, *Institutes of Oratory* 5.12.9–10.

179 · Aristides the Just, as he was known, was an Athenian statesman (ca. 520–468) of sterling reputation.

180 · See also 3.18 (1419a8–12), where Socrates's exchange with Meletus to this effect (Plato, *Apology of Socrates* 26a8–28a1) is referred to.

Iphicrates has it, noblest is he who is best, for both Harmodius and Aristogeiton had no nobility before they performed something noble—and   20
[Iphicrates added] that he himself was more akin to them [than was his
opponent].[181] "At any rate, my deeds are more akin to those of Harmodius and Aristogeiton than are yours." Also as it is in the [speech about]
Alexander, to the effect that all would agree that those lacking orderliness
do not enjoy the delight of just one body.[182] And the reason why Socrates
said that he would not go to Archelaus:[183] insolence, he said, occurs also   25
when those who are treated well are incapable of requiting it in kind, just
as it does in the case of those treated badly. Having thus defined something and grasped what something is, all these people reason syllogistically about the matters they are speaking of.

Another [topic] is based on the number of ways [a term can be taken],
as, for example, what concerns "correctly" in the *Topics*.[184]

Another is based on division—for example, if all commit injustice for   30
three reasons, either for this reason or that one or that one. "Two of these
are impossible, and as for the third, not even [the accusers] themselves
assert it."

Another is based on induction,[185] as, for example, [the argument]
based on the case of the Peparethian woman, namely, that when it comes
to their children women everywhere define what is true. This [is in effect   1398b
what] the mother declared when the Athenian orator Mantias was in a
dispute with his son; and, in Thebes, when Ismenias and Stilbon were
in a dispute, the woman from Dodona demonstrated who the son of Ismenias was, and for this reason they regarded Thettaliscus as the son of   5

181 · The term here translated "nobility" (*gennaion*) is not the usual term so translated
(*kalon*) and suggests, at least, a nobility stemming from good birth. Iphicrates's point,
then, is that, in killing the Athenian tyrant Hippias (actually Hipparchus, the tyrant's
brother, as Thucydides insists: 6.53–59; see also 2.20 above), Harmodius and Aristogeiton established their true nobility, whatever the character of their birth.

182 · The alleged "orderliness" (*kosmios*) of Alexander (Paris) is thus to be shown by the
fact that he did remain content with "one body," that of Helen—another man's wife.

183 · Archelaus was king (or tyrant) of Macedon (413–399) and is portrayed harshly in
Plato's *Gorgias* (470c–471d).

184 · The text is uncertain, part of the difficulty being that no such discussion of the
term in question (*orthōs*) is found in the *Topics*. Kassel suggests emending the text to
read, with Thurot, *oxeos*, which can mean either "sharp" or "high-pitched" and is given
as an example of the ambiguity of terms in the *Topics* (1.15).

185 · That is, reasoning from particulars to a universal. As such, "induction" is akin to
(but not according to Aristotle strictly identical with) argument from example.

Ismenias.[186] And again, from Theodectes's *The Law*: if people do not
hand over their own horses to those who treat badly the horses of others,
nor [their own ships] to those who have capsized the ships of others, and
if it is this way in quite all cases, then surely one must not, when it comes
to one's own safety, deal with those who preserve badly the safety of oth-
10   ers.[187] And as Alcidamas has it, that all honor the wise. At any rate, the
Parians have honored Archilochus, although he spoke ill of others;[188] and
the Chians honor Homer, although he was not a citizen; and the Mytile-
neans honor Sappho, although she was a woman; and the Lacedaemonians made Chilon one of their elders, although they are least of all fond of
15   speeches;[189] and the Italiots honor Pythagoras;[190] and the Lampsacenes
buried Anaxagoras, although he was a foreigner, and they still honor him
even now.[191] And [it has been contended that the wise make the best
rulers][192] because the Athenians were prosperous[193] when they used the
laws of Solon, and the Lacedaemonians those of Lycurgus, and, at Thebes,
as soon as the leaders in the city became philosophers, the city prospered.

Another [topic] is based on a judgment that concerns the same thing
20   as, or something similar to, or the opposite of [the point at issue], especially if all people are always [of that judgment], but, failing that, at least
the greatest number—or the wise, either all or the greatest number of
them—or the good. Or if those rendering the judgment themselves [have

186 · The details of these disputes are lost, although both Ismenias and Stilbon were
prominent Thebans.
187 · The speech or writing here summarized does not survive, but Grimaldi suggests
that the question at issue was Athens' use of mercenary soldiers.
188 · Archilochus was a lyric poet from the island of Paros (ca. 750–700), of whose
work only fragments remain. Aristotle here reports that Archilochus was a "blas-
phemer," that is, one who speaks ill of others including perhaps the gods (as the same
term in English suggests).
189 · Chilon (mentioned also at 1389b3 above), one of the Seven Sages of Greece, was
renowned for his wise sayings.
190 · Italiots are the Greeks of southern Italy and Sicily. The famous pre-Socratic philosopher Pythagoras (ca. 570–495) hailed from Samos, off the Ionian coast. Kassel
brackets this clause, although it is present in the MSS.
191 · Although born in Clazomenae on the Ionian coast, Anaxagoras (ca. 500–428)
spent time in Athens, where he evidently befriended Pericles, and, after being exiled
from there, came finally to Lampsacus, a Greek city located on the eastern side of the
Hellespont.
192 · The transition is abrupt, and I follow the general suggestion of Grimaldi as to
what may be missing. Kassel brackets the entire sentence.
193 · Or "happy" (*eudaemonia* and cognates, here and at the end of the sentence).

had the same judgment in the past], or those whom the judges accept as authorities have done so, or those whose judgment it is not possible to oppose—for example, those who are in positions of authority—or those whom it is not noble to oppose in judgment—for example, the gods or one's father or teachers, just as Autocles[194] said in regard to Meix-   25
idemides, namely, that it was a fine thing in the eyes of the Dread God-desses[195] to submit to the just proceedings of the Areopagus, but not for Meixidemides to do so. Or as Sappho said, dying is bad, for the gods have so judged it: otherwise they would die. Or as Aristippus[196] said to Plato,   30
who (as Aristippus supposed) spoke in too definitive a way: "But our comrade," he said, "was not at all like this"—meaning Socrates. And Ag-esipolis, after having consulted the oracle at Olympia, posed a question to the god at Delphi as to whether the god had the same opinions as the god's father, on the grounds that it would be a shameful thing to contra-   1399a
dict him.[197] And Isocrates wrote of Helen that she was a serious woman, if in fact Theseus so judged her, and he wrote about Alexander as well, whom the goddesses preferred in their judgment.[198] Evagoras, too, was a serious person, just as Isocrates contends; at any rate, when Conon met   5
with misfortune, he left behind all others and went to Evagoras.[199]

194 · Autocles was an Athenian statesman. As Xenophon reports (*Hellenica* 6.3.2 and 6.3.7–9), Autocles, who was "held to be a very incisive orator," was a part of the em-bassy sent to Sparta in 371, prior to the fateful battle of Leuctra. The episode involving Meixidemides is otherwise unknown.

195 · That is, the Erinyes, or Furies, who entrusted the decision of their case against Or-estes, for the murder of his mother Clytemnestra and her lover Aegisthus, to the court of the Areopagus in Athens.

196 · Aristippus of Cyrene (born ca. 435) was a companion of Socrates and is said to have founded the Cyrenaic school of philosophy, which taught a kind of hedonism. Consider Xenophon, *Memorabilia* 2.1 and 3.8.

197 · Agesipolis is a Spartan who became King in 394; see Xenophon, *Hellenica* 4.7.2 for an account of Agesipolis's consultation of the oracle at Olympia and then at Delphi. The oracle at Olympia gave signs of Zeus's will, whereas "the god at Delphi" is Apollo, son of Zeus.

198 · After Eris (Strife) was barred from entering the wedding of Peleus and Thetis, she cast a golden apple among the goddesses, intending it for the one deemed the most beautiful. Hera, Aphrodite, and Athena contended for that title and accepted Alexan-der (Paris) as judge of their beauty. See also 1.6 (1363a18–19).

199 · Isocrates (436–338) was a leading orator or rhetorician in Athens, some of whose works survive: consider in this context *Helen* 18–22 and 41–48 (on Alexander) and *Eva-goras* 51–52. Conon was a distinguished naval commander in Athens (ca. 444–392). For the episode here alluded to, see Xenophon, *Hellenica* 2.1.29.

Another [topic] is that based on parts, just as in the *Topics*:²⁰⁰ what
sort of motion is the soul? For it is either this or that motion. An example
comes from Theodectes's *Socrates*: "In what temple did he act impiously?
Who among the gods believed in by the city has he not honored?"

10   Another [topic] is based on what follows [as a consequence from
something], in exhorting or dissuading, and accusing or defending, and
praising or blaming, since in most cases it turns out that something good
or bad follows as a consequence from the same thing. For example, being envied is a bad thing that follows on one's being educated, whereas
being wise is a good thing. One should not be educated, then, since
15   one should not be envied. Then again, one should be educated, since
one should be wise.²⁰¹ This topic constitutes the art of Callippus, when
the possible is added to it, together with the other points, as stated.²⁰²

Another [topic is involved] when one must exhort or dissuade about
two things that are opposites of one another by using the topic just men-
20   tioned in the case of both. But the difference is that, in the prior case, any
two things just happen to be opposed, whereas here it is opposites [prop-
erly speaking]. For example, a priestess did not allow her son to speak out
in public. "For if," she said, "you say what is just, human beings will hate
you; but if what is unjust, the gods will. You should speak out in public,
then, for if you say what is just, the gods will befriend you, but if what
25   is unjust, human beings will do so." This is the same as the saying "Buy-
ing the marsh and the salt."²⁰³ And when good and bad follow as consequences of each of two opposites, each of the two consequences being
opposite to each other respectively, this amounts to "twisting it back in
retort."²⁰⁴

Since people do not praise the same things out in the open and behind
30   closed doors, but in the open they praise the just and the noble things
especially, while in private they want the advantageous things more, an-

200 · Consider *Topics* 111a33–b11.
201 · Consider again Euripides, *Medea* 294–97 as well as 2.21 (1394a29–30) above.
202 · Consider 2.19 above: in addition to the possible-impossible, Aristotle may have
in mind the future-past and more-less. Nothing is known of this Callippus, although
Aristotle refers to him again at 1400a4.
203 · This proverbial expression means "taking the (necessary) bad with the good, the
chaff with the wheat." In this context it comes close to "Damned if you do, damned if
you don't."
204 · The term Aristotle here uses (*blaisōsis*) is difficult to translate. Its root meaning is
"crooked, curved, or twisted," but (as LSJ suggests) it seems to amount to the "retort-
ing of a dilemma on its proposer."

other [topic] is attempting to draw from these [opposing views] the one or the other as a conclusion. This topic exercises a very great authority in producing paradoxes.

Another [topic] is based on the proportionality in the occurrence of things. For example, when people were compelling Iphicrates's son to undertake public service because he was big, though he was too young to do so, Iphicrates said that if they believe big boys to be men, then they will   35 decree small men to be boys. And Theodectes in *The Law* [says]: "You   1399b make mercenaries citizens, like Strabax and Charidemus, on account of their decency.[205] Won't you make exiles of those among the mercenaries who've done irreparable damage?"

Another [topic] arises from stating that if what results is the same, then   5 what gave rise to the result would be the same too. For example, Xenophanes[206] used to say that those who claim the gods come into being are as impious as those who say they die. For the result either way is that at some point the gods are not. And, in general, taking what results from each thing as though it is always the same: "You are going to judge, not   10 about Socrates,[207] but about a mode of living—whether one ought to philosophize." And that giving "earth and water" is to be enslaved,[208] and that sharing in the common peace amounts to following orders.[209] And one should grasp one or the other alternative in whatever way would be useful.

Another [topic] is based on the fact that the same people do not always choose the same thing later on as they did earlier, but rather conversely, as,   15 for example, in this enthymeme: "If when exiled we fought in order to return home, yet on being returned home we'll prefer exile so that we need not fight." For at one time they chose to remain [citizens] at the price of fighting, at another not to fight at the price of not so remaining.

Another [topic] is asserting that that for the sake of which something

---

205 · Both men are mentioned by Demosthenes: *Against Aristocrates* 89 (among other places) and *Against Leptines* 84.

206 · Xenophanes of Colophon (ca. 570–475) was an important pre-Socratic philosopher-poet.

207 · The reading of the MSS. Spengel reads instead "Isocrates," followed by all the modern editors, on the basis of a comparable passage in Isocrates, *Antidosis* 173–75.

208 · The Persian demanded of newly conquered territories "earth and water" as tokens of submission: see, e.g., Herodotus 4.126; 5.17–18, 73; 7.131, 133, 138, 163.

209 · The "common peace" refers to the submission of most of Greece (Sparta excepted) to Macedonian rule.

20   might be or could come to be *is* the reason it is or has come to be—for
example, if somebody should give someone something so that, in taking
it away, he would cause him pain. Hence this too was said:

> To many, the daemon—not because he bears them goodwill—
> Grants great good fortune, but rather so that
> Their misfortunes may be all the more manifest.[210]

25   And this from Antiphon's *Meleager*:

> Not so that they may kill the beast, but so that they may become
> Witnesses before Greece of the virtue of Meleager.[211]

And this from Theodectes's *Ajax*: that Diomedes chose Odysseus, not because he honored him, but so that the man who accompanied him would
30   be inferior, for it is possible to do this for this reason.[212]

Another [topic] is common to both litigants and advisors, namely, examining the things that urge us on[213] and those that dissuade us, and the
reasons why people both act and avoid doing so. For these are the things
that, if present, mean that one must act, and if they are not present, that one
must not act[214]—for example, if something is possible and easy and advan-
35   tageous, either to oneself or to one's friends, or is harmful to one's enemies,
even if a penalty is involved, provided the penalty is less than what is accom-
1400a   plished thereby. People are urged on by some things and dissuaded by their
opposites;[215] and it is on the basis of these same things that people both
accuse and defend: on the basis of things that dissuade, they make defense
speeches, and on the basis of things that urge one on, they level accusations.
5   This topic constitutes the whole art of Pamphilius and of Callippus.[216]

---

210 · The source of these lines is unknown.

211 · According to the scholiast, prominent men of Aetolia came to Meleager's father,
King Oeneus, not to kill the Calydonian boar themselves but to watch Meleager do it,
and so witness his virtuous act.

212 · The play has not survived, but the episode alluded to is related in Homer, *Iliad*
10.218 and context. Diomedes chooses Odysseus from among the many who volunteer
to join him in a raid of the Trojan camp—though Homer does not suggest a low motive at work in Diomedes.

213 · Or "exhort us" (*ta protreponta*), as elsewhere.

214 · The last clause is found only in a later MS, but it is read by all modern editors.

215 · Kassel brackets this sentence, but it is present in the MSS.

216 · Nothing certain is known of these two orators; Aristotle refers to Callippus also
at 1399a17.

Another [topic] is based on things that are held to happen, on the one hand, but are incredible, on the other. [One can argue] that people would not have held [such things] to exist if they had not in fact happened or nearly happened. [One can argue even] that these incredible things are all the more the case [for the very reason that they are incredible], since people suppose [that the only things that exist are] either the things that now are or those that are likely to be. If, then, something is incredible and not likely, it would be true, since it is not on account of its being likely and persuasive that it is held to be [true]. For example, Androcles the Pithean[217] said, when accusing the law, after people made an uproar be-   10 cause he contended that "the laws need a law that will set them aright," "for fish too need salt," although it is not likely or persuasive that things reared in the briny sea need salt, and "crushed olives need olive oil," although it is hard to credit that the things from which olive oil is derived need olive oil.

Another [topic] is refutative in that it examines the inconsistencies   15 involved, taking up separately what pertains to the disputant, on the one hand, if there is some inconsistency in all the dates, actions, and arguments [he cites] (for example, "And he says that he is the friend of you all, but he has sworn fealty to the Thirty"[218]) and what pertains to oneself, on the other: "And he asserts that I am litigious, but he can offer no demonstration of my having brought suit against anyone." [One should take   20 up separately also] what pertains to oneself and the disputant: "And this fellow has never loaned anything, but I have in fact bailed out many of you."

Another [topic], pertaining to human beings and affairs that have been prejudged or are held to have been prejudged,[219] is to state the cause of the false opinion, since there is some reason why it appears to be so. For

217 · Androcles hailed from the Athenian district of Pitheus. A prominent democrat and orator, he was a staunch opponent of Alcibiades: see, e.g., Thucydides 8.65 and Plutarch, *Alcibiades* 19.

218 · At the end of the Peloponnesian War (404), Sparta installed a harsh oligarchy in Athens, dubbed "the Thirty" (or "Thirty Tyrants"). The fellow in question, then, may claim to be a friend to "you"—presumably the *demos* or people—but is in fact aligned with the oligarchy.

219 · The term (*prodiaballō*) has as its root a word (*diabolē*) that can mean "slander" or "false accusation"; hence "to slander or falsely accuse in advance." *Diabolē* is rendered as "slander" at the end of the next sentence.

25   example, a certain woman who had given her own son away[220] was held to
be sleeping with the youth, on account of the [intensity with which] she
greeted him, but when the cause of this was stated, the slander was undone. Also, for example, in Theodectes's *Ajax*, Odysseus says to Ajax why,
although he is in fact more courageous than Ajax, he is not held to be so.

          Another [topic] is based on cause: if the cause is present, then [the re-
30   sult] is so, but if it is not present, then it is not so. For the cause and that
of which it is the cause go together, and there is nothing without a cause.
For example, Leodamas, in defending himself against Thrasyboulus's accusation that his name had been inscribed on a stele on the Acropolis but
that he had had it removed during the time of the Thirty, said that this
35   was not possible. For the Thirty would have had *more* trust in him if he
had been recorded as an enemy of the *demos*.[221]

          Another [topic] consists in examining whether what one is advising or
doing or has done admits of being done better some other way. For it is
1400b manifest that if there is [some better way],[222] then [the accused] did not
perform the act, since no one voluntarily and knowingly chooses things
that are inferior. But this is false. For it often becomes clear [only] later on
how it would have been better to act, whereas previously it was unclear.

5   Whenever something is about to be done that is contrary to things
that have been done, another [topic] is to examine both together. For ex-

220 · The meaning of the participle here (*hypobeblēmenēs*) is disputed: it is taken to
mean "palming off her son on another woman," but, as Grimaldi notes, "the usual meaning of the middle [voice], however, is not this but 'to bring in another's child as one's
own.'" The sixteenth-century commentary of Victorius suggests that the mother "threw
herself under" the young man—another possible meaning of the term—but this would
seem to corroborate rather than undermine the prejudice in question. Perhaps better
is the reading, adopted by no modern editors but enjoying some manuscript support
(see Cope, 289 and the apparatus criticus of Grimaldi), *diabeblēmenēs*: "when a certain woman had been slandered with regard to her son because of her greeting of him."
221 · Names of traitors were inscribed on a stele or pillar on the Acropolis. Leodamas
was a supporter of the oligarchy in Athens (see n. 218 above), Thrasyboulus of the democracy.
222 · The reading of Kassel's text. All the MSS, however, read a negative. One might
then translate as follows: "For it is manifest that if this is not so [i.e., if the person has
not followed the better course], then he did not perform the act." Although Grimaldi
argues that this topic could apply to all three kinds of rhetoric, Cope (among others)
contends that it applies best to judicial rhetoric. If someone is accused of doing or advising what was not best, the accusation must be false, i.e., the accused is not culpable,
since no one voluntarily chooses to do the lesser good—a fallacious argument, as Aristotle points out.

ample, when the Eleans asked Xenophanes whether or not they should sacrifice to Leucothea[223] and sing dirges for her, he advised them, if they suppose her to be a goddess, not to sing dirges for her, but if a human being, not to sacrifice to her.

Another topic is making accusations or defense speeches on the basis of errors committed. For example, in Carcinus's *Medea*, some people level the accusation that she killed her children—they ceased to appear, at any rate, for Medea erred in sending her children away. But she defends herself by saying that she would have killed, not her children, but Jason; she would have erred in not doing this, if in fact she had done the other. This topic and form of enthymeme constitute the whole art prior to Theodorus.[224]

Another [topic] is based on a proper name—for example, as Sophocles says, "Clearly, Sidero [i.e., of iron], you even bear the name";[225] and as people are accustomed to saying in their praises of the gods;[226] and as Conon used to call Thrasyboulus "bold counselor" [*thrasuboulos*]; and as Herodicus said to Thrasymachus, "You are always a bold fighter [*thrasumachos*]" and to Polus "You are always a colt,"[227] and of Dracon the lawgiver, "His laws were not of a human being but of a dragon [*drakon*]," for they were harsh.[228] And as Euripides's Hecuba [said] in regard to Aphrodite, "And the name of the goddess correctly begins 'folly' [*aphrosunēs*]." And as Chaeremon[229] [has it], "Pentheus, named from future misfortune."[230]

223 · Leucothea ("White Goddess") is an alternative name of Ino, daughter of Cadmus and the wife of the king of Thebes. Ino threw herself into the sea, with her infant son, and was transformed into a goddess of the sea (Homer, *Odyssey* 5.333 and following). Since Leucothea is (now) an immortal goddess, a song of mourning would be inappropriate, as is sacrificing to a human being (as distinguished from a goddess).

224 · The text is somewhat uncertain and could be rendered: "the whole earlier art of Theodorus." Theodorus of Byzantium (fl. 430–400) spent much time in Athens.

225 · A fragment from the lost *Tyro*: Nauck fr. 597. Sidero is the name of Tyro's stepmother.

226 · Here the scholiast, cited by Grimaldi, adds: "as Zeus is given his name as the cause of our life (*zōēs*)." Consider also Plato, *Cratylus* 395e5–396a3.

227 · On this meaning of Polus's name, consider Plato, *Gorgias* 463e.

228 · Dracon (or Draco) was one of the earliest Athenian lawgivers, known for the severity of his laws (hence our "draconian measures"): see, e.g., Aristotle, *Politics* 1274b15–19.

229 · A tragic poet of the middle of the fourth century. Aristotle mentions him twice in the *Poetics*: 1447b21 and 1460a2. See also 3.12 (1413b13) below.

230 · The name of Pentheus, king of Thebes, is derived from *penthos*, "sorrow." In Euripides's *Bacchae*, King Pentheus bans the worship of Dionysus, which leads eventually to Pentheus's being torn apart limb from limb by crazed Bacchic celebrants.

Refutative enthymemes are held in higher regard than are demonstrative ones because the refutative enthymeme draws a conclusion from opposing things in a short compass, and because statements put side by side are more readily manifest to the listener. And when it comes to all syllogistic reasoning, both that which is refutative and that which establishes something, people applaud above all the sorts of syllogisms they foresee from the beginning and not by dint of the syllogisms' being superficial (for as people perceive [the conclusion] in advance, they are simultaneously pleased with themselves), as well as all those syllogisms they are slower to grasp, though only to the extent that they understand them immediately upon their having been stated.

CHAPTER 24

Now, since it is possible for something to be a syllogism, but also for something not to be one but merely appear to be, there can of necessity be an enthymeme as well as something that merely appears to be an enthymeme but is not one, since the enthymeme is in fact a syllogism of a sort. There are topics belonging to apparent enthymemes, one of which bears on diction.[231] And one part of this [fallacy] is akin to making, in dialectics, a final statement in the manner of a conclusion when there has been no syllogistic reasoning in fact—"Since such and such is not the case, therefore such and such is necessarily so"—namely, in the case of enthymemes, making a terse and antithetical statement that appears to be an enthymeme. For such diction as that is the province of an enthymeme; and it seems to be such by virtue of the character of the diction at issue. When it comes to speaking in a syllogistic way by means of the diction employed, it is useful to state the key points of many syllogisms: "Some he saved, others he avenged, the Greeks he freed."[232] Each of these points was set forth on the basis of other things, but when they are put together, a certain [conclusion] appears to arise on the basis of them.

Another part [of the topic bound up with diction in apparent enthymemes] bears on homonymy:[233] asserting that a mouse is a serious thing—from it, at any rate, is derived the most honorable rite of all, since

231 · That is, "wording" or "style of expression" or "phrasing" (*lexis*); see 3.1–12 for Aristotle's extended treatment of diction.

232 · See Isocrates, *Evagoras* 65–69. Evagoras was king of Salamis (411–374).

233 · Or "equivocation," i.e., when one word has two or more meanings.

the Mysteries are the most honorable rite of all.[234] Or if someone, in prais-   15
ing a dog, should adduce alongside it the one in the heaven,[235] or Pan,
because Pindar said, "O blessed one, you whom Olympians call manifold dog of the great goddess."[236] Or the fact that being without a dog is
most dishonorable, with the result that the dog is clearly honorable.[237]
Or asserting that Hermes is the most sociable of the gods, since he alone   20
is called "common Hermes."[238] And that reason [*logos*] is a most serious
thing because good men are deserving, not of money, but of an account
[*logos*], for being "worthy of account" is not meant in a simple fashion.[239]

Another [topic belonging to apparent enthymemes] is to speak by putting together what was divided or by dividing what was put together. For   25
since what is not in fact the same thing often seems to be the same, one
should do whichever is the more useful. This is the argument of Euthydemus, that he knows that there is a trireme in the Piraeus, for he knows
each particular.[240] And that he who knows the letters knows the word,
since the word is the same thing [as the letters making it up]. And con-   30
tending that, since twice the amount of something is unhealthful, even
the original amount is not healthful, for it is absurd if [each of] the two
is good, but, taken as one [thing together], they are bad. In this way, [the

---

234 · "Mysteries" (*mustēria*)—most solemn religious rites—is allegedly derived from
"mouse" (*mus*), when in fact the term is linked to *muein*, "to close" (one's lips or eyes).

235 · That is, the Dog Star (Sirius).

236 · Pindar thus calls Pan the "dog" of Cybele, her constant companion.

237 · No commentator can shed much light on this enigmatic sentence: "In itself the
statement is a puzzle" (Cope). Some suggest that a reference to the Cynic philosophers
is intended, since Diogenes the Cynic was also known as "dog" ("Cynic" being derived
from the word for "dog").

238 · The homonymy here concerns the word *koinos* (common, general, shared):
Hermes is most *koinos* of the gods because he alone is called *koinos* Hermes. Hermes
was the god of luck, among other things, and a stroke of good luck was called *to her-
maion*; when someone found money lying about, for example, people would cry out
"*koinos* Hermes!"—meaning that they claimed a share in the find.

239 · The expression "worthy of account" (*logou axion*) means "noteworthy," "impressive," but it literally means "worthy of an account, a speech" (*logos*), and so is in this way
connected to *logos* in the sense of "reason."

240 · Euthydemus was a sophist from Chios, best known from the Platonic dialogue
named after him. Aristotle's statement here is highly compressed. Perhaps the suggestion is this: someone knows that a trireme (a warship) is; he knows that the Piraeus (the
port of Athens) is; therefore he knows that there is a trireme in the Piraeus. Consider
also Aristotle, *Sophistic Refutations* 177b12–13, where another and perhaps related argument of Euthydemus is mentioned.

argument] is refutative, but in the following way it establishes something: one good thing is not [made up of] two bad things.²⁴¹ But the
whole topic is contrary to reason. Again, there is what Polycrates said in
35   regard to Thrasyboulus, that he put down thirty tyrants, for he combines
them.²⁴² Or the remark in Theodectes's *Orestes*, for it is based on division:
"It is just for any woman who kills her husband"²⁴³ to die, *and* for a son
1401b to avenge his father; and this is what in fact was done. Yet once these are
combined, perhaps it is no longer just. But this might also bear on [the
fallacy of] omission, for it leaves out the "by whom" [the guilty wife is to
be put to death—not by her own son].

Another topic involves establishing or dismantling [an argument]
by means of exaggeration.²⁴⁴ This is when [the speaker], without hav-
5   ing established that [his opponent] did something, amplifies the matter
in question. For it is made to appear either that the deed was not done,
when the accused himself amplifies the matter, or that it was done, when
the accuser is enraged.²⁴⁵ This is not an enthymeme, then, for the listener
wrongly reasons that something was or was not done, when that was not
shown to be so.

Another [topic belonging to apparent enthymemes] is based on the
10   sign, for this too is illogical.²⁴⁶ For example, if someone should say, "Lovers are advantageous to cities, since the love of Harmodius and Aristo-

241 · The first formulation is (apparently) refutative because it rejects what must have
been the original proposition—that one portion of something is good for you, but
double the portion of it is bad—whereas the second is (apparently) demonstrative in
that it attempts positively to establish that the double amount is good on the grounds
that the two good things making it up cannot in combination produce one bad thing.
Yet, as Aristotle adds immediately, the whole *topos* is fallacious.

242 · Polycrates was a fourth-century rhetorician. Evidently Thrasyboulus (see n. 221
above) claimed, in putting down the tyranny in Athenians, that he put down not one
but thirty tyrants or thirty tyrannies—and so deserves thirty times the credit (for this
interpretation, see Quintilian, *Institutes* 3.6.26 and 7.4.44).

243 · The play is not extant; see Nauck fr. 5.

244 · The term is *deinōsis*; see n. 140 above.

245 · The reading of most MSS. One MS, accepted by Kassel, has, instead of "the accuser is enraged," "the accuser rouses [the audience]." Some suggest emending the text
to make it parallel to the immediately previous clause: "or that it was done, when the
accuser amplifies the deed."

246 · Literally, "asyllogistic," here and below. Presumably Aristotle has in mind here the
non-necessary sign, as distinguished from the necessary sign that constitutes "decisive
evidence": see 1.2 (1357b1 and following).

geiton brought down the tyrant Hipparchus."[247] Or if someone should say that Dionysius is a thief, since he is base, for this is indeed illogical: not every base person is a thief, although every thief is base.   15

Another [topic] arises through what is accidental—for example, what Polycrates said in regard to the mice, that they came to the assistance [of the soldiers] because they gnawed through the bowstrings.[248] Or if someone should contend that being invited to dine is a most honorable thing, since it was on account of the fact that he had not been invited that Achilles was enraged at the Achaeans in Tenedos.[249] He was angry on the grounds that he was being dishonored, but the occasion of his not being invited was accidental to this.   20

Another [topic] is that which bears on the consequence—for example, in the *Alexander*, [it is said] that he is great-souled because he looked down on associating with the many and spent his time by himself on Mount Ida.[250] For because the great-souled are such, he, too, would seem to be great-souled. And since someone is a dandy and goes about at night, he is an adulterer, for such [are adulterers]. Similarly, since beggars in the   25 temples sing and dance, and since it is possible for exiles to live wherever they like, they would seem to be happy because such things are available to those who seem to be happy, and these things are available to beggars and exiles. But *how* they are available makes a difference. Hence this too falls into the class of [the fallacy of] omission.

Another [topic belonging to apparent enthymemes] bears on taking   30 what is not the cause as the cause—for example, when something has come into being simultaneously with or after something else. For people take "after this" as though it were "on account of this," and especially those in positions of governance—as Demades, for example, said that the policy of Demosthenes was the cause of all ills, for after it the war happened.[251]

247 · For the story, see n. 181 above. Hipparchus was not in fact tyrant when he was killed by Harmodius and Aristogeiton.

248 · It is said that the inhabitants of Troy honored mice for this reason. Consider also Herodotus 2.141: when King Sennacherib invaded Egypt, King Sethos was saved, in accordance with a prophetic dream, by a swarm of field mice, who proceeded to gnaw through the quivers, bows, and shield handles, leaving the invading army defenseless.

249 · Grimaldi suggests that this alludes to a lost play of Sophocles, the *Syndeipnoi* (*Fellow Diners*), the subject of which is a gathering of Greek soldiers at Tenedos prior to the invasion of Troy.

250 · Evidently a reference to the lost *Alexander* (i.e., Paris) of Polycrates.

251 · Demades was an Athenian orator and demagogue (ca. 380–318), perhaps in the pay of Macedon. Demosthenes (384–322) was the greatest Athenian orator of his day.

35   Another [topic] bears on the omission of "when" and "how"—for example, that Alexander justly took Helen, for the choice [of a husband] was given to her by her father.²⁵² For [this granting of a choice does not apply] equally forever, but for the first [marriage only], since the father

1402a   has authority until that time. Or if someone should assert that striking freemen is an act of insolence, since this is not always so, but only when one strikes the first blow.

Further, just as in eristic disputations, an apparent syllogism arises when something is stated both simply and not simply except as pertains
5   to a given case: for example, in dialectics, that that which is not *is*, for that which is not *is* that which is not, and that the unknown is known, since it is known that the unknown is unknown. So also in matters of rhetoric, an apparent enthymeme arises from what is not simply likely, but rather from what is likely [only] in a given case. But this [particular likelihood]
10   is not universal, just as Agathon,²⁵³ too, says:

Perhaps somebody might say that this very thing is likely:
To mortals many unlikely things happen.

For something contrary to what is likely does come into being, so that even what is contrary to what is likely is likely. But this is not simply so.
15   Rather, just as in eristic disputations, failing to add "in respect of what" and "in relation to what" and "how" produces monkey business,²⁵⁴ so also here [in matters of rhetoric the monkey business is produced by the fact that] the likelihood is not simply such but likely [only] in a given case. It is on the basis of this topic that Corax's *Art* has been composed.²⁵⁵ For if someone is not liable to being blamed for something—for example, if someone weak is accused of assault—[then he can say that] it is not
20   likely [that he did it]. And if he is liable because, for example, he is strong, [then in that case] it is not likely [that he is guilty], since it *is* likely that

---

The war in question may be the conflict with Philip II of Macedon that ended at Chaeronea in 338, a decisive victory for the Macedonians.

252 · See Euripides, *Iphigenia in Aulis* 49–79.

253 · A celebrated tragedian of Athens, depicted by Plato in his *Symposium*. The source of the quotation is unknown.

254 · Literally, "sycophancy," a sycophant being one who threatened the rich with frivolous lawsuits in order to be paid off. Consider, e.g., Plato, *Republic* 340d1.

255 · According to Cicero (*De oratore* 1.20.91 and *Brutus* 46), Corax of Syracuse was one of the founders of rhetoric as an art.

he would seem to be guilty. And similarly also in the other cases. For it is necessary that one be either liable to being blamed for something or not liable. Both alternatives appear likely, then, the one really being likely, the other not simply so but in the way stated. "Making the weaker argument the stronger" also amounts to this, and hence human beings were justly   25 disgusted by what Protagoras professed,[256] since it is both a falsehood and not a true, but only an apparent, likelihood, and it is found in no art except[257] rhetoric and eristics.

What concerns enthymemes, both those that really are enthymemes and those that only appear to be, has been stated.

CHAPTER 25

It follows on the points stated to speak about refutation. It is possible   30 to refute something either by constructing a counter-syllogism[258] or by adducing an objection. Now, it is clear that it is possible to construct a counter-syllogism from the same topics [as used by one's opponent], for syllogisms are based on generally held opinions, and many such opinions contradict one another. Objections, on the other hand, are brought to   35 bear in four ways, just as also in what pertains to topics.[259] For an objection [may be derived] either from [the opponent's enthymeme] itself; or

256 · Protagoras of Abdera (ca. 490–420), featured in Plato's *Protagoras* and *Theaetetus,* was the most famous sophist of antiquity. Although Aristotle here implies that Protagoras claimed to be able to make the weaker argument the stronger, the sophist is best known for his dictum that "human being is the measure, of the things that are, that they are, and of the things that are not, that they are not." Protagoras himself refers to what it is he "professes," i.e., the public claim he makes about his teaching in general, at *Protagoras* 319a6–7.

257 · A more literal rendering of the reading of the MSS here is "it is found in no art but in rhetoric and eristics." Denniston (p. 4) defends taking *alla* ("but") here as "except," however rare such a usage. Ross alters the text so as to read "in no art other than rhetoric and eristics." At stake is whether Aristotle is excluding rhetoric (and eristics) from the class of arts—striking, given the title of the present work.

258 · A counter-syllogism (*antisyllogisamenos*) establishes the contrary of an opponent's conclusion.

259 · Grimaldi argues that this must be a general reference to "topics," i.e., to "the larger body of his writings on dialectics in general," in part because no comparable division pertaining to objections is found in the *Topics.* Consider, however, *Topics* 8.10, especially 161a1 and following.

from one similar to it; or from its opposite; or from judgments previously
rendered. I mean by "itself," this: if, for example, the enthymeme should
be about love's being a serious thing, the objection could be twofold, for
either (speaking universally) every neediness is base or (speaking about a
particular case) Caunian love[260] would not have been spoken of, if there
were not in fact base loves. An objection based on the opposite is brought
to bear if, for example, the enthymeme held that the good man benefits all
his friends—but not even the scoundrel harms [his friends]. In the case of
similar things, if the enthymeme held that those who have suffered badly
always feel hatred, [the objection would be that] not even those who have
been treated well always feel friendly affection. As for the judgments rendered by well-known men, if, for example, a certain enthymeme said that
there should always be some forgiveness for those who are drunk, for the
errors they make are done in ignorance, an objection is that then Pittacus
was unintelligent, for otherwise he would not have legislated greater penalties if somebody errs while drunk.[261]

Since enthymemes are stated on the basis of four things (and these
four are likelihood, example,[262] decisive evidence, [and] a sign), the enthymemes drawn from what is for the most part the case, in fact or seem-
ingly so, have conclusions based on likelihoods; other enthymemes come
by way of induction from what is a similar case, either one or more than
one such case, whenever one assumes the universal and then reasons syllogistically to the particular, by way of an example; other enthymemes,
based on what is necessary and [always] in existence,[263] proceed by way
of decisive evidence; other enthymemes proceed by way of a universal or
particular [proposition], whether it is or is not really so, through signs.

260 · That is, incest. Caunus was in love with his sister Byblis; see Ovid, *Metamorphoses* 9.454–665.

261 · On the legislator Pittacus, see Aristotle, *Politics* 2.12 (1274b18–23), where this law
is discussed.

262 · That Aristotle here includes "example" under the heading of the enthymeme, as
distinguished from being a source of arguments separate from enthymemes (see 2.20
beg.), has prompted much discussion among scholars. Grimaldi, however, contends
that example "remains one of the two *koinai pisteis* [common modes of persuasion]. . . .
Example may be a source of enthymeme insofar as example . . . can give you a probable universal principle or truth from which you may then reason by the use of the enthymeme to a particular conclusion" (*Studies*, 104).

263 · All modern editors accept the addition of "always" here first suggested by Vahlen.
The MSS read, simply, "what is necessary and existing."

And [since] "likely" is what is not always but only for the most part so, it is manifest that enthymemes of this sort can always be refuted by bringing an objection to bear. But the refutation is apparent and not always true, for the objector refutes [the argument], not because it is not likely, but because it is not necessarily so. Hence the defendant always has more 25 of an advantage than does the accuser through this false reasoning. For since the accuser proves his case through likelihoods, and since it is not the same thing to refute something [by arguing] that it is not likely as it is to argue that it is not necessary, what is for the most part so can always be objected to—for otherwise it would not be likely but always so and necessary. The judge supposes that, if [the argument] is thus refuted, either 30 it is not likely or it is not for him to judge, though in this his reasoning is faulty, just as we were saying. For he should not judge on the basis of necessities alone, but also on the basis of likelihoods, since this *is* to "judge by one's best judgment."[264] It is not sufficient, then, if one refutes an argument on the grounds that it is not necessary; rather, one should refute it 35 because it is not likely. This will occur if the objection is to a greater degree based on what is for the most part the case, and such an objection is possible in two ways: either by reference to the time[265] involved or to the facts. But what exercises the greatest authority is referring to both, for if 1403a such things happen this way often, it is more likely [to have happened this way also in the case at hand].

Both signs and the enthymemes stated by way of signs are, even if they are relevant, refutable, just as was stated in the first [arguments].[266] For that no sign [by itself] forms a syllogism is clear to us from the *Analytics*.[267] 5 In the case of enthymemes formed from examples, the refutation of them is the same as in that of likelihoods. For if we have some one thing that is not thus, [the enthymeme from example] has been refuted, because it is not necessary, even if there are more examples or frequent instances of the example [on the opponent's side]; on the other hand, if there are more examples and more frequent instances of the example [on the opponent's side], one must contend against him either that his present ex-

264 · A part of the oath taken by Athenian jurors; see also 1375a29–30.

265 · Some commentators, including Grimaldi, take "time" to mean not the date of the alleged deed (in judicial proceedings) but rather the frequency of the action in question.

266 · Consider 1.2 (1357b10–14, 17–21) on "signs."

267 · Consider *Prior Analytics* 2.27 (70a24–26 and context).

10   ample is not similar to those, or that it proceeds dissimilarly or has *some*
difference, at least.[268]

Decisive evidence, and the enthymemes formed from decisive evidence, will not be subject to refutation on the grounds that they do not
form a [valid] syllogism (and this too is clear to us from the *Analytics*[269]).
It remains only to show that the fact alleged is not so. But if it is manifest both that it is so and that it constitutes decisive evidence, then this is
15   already irrefutable, for all of it then becomes a manifest demonstration.

CHAPTER 26

Amplifying or downplaying is not an element of an enthymeme. (I mean
by "element" and "topic" the same thing, for "element" and "topic" are
20   [headings] under which many enthymemes fall.) But amplifying and
downplaying bear on showing that something is great or petty, just as
one shows also that something is good or bad, or just or unjust, and anything else whatever. All these constitute subject matters of syllogisms and
enthymemes. As a result, if none of these is a topic of an enthymeme,
25   then neither would amplifying or downplaying be.[270] And refutative [en-
thymemes] are not some one specific form either, for it is clear that someone refutes something either by establishing something else or by bringing an objection to bear, and by the former they demonstrate in response
[to the opponent] the opposite [of his conclusion]—for example, if the
one fellow has shown that something has happened, the other shows that
it has not happened; and if the one fellow shows that it has not happened,
the other shows that it has. As a result, then, this will not be the difference
30   [between the two speakers]; for both make use of the same things, seeing
that they adduce enthymemes [to show] that something is or is not so.
As for the objection, it is not an enthymeme, but (just as in the *Topics*) it
is stating a certain opinion on the basis of which it will be clear that [the
opponent] has not reasoned syllogistically or that he has taken hold of
something false.

268 · This difficult sentence has prompted several emendations and interpretations; I
follow Grimaldi's reading and rendering.
269 · See *Prior Analytics* 2.27.
270 · Aristotle includes amplification and downplaying (and hence what is great or
small, greater or smaller) among the "points common [to the various ends of rhetoric],"
together with possible-impossible and past or future fact, and in contrast to the specific
topics; see 1.3 (1359a11–26), 2.18 (1391b32–1392a1 and context), and 2.19 (1393a8–18).

Now, since there are three things that one must concern oneself
with pertaining to the speech —namely, examples and maxims and en-   35
thymemes; or, in general, matters pertaining to the understanding, which
will give us a ready supply [of arguments] and indicate how we will re-   1403b
fute [the arguments of others] —let this much be stated by us. It remains
to go through what concerns diction and arrangement [of the parts of a
speech].

Outline of Book 3

A. Diction 3.1–12
  1. Diction and delivery in poetry and prose: 3.1–2
     a) The necessity of concern for diction
     b) Clarity as the virtue of diction
     c) Appropriateness of the language to the subject
     d) Dialect, compound, made-up words
     e) Metaphors and epithets
  2. Frigid or corny expressions: 3.3
     a) Compound words
     b) Special dialects
     c) Inappropriate epithets
     d) Inappropriate metaphors
  3. Similes: 3.4
  4. Speaking correctly: 3.5
     a) Connective particles
     b) Specific names for specific things
     c) Nouns and gender
     d) Avoiding solecism
  5. Expansion and concision: 3.6
  6. Passion and character appropriately conveyed: 3.7
  7. Rhythm: 3.8
  8. Periods and clauses: 3.9
  9. Urbane and well-regarded sayings: 3.10–11
     a) Metaphors
     b) Enthymemes
     c) Antitheses
     d) Vivid expressions

Book 3

Since there are three things one must concern oneself with pertaining to the speech—first, the things on which the modes of persuasion will be based; second, what concerns diction; and, third, how one ought to arrange the parts of the speech—what concerns the modes of persuasion has been stated, both how many are the things they can be based on (the fact that there are three such bases), and what sorts of things these are, and why they are only this many. For all people are persuaded either because they themselves as judges have been affected in some respect; or because they suppose that the speakers are of a certain sort; or because something has been demonstrated.

Enthymemes, too, have been spoken of, as to where a ready supply of them is to be found, for there are the specific kinds [of topics] for enthymemes, on the one hand, and the [general] topics, on the other.

But speaking about what concerns diction follows next. For being in possession of the points one must say is not sufficient; rather, it is necessary [to know] also *how* one must say them, and this contributes much to making the speech appear to be of a given character. The first consideration, then, was sought out according to nature, what in fact is first by nature, namely, what gives the subject matters themselves their persuasiveness. Second is to set these things down with reference to diction. Third among these—what has a very great power but has not yet been taken up—is what pertains to the delivery. For even in tragedy and rhapsody, [attention to delivery] arose only at length, since at first the poets themselves used to deliver[1] their tragedies. It is clear, then, that this sort

1403b

5

10

15

20

25

---

1 · The word translated as "deliver" (*hupekrinonto*) can also mean "act" or "perform."

[of concern] pertains to rhetoric too, just as it does also to poetry, this latter, in fact, having been the concern of Glaucon of Teos,² among others.

Now, [delivery] resides in the voice—how one ought to use it relative to each passion (that is, when to use a loud voice, when a quiet one,
and when a middling), and how to use different tones (that is, high-
30   pitched, deep, and middling), and what rhythms relate to each. For there
are three things [that people] consider, and these are volume, harmony,
[and] rhythm. Those [who master these three things] almost always take
the prizes in competitions, and just as nowadays those who deliver³ the
poems there have a greater power than do the poets, so also [it is delivery
35   that has greater power] in political contests, on account of the depravity
of the regimes.⁴ An art about these things has not yet been composed,
since even what concerns diction [in poetry] arose only at length. In fact
1404a   it is held to be a vulgar thing, which is a fine supposition. But since the
whole matter of concern in rhetoric is related to opinion, one should be
concerned with [diction], not on the grounds that it is correct to do so,
but on the grounds that it is necessary. Justice, at any rate, seeks out noth-
5   ing more, when it comes to the speech, than not causing [the listeners]
pain or delight, for it is just to contend [against one's opponent] with the
facts themselves, such that anything apart from the demonstration is superfluous. But, nevertheless, [diction] has great power, as has been said,
on account of the depravity of the listener. The matter of diction, then,
10   has some small necessary presence in all instruction, for speaking in this
or that way does make some difference in making one's point clear—but
only some. All these things are [a matter of] imagination and geared toward the listener, which is why nobody teaches geometry in this way.

Now, when [delivery] does come [into its own in rhetoric], it will accomplish the same thing as it did for the art of acting [or reciting lines
of poetry], and in fact some have undertaken to speak about it to a small
15   extent—for example, Thrasymachus in his *Pitiable Ones*.⁵ Being a skilled
actor belongs to one's nature and is less a matter of technical art, whereas

2 · This Glaucon, who is not of course the brother of Plato featured in the *Republic*, may
be the same one mentioned by Plato at *Ion* 530d; nothing is known of the work Aristotle alludes to.

3 · That is, the actors or rhapsodes.

4 · Spengel suggests reading "citizens" rather than "regimes," partly on the basis of
1404a8, where Aristotle speaks of the depravity of the listener.

5 · *Eleoi*. The rhetorician Thrasymachus of Chalcedon (ca. 459–400) is best known
from his dramatic appearance in the first book of Plato's *Republic*. The work mentioned

what pertains to diction *is* subject to a technical art. So it is that prizes again go to those who are capable in this respect, just as they do also to rhetoricians for their delivery, since written speeches [when they are delivered] have greater effect on account of their diction than they do on account of the understanding [present in them].

Those who first began to set in motion [the concern for diction] were, as is only natural, the poets, for words are imitations, and the voice, which is the most imitative of all our parts, was ready to hand [for their use]. Hence the relevant arts were established—rhapsody and acting and the others. And since the poets, though they spoke naïvely, seemed to gain their reputation on account of their diction, it was for this reason that a poetical diction first arose [in rhetoric]—that of Gorgias, for example. And still, even now, the many among the uneducated suppose that such people converse most beautifully. But this is not so. Rather, the diction involved in speech and that involved in poetry are different. What has transpired makes this clear: not even those who write tragedies still make use of it in the same manner, but just as they changed from tetrameters to iambic meter because this latter is, of all the meters, the one most similar to speech, so also have they dispensed with all such words as go against the conversational, with which the poets used to adorn [their writings], as do even now those who write hexameters. Hence it is laughable to imitate those who themselves no longer make use of that manner [of writing]. It is manifest as a result that we need not be precise about *all* the things it is possible to speak of in connection with diction, but only about those that concern the sort of diction we are speaking of; what concerns that other [diction proper to poetry] has been spoken of in the *Poetics.*[6]

CHAPTER 2

Let those matters stand as having been considered, then, and let a virtue of diction be defined as clarity, for argument or speech is a sort of sign, such that if it is not clear, it will not perform the task that is its own; and let the diction [proper to rhetoric] be neither humble nor above the worth [of the subject matter in question] but appropriate to it. For poetic diction may not be humble, but neither is it appropriate for a speech. In

does not survive. Consider also Plato, *Phaedrus* 267c (on the abilities of Thrasymachus, including the capacity to arouse pity).

6 · Consider *Poetics* 20–22.

the case of nouns and verbs, the terms in their prevailing senses make for clarity, whereas all those other nouns spoken of in the *Poetics*[7] render the diction, not humble, but ornate, since departing from [ordinary words] makes [the writing] appear more august. For what human beings feel in relation to foreigners and their fellow citizens is the same in matters of diction: so it is [according to them] that one must give to one's conversation a foreign character. For human beings wonder at what is far-off, and the object of wonder is pleasant.

Now, in meters [or verse], many things bring this effect about,[8] and there it is fitting, since the subject matter of the speech and the characters it deals with stand out more [from the ordinary]. But in prose speeches, these things are much less fitting, since the hypothesis[9] involved is a lesser thing. For even in poetry, if a slave were to use gussied-up language, or someone too young were to do so, it would be rather inappropriate, or in connection with subjects too petty for it. Instead, what is fitting even in these [poetical] writings [lies between] contraction and amplification.[10] Hence the writers should go unnoticed [by the audience] and be held to be speaking, not artificially, but naturally (since this latter is persuasive, the former the opposite: people are suspicious of [those who employ such artifice] as of those who are hatching a plot, just as they are suspicious also of wines that have been adulterated). And as an example, there is the affect of Theodorus's[11] voice in comparison to the voices of the other actors, for his seems to belong to the [character] speaking, whereas the others'

---

7 · Consider *Poetics* 21.

8 · The reading of the MSS, accepted by Kassel. Ross, following a suggestion of Bywater, gives a text that would read, in translation, "Now, in meters [or verse], many things are written in this way."

9 · *Hypothesis*: the foundation, supposition, or basis of an argument.

10 · Here Kassel inserts the sentence beginning "But in prose speeches" such that his text reads, in translation, "Now, in meters [or verse], many things bring this effect about, and there it is fitting, since the subject matter of the speech and the characters it deals with stand out more [from the ordinary]. For even in poetry, if a slave were to use gussied-up language, or someone too young were to do so, it would be rather inappropriate, or in connection with subjects too petty for it. Instead, what is fitting even in these [poetical] writings is a certain contraction and amplification. But in prose speeches, these things are much less fitting, since the hypothesis involved is a lesser thing." I follow the reading of the MSS.

11 · Theodorus was a celebrated actor in tragedies; Aristotle mentions him also at *Politics* 1336b28.

seem to belong to others. He conceals[12] something well, whoever composes by selecting from the customary language of conversation, which   25
is in fact what Euripides does and what he first showed the way toward.

Now, since the speech is composed of nouns and verbs (the number
of forms of nouns having been a subject of study in the writings concerning poetry),[13] those words that are of a special dialect [or are unusual],[14]
compound words, and made-up words, one must use only rarely and in   30
few places (where to use them we will say later,[15] but the reason for this
was stated [already]: otherwise one departs from what is fitting in the direction of what is too grand). But the prevailing [sense of a term] and the
term that belongs properly to a thing, and metaphor, alone are useful for
the diction belonging to prose speeches. A sign of this is that all make
use of only these, for everyone engages in conversation by using metaphors, terms that properly belong to the thing, and terms in their prevail-   35
ing sense. It is clear as a result that if someone composes [a speech] well,
there will be something of a foreign character to it, and [yet] this admits
of going unnoticed, and [his meaning] will in fact be clear. And [such
clarity] is, as we saw, the virtue of rhetorical speech. As for nouns, hom-
onyms are useful to the sophist (since it is with these that he performs
his tricky business), whereas to the poet synonyms are useful. I mean by
terms in their prevailing sense as well as synonyms, "making one's way"   1405a
and "going," [for example,] since both [are used in] their prevailing senses
and are synonyms of one another.

What each of these is, then, and how many forms of metaphor there
are, and that metaphors have the greatest effect in both poetry and
speeches, have been stated in the writings concerning the art of poetry,   5
just as we were saying.[16] One must bestow all the more diligent labor on
[metaphors] in a speech, inasmuch as the speech can rely on fewer sources
to aid it than can meters [or verse]. Clarity, pleasure, and the foreign are
conveyed by metaphor especially, and it is not possible to grasp metaphor   10

12 · The "concealment" (literally, "steals": *kleptetai*) in this case consists in obscuring
the fact that the speech is an artful composition and not at all a product of ordinary
conversation. See also n. 20 below.

13 · Consider *Poetics* 20–22.

14 · *Glōttai*: the term means literally "tongues" and, by extension, "languages." Here
Aristotle means by it any term that is odd, foreign, or would require explanation.

15 · Consider 3.7 below.

16 · Consider *Poetics* 21 (1456b20 and following).

from someone else.[17] One should state both epithets and metaphors in a fitting way, and this will proceed from the proportion [or analogy] involved. Otherwise, the inappropriateness will be apparent because things that are in opposition will be especially apparent when set side by side. But one must examine what is fitting for an old man in the way that the scarlet cloak is appropriate for the young,[18] for the same clothing is not

15   suitable [for both]. And if you want to adorn [someone or something], you must apply the metaphor derived from the better things that belong to the same genus, and if to blame [someone or something], from those that are worse. I mean, for example—since opposites fall in the same genus—asserting that he who begs "prays" and that he who prays "begs" is to compose [in the way] described, because both begging and praying are solicitations [but are the opposites of one another in what they con-

20   note]; so also when Iphicrates asserted that Callias was a "begging priest" but not a "bearer of the torch."[19] But Callias asserted that Iphicrates was not initiated into the Mysteries, for if he were he would not call him a begging priest but rather a bearer of the torch. For both are concerned with a god, but the one is honorable, the other dishonorable. And one [may call actors] "Dionysus-flatterers," but they call themselves "skilled

25   artisans." These are both metaphors, the one disparaging, the other the opposite. And pirates nowadays call themselves "suppliers." Hence it is possible to say that someone who has committed an injustice "makes a mistake," and that one who makes a mistake "commits an injustice," and that someone who stole something both "gained possession of it" and "supplied himself" with it. And there is what Euripides's Telephus asserts:

30   Being lord of the oar, and having landed in Mysia.

17 · Aristotle does not evidently mean that one cannot borrow a metaphor from another speaker, but rather that one cannot acquire the ability to come up with metaphors from someone else.

18 · "Scarlet (or red) cloak" signified military garb, among the Spartans and Persians, for example, and so would be suitable for a young man eligible for military service, as an elder would no longer be.

19 · Callias, son of Hipponicus, features in the writings of Plato and Xenophon, where he appears as a very wealthy patron of the sophists (in the *Protagoras*, e.g.) and prominent citizen of democratic Athens. Xenophon (*Hellenica* 6.3.3) refers to Callias as "the bearer of the torch," the official responsible for leading the procession of initiates "from Athens to Eleusis on the fifth day of the great Eleusinia, the *torch-day*" (so Cope; emphasis original). To "confuse" the bearer of the torch with a begging priest or mendicant is thus to denigrate or insult Callias considerably. See also book 2, n. 31 above.

This is inappropriate, for "being lord" is grander than what is merited. No concealment[20] has been carried out in this case, then. Error may reside also in the syllables, if they are not indicative of a pleasing vocal sound— for example, Dionysius the Brazen in his elegies addresses poetry as "Calliope's screeching," because both [poetry and screeching] are sounds of the voice, but the metaphor of meaningless vocal sounds is a poor one.[21]   35

Further, when it comes to naming nameless things, one should apply metaphors that are not far-fetched but derived from things that are akin to them and of like form, which, once they have been stated, are clearly akin—for example, in the well-regarded riddle: "A man I saw gluing   1405b bronze on a man with fire."[22] For the experience has no name, but both [gluing and cupping] are a sort of attaching, and so it spoke of the application of the cupping instrument as "gluing." And in general it is possible to grasp suitable metaphors from well-turned riddles. For metaphors   5 pose riddles, the result being that the transference [of the meaning contained in the metaphor] has clearly been well done. [It is possible to fashion metaphors] also from beautiful [words].[23] The beauty of a word, just as Licymnius[24] says, resides in the sounds [it makes] or in what is signified, and similarly with the ugliness of a word.

Further, and third, there is the consideration that refutes the sophistic argument on this score. For it is not as Bryson[25] contended, that there   10 is no ugly speech, if in fact saying *this* instead of *that* signifies the same thing. This is false: one word is more prevalent than another and bears a greater similarity [to the thing referred to] and is more appropriate for

20 · Here Aristotle refers to his formulation at 1404b24–25, according to which "he conceals something well, whoever composes by selecting from the customary language of conversation, which is in fact what Euripides does and what he first showed the way toward."

21 · So called [Dionysius the Brazen] because he evidently first suggested the use of bronze coins in Athens: see Athenaeus 669d and Cope ad loc. Calliope, one of the Muses, was associated with epic poetry in particular.

22 · The riddle refers to the practice of "cupping," the application of a metal cup on the skin that, when heated, is sealed to it and draws the blood up.

23 · Or "noble [words]," here and throughout this section, just as "ugly" could be "shameful."

24 · Little is known of Licymnius of Chios, a dithyrambic poet. See below 3.12 (1413b13) and 3.13 (1414b17) for additional references. See also Plato, *Phaedrus* 267c2 as well as E. M. Cope, "On the Sophistical Rhetoric," *Cambridge Journal of Classical and Sacred Philology* 3.9 (1856): 255–57.

25 · For the little that is known of this rhetorician, see E. M. Cope, "On the Sophistical Rhetoric," *Cambridge Journal of Classical and Sacred Philology* 2.5 (1855): 143–46.

making the thing appear before one's eyes. Further, *this* or *that* may not
signify things in the same state, such that one word must thus be posited

15   as being more beautiful or uglier than another. For both do signify the
beautiful or the ugly, but not in the respect in which a given thing is beautiful or ugly; or, if they do this, then they do so in varying degrees, more
and less. So metaphors should be applied from these sources, from beautiful words either in vocal sound or their power or the sight [they conjure
in the listener], or in reference to some other perception. And it is supe-

20   rior to say, for example, "rosy-fingered dawn" rather than "scarlet-fingered
dawn," or, poorer still, "red-fingered dawn."²⁶

        And in the matter of epithets, it is possible to fashion epithets from
what is low or ugly—for example, "the mother-killer"—as also from what
is better—for example, "the father-avenger." And when someone who
had won the mule race gave Simonides a little money [to write verses in

25   praise of the victory], Simonides was unwilling to do so on the grounds
that he was disgusted at writing about half-asses; but when the fellow gave
him enough money, Simonides wrote: "Hail! Daughters of storm-footed
steeds!"—although they were daughters of asses too. Further, the use of di-
minutives [accomplishes] the same thing [as do epithets]. The diminutive

30   is that which makes both the bad and the good less, just as Aristophanes
jokes in the *Babylonians*,²⁷ "gold-let" instead of gold coin, "cloak-let" instead of cloak, "insult-let" for insult, and "disease-let." But one should be
cautious and observe due measure in both [metaphors and epithets].

CHAPTER 3

        Corny [or frigid] expressions²⁸ in matters of diction arise in four [in-
35   stances]: [first,] in compound words. For example, Lycophron's the "many-
faced heaven of the great-peaked earth" and "narrow-passaged headland";
1406a   and [the way] Gorgias named "begging-Muse-flatterers" and "swearing
false oaths even while swearing right solemnly"; and as Alcidamas [spoke
of] "the wrath-filled soul and the face become fire-hued," and "he supposed their zeal would become end-fulfilling," and "he made the persua-

---

26 · "The latter suggests cooks' hands, or other vulgar associations" (Cope).

27 · This comic play does not survive.

28 · *Psychra*: literally, "cold," hence also "frigid," i.e., expressions that fall flat. In Xenophon's *Symposium*, Socrates attempts to deflect the accusation that he does not care
about the gods by making a bad pun; he then adds that, if what he says is *psychra*, that
is not his fault: 6.7, end.

siveness of the speeches end-fulfilling," and "the foundation of the sea was   5
blue-hued." All these appear poetic because they are compound words.

This, then, is one cause [of corny expressions], and another is the use of special dialects [or unusual terms]. For example, Lycophron [called] Xerxes "the
prodigious-monster man," Sciron "a thievery man," and Alcidamas [speaks
of] a "plaything to poetry," and "the presumptuous recklessness of [his] nature," and "whetted with the undiluted anger of [his] understanding."[29]   10

Third is the use of epithets that are either long or inapt or frequent.
In poetry it is fitting to say "white milk," but in speech these things are,
some of them, rather inappropriate, while others, if used to excess, convict [the writer] and make it manifest that it is poetry. Now, one must in-   15
deed make use of epithets, since doing so effects a change from the usual
and creates a diction marked by something foreign, but one must aim at
the due measure in this, since [failing to do so] fosters something worse
than does speaking at random: the one is not good, the other actually
bad.[30] It is from this that the corny expressions of Alcidamas arise, for
he uses epithets not as seasonings but as a main course, and thus they are   20
long and too grand and conspicuous. For example, it is not "sweat" but
"damp sweat," and not "to the Isthmian games" but "to the festive cele-
bration of the Isthmian games," and not "laws" but "laws, kings of the cities," and not "at a run" but "with the running impulse of his soul," and not
"museum"[31] but "receiving the museum of nature," and "the sullen-faced   25

29 · Lycophron the sophist applies a term from epic poetry (pelōr)—Homer uses it to
describe the Cyclops (Odyssey 9.428)—to the Persian King. Sciron was a notorious
thief whom Lycophron calls by an adjective (sinis) derived from the name of another
such thief, Sinnis; both Sciron and Sinnis, as it happens, were killed by Theseus. "Presumptuous recklessness" attempts to convey the sense of the poetic word (atasthalia)
Alcidamas here uses. Cope suggests that, in the last example, the word translated as
"whetted" (tethēgmenon) is the special term, used mostly in poetry and being a metaphor for "exasperated, excited, provoked, irritated."
30 · The clause is ambiguous, and Burkett, following Kennedy, renders it this way: "one
should aim at the mean, for it does less harm than speaking carelessly; carelessness
lacks merit, moderation lacks fault." There are two difficulties. First, the subject of the
second clause is unstated ("the other": hē de) and may refer either to the failure to observe due measure or to observing it; and, second, there is no explicit verb in the second clause. If one assumes that the verb implied there is the same as is in the first, then
Burkett's rendering would be correct.
31 · "Museum" means in the first place "a shrine of the Muses" and, by extension, "a
library or school for instruction in the arts." Commentators are puzzled by the phrase
in general (Cope: "I do not fully understand it") and by the meaning of the participle
(paralabōn) in particular.

soul's concern," and a craftsman, not of "favor," but of "all-popular favor,"
and "manager of the listeners' pleasure," and "he concealed" something,
not "with branches," but "with branches of the wood," and "he covered
with a cloak," not "his body," but "the shame of his body," and "the desire
of his soul" was "imitating-in-response"[32] (and this is at once both a compound word and an epithet, and so the result becomes a poem), and "so
extravagant the excess of depravity."

Hence by speaking poetically in an inappropriate way, people foster
what is laughable and corny, as well as a lack of clarity traceable to empty
verbiage. For whenever somebody throws [words] at one who already understands [the point], he does away with clarity through the murkiness
[of his words]. Human beings use compound words whenever something
is nameless and the account of it is readily put together—for example,
"time-wasting."[33] But if there is much of this, the effect is altogether poetic. Hence compound words are most useful for dithyrambic poets, since
they are full of noisy sound.[34] Dialect [or unusual] terms are most useful
to epic poets, for [epic poetry] is solemn and high-flown. Metaphor is
most useful to iambic poets, for this is what they use now, as was said.[35]

And, further, fourth, what is corny arises in [the use of] metaphors,
for metaphors, too, may be inappropriate, some on account of being
laughable—comic poets also use metaphors—others because they are
excessively solemn and tragic. They are also unclear if far-fetched—for
example, Gorgias's "unripe and bloodless affairs." And "these things you
shamefully sowed, and badly did you reap"—for this is excessively poetic. And as Alcidamas [calls] philosophy a "fortress against[36] the laws,"
and the *Odyssey* a "noble mirror of human life," and applying "no such
plaything to poetry."[37] Quite all of these are unpersuasive for the reasons
stated. And Gorgias's remark to the swallow, when it let go its excrement

32 · *Antimimon* (as most MSS have it) is evidently a coinage containing the prefix *anti*-
meaning "corresponding to," "in response to," or "counter" (as *antistrophē* corresponds
to *strophē* in Greek theater) and -*mimon*, pertaining to imitation or mimicry.

33 · The compound Aristotle here coins is simply *chronotribein*, *chronos* meaning
"time," *tribein* meaning "to spend (time) at something," "to while away (the time)."

34 · Originally sung in honor of Bacchus, dithyrambs were the "most licentious and
most extravagant of all the kinds of poetry" (Cope).

35 · Kassel brackets this sentence as a marginal gloss, but it is present in the MSS.

36 · Alcidamas's expression is ambiguous: it could mean that philosophy is a "fortress
[*epiteichisma*] against" the laws or a "bulwark of" the laws. Cope suggests the former:
"'fortress to threaten' (a standing menace to), the laws."

37 · A part of the same line is quoted above at 1406a9.

as it flew over him, belongs to the best of tragic poetry. For he said: "A shameful thing, O Philomela," since it is not a shameful thing if a bird did that, but for a maiden it is shameful. He rebuked her well, then, by stating what she was and not what she is.[38]

CHAPTER 4

The simile[39] is a metaphor too, since the difference involved is slight: 20
whenever [the poet] says of Achilles, "And like a lion he rushed on," it is a simile, but when he says, "A lion rushed on," it is a metaphor. For since both [Achilles and a lion] are courageous, he addressed him [in the latter verse] by transferring "lion" to Achilles.[40] But the simile is useful also in a speech—used rarely, however, since it is poetic. They should be applied   25
as metaphors are applied, for they *are* metaphors, differing [only] in the respect stated. These are similes: for example, Androtion [said] of Idreus that he was "similar to little dogs unleashed," since they lunge and bite, and Idreus, once freed from his bonds, was harsh.[41] And as Theodamas   30
likened Archidamus to a Euxenus who did not understand geometry, by analogy, for Euxenus will also be an Archidamus skilled in geometry.[42] And the remark in Plato's *Republic* that those who strip the dead [on the battlefield] are like little dogs that snap at the stones but without set- ting upon him who threw them; and the [simile] pertaining to the com-   35
mon people, that they are similar to a ship's pilot who is strong but deaf; and the one pertaining to the meters [or verse] of the poets, that they are like those in the bloom of youth without beauty (for when the latter lose their bloom, and the former are broken up, they do not appear as what   1407a

38 · Philomela was a maiden whom the Olympic gods turned into a bird after her brother-in-law raped her. See Ovid, *Metamorphoses* 6.545.
39 · Literally, "image" (*eikōn*).
40 · Aristotle does not identify the poet in question, and the exact quotation does not appear in our texts of Homer (but consider the simile of the lion at *Iliad* 20.164). "Transferring" translates a participle derived from the verb (*metapherō*) related to the noun "metaphor," literally, "carrying across."
41 · Androtion (ca. 410–340) was an Athenian statesman and orator, a student of Isocrates. Idreus was a prince of Caria who became king on the death of his brother Mau- solus in 351. Presumably he had been imprisoned at some point prior to his accession.
42 · Nothing is known of these three men, and so the joke is difficult to reconstruct. Cope, Kennedy, and Burkett all suggest that Theodamas is insulting both men: both are unimpressive, one knows a little geometry. Sachs (254 n. 199) suggests that Euxenus is the butt of the joke.

they were).[43] Also Pericles's [simile] pertaining to the Samians, that they
are like children who accept some morsels but cry nonetheless; and about
the Boeotians, that they are similar to oaks: oaks are cut down by their
own wood, and the Boeotians are fighting one another.[44] And what Demosthenes [said about] the common people, that they are similar to the
seasick aboard ships.[45] And as Democrates[46] likened orators to wet nurses
who swallow up the little morsel and then daub the children with their
saliva. And as Antisthenes likened Cephisodotus the Skinny to frankin-
cense, because he brings delight as he grows less and less.

All these it is possible to state both as similes and as metaphors, such
that all those that are approved of when stated as metaphors will clearly
be approved of also as similes—and similes are metaphors lacking the
[explanatory] account.[47] But the metaphor based on analogy must always
be reciprocally applicable and apply to either of the two things of the
same genus. For example, if the drinking cup is a shield of Dionysus, then
it is fitting to say that the shield is a drinking cup of Ares.[48]

CHAPTER 5

The speech, then, is composed of these things, and the principle of diction is to speak correctly.[49] This consists in five things. First is [the proper
use of] connective particles, if someone assigns them as they naturally
arise in relation to one another, the earlier and the later—the sort of thing
some of them require, just as "on the one hand" [*men*] requires "on the
other hand" [*de*] and "I, on the one hand" [*egō men*] requires "he, on the
other hand" [*ho de*]. [The speaker] must also assign this reciprocal relation while [the listener] still remembers [the first particle], and he must

43 · See Plato, *Republic* 469c-e, 488a-b, and 601a-b; in each case Aristotle's rendering
differs slightly from the original as we have it.
44 · Pericles (ca. 495–429) was the great statesman leading democratic Athens. Presumably oaks are cut down by oak-handled axes.
45 · Evidently not the great orator, but the renowned Athenian general (d. 413) whose
exploits appear in Thucydides' *War of the Peloponnesians and Athenians*.
46 · An Athenian orator about whom little is known.
47 · Literally, "lacking a *logos*." As Cope suggests, "Similes [are] metaphors without the
descriptive details (the detailed explanation)."
48 · The drinking cup is to Dionysus (god of wine) as the shield is to Ares (god of war).
The metaphor involves transferring to the drinking cup the name associated with its
analogue, the shield.
49 · Literally, "to Hellenize," that is, to speak (correct) Greek.

not separate them by a great distance or assign another connective par-   25
ticle ahead of the necessary one, for this is rarely fitting. "But [*de*] I, since
he told me—for Cleon came in, asking as well as demanding—went off,
taking them with me": in these [clauses] there are many connective particles that have been set ahead of the particle to be assigned, and if [the
clauses] that intervene before the phrase "went off" are numerous, it becomes unclear.   30

So one part of [speaking] well is bound up with connective particles,
and a second is to speak using specific names for things and not generic
ones. Third, not using ambiguous terms, and [avoiding] these unless one
chooses to do the contrary, which is in fact what people do when they have
nothing to say but pretend to say something nonetheless. For such people
say these things in poetry—for example, Empedocles.[50] For what is long   35
and circuitous hoodwinks people, and his listeners suffer what in fact the
many do with the prophets: when the prophets speak ambiguously, the
people go right along with it.

Croesus, in crossing the Halys, will destroy a great empire.[51]   1407b

And because speaking generally is less prone to error, the prophets speak
of a given matter by way of general terms,[52] for in games of even-or-odd,
someone would more likely hit upon [the right answer] by saying "even"
or "odd" rather than a specific quantity, or *that* something will be rather
than *when* it will be, so that those who utter prophecies do not specify the   5
when. So quite all of these are similar and—unless they [are chosen] for
some such reason [as the one stated]—should be avoided.

Fourth, as Protagoras used to divide the genera of nouns, male and
female and inanimate,[53] for one must assign these things correctly too.

---

50 · Empedocles of Agrigentum (ca. 495–430) was among the greatest of the pre-
Socratic philosophers.

51 · Croesus, king of Lydia (ca. 595–546), famously asked the oracles of Delphi and
Amphiaraus whether he would succeed in conquering Cyrus the Great, King of Persia
(as is implied by "crossing the Halys" river). The reply here recorded (see also Herodotus 1.53) is a famous example of the ambiguity of oracles: the empire that Croesus destroyed was, of course, his own.

52 · Literally, "the genera."

53 · Literally, "implements," "inanimate objects" (*skeuē*). Greek nouns were either masculine, feminine, or neuter—although Cope contends that "genera" here is "*not* the now recognized grammatical classification of 'genders of nouns', masculine, feminine, and neuter.
[Genera] is ... simply 'classes'" (emphasis original). Evidently Protagoras was concerned,

"And upon arriving and then conversing, she left."[54] Fifth is the correct
10   expression pertaining to many and few and one: "Upon arriving, they began to beat me."[55] In general, what has been written must be easy to read
and easy to recite—in fact these are the same thing. It is this that [writ-
ings with] many connective particles, and that are not easy to punctuate,
lack—as with the writings of Heraclitus. For it is a task to punctuate Her-
15   aclitus's writings, owing to the lack of clarity as to just what he has placed
with which of two words, whether to this one that follows or that one that
precedes—for example, at the very beginning of his composition. For he
there asserts: "Of this *logos* that is always human beings are uncomprehending," and it is unclear to which word the "always" belongs.[56]

Further, not assigning [the correct term] creates a solecism, if you fail
20   to link [two] words with what can fit with both—for example, in the case
of sound and color, "seeing" is not common to them, whereas "perceiving" is common to them. It is unclear, too, if you do not say what you are
proposing when you then go on to throw in many things in the middle
[of the sentence]. For example, "I was going to—once I'd conversed with
him about this and that and thus—go on my way" rather than "I was going to be on my way, once I'd conversed with him, and then this and that
25   happened in this way."

CHAPTER 6

These things contribute to an expansive[57] sort of diction: using a definition of something rather than its name—for example, not "circle," but "a

---

not with grammatical gender, but with "natural gender of nouns based on gender-based
word endings" (Burkett ad loc.). Consider also *Sophistical Refutations* 173b18–25.

54 · The two participles ("arriving" and "conversing") are in the feminine singular, as
required by the feminine singular subject (compare the preceding note).

55 · The plural participle agrees with the plural main verb. "Few," which is bracketed
by some editors, may (according to the medieval commentator Victorius) be alluding
to the dual voice in Greek, which refers to two, and so is between the singular subject
and the plural (more than two).

56 · The "always" may go together with the *logos* that is always, or with the human beings who are always uncomprehending.

57 · The term Aristotle here uses (*ongkos*) is ambiguous. It means, literally, "bulk" or
"mass" and can have either a positive ("expansive," "lofty") or negative ("bulky," "in-
flated," "overdone") connotation. Here it seems closely akin to amplification, since its
opposite contributes to "concision."

plane [all of whose points] are an equal distance from the center." The opposite contributes to concision—that is, using a name instead of the definition. Also, if something is shameful or inappropriate: if what is shameful resides in the definition, say the name, but if in the name, use the definition. Clarify by means of metaphor and epithets, while guarding against the poetic. Make the one thing many, just as the poets write; although there is only one harbor, they say "to Achaean harbors" and "of [my] writing tablet these are the many-leaved folds."[58] And do not link up [two words with a single definite article] but give each one its own: "of that wife of ours." But if [one wishes to speak] concisely, do the opposite: "of our wife." And speak with connective particles, or without them for concision, but do not omit a grammatical connection: "having left and having conversed," "having left, I conversed."[59] And there is Antimachus's useful [device] of speaking on the basis of [qualities] something does not possess, as he does in regard to Teumessus: "There is a windy little hill."[60] For in this way amplification may be carried out indefinitely. And this [use of] what something is not, is applicable to things good and bad, whichever way may be more useful. Hence also the names that the poets apply, the "stringless" and "lyreless" tune, for they apply [adjectives] to things based on what they lack. This way of speaking in metaphors by way of analogy is well regarded—for example, asserting that the [sound of the] trumpet is a "lyreless tune."

CHAPTER 7

Diction will also comprise what is fitting if it conveys [the speaker's] passion [or emotion] and character, and is proportional to the underlying subject matter. "Proportional" means if what concerns weighty matters is not spoken of offhandedly nor what concerns trivial ones solemnly; and if no ornamentation is attached to a trivial noun. Otherwise it appears to

58 · Cope indicates that Euripides uses the plural of "harbor" (when he means the singular) five times, Sophocles once—though this precise line is found in neither poet. The second quotation is found in Euripides, *Iphigenia in Taurus* 727.

59 · The suggestion seems to be that the latter expression, which is without an explicit conjunction, is the more concise. The "grammatical connection" in this case is the relation between the participle and the finite verb.

60 · Antimachus was an Athenian orator and poet (fl. ca. 400) about whom little is known. It is said that the line quoted comes from his epic *Thebaid*. Apparently Antimachus devoted several lines to describing the qualities the hill did *not* possess.

15   be comedy—for example, what Cleophon[61] writes, for he used to speak
     of some things just as one might say, "O Lady fig!"
         [Diction] is marked by passion [or emotion] if there is insolence at is-
     sue and the diction is that of someone angry; and if there are impious and
     shameful things involved, [the diction] is that of a disgusted person who
     is wary even of speaking of them; and if there are praiseworthy things,
     then [one speaks] admiringly, and if pitiable things, humbly, and similarly
20   in the other cases. The appropriate diction also makes the matter at hand
     credible. For the soul reasons mistakenly that what is being said is true be-
     cause people are themselves in a similar state under such and such circum-
     stances, and so they suppose that the matters at issue are just as the speaker
     says—even if that is not the case; and the listener always shares in the pas-
     sion of the passionate speaker, even if the latter makes no sense. Hence
25   many speakers leave the listeners dumbstruck by creating a tumultuous
     uproar.
         And this way of establishing something, based on the relevant signs,
     is indicative also of character in that that which is fitting for each genus
30   and characteristic state accompanies it. I mean by "genus" what pertains
     to age—for example, a boy or a man or an elder—and a woman or a man,
     and a Laconian[62] or Thessalian; and by "characteristic states," those things
     in reference to which someone is a certain sort of person in his life, since
     it is not in reference to each and every characteristic state that lives are of
     a certain sort. If then someone states the words appropriate to his char-
     acteristic state, he will foster [a sense of his] character. For a rube and an
     educated person would not say the same things or even speak in a similar
     way. And listeners are affected in some way by the device the speechwrit-
     ers use to excess: "Who does not know . . . ?" [and] "things that everybody
35   knows." For the listener, in his shame, agrees so that he may share in what
     everybody else [is said to know] too.
         And using these things in a timely or untimely way belongs in com-
1408b mon to quite all the kinds [of rhetoric]. A remedy for every hyperbole is
     the well-worn [device] of the speaker himself being the first to criticize[63]

61 · An Athenian tragic poet about whom little is known. Aristotle mentions him also
at *Poetics* 1448a12 and 1458a19.

62 · That is, a Spartan.

63 · The MSS read *prosepiplēttein* ("criticize in addition") instead of the modern emendation *proepiplēttein*, based in part on Quintilian's quotation of the phrase in Greek
(*Institutes* 8.3.37)—although he does not cite Aristotle by name.

himself, for then [the point expressed by the hyperbole] seems to be true, since the speaker is not unaware of what he is doing. Further, one must not make simultaneous use of all these proportions [that is, of analogous   5 effects of sense and sound], for in refraining from doing so the [artifice] is kept concealed from the listener. I mean, for example, if the words are harsh, then the tone of voice and the countenance must not accord with them too.[64] Otherwise, what each of them is becomes manifest. But if [the speaker does] the one but not the other, then it escapes the notice [of the listener] that what [the speaker] is doing amounts to the same thing. (Now, if gentle things are stated harshly and harsh things gently, [it is true,] it becomes unpersuasive.[65]) Compound words and   10 a greater number of epithets and especially foreign terms are fitting for someone speaking in a passionate [or emotional] way, for there is latitude granted to someone who, in his anger, states that an evil is "heavenhigh" or saying that it is a "monstrosity."[66] And whenever he already has a hold on his audience and puts them in an enthusiastic state by means of either praise or blame or anger or friendship—as also Isocrates does,   15 for example, at the end of the *Panegyricus*: "fame and judgment"[67] and "they who dared."[68] For those in the grip of enthusiasm utter such things, and it is clear as a result that people accept them [from the speaker] because they are in a similar state themselves. Hence it fits with poetry, for poetry is marked by enthusiasm. So either it must be used in this way, or ironically—just as Gorgias used to use it, and like the remarks in the   20 *Phaedrus*.[69]

64 · Reading Kassel's text. The MSS would read, in translation, "the tone of voice and the face, and the things that accord with these, [must not be harsh too]."

65 · The reading of the MSS. Thurot suggests reading "persuasive" instead of "unpersuasive," since this would seem to accord better with the immediately preceding sentence.

66 · "Heaven-high" is a compound word, and the form of the word here translated as "monstrosity" is an alternative form (*pelōrion* for *pelōr*) and to that extent "foreign"; see also 3.3 (1406a8), where the latter term is used as an example of a "dialect" or unusual term.

67 · The reading of the MSS (*phēmē de kai gnōmē*). But the text of the *Panegyricus* (186) as we have it reads instead "fame and memory" (*phēmē de kai mnēmē*).

68 · Isocrates, *Panegyricus* 96; the verb (*etlēsan*) is poetic and rare in Attic prose. (In fact the MSS of Isocrates read the regular prose form of the verb, *etolmēsan*, although they have been "corrected" by editors on the basis of this passage of the *Rhetoric*.)

69 · For a possible example of Gorgias's irony, cited by Aristotle, see *Politics* 1275b25–30. For the relevant passages in Plato's *Phaedrus*, consider 231d and 241e.

CHAPTER 8

The form of diction should be neither in meter nor altogether without
rhythm. The former is unpersuasive—it seems to have been fabricated—
and is at the same time distracting. For it prompts [the listener] to pay
attention to the reoccurrence of the similar [rhythm, instead of to the
25 speech itself], just as when children anticipate the cry of the heralds—
"Whom does the freedman choose as his representative?"—with their
"Cleon!"[70] As for what is without rhythm, it is unlimited [or indefinite],
whereas it must be limited [or made definite] (though not by meter), for
what is unlimited [or indefinite] is unpleasing and unknowable. Now, all
things are limited [or made definite] by number, and the number char-
30 acteristic of diction is rhythm, of which meters are divisions. Hence the
speech must have rhythm but not meter, for in that case it will be a poem.
And the rhythm should not be a precise one, and this will be the case if it
is rhythmic only up to a certain point.

As for rhythms, the heroic is solemn and lacking in the harmony characteristic of conversation,[71] whereas the iambic is the very diction of
35 the many. Hence all speakers give voice to iambic meters especially. But
[a speech] must have solemnity and be moving. The trochaic is too much
1409a like the cordax,[72] as [trochaic] tetrameters make clear, for tetrameters are
a tripping rhythm.[73] There remains the paean, which those beginning
from Thrasymachus on used to use, but they were unable to say what its
defining character was. But the paean is the third kind of rhythm, since it
5 is connected to the ones mentioned. For it is three-to-two, whereas, of the
other rhythms, the one is one-to-one, the other two-to-one; and the one-
and-a-half is [between] these ratios—and this is the paean.[74] The other

70 · A freed slave could not represent himself in court proceedings. Cleon (d. 422) was
a notorious leader of the Athenian *demos* in the Peloponnesian War. For speculation as
to the meaning of this remark, consider Cope (ad loc.).

71 · Here I adopt the reading suggested by Cope. The MSS read "the heroic is solemn
and conversational [*lektikos*] and lacking in harmony." But it is odd to think of, say,
Homer's *Iliad* as either conversational or lacking in harmony. Various emendations
have been proposed, including the addition of a negative before "conversational."

72 · That is, a comic dance.

73 · A trochaic tetrameter is a line of poetry consisting of four long-short feet.

74 · The heroic rhythm, which includes dactyls (one long, two short syllables), spond-
ees (two long), and anapests (two short, one long), is characterized by a ratio of 1:1,
since two short syllables are equivalent to one long syllable. The trochaic (one long,
one short) and iambic (one short, one long) are characterized by a ratio of 2:1 for the

rhythms must be set aside both for the reasons stated and because they are characteristic of meter. The paean, however, must be retained. For of the rhythms mentioned it alone is not a meter, and as a result it most of all goes unnoticed. Nowadays people make use of a single [kind of] paean   10 both when they begin and when they come to the end [of a sentence],[75] but the end should differ from the beginning. There are two forms of paean that lie opposite one another, of which the one does fit with the beginning, just as people in fact use it; and this is the paean that begins with the long [syllable] and ends with three short:

Delos-born or perhaps Lycian

and   15

Golden-haired far-darter, son of Zeus.

But the other paean proceeds in the opposite way, with three short syllables at the beginning and the long one at the end:

After earth and [her] waters / Night obscured Oceanus.[76]

And this creates the ending, for the short syllable, because it is incomplete, creates a truncated [rhythm]; one should instead break off the line with the long syllable and make the ending clear, not by way of the scribe   20 or a marginal annotation but by the rhythm [itself].

That diction, then, should have a good rhythm and not be without rhythm, and what rhythms create good rhythm, and what they are like, have been stated.

CHAPTER 9

Diction is necessarily either "strung together" and made one by the connective particle, just as with the preludes in dithyrambs, or "turned down"   25 and similar to the antistrophes of the ancient poets. Now, the strung to-

---

same reason. Hence the paean, being composed of three short and one long syllable, is characterized by a ratio 3:2 or 1½:1.

75 · The phrase "and when they come to the end" does not appear in the MSS, but modern editors, following Spengel, adopt it.

76 · It is impossible to convey the meters in translation. The lines transliterated are as follows: *Dālŏgĕnĕs / eī tĕ Lŭkĭan* and *khrŭsĕŏkŏmā Hĕkătĕ / pai Dios* and *mĕtă dĕ gān / hŭdătă ōkĕŏnŏn ĕphănĭsĕ nŭx*. The first two quotations are paeans to Apollo; all three quotations have been attributed to Simonides.

gether sort of diction is the ancient one: "This is the setting-forth of the inquiry of Herodotus of Thurii."[77] For quite all used this previously, but
30   now not many do. I mean by "strung together" that which has no end in itself, unless the matter being spoken of comes to an end. But this is unpleasant because it is unlimited, since everyone wishes to glimpse the end. That is why people gasp for breath and collapse only at the finish line, for when seeing the goal ahead of them they do not flag before [they reach it].

35   This, then, is the strung-together sort of diction, but the "turned-down" sort of diction consists of periods. I mean by "period" diction that has a beginning and an end, itself in itself, and that is of a size that is read-
1409b ily surveyable at a glance. Such diction is pleasant and easy to learn—pleasant on account of its being the opposite of the limitless and because the listener always supposes that he has got hold of something and that he is always drawing some conclusion for himself, whereas it is unpleasant not to foresee something or not to finish something. Such diction is
5   easy to learn because it is easy to commit to memory; this is so because periodic diction has number, which is the easiest thing of all to remember. Hence everyone remembers meters [or verse] to a greater degree than what is set forth in prose, since verses have number by which they are measured. The period must come to completion also with the thought
10   involved and not be cut off abruptly, as with Sophocles's iambs:

Calydon is this land of the territory of Pelops.

For the contrary supposition [to what is actually meant] is caused by a line's being divided, just as in the case mentioned—that the Calydonian land belongs to the Peloponnesus.[78]

    A period consists of clauses, on the one hand, or it is simple, on the

77 · An approximation of the first sentence of Herodotus's *Histories* as it has come down to us (although our MSS read "Halicarnassus" instead of "Thurii"). Kassel brackets the phrase, but it is present in the MSS. As Kennedy (240 n. 95) observes, "Though Herodotus' work in general is an example of strung-on diction, the opening sentence does not illustrate the use of connectives."

78 · Although Aristotle attributes the line to Sophocles, it is apparently the first line of Euripides's lost *Meleager* (Nauck fr. 515). As the next line of the play makes clear (cited in Freese ad loc.), Calydon is separated from the Peloponnesus by the Straits of Corinth: "Calydon is this land, from the territory of Pelops / Across the strait, with its prosperous fields." The line in isolation, however, is misleading, since the word for "territory," in the genitive case, would seem to mean "*of* the territory of Pelops," rather than (as the next line makes clear) "across the strait *from* the territory of Pelops."

other.[79] Diction [characterized by a period consisting of] clauses is both complete and distinct as well as readily stated in one breath—not, how-   15
ever, in [an arbitrary] division (just as is the case with the period men-
tioned above) but as a whole.[80] A clause is one or the other part of this
period, and I mean by a "simple" [period one that has only] a single clause.
The clauses and the periods must be neither curtailed nor long, for the
short one often causes the listener to stumble. This is necessarily the case   20
whenever [the listener] is still hurrying on toward what comes next and
in accord with the meter, of which the listener has within himself his own
[sense of its] demarcation, and he is drawn up short when [the speaker]
stops—it is as if he stumbles, on account of the abrupt ending. But as
for long clauses, they make it so that [the listener] is left behind, just like
those who turn back only once they are well beyond the goal post [in a
chariot race], for they, too, leave behind those who are going along with
them. Similarly, periods that are long amount to a speech and are similar   25
to a dithyrambic prelude. As a result, there is the joke that Democritus
the Chian made about Melanippides, who wrote preludes instead of antistrophes:

> A man does bad things to himself in doing bad things to another,
> And the long prelude is worst for him who wrote it.[81]

For this sort of thing applies also to stating long clauses. And clauses that   30
are excessively short do not constitute a period. These latter, then, carry
the listener along at a breakneck speed.

Of the diction consisting in clauses, the one is "divided," the other
"opposed"—divided being, for example: "Many times I wondered at
those who gathered the general assemblies together and instituted the   35
gymnastic contests"; opposed, that in which, in each clause, one opposite
is set together with the other, or the same word has been yoked to oppo-   1410a
sites, for example: "They benefited both, both those who stayed behind
and those who followed along. For the latter they caused to acquire more

79 · Kōla (literally, "limbs" or "members of a body") are either clauses or phrases that
have "some grammatical independence" (Kennedy 241 n. 100). A single clause (kōlon)
may constitute a period, but where two clauses do so, they may be either "divided"
(i.e., parallel to one another) or "contrasted": see just below at 1409b32 and following.
80 · Kassel brackets the clause, "just as . . . ," but it is present in the MSS.
81 · Democritus of Chios was evidently a musician. Melanippides, a dithyrambic poet
from Melos, is mentioned by Xenophon at Memorabilia 1.4.3. The second line is a par-
ody of Hesiod, Works and Days 265: "And the bad plan is worst for him who planned it."

than they had at home, and the former they left with enough at home."
"Staying behind" and "following along" are opposed, as are "enough" and
"more." "As a result, [they are beneficial] both to those who need money
and to those who wish to enjoy it"—"enjoyment" lying opposite "acquisition." And, further: "It often happens that in these circumstances the
prudent miss the mark and the imprudent succeed." "Immediately they
were deemed to deserve the first prizes, and not long after they gained the
rule of the sea." "Sailing over the mainland and marching across the sea,
yoking the Hellespont and digging through Athos." "And being by nature
citizens, by law they were deprived of their city." "For some of them badly
perished, the others were shamefully saved." And: "privately to use barbarian servants, but publicly to overlook the enslavement of many allies."
"Either to possess it while alive or to bequeath it when dead."[82] And what
someone said in regard to Pitholaus and Lycophron in the courtroom:
"These men, when at home, sold you, but having come here they bought
you."[83] All of these together do what was stated. And this sort of diction is
pleasing because the opposites are very readily recognized and even more
so when placed side by side, and because it is like a syllogism, for refutation is a bringing together of opposites.

Such, then, is "antithesis," and it is "parisosis" if the clauses are equal,
"paromoiosis" if each clause has endings that are similar, and this is necessarily so either at the beginning or at the end. At the beginning, the words
[in their entirety] are always [similar]; at the end, the similarity appears
in the last syllables or in the inflection of the same word or [the repetition of] the same word. At the beginning, there are such things as "For he
got idle land from him."[84] "They were both open to gifts and movable by
words."[85] At the end: "You might have supposed him not to have fathered
a child, but to have been a child himself."[86] "Amid the greatest concerns

82 · All the quotations in the paragraph to this point are taken, more or less exactly,
from Isocrates, *Panegyricus* (see 1, 35, 41, 48, 72, 89, 105, 149, 181, 186).
83 · Pitholaus and Lycophron were brothers of Thebe, wife of Alexander of Pherae.
Urged on by her, they assassinated their brother-in-law and thus came to power. The
precise meaning of the quotation is uncertain, although the general sense—that
the very people who were once sold out (or into slavery?) by the two men have now
been bribed by them—seems clear enough.
84 · Aristophanes fr. 649 (Kock). The word for "land" is *agron*, that for "idle" is *argon*.
Thus the line is a sort of jingle.
85 · Homer, *Iliad* 9.526. Here "open to gifts" is *dōrētoi*; "movable," *pararrētoi*.
86 · The text is uncertain, as is the authorship. The first clause ends with the infinitive
tetokenai, the second with the infinitive *gegonenai*.

and the slightest hopes."[87] Inflections of the same word: "Worthy of being set up as a statue in bronze, while not being worth a bronze penny?"[88] And the same word: "You used to speak ill of him even when he was alive and now too you write ill of him." And based on the [same] syllable: "What terrible thing would you have suffered, if you had seen a man idle?"[89] It is also possible for the same [period] to have all these things at the same time, that is, antithesis and equality of clauses [*parisos*] and similarity of endings. The beginnings of periods were fairly thoroughly enumerated in the *Theodectea*.[90] But there are also false antitheses—for example, as Epicharmus once wrote:

At one time I was among them, at another I was with them.[91]

CHAPTER 10

Since what concerns these things has been defined, the source of urbane and well-regarded sayings must be stated. Now, producing such sayings belongs to someone with the natural gift for it or to one who has been so trained, but showing what they are belongs to this inquiry. Let us speak of this, then, and give a thorough enumeration; and let this be our starting point: learning something easily is pleasant by nature for everyone, and words signify something; the result is that all those words that prompt us to learn something are most pleasant. Dialect [or unusual] terms are unknown, but we do know words whose meaning is prevalent. It is metaphor that does this especially, for when [the poet] says that old age is a "dried stalk,"[92] he fosters learning and understanding through the genus involved in the metaphor, for both are withered. The similes of the poets do the same thing; and therefore, if it is well done, it appears urbane.

35

1410b

5

10

15

87 · "Concerns" is *phrontesi*; "hopes," *elpisin*. The source is unknown.
88 · That is, the subject in question is thought to be worth a bronze statue (*chalkous*), when in fact he is not worth a bronze (*chalkou*) penny.
89 · Here the last syllable of the word at the end of one clause (*deinon*: "terrible") is repeated in the last syllable of the last word at the end of the other clause (*argon*: "idle").
90 · A work thought to have been composed by Aristotle in honor of his deceased friend Theodectes, whom Aristotle quotes several times in the *Rhetoric*.
91 · Epicharmus was a comic writer and playwright from Sicily, active in the first quarter of the fifth century; see also 1365a16 above. The first part of the clause suggests "in their home," the second more broadly being with them. But since the latter surely can include the former, the antithesis is a false one.
92 · Homer, *Odyssey* 14.214.

For the simile—just as was said before[93]—is a metaphor that differs in the way it is set forth.[94] Hence it is less pleasant because it is longer; it does not say that *this* is *that*, and so the soul [of the listener] does not inquire about it. And so it is necessarily the case that, when it comes to both diction and enthymemes, all those are urbane that foster in us rapid learning. Hence superficial enthymemes are not well regarded (for we say that things clear to everyone, and which nobody need inquire about, are superficial), nor are all those that, when stated, are not understood. Instead, all those enthymemes that are understood as soon as they are stated (although there was no such understanding before) or that are grasped shortly thereafter, *are* well regarded. For [in these ways] a sort of learning arises; otherwise, there is neither [immediate nor all-but-immediate learning]. As regards the understanding of what is being said, then, such enthymemes are well regarded.

But as for diction, in regard to the form [of the period or its clauses], if it is stated antithetically, [it will be well regarded]. For example, "believing the peace shared by the others to be a war against their own private [interests]"[95]—"war" being antithetical to "peace." As for words, [they are well regarded] if they contain a metaphor, and this not a foreign one (for then it is difficult to comprehend), nor superficial (for then it does not produce any effect [in the listener]). Further, [expressions will be well regarded] by making things appear before the eyes [of the audience]: they should see things actually being done rather than what is going to be done. One must therefore aim at these three things: metaphor, antithesis, [and] realized activity.[96]

Of the four kinds of metaphors, the most well-regarded are those based on analogy, as Pericles said that the youth that perished in the war had vanished from the city just as if someone should remove the spring from the year.[97] And [as] Leptines said about the Lacedaemonians, that

---

93 · Consider 3.4 above.

94 · Reading *prothesi* with some MSS and most modern editors. Also possible is the slight variant *prosthesi*: "that differs in what is added to it," namely, the word *hōs* ("as" or "like").

95 · See Isocrates, *Philippus* 73; Aristotle has altered the wording slightly.

96 · "Realized activity" attempts to translate the famous Aristotelian term *energeia*, a state of being active, a potential or capacity realized. Here the stress is on the lively image created in the mind of the audience by the speaker's language. See also 3.11 below.

97 · The same line, which does not appear in Pericles' funeral oration as recorded by Thucydides, is referred to above at 1365a31–33.

he would not allow [the Athenian assembly] to overlook Greece's becom-   5
ing one-eyed.[98] When Chares was seriously urging that he be audited in
connection with [his conduct] of affairs during the Olynthian war, Cephisodotus was indignant, claiming that Chares was trying to have his
audit conducted while he had the *demos* by the throat.[99] [Cephisodotus]
also once encouraged the Athenians to march out to Euboea [immedi-
ately], saying that they must there provision themselves, in the manner   10
of Miltiades's decree.[100] And Iphicrates, after the Athenians had signed a
treaty with Epidaurus and the coastal [cities], was indignant,[101] claiming
that they had deprived themselves of a daily allowance for the war.[102] And
Peitholaus [called] the *Paralus*[103] "cudgel of the *demos*" and Sestos "the
corn-bin of the Piraeus."[104] And Pericles bade [the Athenians] get rid of   15
Aegina, "the eyesore of the Piraeus." Moerocles asserted that he was no
more a scoundrel than (naming someone among the respectable), for that
fellow is a scoundrel at 33 percent interest, whereas he himself takes only
10 percent. And the iambic line of Anaxandrides,[105] on daughters who
delay getting married:

98 · After the disastrous Athenian defeat at Leuctra in 371 and subsequent invasion of
the Thebans, the Lacedaemonians sent an embassy to Athens; the metaphor suggests
that the defeat of Athens amounts to Greece losing one of her two eyes, the other of
course being or belonging to the Lacedaemonians.

99 · A Cephisodotus is mentioned also at 1407a9, where he is identified as "the Skinny."
The text here is uncertain; some editors suggest a reading that would have Cephi-
sodotus accusing Chares of trying to shove his accounts down the throat of the people.
An "audit" was an official review at the conclusion of a public official's term of office.

100 · As the scholiast on this passage indicates, Miltiades (ca. 550–489) marched out
from Athens to ward off the attacking Persians, without permitting debate and hence
without delay. The text is somewhat uncertain, although the general point seems clear.

101 · Not the word elsewhere translated as "indignation" (*nemesis*: see 2.9) but
aganakteō—"to be vexed or indignantly angry."

102 · The word translated "daily allowance" means more literally "the supplies one
takes on a journey, one's daily rations." Epidaurus was a Spartan ally and hence enemy
of Athens; Iphicrates is indignant because he thinks the truce struck amounts to Athens voluntarily giving up the resources it could gain from plundering it and such other
coastal cities as are easily within its grasp.

103 · One of the two official state ships of Athens, the other being the *Salaminia*.

104 · Sestos was a town on the Hellespont, evidently the site of corn sales; the Piraeus was
the seaport of Athens through which the many supplies on which it depended would pass.

105 · A comic poet (Kock fr. 68); see also 3.11 (1412b16). The term here translated as "in
arrears" is a legal term of Athenian law and indicates someone who has failed to pay a
fine by the court-appointed date.

20   When it comes to marriage my maidens are in arrears.

And the remark of Polyeuctes concerning a certain paralyzed man, Speu-
sippus, that "he can't keep still, bound by chance in a five-holed pillory
of illness." Cephisodotus used to call the triremes "multicolored mills,"[106]
25   and the Cynic used to call taverns "the Attic common messes."[107] And Ae-
sion [used to say] that they had "drained the city into Sicily," for this is a
metaphor and puts the matter before one's eyes.[108] And "so that Greece
cried out." This too is in a certain manner a metaphor and puts the matter before one's eyes. And just as Cephisodotus bade [the Athenians]
30   be careful lest they make of their many unruly mobs an assembly. Also,
as Isocrates [said] in regard to those who "run together" in public festivals.[109] And, for example, in the funeral oration, that it was right for
Greece to cut its hair in mourning over the tomb of those who met their
end at Salamis, on the grounds that its freedom was being buried alongside their virtue.[110] For if he had said [only] that it was right [for Greece]
35   to weep for the virtue being buried alongside [them], it would be a meta-
1411b   phor and put the matter before one's eyes, but the "freedom . . . virtue"
clause contains a certain antithesis. And as Iphicrates said, "the path of
my speeches is right through the middle of the deeds done by Chares": it
is a metaphor involving analogy, and the "right through the middle" puts
5   the matter before one's eyes. And asserting that "dangers call in dangers
for assistance" puts the matter before one's eyes and is a metaphor. And
Lycoleon on behalf of Chabrias [said]: "They feel no respectful awe at all
before his suppliant [statue], the bronze image"—a metaphor for that

106 · Triremes were warships, the backbone of the Athenian naval empire, and evidently were brightly colored. The implication of the metaphor is that the ships were
used for grinding down the tributary allies.

107 · Teetotaling Sparta was famous for its common messes, where all male citizens ate
together; the Attic (or Athenian) equivalent is here said to be the taverns.

108 · A reference to Athens' disastrous attempt to subdue the island of Sicily in the
course of the Peloponnesian War.

109 · See Isocrates, *Philippus* 12: "But nevertheless, overlooking all these difficulties, I
have become so ambitious in old age that I wished, by addressing my remarks to you,
at the same time to make it manifest, to those who spend time with me, that to burden
our public festivals with oratory and to address quite all those who there run together
is really to address no one at all in them; rather, such speeches are as ineffective as the
regimes written by the sophists."

110 · The line is attributed to Lysias.

moment but not forever, though it is before one's eyes, for it is only while
[Chabrias] is in danger that the statue supplicates, the inanimate being in-   10
deed animate, a reminder of his deeds done on behalf of the city.[111] And
"in every way practicing to be small-minded," since "practicing" is to in-
crease something. And that "the god kindled the mind as a light in the
soul," for both make something clear. "For we do not end wars but post-
pone them," for both are bound up with what is going to happen—both   15
postponement and a peace of that sort. And asserting that "treaties are a
much more beautiful trophy than the kind that arises in warfare," for the
latter concern small things and a single stroke of luck, whereas the former
concerns the entire war, both being a sign of victory. And that "cities must
pay a great assessment[112] through the blame placed on them by human be-   20
ings," for such an assessment is a sort of judicial penalty.

That urbane sayings arise from metaphor by analogy, and by setting
things before one's eyes, has been stated.

CHAPTER 11

But it must be stated what we mean by "before one's eyes," and what makes
this happen. So I say that all those [expressions] that signify things in a   25
state of activity or actuality in effect put things "before one's eyes."[113] For
example, contending that the good man is "four-square"[114] is a metaphor,
for both [the good man and the square] are complete, but [the metaphor]
does not signify any activity. Instead, "with his flower in full bloom"[115]

---

111 · Chabrias was an Athenian general (d. 357). In recognition of an earlier military
victory near Thebes in 378, the Athenian people had erected a statue of Chabrias in
a kneeling posture, the same one in which his soldiers had faced the enemy. Later, in
366, he was brought to trial on a charge of military misconduct, and Lycoleon defended
him, in part by appealing to the statue that Lycoleon then interpreted as being in a sup-
plicating (rather than defiant) posture. Cope calls the last part of this sentence "very
obscure"—and with reason.

112 · The phrase includes the word (*euthuna*) translated just above (at 1411a6) as "audit." The idea is that cities held in low regard by human beings pay a heavy price, and
justly so.

113 · "A state of activity or actuality" attempts to convey the meaning here of *energeia*;
see also n. 96 above.

114 · Consider, e.g., the discussion of a line of Simonides that describes a man as being
"four-square": Plato, *Protagoras* 339b1–3 and context.

115 · Isocrates, *Philippus* 10.

conveys such activity or actuality, as does "you, just like an animal grazing
30   at will";[116] "now then the Greeks, darting forward on their feet":[117] the
"darting forward" is an activity and a metaphor, for it means "quickly."
Homer has also used this in many places, making inanimate things animate by way of a metaphor; in all cases he is well regarded by dint of putting
something into a state of activity, as, for example, in these lines: "Again to-
35   ward the plain rolled the remorseless stone"[118] and an "arrow flew"[119] and
1412a [an arrow] "eagerly fell upon,"[120] and "In the earth [the spears] stood,
longing for their fill of flesh,"[121] and "The point of the spear eagerly sped
through his chest."[122] In all these lines, things appear to be engaged in activity, on account of their being animate, for being shameless and eager
5   and the rest are activities. He applied these things by way of the metaphor
based on analogy, for as the stone is to Sisyphus, so he who acts shamelessly is to one treated shamelessly. And in his well-regarded similes too,
[Homer] does the same with inanimate things: "swelling, foam-speckled;
some in front, but others upon others behind."[123] For he makes all things
10   moving and alive, and activity is motion. But one should form a metaphor (as was said previously) from things that are related but not manifestly so — for example, in philosophy, too, it belongs to a shrewd person
to contemplate that which is similar even in things that are far apart, just
as Archytas[124] said that an arbitrator and an altar are the same thing, for
with both the victim of injustice seeks refuge. Or if someone should assert
15   that an anchor and a hook are the same thing, for in a sense they are the
same thing, but they differ in that one [does what it does] from above, the

116 · Isocrates, *Philippus* 10. "An animal grazing at will" attempts to convey the sense of
apheton, which applied especially to sacred flocks that as such did not labor. Socrates
uses the term to describe the state of Pericles's two sons, left to their own devices in the
hope that they might spontaneously stumble on virtue (Plato, *Protagoras* 320a2 and
context).
117 · Euripides, *Iphigenia in Aulis* 80.
118 · Homer, *Odyssey* 9.598.
119 · Homer, *Iliad* 13.587.
120 · Homer, *Iliad* 4.126.
121 · Homer, *Iliad* 11.574.
122 · Homer, *Iliad* 15.541.
123 · Homer, *Iliad* 13.799. The poet here refers to the waves of the sea, as part of a simile
comparing combat to the motion of the sea.
124 · A Pythagorean philosopher from Tarentum, active in the first half of the fourth
century. See Diogenes Laertius 8.4.79–83.

other from below.[125] And when cities that are far apart from one another are put on an equal footing, this is the same thing as equality in the case of superficies and powers.[126]

Most urbane expressions arise from metaphors and from [the listener's] being deceived [in a sense]. For it becomes clearer that he learned something contrary to what [he thought] was the case, and the soul seems   20
to say, "That's true! But I was wrong." Apothegms marked by urbanity arise from the fact that the speaker does not mean what he [literally] says—for example, the remark of Stesichorus that "the cicadas will sing to themselves from the ground."[127] And those apothegms that pose a good riddle are pleasing for the same reason, for learning occurs [once their meaning is understood], and they are stated by means of a metaphor. This   25
is what Theodorus[128] means by "saying novel things"; this occurs when the remark is paradoxical and is not (as that fellow puts it) "in line with one's prior opinion," but is just like wordplay made up by jokesters.

And jokes [or puns] involving the change of a letter also bring this about, for they involve tricking [the listener]. This occurs in meters [or verse] too, for [the verses do not proceed] as the listener presumed they   30
would: "And he walked on, having on his feet—chilbains," but one supposed that he would say "sandals."[129] This must be clear as soon as it is stated. Those jokes that depend on the change of a letter bring it about that [the speaker] does not mean what he says but what the word means when it is twisted around—for example, the remark of Theodorus about Nicon the citharist: *thrattei se*. For he pretends to be saying, "Something   35
troubles you," and tricks [the listener], since he means something else.[130]

125 · That is, the ship is made stationary from below, whatever is placed on the hook, from above.

126 · The sentence has occasioned much commentary and some emendation. Cope suggests that Aristotle is here speaking of the redistribution of wealth or property and that the word translated as "superficies" (a term from Euclid) means in this context "(surface) area," i.e., land allotments, just as "powers" refers to political offices.

127 · A lyric poet (dates uncertain). The suggestion is that the land will be devastated. The same line, with its context, is stated at 2.21 (1395a1–2), where Aristotle identifies it as an enigmatic or riddling apothegm.

128 · On Theodorus of Byzantium, see 2.23 (1400b16)—a reference to his "art"—as well as 3.13 (1414b13).

129 · "Chilbains" is *chimethla*; "sandals," *pedila*.

130 · As Cope suggests, the same words produce a sound that could mean "You are a Thracian [slave] girl": *Thratt' ei se*.

1412b   Hence it is pleasant to the person who comes to understand it, since if
he does not take Nicon to be a Thracian, [the line] will not seem urbane.
And "you want him to perish."[131]

Both[132] must be stated in an appropriate way, and so too also with
[other] urbane remarks—for example, asserting that, for the Athenians,
5   "the empire [*archē*] of the sea was not the beginning [*archē*] of evils [for
them]," for it benefited them.[133] Or as Isocrates [said] that the city's empire [*archē*] was the beginning [*archē*] of evil things [for it]. For in both
cases, what somebody supposes will not be said *is* said, and then it is recognized to be true. For [in the second example] asserting that the *archē*
is the *archē* is nothing particularly wise, but he means the word in differ-
10   ent senses; and [in the first example] the *archē* that he negates is meant
in a different sense [from the other instance of *archē* in the sentence that
he affirms].

But in quite all these cases, if [the speaker] introduces the word appropriately, by means of homonymy or metaphor, then it is well done. For
example, "unpleasant Pleasance";[134] the homonym is negated, but appropriately, if [the person in question] is unpleasant. And "You should be no
stranger than a stranger" or "not more than you need to be"; this is the
15   same thing as saying, "The stranger should not always be strange," for this
[word "stranger"] is used in a different sense.[135] The same holds for the
lauded remark of Anaxandrides:[136] "Noble indeed it is to die before doing something that is worthy of death." For this is the same thing as saying that it is a worthy thing, for one who is not worthy of dying, to die, or
that it is a worthy thing for him to die, though he is not worthy of dying or

131 · Cope contends that "no satisfactory explanation has hitherto been given of this
pun." The aorist infinitive of the verb *perthō*, here translated as "to perish," is the same
as the noun meaning "Persian women" (*persai*). But Cope wonders whether the pun
consists in the ambiguity of the main verb (*boulei*), which sounds similar to the noun
for Council (*boulē*): "may the Council destroy him."

132 · The referent is ambiguous: either both of the two prior examples, or both statements that are metaphorical and those that turn on the change of a letter (puns).

133 · The word for "empire" (or "rule") is the same as the word for "beginning": *archē*.

134 · This does no more than very loosely approximate the Greek: Anaschetos (a man's
name) is not *anaschetos* ("bearable," "tolerable," "endurable"): Mr. Bearable is unbear-
able.

135 · The word is *xenos*—"foreigner" or "stranger"—and commentators divide on Aristotle's meaning here.

136 · A comic poet, first mentioned at 3.10 (1411a18); his play *Old Man's Madness*
(*Gerontomania*) is mentioned at 3.12 (1413b25).

has not done things worthy of death.[137] The form of diction in these is the   20
same, but insofar as they are stated in fewer words and antithetically, they
are to a greater degree well regarded. The cause of this is that the learning involved arises to a greater degree through such antitheses and arises
more quickly [when stated in] few words. And if what is said is [going to
be seen as] true and not superficial, it must always be related to the person addressed or be correctly stated. It is possible for these things to be   25
separate—for example, "He who has committed no fault must die"—but
that is not urbane. "The worthy man must marry the worthy woman"—
but that is not urbane. If, however, both are present simultaneously, [then
it will be an urbane remark]: "It is a worthy thing to die when one is not
worthy of dying." The more the remark has this [characteristic], the more   30
urbane it appears—for example, if the words should [constitute] a metaphor and a metaphor of a given sort, as well as antithesis and parisosis,
and if it should be characterized by activity.

Similes, as was said also above, are always in a certain manner well-
regarded metaphors.[138] For they are always stated on the basis of two
terms, just as is the metaphor involving analogy. For example, the shield,   35
we contend, is the drinking cup of Ares,[139] and a bow a string-less lyre;   1413a
in this way they are not stated simply, but saying that the bow is a lyre or
the shield a drinking cup is [to speak] simply.[140] And in this way [such ex-
pressions] liken things [to other things]—for example, an aulos-player to
an ape, a nearsighted man to a sputtering lamp, for both [such a man and
lamp] are contracted.[141] The remark is well made when it involves a meta-   5
phor: it is possible to liken the shield to Ares's drinking cup and a fallen
ruin to a household rag; and to assert that Niceratus is a Philoctetes bit-
ten by Pratys, in the image Thrasymachus made on seeing Niceratus de-

137 · The example depends on an ambiguity in the Greek word repeated throughout
here, *axion*, which can mean both "worthy of" (something good) and "deserving"
(something bad): it is a worthy thing to die (nobly) when you haven't done anything
that deserves the death penalty.
138 · The reading of the MSS. Kassel's emendation would translate as "Similes, as was
also said above, that are well regarded are in a certain manner metaphors."
139 · See 3.4, at the end.
140 · The distinction seems to be this: "the shield is the drinking cup of Ares" is a metaphor, but if one speaks of "the drinking cup of Ares," when one means a shield, then
one is speaking "simply."
141 · The commentators suggest that this means an aulos-player leans over as he plays,
in the manner of an ape, and that the eyes of the nearsighted man contract, just as the
flame of a sputtering lamp contracts.

feated by Pratys in a rhapsodic competition, long-haired and unkempt
10   still.[142] It is in these especially that poets fall flat, if they do not do this
well, and are well regarded if they do—I mean whenever they make [two
things] correspond: "He carries his legs like twisty celery"; "like Philammon quarreling with the punching bag." And all such things are similes,
and similes are metaphors, as has been said many times. Proverbs, too, are
15   metaphors taken from one species and applied to another species. For example, if someone takes home something that he has persuaded himself
will be good, and then is harmed by it, it is as the Carpathian says about
the hare,[143] for both suffered what was mentioned.

The sources, then, of urbane remarks, and the cause of their being urbane, have pretty much been stated. But well-regarded hyperboles are
20   metaphors too—for example, regarding someone with a black eye, "you'd
have supposed he's a basket of mulberries." For a black eye is a bit pur-
plish, but the considerable intensity [or vehemence of the characteriza-
tion constitutes the hyperbole]. "This is like *this* or *that*" is a hyperbole
when it differs [from other metaphors] in the diction used: "like Philam-
25   mon quarreling with the punching bag" [is a simile] but "you'd have supposed him to be Philammon battling the punching bag" [is hyperbole].
"He carries his legs like twisty celery" [is a simile] but "you'd have supposed him to have, not legs, but celery stalks, so twisty are they." And hyperboles are characteristic of youth, for they clarify in a most intense [or
30   vehement] way. Hence those who are angry state them most of all.

> Not even if he should give me as many things as are the grains of sand and
>   dust.

> But I will not marry a maiden daughter of Agamemnon, son of Atreus,
> Not even if in beauty she should contend with golden Aphrodite
> And, in her works, with Athena.[144]

142 · Thrasymachus is presumably the famous rhetorician, and the Niceratus here mentioned may be the son of the famous general Nicias; for Niceratus's ability to recite
the whole of the *Iliad* and *Odyssey* from memory, see Xenophon, *Symposium* 3.5–6. Although accounts of Philoctetes vary, most agree that he was stranded on the island of
Lemnos and suffered terribly from a snakebite he there received.
143 · The reading of the MSS. Kassel follows Ross's emendation: "people assert that it
is like the Carpathian and the hare." The details of the proverb are uncertain, though
the gist of it seems clear enough.
144 · Homer, *Iliad* 9.385, 388–90.

(The Attic orators make use of this especially.) Hence it is inappropriate   1413b
for an elder to speak in hyperbole.

CHAPTER 12

It must not have escaped one's notice that a different diction fits with
each kind [of rhetoric]. The diction belonging to written [arguments] is
not the same as that for debate contests—nor for public addresses or ju-   5
dicial proceedings. But it is necessary to know both: the one amounts to
knowing how to speak [the language] correctly,[145] the other to not being compelled to remain silent, if someone wishes to convey something
to others—which is just what happens to those who do not know how
to write. The diction belonging to writing is the most precise; the diction belonging to debate is most appropriate for delivery. Of this latter,   10
there are two forms: that bound up with character and that bound up
with the passions. Hence actors seek out plays of this kind, and poets
seek out such [actors]. But those poets who write to be read are popular
[too]—like Chaeremon[146] (for he is as precise as a speechwriter), and Licymnius among the dithyrambic poets. When they are compared, some
written speeches appear meager in public contests, whereas some orators'   15
speeches, though they may be well delivered, appear amateurish when
read.[147] The cause of this is that [their diction] fits with the public contest [only]. Hence things intended for delivery, when there is no such delivery, appear naïve [or silly] because they do not perform the work that
is theirs—for example, words unconnected [by conjunctions][148] and repeating the same [word] frequently are correctly disapproved of in writ-   20
ing, but in debate they are not disapproved of, and in fact orators use
[these devices], since they are suitable for delivery. (But it is necessary for
those who repeat the same [word] to introduce changes, which paves the
way, as it were, for the delivery.) "This is the fellow who stole from you,
this is the fellow who deceived you, this is the fellow who attempted the
utmost betrayal." Such is what the actor Philemon used to do in Anax-   25
andrides's *Old Man's Madness*, when he says "Rhadamanthus and Pala-

---

145 · Literally, "to Hellenize," that is, to speak correct Greek. See also n. 49 above.
146 · A tragic poet; see also 2.23 (1400b24) and the note there.
147 · Literally, "when in the hands," i.e., when one holds them as written speeches in
one's hands.
148 · Or "asyndeton," our technical term derived from the Greek, here and throughout.

medes," and the "I" in the prologue of *The Pious*.[149] For if someone does not deliver [or act out] such lines, he becomes "the fellow carrying the beam."[150]

Similar, too, is the case of words unconnected [by conjunctions, or asyndeta]. "I came, I met, I asked." For it is necessary to deliver [or act out] these things and not to speak as though one were saying one thing in the same character and tone. Further, words unconnected [by conjunctions] have something peculiar to them: many things seem to have been said in an equal amount of time, since the conjunction makes many things one, such that if it is removed, the opposite will clearly arise, namely, that one will be many; in that case, there is amplification. "I came, I conversed, I supplicated": [the listener] seems to survey the many things [the speaker] said.[151] This is what Homer, too, wishes to do in [the following passage]:

> Nireus, in turn, from Syme . . .
> Nireus son of Aglaia . . .
> Nireus who is most handsome.[152]

For it is necessary that he, about whom many things have been said, be spoken of repeatedly. If he is spoken of repeatedly, then, it also seems that much has been said of him, and the result of this fallacy is that [Nireus] is magnified, though [Homer] mentioned him only in this one instance and thus preserved his memory, though he gave no subsequent account of him anywhere.

Now, diction associated with public speaking is altogether like sketching something in outline, for the greater the crowd, the more distant is their viewpoint; hence in both [public speaking and sketching] precision is beside the point and in fact appears worse. Judicial diction is more precise; that before a single judge is still more so, since rhetoric is least involved there: what is germane to the matter at hand and foreign to it are more readily surveyable [by a single judge], and since the element of a contest is absent, the judgment is unsullied. Hence the same orators are not well regarded in all these [kinds of speaking]. Instead, wherever acting [or performance] is most at work, there precision will least be present,

---

149 · These (comic) plays do not survive.

150 · A proverbial expression suggesting a clumsy or awkward speaker.

151 · The text is uncertain. I follow Cope's reading and suggested translation. Kassel, following Spengel, prints a text that would translate as "I came, I conversed, I supplicated" (these seem to be many things) "he disregarded all that I said."

152 · Homer, *Iliad* 2.671–73.

but it is in such a performance that a voice, and especially a loud voice, is needed.

The diction characteristic of epideictic rhetoric is most like writing, for its proper work is to be read. Second [in similarity to writing] is the judicial. But it is superfluous to specify further that the diction must be pleasing and magnificent.[153] For why this any more than "moderate" and "liberal" or any other moral virtue? It is clear that the points stated will render [the speech] pleasant, if in fact the virtue of diction was correctly defined. For the sake of what, [other than being pleasing], must it be clear and not humble but instead fitting [to its subject matter]? And if it is long-winded, it will not be clear, nor will it be if it is [too] concise. It is clear instead that the middle course is fitting. The points stated will render it pleasing, if the customary and the foreign are well mixed, as well as the rhythm and persuasiveness stemming from what is appropriate to it.

What concerns diction has been stated, then, concerning all [speeches] in common and each kind in particular. It remains to speak about arrangement.

CHAPTER 13

Of the speech there are two parts: it is necessary both to state the subject matter of the speech and to demonstrate it. Hence it is impossible to state [the subject matter] but not offer a demonstration of it or to make a demonstration without initially stating[154] [the subject matter]. For he who demonstrates, demonstrates *something*, and he who initially states something does so for the sake of demonstrating something. Of these, the one is the proposition [concerning the matter at hand], the other the mode of persuasion [or proof], just as if one should define the one as the problem and the other as the demonstration.

But at present people define [these things] in a laughable way. For narration doubtless belongs only to judicial speech, and how can narration, such as they speak of it, belong to epideictic speech or to speech in a public assembly, or to matters pertaining to the rebuttal of an opponent, or to an epilogue attached to demonstrations? A preface, comparison, and recapitulation occur in speeches in the public assembly whenever there is also a speech opposing one's own, for both accusation and

153 · That is, "befitting greatness" (*megaloprepē*).
154 · The verb (*prolegein*) can also mean "proclaim" or "propose."

defense occur frequently [there], but these do not arise insofar as there is
5   the giving of advice [only]. But an epilogue, in addition, does not belong
even in every judicial speech—for example, if the speech is short or the
matter at issue is easily remembered, for [the epilogue] in effect reduces
the length [of the speech that precedes it by summing it up].

The necessary parts [of the speech], therefore, are the proposition
and the mode of persuasion [or proof]. These, then, are proper [to every
speech], and at most there is a preface, proposition, mode of persuasion
[or proof], [and] epilogue. For matters bearing on the rebuttal of an op-
10 ponent belong to the modes of persuasion, and comparison is an amplification of one's own [arguments] such that it [too] is a certain part of the
modes of persuasion, since he who does this demonstrates something,
whereas neither the preface nor the epilogue [is a part of the mode of per-
suasion]; instead, these serve to call things to mind. If, then, one [further]
distinguishes such things, there will be (as in fact Theodorus[155] and his
circle used to have it) a distinction between narration and post-narration
and pre-narration, and refutation and post-refutation. But one must set
15 down a name [only] when one speaks of something with a particular form
and distinct difference; otherwise the name becomes empty and silly—
such as what Licymnius does in his *Art*, using the names "waftings" and
"wandering off" and "branches."

CHAPTER 14

20 The preface is the beginning of a speech—what in poetry is the prologue
and in aulos-playing the prelude. For all of these are beginnings and a sort
of paving of the way for what is to come. The prelude, then, is similar to
the preface in epideictic speeches, for aulos-players, too, start off playing whatever they are good at and attach that to what gives the key to the
25 tune, and one must write epideictic speeches in this way: by stating immediately whatever it is he wishes to say, [the speaker] states the key note
[of the whole speech] and connects it [to what is to come], which is in fact
what everyone does. An example is the preface of Isocrates's *Helen*, for eristic speakers and Helen have nothing in common.[156] At the same time,
even if one departs from the topic, it is fitting for the whole speech not to
be of like form [throughout and hence monotonous].

155 · A rhetorician mentioned also at 2.23 (1400b16) and 3.11 (1412a25).
156 · In the preface (1–13), Isocrates criticizes those given to "eristic" or quarrelsome
speech, before turning to his defense of Helen.

What is said in the prefaces to epideictic speeches proceeds from   30
praise or blame. For example, Gorgias in his *Olympics* speech: "You deserve to be admired by many, Greek men,"[157] for he is praising those who
instituted the public festivals. But Isocrates blames them because they
honored the bodily virtues with gifts, but to those who think well they   35
gave no prize at all.[158] [Such prefaces may proceed] also from advice. For
example, [saying] that "one must honor those who are good"—hence [the
speaker] himself praises Aristides—or [saying that one must honor] those
who are neither well regarded nor base but all those who, though they are
good, are obscure, like Alexander son of Priam.[159] For this [speaker] is [in   1415a
effect] giving advice.

Further, [prefaces to epideictic speeches] may also be based on judicial prefaces. This occurs when they are based on appeals to the listener, if
the speech is about something paradoxical or difficult[160] or already ban-
died about by many, the result being that [the audience] is sympathetic
to the speaker—as with Choerilus's "But nowadays, when all things have
been divvied up."[161] The prefaces of epideictic speeches, then, are based   5
on these things—on praise, blame, exhortation, dissuasion, [and] on appeals to the listener. And the keynotes struck [in the prefaces] must be
either foreign or germane to the speech.

As for the prefaces of judicial speeches, one must grasp that these accomplish the same thing as do dramatic prologues and the prefaces of epic   10
poems (for those belonging to dithyrambs are similar to epideictic prefaces): "on account of you and your gifts and booty."[162] But in speeches[163]
and epic poems, [the preface] is a sample of the argument so that [the au-

157 · This speech delivered by the famous orator does not survive.

158 · Consider Isocrates, *Panegyricus* 1.

159 · "Aristides the Just," as he was known; see also 2.23 above. It is strange that Aristotle calls Alexander (or Paris) "obscure," he who was the immediate cause of the Trojan War. Burkett (ad loc.) suggests that "Aristotle is probably referring to [Alexander's]
early, obscure background on Anatolian Mount Ida before being thrust into history."

160 · As Cope notes, "difficult" here (*chalepos*) may mean either difficult (for the
speaker) to state or difficult (for the listener) to hear.

161 · Choerilus was an epic poet of the late fifth century who hailed from Samos. He
was best known as author of a poem about the Persian War, from which (according to
the scholiast) this line is taken. The poet is here complaining that, in contrast to the poets of old, all the subjects of poetry have by now been taken up by others.

162 · The quotation has been attributed to the dithyrambic poet Timotheus.

163 · The reading of most MSS. Emendations or alternative readings include "prologues and speeches" and "[judicial] speeches."

dience] may know in advance what the speech concerns and their understanding not be kept in suspense, for that which is undetermined leads
[the audience] astray. He, then, who places the beginning into [the listen-
15   er's] hand, as it were, permits him who holds on to it to follow the speech.
So for this reason [there are such beginnings as these]:

> Sing, goddess, of the anger.[164]

> Tell me of the man, Muse.[165]

> Lead me to another account, how from Asian land a great war came to
> Europe.[166]

And tragedians make clear what the drama is about, even if not immedi-
20   ately, as does Euripides, then at least somewhere in the prologue, as in fact
Sophocles does: "My father was Polybus."[167] The case is similar also with
comedy. The most necessary task of the preface, then, and this is peculiar
to it, is to make clear what the end is for the sake of which the speech [is
being made]. Hence if in fact the matter at issue is clear, or petty, the preface should not be used.

25   The other forms [of preface] that people use are in effect remedies[168]
and are common [to rhetoric as a whole]; these are stated with an eye to
the speaker; to the listener; to the matter at hand; and to the opponent.
As for what pertains to oneself and one's adversary, [the prefaces in ques-
tion] concern all such things as either dissolve slander[169] or foster it. But
these do not proceed in similar ways: for the person defending himself,
matters bearing on the slander [or accusation] are first, whereas for the
30   accuser, these appear in the epilogue. The reason for this is not unclear,

164 · From the first line of Homer's *Iliad*.

165 · From the first line of Homer's *Odyssey*.

166 · Evidently from Choerilus's lost poem about the Persian War.

167 · Sophocles, *Oedipus the Tyrant* 774. The obvious difficulty here is that the line appears, not at the beginning, but at about the midpoint of the play. Hence Cope's com-
ment on the passage: "Aristotle has here used *prologos* [prologue] in a more comprehensive sense than that which it usually bears, for an 'explanatory introduction,' in general,
wherever it may occur."

168 · Remedies, that is, for the various defects of the audience: consider in this regard
Aristotle's earlier reference to the "depravity of the listener": 3.1 (1404a8).

169 · The term (*diabolē*) often means "a false or malicious charge," hence "slander," but
it can also mean simply "a legal accusation," an ambiguity that should be kept in mind
throughout.

for when the defendant is about to introduce himself it is necessary for him to remove any obstacles, the result being that the slander must be dissolved at the outset. For the slanderer, by contrast, he must slander the accused in the epilogue so that people may remember it to a greater degree.

What pertains to the listener proceeds from making him both well disposed and angry,[170] and sometimes also making him attentive or the opposite, for it is not always advantageous to make [the listener] attentive. Hence many attempt to prompt him to laugh. As for his being readily open to instruction, quite all things will lead to this, if someone wishes, in particular [the speaker's] appearing decent, for people pay greater heed to those who are decent. They are apt to pay attention to great matters, to matters of particular interest to them, to things that provoke wonder [or admiration], and to pleasant things. Hence one must instill [the thought] that the speech is concerned with such things.

But if [it is advantageous that] they not be attentive, [the speaker must convince the audience] that the matter is petty, that it has nothing to do with them, that it is painful. Yet it must not escape one's notice that all such things are extraneous to the speech, for they are aimed at a paltry listener who listens to what is extraneous to the speech; if he is not such a fellow, there is no need at all of a preface, except to state in summary fashion the matter at hand so that, as with a body, the speech may have a head.

Further, making [the audience] attentive is common to all the parts [of the speech], if need be; for they are more inclined to relax their attention anywhere than at the beginning. Hence it is laughable to arrange this [call on their attention] at the beginning, when all are paying particular attention as they listen. As a result, whenever the right moment occurs, one must say, "And pay attention to me, for this pertains no less to you than to me" and "I'll tell you a terrible thing such as you've never heard before," or something "so amazing." And this is, just as Prodicus said, to throw in a bit of the fifty-drachma lecture when the listeners are dozing off.[171] But that [one is thus speaking] to the listener not qua listener is clear, for all in their prefaces either utter slanders or allay fears:

35

1415b

5

10

15

20

170 · The phrase "and angry" is deleted by Kassel but present in the MSS.
171 · Consider Plato, *Cratylus* 384b for a reference to Prodicus's fifty-drachma lecture—too expensive for Socrates.

Lord, I'll not say that I in haste...[172]

What are you prefacing...?[173]

And it is those who have a poor case, or seem to, [who do this], for it is better to spend time on anything other than the case at hand. Hence slaves do not speak to the questions asked but beat around the bush and preface
25   what they say. But how one ought to render [the listener] well disposed has already been stated, as well as each of the other points of this sort.[174] Now, since this is well stated—"Grant to me, when I come to the Phaeacians, friendship or pity"[175]—it is these two things that one must aim at.

But in epideictic [prefaces], one must make the listener suppose that he is sharing in the praise, either he himself or his familial line or his usual
30   practices, or in some other way. For what Socrates says in his funeral oration[176] is true, that it is not difficult to praise Athenians among Athenians, but [it is difficult to do so] among Lacedaemonians. Prefaces in speeches for the public assembly are based on those in judicial speeches, but by nature they least have prefaces. For in fact [listeners] know what the speech
35   concerns, so that the case at hand needs no preface at all, except on account of [the speaker] himself or his opponents, or if they suppose that the matter is not of such import as you wish it to be, either too great or too little. Hence it is necessary either to slander it or to do away with [such slander] and either to amplify [the importance of the matter at hand] or to diminish it. For these reasons a preface is needed, or for the sake of a certain
1416a adornment, since [the speech] appears off the cuff if it does not have a preface. For such is Gorgias's encomium of the Eleans, which starts off immediately, without any preliminary sparring or warm-up, "Elis, happy city."

CHAPTER 15

When it comes to slander, one matter concerns the [arguments by]
5   which someone might do away with a harsh insinuation, for it makes

---

172 · Sophocles, *Antigone* 223. The speaker is a guard, who is frightened to tell Creon the news that Polyneices has been buried against the command of the king.

173 · Euripides, *Iphigenia in Taurus* 1162. Here Thoas, king of the Taurians, addresses Iphigenia; the full line in the original runs as follows: "What news are you prefacing? Speak out clearly."

174 · Consider 2.4 (on friendly affection) and 2.8 (on what elicits pity).

175 · Homer, *Odyssey* 7.327.

176 · See Plato, *Menexenus* 235d as well as 1.9 (1367b8–9) above.

no difference whether [the slander or accusation] has [actually] been stated or not. This is, as a result, a general concern. Another way[177] is to confront the points in dispute, either [by contending] that the matter is not so, or that it is not harmful (or not harmful to *this* person or not to such a degree), or that it is not unjust (or not a great injustice) or is not a shameful thing (or is such to no great degree). The dispute concerns such things, just as Iphicrates [put it] to Nausicrates.[178] For he said that he did do what [Nausicrates] said, and so caused harm, but he committed no injustice thereby. Or when one has committed an injustice, one can strike a balance [by contending that], if there was harm done, [the deed] was noble nonetheless, [or] if productive of pain, also of advantage, or some other such thing. Another way[179] is [to contend] that the matter at issue was an error, or a misfortune, or a necessity, such as when Sophocles said that he trembled, not as his accuser said, so that he might be held to be an old man, but of necessity, since it was not his wish to be eighty years old.

[One can] strike a balance also as regards the end involved—that he did not wish to do any harm but acted instead for this or that reason and not for the reason [the accuser] stated in his slander, though it turned out that harm was indeed done. "And it would be just to hate me, if I had acted so that this came about." Another [way to deal with slander or accusation] is if the accuser has been implicated in the same charge, either now or previously, either he himself or those in his circle. Another, if others are implicated in the same charge, others whom people agree are not liable to the slander in question—if, for example, someone is an adulterer because he is dapper, then so-and-so would be an adulterer too [but clearly he is not]. Another [way to deal with slander is] if either another person or [the accuser] himself slandered certain others[180] [in the past who subsequently were revealed to be not guilty] or if, without a formal charge[181] being brought against them, others were under suspicion who subsequently were revealed to be not guilty, just as [the accused] him-

10

15

20

25

---

177 · Here some MSS read "topic" (*topos*) rather than "way" (*tropos*), perhaps rightly.

178 · Nausicrates (or Naucrates) is mentioned by Cicero as being a student of Isocrates. On the Athenian general Iphicrates, see, e.g., 1365a27 and context.

179 · Here too some MSS read "topic" (*topos*) rather than "way" (*tropos*).

180 · The MSS differ somewhat; another possible reading would give the translation "if he slandered others or another slandered them."

181 · The term translated here as "formal charge" is the same term otherwise translated as "slander" (*diabolē*).

self now is under suspicion. Another proceeds from counter-slandering the slanderer, for it would be absurd if the arguments of someone who is himself not credible will be credible. Another [way to deal with slander] is if a judgment has already occurred, just as Euripides [said] against Hygaenon, who, in the matter of a property exchange,[182] accused [Euripides] of impiety because he had recommended committing perjury when he wrote: "The tongue swore an oath, but the mind is unsworn."[183] For [Euripides] asserted that [Hygaenon] was guilty of injustice by bringing the judgments of the Dionysian contest into the courtroom, since he had already given an account of his words in the former, or would do so, if one wished to accuse him there.[184]

Another [way] is to form an accusation on the basis of [the use of] slander [itself], as to how great a thing it is, and this because slander alters judgments,[185] and because it in effect does not trust in the matter actually at hand. Common to both [accuser and accused] is the topic of stating "tokens," as does Odysseus in *Teucer*, for example, because [Teucer] was a relative of Priam (since Hesione was Priam's sister).[186] But Teucer countered that his father, Telamon, was an enemy of Priam, and that he himself did not denounce the spies.[187]

182 · Wealthy citizens in Athens were required to fund various public events or services—the outfitting of a trireme or warship, for example, or a dramatic chorus—but one could challenge the requirement on the grounds that another, wealthier citizen had been passed over. The challenger could summon the other person to court and offer to exchange properties with him (*antidosis*).

183 · For the line, see Euripides, *Hippolytus* 612. See also, e.g., Plato, *Theaetetus* 154d4–6. Euripides's accuser means to suggest that, since, in a play of his, Euripides apparently recommends making insincere oaths, his oaths in a courtroom cannot be trusted.

184 · In the Dionysian festival of 428, the trilogy of which the *Hippolytus* forms a part was awarded first place.

185 · The Greek is ambiguous; it might also mean "because it fosters other [i.e., extraneous] judgments."

186 · Teucer was son of King Telamon and Hesione. Aristotle here refers to a lost play of Sophocles; see also 2.23 (1398a4).

187 · To incriminate Teucer on a charge of treachery, Odysseus makes use of the "token" (*symbolon*) that Teucer is related to Priam of Troy; to vindicate himself, Teucer makes use of the "token" that his father hated Priam and that he himself did not reveal the presence of Greek spies in Troy. Burkett here suggests that "*symbola* ["tokens"] refer to speculative or probable knowledge derived from signs that may serve as circumstantial evidence."

Another way, pertaining to the slanderer, is to praise something petty [about the opponent] at length while criticizing a great thing concisely,   5 or setting forth many good things [about the opponent] but then criticizing one thing about him that actually pertains to the case at hand. Such are those who are most skilled in the art [of rhetoric] and most unjust, for they attempt to do harm to one's good points by mixing them with what is bad.

[A topic] common to both the slanderer and him who does away with the slander [occurs] when the same thing admits of being done for several reasons: the slanderer must put a bad construction on it, taking it as serv-   10 ing the worse motive, whereas he who does away with the slander must take it as serving the better one. For example, that Diomedes chose Odysseus: to the one, Diomedes did so because he supposed Odysseus to be best, to the other, it was not for this reason but because he supposed that only Odysseus, being a paltry fellow, would be no rival to him.[188]

Let this much be said about slander.   15

CHAPTER 16

Narration in epideictic speeches is not continuous but proceeds part by part, for one must go through the relevant actions that form the basis of the speech. The speech is composed in part of what is non-technical (since the speaker is not at all a cause of the actions in question), in part of what is based on technical art. And this latter amounts to showing ei-   20 ther that [the action] really is so, if it seems otherwise not credible, or that it is of a certain character, or import, or all of these together. It is for this reason that one sometimes must not narrate all things continuously, since showing things in this way is difficult to remember. From these [given actions], then, one is courageous; from those, one is wise or just, and in this way the speech is simpler, whereas in the other way it is complicated and   25 not straightforward. One must [merely] call to mind actions that are well known. Hence the majority [of epideictic speeches] need no narration at all—for example, if you want to praise Achilles, since everyone knows his actions—though one must make use of those actions. But if one wants

---

188 · Diomedes selects Odysseus, from among many volunteers, to accompany him behind enemy lines: Homer, *Iliad* 10.242–46. See also the earlier reference to this in 2.23 (1399b28–29), where Aristotle cites as his source the *Ajax* of Theodectes.

to praise Critias,[189] [narration] is needed, for many people do not know [his actions].[190]

30   But at present people laughably contend that the narration [in judicial speeches] must be quick. Yet, just as a fellow said to the baker, who asked whether he should knead the dough hard or softly, "What's that? Is it impossible to do it well?"—the case is similar here too: one must not narrate at length, just as one must not state prefaces at length either, or modes of persuasion. For doing so well does not consist in do-

35 ing it either quickly or concisely, but in due measure. And this is to state so many things as will make the matter at hand clear, or so many as will

1417a make [the listener] suppose that something has happened, or some harm has been done, or some injustice committed, or that things are of so great an import as you wish. But for the opponent, the opposite things [must be done]. And you must slip into the narration all that bears on your virtue—for example, "But I used to chastise him, because I was always affirming the just course—not to abandon his offspring," or [you must

5 narrate] the vice of the other fellow: "But he replied to me that, wherever he may be, there will be other children," which is what Herodotus contends the Egyptian rebels replied[191]—or [narrate] so many things as the jurors find pleasant.

    But the defendant's narration must be less extensive, for the points in dispute are whether or not something has happened or caused harm or

10 was unjust or was of such great import, the result being that one should not use up time on an agreed-on point—unless it is in some way relevant [to the defense]—for example, that something was indeed done, but it was not unjust. Further, one must speak of all such things as having been

189 · Critias was a sometime associate of Socrates best known as a member of the oligarchic Thirty, who ruled Athens harshly (and briefly) at the conclusion of the Peloponnesian War. Critias, then, was no Achilles.

190 · Here Kassel (and other editors) posit a lacuna in the text as it has come down to us, since the unannounced subject of the next paragraph is judicial speeches. Some MSS attempt to fill the lacuna by repeating lines found at 1367b26–31 (and even beyond): "And praise is speech that indicates greatness of virtue. One must, then, point out that the actions are of such a character. But an encomium is of one's deeds. Attendant circumstances are conducive to a mode of persuasion—for example, good birth and education, for it is likely that good human beings arise from those who are good, and one who has thus been reared is such himself. Hence we offer encomiums over those who have carried out certain actions."

191 · Herodotus 2.30.

done [in the past], not as being done [currently], unless doing so brings either pity or dread. An example is the story told to Alcinous, because in front of Penelope it was written in sixty lines;[192] and as Phayllus narrated   15
the epic cycle; and the prologue of *Oeneus*.[193]

The narration also ought to bear on [moral] character. This will be the case if we know what fosters [a sense of one's] character. Now, one thing is to make clear the choice involved; and the sort of character one has relates to the sort of choices one makes, and the sort of choice one makes is related to one's end or goal. It is for this reason that mathematical arguments do not involve matters of character, because they do not involve choice either (since they do not have the "for the sake of which" [or end]),   20
whereas Socratic arguments do, since they speak about such things.[194] But matters pertaining to character follow on each sort of character— for example, that he was walking while simultaneously talking, for this makes clear his brashness and rude character. And one should not speak as though on the basis of one's understanding or intellect, as people nowadays do, but rather on the basis of the choice [one has made]: "But I wished it, for this is in fact what I chose. But if I did not benefit by it, it   25
is better [nonetheless]." For the former statement [reflective of one's understanding] belongs to a prudent person, the latter to a good one; [the character] of a prudent person resides, that is, in the pursuit of the advantageous, whereas that of a good person resides in the pursuit of the noble. And if it does not seem credible, then the cause of that must be stated in addition, just as Sophocles does: an example is from *Antigone*, that she cared more for her brother than her husband or offspring, since, should   30
the latter perish, they might come to be [again],

But when one's mother and father have gone to Hades,
There is no brother who could ever come to be.[195]

192 · The "story told to Alcinous" refers to the events narrated in books 9–12 of the *Odyssey*, whereas the same account is told to Penelope in some fifty-five or so lines: see *Odyssey* 23.264–84 and 310–43. A "story told to Alcinous" became a proverbial expression meaning "a long-winded tale" (see, e.g., Plato, *Republic* 614b2–3).
193 · Nothing is known of Phayllus; presumably he greatly condensed a long poem. *Oeneus* is a lost play of Euripides.
194 · Kassel excludes the phrase translated as "since they speak about such things," but it is present in the MSS.
195 · Sophocles, *Antigone* 911–12, although the MSS of Sophocles read *kekeuthotoin* ("have been covered over") for Aristotle's *bebēkotōn* ("have gone").

But if you have no such cause [to state], at least [say] that you are not ig-
35   norant of the fact that what you are saying is not credible, but that such
is the sort of fellow you are by nature, for people do not credit that anyone voluntarily does anything apart from what is beneficial [to himself].

Further, speak on the basis of what is marked by passion [or emo-
tion], narrating the things that both follow on the passions and that are
known to people, as well as things peculiarly characteristic of either one-
1417b   self or the other fellow: "And he went off, while glaring at me." And as
Aeschines [said] about Cratylus, that he hissed violently, with both hands
shaking:[196] these are persuasive, because, being known to people, they become tokens of things that are unknown to them. One can grasp a very
great number of such things from Homer:

5   Thus she spoke, and the old woman covered her face with her hands.[197]

For those who are beginning to cry put [their hands] over their eyes. And
immediately introduce yourself as being a certain sort of person—so that
people may look on you as such—and introduce your adversary as well.
But do this in such a way as to escape notice in doing it. That this is easy
to do one should see from the case of messengers: we know nothing about
10   them, but nonetheless we gain a certain supposition about them.[198] One
should offer narration in many places, and sometimes not at the beginning.

There is least narration in speaking before the public assembly because
nobody narrates what concerns the future. But if in fact there is narration
there, it will be of past events so that, when people remember them, they
15   may deliberate better about what is to come—whether [speakers] slander
or praise it. But then [the speaker] does not carry out the task of the advisor strictly speaking. And if [what one says] is not credible, promise both
to state a cause of this immediately and to set things out in order as they
wish—as, for example, Jocasta is always promising to do in the *Oedipus* of

196 · Aeschines is presumably the Athenian orator (ca. 397–322), at odds with Demosthenes over the conduct of Athenian foreign policy. In the *Cratylus*, Plato portrays a
young man of that name much influenced by Heraclitus—but the Cratylus here mentioned may well be a different person.

197 · Homer, *Odyssey* 19.361.

198 · Or, perhaps, "we know nothing about what [they are going to say], but nonetheless we gain a certain supposition [about it]."

Carcinus,[199] when the person seeking her son puts questions to her. [The
same is true] also of Sophocles's Haemon.[200]   20

CHAPTER 17

Modes of persuasion should be demonstrative, and since the [judicial]
dispute concerns four things,[201] he who brings a demonstration to bear
ought to do so concerning the point in dispute. For example, if in a given
judgment it is disputed whether something happened, one should make
the demonstration bear on this especially; but if it is that no harm was   25
done, then it should bear on this, and, similarly, if the point in dispute
is that the matter is not so great, or that it was in fact done justly, [then
the demonstration should establish this]. And if the dispute concerns
whether this particular thing was done [as a matter of fact], let it not go
unnoticed that, in this dispute alone, it is necessarily the case that one or
the other of the two disputants is a base fellow, for ignorance is not the
cause [of the dispute], as it might be if some people should dispute the
justice of something. As a result, one must use [the baseness of one's op-   30
ponent] in this case [of a dispute over fact], though not in the others.
     In epideictic speeches there will be much amplification, as regards
what is noble and advantageous. For the matters at hand must be trusted
in[202] [by the audience], since [speakers] rarely bring demonstrations of
these to bear—[only] if they are not credible or if someone else bears responsibility for them.
     As for speeches in the public assembly, someone may dispute either
that [what has been predicted] will be in fact or, if the things [the oppo-   35
nent] recommends *will* come to pass, one may dispute whether they will
be just or advantageous or as important [as he claims]. One must also see
if he is lying in some matter that falls outside the question at hand, for
such things appear to be decisive evidence that he is lying also in other
regards.   1418a

199 · A prolific tragic poet, none of whose plays survive. Aristotle refers to him also at
2.23 (1400b9–10) above.
200 · Cope calls this last example "hopeless": "there is nothing in the extant play which
could be interpreted as required here." Consider, however, Sophocles, *Antigone* 683–723.
201 · The "four things" are questions of fact (whether something happened); harm; importance or "greatness" of the matter at hand; and justice.
202 · *Pisteuesthai*: to be convinced (rightly or wrongly) that something is so.

Examples are most characteristic of rhetoric in the public assembly, enthymemes of judicial rhetoric. For the former sort of rhetoric concerns what will be, such that it is necessary to speak of examples on the basis of past events, whereas the latter sort of rhetoric concerns things that [either] are or are not, to which demonstration and necessity belong to a greater degree. For what has happened involves necessity. One should not state [a series of] enthymemes in succession, but rather mix them in [in the rest of the speech]; otherwise they do damage to one another, since there is a limit when it comes to quantity:

O friend, since you said as many things as a sagacious man would,[203]

but not "such sorts of things." And neither should one seek out enthymemes about everything; otherwise you will do what some of those who philosophize do, they who conclude syllogistically about things that are better known and more credible than are the [premises] on the basis of which they speak. And whenever you are fostering passion [in the audience], do not state an enthymeme, for either the enthymeme will drive out the passion or the enthymeme will have been stated in vain: motions that are simultaneous drive one another out, and they either obscure or weaken one another. And neither when the argument bears on [moral] character should one seek out at the same time a given enthymeme, for the demonstration [resulting from an enthymeme] involves neither one's [moral] character nor one's choice. But one should make use of maxims in both narration and a mode of persuasion [or proof], for these do involve character: "In fact I gave, and this even though I know that 'one mustn't trust.'" And if [one is speaking] in a passionate way: "In fact I have no regret, even though I am the victim of injustice: with this fellow lies the profit, but with me, the just!"

Speaking in a public assembly is more difficult than doing so in a courtroom, as is only likely, because the former concerns the future, the latter what has happened in the past, which is already known even to the prophets, as Epimenides the Cretan[204] said (for he did not use to prophesy about the things that will be, but about past events that were, however, unclear). And the law amounts to the hypothesis in judicial rhetoric; when one has a starting point, it is easier to discover a demonstration.

203 · Homer, *Odyssey* 4.204.
204 · Compare, e.g., Plato, *Laws* 642d, where Kleinias tells the Athenian Stranger that Epimenides correctly foretold, a decade before the fact, that the Persians would invade Greece—and that the Greeks would prevail.

And [speaking in the public assembly] does not admit of many delay tactics, such as speaking against one's opponent or about oneself, or making a passionate speech. Instead, such speaking admits of these things least of all—unless one digresses. One must do this, then, when at a loss—which is just what the Athenian orators, including Isocrates, do. For even   30
when giving advice [to the assembly], he levels accusations—for example, against the Lacedaemonians in the *Panegyricus* and against Chares in the *Symmachicus*.[205]

But in epideictic rhetoric, one must intersperse praises into the speech, as, for example, Isocrates does, for he is always bringing up someone [in his speech]. And this is the same thing that Gorgias used to say, that the argument never leaves him high and dry. For if he is speaking of Achilles,   35
he praises Peleus, then Aeacus, then the god;[206] and similarly also [if he is speaking of] courage, which performs these or those things, or is of this or that character.[207]

If, then, one has demonstrations at one's disposal, one must speak in a manner bearing on [moral] character and demonstratively; if you have no enthymemes, speak as regards character [only]. In fact it is more fit-   1418b
ting for a decent person to appear to be a fine fellow than for his argument to be precise. Refutative enthymemes are to a greater degree well regarded than are demonstrative ones because all those that effect a refutation make clearer that a syllogistic conclusion has been reached, since opposites are more recognizable when placed beside one another. [Enthymemes] against one's adversary are not some other form [of argument]   5
but belong to the modes of persuasion; some [refutative enthymemes] do away with [the opponent's argument] by way of objection, some by way of syllogism.[208] In both the assembly and the courtroom, the first speaker must state his own modes of persuasion [or proofs] first, then meet those of his opponent by refuting them and pulling them apart in anticipation.

205 · See *Panegyricus* 110–14 and *Symmachicus* (better known as *On the Peace*) 27.

206 · That is, Gorgias would praise first Achilles's father, Peleus, then his grandfather, Aeacus, then the grandfather's father, Zeus.

207 · The reading of Kassel's text. Some mark the text differently so as to give this reading in translation: "it either performs these or those things, or is of this or that character."

208 · The sentence is somewhat ambiguous and might be rendered also as follows: "[Enthymemes] against one's adversary are not some other form [of argument]; but some modes of persuasion do away with [the opponent's argument] by way of objection, some by way of syllogism." Kassel excises the whole clause that follows the semicolon in the text above.

10   But if the opposition is manifold, speak against the opposing points first, the sort of thing Callistratus did in the Messenian assembly. For only once he took up the points they were going to say did he himself then say [what he was going to say].[209]

But he who speaks subsequently must first speak against the opposing argument, doing away with it and offering a counter-syllogism, especially if that opposing argument was well regarded. For just as the soul is
15   not receptive to a human being who has been slandered in advance, [so] in the same manner it does not accept one's speech either, if the opponent is held to have spoken well. The person going to speak, then, must make room in the [soul of] the listener, and this will occur if he does away with [the opponent's previous argument]. Hence he must make his own points credible by waging war accordingly against either all [the oppo-
20   nent's] points or the greatest of them or those that were well regarded or are easily refuted.

Of the goddesses I will first become an ally . . .

For I, [. . .] Hera . . .

In these lines, she touched first on what is most naïve.[210] These things, then, concern modes of persuasion.

As for what bears on character, since some things one says about one-
25   self may either arouse envy or be long-winded or open to contradiction, and since what concerns another person may be abusive or rude, one

209 · The reference seems to be to the embassy on which Callistratus was sent before the battle of Mantineia in 362. Callistratus is mentioned also above at 1.7 (1364a19) and 1.14 (1374b26).
210 · See Euripides, *Trojan Women* 969 and 971. Hecuba is here addressing herself to Helen. The broader context is as follows:

> Of the goddesses I will first become an ally,
> And show that she [i.e., Helen] does not state what is just,
> For I do not think that Hera and the maiden Pallas
> Have come to so great a degree of folly
> Such that the one sold Argos to the barbarians,
> And Pallas sold Athens into slavery to Phrygia.

The weak or "naïve" argument in question was placed by Helen in the middle of her speech—that in the beauty contest between Pallas (Athena), Hera, and Cypris (i.e., Aphrodite), Pallas offered Paris the rule of all of Phrygia and the destruction of Hellas, while Hera offered him the rule of Asia and Europe. This argument Hecuba skillfully takes up first, and so makes most prominent.

ought to have someone else say them, just as Isocrates does in the *Philippus* and *Antidosis*,[211] and as Archilochus does in uttering blame. For he makes the father say about his daughter (in the iambic poem): "There is nothing that cannot be expected, nor declared impossible under oath," 30 and [there is what] Charon the carpenter [says], in the iambic poem that begins, "Not for me the things of Gyges."[212] And the way Sophocles has Haemon speak to his father on behalf of Antigone, on the supposition that it is what others are saying.[213] One must also alter the enthymemes and sometimes make them into maxims—for example, "Those with intelligence ought to be reconciled when they enjoy good fortune, since in this 35 way they might gain most greatly." But expressed as an enthymeme: "For if one ought to be reconciled when such reconciliation is most profitable and gainful, then those who enjoy good fortune ought to be reconciled."

CHAPTER 18

Concerning interrogation,[214] it is especially opportune to make use of it when the other person has already spoken, so that, when one additional 1419a question is posed, an absurdity [in the opponent's argument] results. For example, Pericles interrogated Lampon[215] about initiation into the rites of the savior goddess, and when he said that it was not possible for someone uninitiated to hear about it, Pericles asked if he himself knew it; Lampon claimed that he did, and so Pericles asked: "And how is that, you who 5 are uninitiated?" Second, [it is opportune to use interrogation] whenever one remark is manifest and it is clear to the questioner that [the person being interrogated] will grant the other; for once one has gained from him the one statement, do not ask in addition about the other that is manifest but rather state the conclusion oneself, as Socrates did. When Meletus claimed that Socrates did not believe in gods, [Socrates], hav-

---

211 · The exact references are somewhat controversial, but consider *Philippus* 4–7 and *Antidosis* 132–39 and 141–49.

212 · Only fragments of the poems survive. Evidently Archilochus has the girl's father utter the criticism that the poet himself declined to state in his own name, and it is Charon, not the poet, who rebukes the love of wealth; on Gyges, see, e.g., Herodotus 1.12 and context.

213 · Consider Sophocles, *Antigone* 688–700.

214 · The noun (*erōtēsis*) means simply "questioning," but in a legal context can also mean "interrogation" or "cross-examination."

215 · Lampon the soothsayer or prophet is mentioned at Aristophanes, *Birds* 521.

10   ing said that he speaks of a certain *daemonion*,²¹⁶ then asked if *daemones*
are not either children of gods or something divine, and when Meletus
said, "They are," [Socrates] said, "Whoever supposes that there are children of gods, but not gods?"²¹⁷ Further, [it is opportune to use interroga-
tion] when one is going to show that [the opponent] is either contradict-
ing himself or speaking paradoxically. And, fourth, when [the opponent]
cannot help but do away [with his argument] by answering in a sophistic
15   manner. For if he answers in this way—"on the one hand, it is so, on the
other, it is not," or "in some respects, yes, in other respects, no," or "in one
respect, yes, in another, no"—people make an uproar on the grounds that
he is at a loss. But otherwise one should not undertake [to interrogate the
opponent], for if he raises an objection, it seems that you have been over-
powered. For it is not possible to pose many questions, on account of the
weakness of the listener. Hence one must make enthymemes, too, as concise as possible.

20   But when it comes to ambiguous questions, one must answer by defining them in speech, and not tersely; those questions that seem to contradict [one's own position] must immediately be done away with in one's
answer, before the opponent can pose the next question or draw a syllogistic conclusion, since it is not difficult to foresee what the argument
amounts to. But let both this and the solutions [to such difficulties] be
25   manifest to us on the basis of the *Topics*.²¹⁸

        And when [the opponent] is drawing a conclusion, if the conclu-
sion poses a question, state the relevant cause—for example, when
Sophocles²¹⁹ was asked by Peisander if it seemed best to him, just as it
had seemed best also to the other committee members, to establish the
Four Hundred, he said that it did.

        "What then? Wasn't it your opinion that these were base [actions]?" He
        said that it was.
30   "So then you engaged in these base actions?"
        "Yes," he said. "For there were no other, better ones."

216 · The readings of the MSS differ here, and I translate what I take to be the general
sense of the clause; Kassel brackets it.
217 · Consider Plato, *Apology of Socrates* 27c-d as well as 2.23 (1398a15–17).
218 · Consider *Topics* 8.4–7.
219 · Not the tragic poet but the Athenian politician, mentioned also above at 1.14
(1374b36). The oligarchic Four Hundred was established in Athens in 411, during a
time of great political upheaval subsequent to Athens' terrible defeat in Sicily. The coup
thus put an end to Athenian democracy, albeit temporarily.

And the Laconian who, when undergoing an audit for his time as ephor, was asked if in his opinion the other [ephors] were justly put to death, said that that was his opinion. The questioner: "Didn't you vote for these same things?" And he said that he did. "So then," he said, "wouldn't you too justly die?" "No indeed," he said. "For they did these things because   35 they took money, whereas I did not do that but instead acted according to my judgment." Hence one should neither pose an additional question af- ter the conclusion nor pose the conclusion as a question, unless the truth   1419b of the matter is much in one's favor.

As for jokes, since they seem to have a certain utility in contests, and [since] Gorgias was correct when he said that one ought to ruin the seri- ousness of one's opponents with laughter and their laughter with serious- ness, the number of forms of jokes there are was stated in what concerns   5 the art of poetry,[220] of which the one sort suits the free human being, the other does not. One will thus be able to find the kind of joke that suits oneself. And irony is more liberal than is buffoonery, for the ironist makes a joke for his own sake, the buffoon for that of another.[221]

CHAPTER 19

The epilogue is composed of four things: of rendering the listener well   10 disposed toward oneself and badly disposed toward the opponent; of am- plifying or diminishing [the matter at hand]; of establishing certain pas- sions in the listener; and of recalling to mind [points made in the speech]. For after demonstrating that one is truthful, the opponent false, it is nat-   15 ural to offer praise and blame accordingly and to drive home the point. And you must aim at one of two things: either that you are good in these specific respects or good simply; and either that the other fellow is bad in these respects or bad simply. The topics on the basis of which one ought to establish that [human beings] are serious or base have been stated.[222] What naturally follows is to amplify [the importance of] points that have   20 already been shown or to diminish their importance. For the deeds done must be agreed to, if one is going to speak about their import, just as the amplification [or expansion] of bodies proceeds from preexisting things.

220 · Aristotle's treatment of jokes (or comedy) in the *Poetics* has not survived.
221 · On irony (*eirōneia*) and buffoonery (*bōmolochia*), see also *Nicomachean Ethics* (on irony) 4.7 (1127b22–32) and (on buffoonery) 4.8 (1128a4–16).
222 · The Greek text is difficult, although the general sense seems clear. For the topics in question, consider 1.9 above.

As for the sources one ought to use to amplify and diminish, the relevant topics were set out previously.[223]

25   After this, once the character and import of the things in question are clear, one must lead the listener to certain passions. And these are pity and fear[224] and anger and hatred and envy and emulation and contentious strife; the topics about these too were stated previously.[225] It remains, as a result, for the speaker to call to mind points made previously. It is fitting to do this in the way that people contend [should be done] in pref-
30 aces, though they are not correct to say that, for they recommend that one repeat oneself so that [the speech] may be easy to understand. There, [in the preface], one ought to state what the matter at hand is so that it not escape anyone's attention what the judgment concerns, but here, [in the epilogue], one should speak, in summing things up, of the points that have established one's case.

    A starting point [of the epilogue] is that one has demonstrated the things one promised to demonstrate, so that one should speak of both those points and the reason for them. [The epilogue] is stated on the ba-
35 sis of a reply to the opponent by way of contrast, and one may compare the points that both [speakers] have said about the same thing, or do so without direct comparison:[226] "But this fellow said these things about it,
1420a whereas I said this, and for these reasons." Or on the basis of irony, such as "For this fellow said *this*, whereas I said *that*. And what would he have done, if he had in fact proved *this* but not *that*?" Or on the basis of inter-rogation: "What has not been shown?" or "What did this fellow show?" So one may thus [state an epilogue] on the basis of a comparison or, as
1420b accords with the nature of the thing, just as they were stated, one's own points [first] and then, separately, if you wish, the points in the oppo-nent's speech.

    For the end [of the speech], the absence of connecting particles[227] is fit-ting as regards diction, so that it is an epilogue rather than an argument [*logos*]: "I have spoken; you have heard; grasp it; judge."

223 · Consider 2.19 as well as 2.26 above.
224 · The word is *deinōsis*: it can mean "exaggeration"—see book 2, n. 140 above—but also the passion evoked by the presence of what is *deinos*, "terrible." "Indignation" is another possible translation.
225 · Consider, above, 2.1–11.
226 · The text here is uncertain, with several emendations suggested. I follow in the main the reading and translation of Cope-Sandys.
227 · Or "asyndeton."

INTERPRETIVE ESSAY

Aristotle's *Art of Rhetoric* as it has come down to us is divided into three principal sections or books. The first book is devoted in part to answering the question "What is rhetoric?" and includes an extensive discussion of the three kinds of rhetoric—deliberative, judicial, and epideictic—together with their characteristic subject matters. These subject matters, or "specific topics," supply the material to be shaped into a persuasive *logos*, a speech or argument, by the skilled rhetorician. The central book features an extended analysis of the three rhetorical "modes of persuasion" or, as the term is often translated, "proofs" (*pisteis*). The third and shortest book discusses diction or style of expression (*lexis*) and, somewhat more briefly, the necessary parts of a speech in their proper arrangement. The first two books are united in their attention to the intellectual component of a speech or to the "understanding" (*dianoia*) reflected in it (1403a34–b2; consider also 1404a18–19 and 1410b27–29); the third book looks more to practical matters, on the grounds that "being in possession of the points one must say is not sufficient; rather, it is necessary to know also *how* one must say them" (1403b15–17). In this way Aristotle's treatment of rhetoric is at once theoretical and practical, which means that the *Art of Rhetoric* is neither a strictly philosophic inquiry nor yet a handy guidebook for rhetoricians.

WHAT IS RHETORIC? (1.1–3)

The first thing that must strike the reader of Aristotle's treatise is its title, as recorded in the principal manuscripts: *Art of Rhetoric* (*technē rhetorikēs*).[1]

1 · I have used Kassel's critical edition of the Greek text, including his invaluable apparatus criticus: Rudolf Kassel, *Aristotelis Ars rhetorica* (Berlin: Walter de Gruyter, 1976).

In this way Aristotle announces that rhetoric is or can be made into an art properly speaking—a characteristic or disposition of soul that is bound up with making or production and is accompanied by a *logos*, a "true *logos*" (see *Nicomachean Ethics* 1140a6–10). Of the extant works of Aristotle, the *Rhetoric* is the one that most obviously claims to teach an art. But he thereby also implies, at least, that Plato's Socrates was wrong to contend that rhetoric is not an art at all but merely a "knack" (*tribē*), gained by trial-and-error experience, and intended to persuade an audience by flattering them while teaching them nothing (Plato, *Gorgias* 463b4 and context). The first sentence of the *Art of Rhetoric*, moreover, continues this defense or elevation of its subject matter: "Rhetoric is a counterpart [*antistrophos*] of dialectic" (1354a1). To begin to understand this, it is helpful to recall that Socrates had classified rhetoric as the "counterpart" (*antistrophos*) of nothing more exalted than fancy cooking; this is so, according to Socrates, inasmuch as rhetoric seeks to flatter or please the soul, just as such cooking seeks to flatter or please the body, each being indifferent to the health of what it caters to (*Gorgias* 465d7–e1; consider also 464b8). By contrast, then, Aristotle links rhetoric, the art of rhetoric, with nothing less than dialectic, which is a branch of the science of "analytics" or logic (consider 1359b10).

Rhetoric and dialectic are brought together in the first place because both are concerned with the characteristically human capacity for speech (*logos*), be it scrutinizing and maintaining an argument, in dialectic, or defending oneself and accusing another, in rhetoric (1354a4–6). Rhetoric and dialectic, then, are concerned with what all human beings are "in a way" already cognizant of, and hence all human beings "in a way" have a share in both. That some may make a good speech by a lucky stroke, others through a certain facility gained by habit—Aristotle might have used the word "knack"—suggests that it is also possible to make such speeches by means of a "method" (1354a8). This one could do as the result of considering, as only an art permits one to do (1354a11), how it is that certain speeches hit the mark. It is evidently the purpose of Aristotle's *Art of Rhetoric*, then, to sketch the outlines of such an art and so permit us to do by means of a "technical method" (1355a4) what others may do either from time to time or even regularly, without, however, being able to explain to themselves or others how it is they speak as they do.

Aristotle also stresses in the first chapter that only rhetoric and dialectic take as their subject matter whatever may fall within the purview of human speech or reason. This amounts to saying that rhetoric and dialectic do not take as their characteristic subject matters whatever belongs to "a distinct science" (1354a3) like medicine or geometry: it is the skilled doctor, not the rhetorician as rhetorician, who will make good arguments about medicine. As Aristotle puts it in 1.2, "Neither rhetoric nor dialectic is a science concerned with how any particular subject stands, but they are instead certain capacities for supplying arguments" (1356a32–34). This formulation raises a doubt, it is true, whether rhetoric is a science (*epistēmē*) at all, as distinguished from a capacity or potential or power (*dunamis*). This doubt would seem to be strengthened by the fact that the more rhetoric (or dialectic) attempts to speak of the things that do belong to "a distinct science," the more it will become that very science and hence cease to be rhetoric (or dialectic): "Insofar as someone attempts to fashion either dialectic or this [art of rhetoric], not into capacities but sciences, he will unawares obscure their nature by effecting the change, reconstructing them as sciences of the given underlying subject matters rather than of arguments or speeches [*logoi*] alone" (1359b12–16). The beginning of this remark suggests that rhetoric is a capacity as distinguished from a science; its conclusion suggests rather that rhetoric, like dialectic, is indeed a science—"of *logoi*," as distinguished from any (other) particular subject matter. Indeed, in 1.1 Aristotle unambiguously calls rhetoric a "science" (1355b19; consider also *Topics* 101b5–10). Let us grant the point, then, assuming for the purpose that there can be a science of things that are not necessary or therefore eternal but are as they are only "for the most part," as the matters treated by rhetoric prove largely to be (compare *Nicomachean Ethics* 1139b18–24 with *Metaphysics* 1027a19–21; *Rhetoric* 1357a30–34); as for the existence of speeches as such, regardless of subject matter, these depend of course on the existence of human beings. This, however, only underscores the question, not of what brings rhetoric and dialectic together as capacities or arts or indeed sciences, but of what separates them. If rhetoric is related to dialectic by likewise being a concern with the analysis and formulation of speeches as such, the specific subject matter of those speeches being of no import to rhetoric or dialectic as sciences, in what respect is rhetoric also distinct from dialectic precisely as its "counterpart"?

Aristotle's answer to the question "What is rhetoric?" unfolds gradually and is to a degree shaped by the art it means to describe. He eventually expands on the relation between dialectic and rhetoric in the course of his response to certain unnamed "technical writers" with whom he disagrees. For immediately after he has asserted rhetoric's relation to di-

alectic, he turns to discuss at some length the misunderstanding or mis-
representation of rhetoric on the part of these writers, who are evidently
responsible for the need to defend rhetoric in the first place (1354a11–
1355a20). In other words, Aristotle in effect acknowledges the controversial character of rhetoric just after he has affirmed its status as both an art
and a cousin of dialectic: not rhetoric itself or as it should be, but rhetoric
as it is frequently treated today *is* a questionable thing.

Aristotle's criticism has two parts. First, the technical writers have neglected precisely the technical part of rhetoric, namely, the "mode of persuasion" (*pistis*) together with its "body" or core, what Aristotle famously
dubs here the "enthymeme" (1354a13–16). Rather than elaborate on these
terms now, however, Aristotle instead sketches the extraneous matter that
takes the place of rhetoric's technical core in these writers: the manipulation of the passions of the judges or jurors, including their anger and envy
or pity. To "warp the juror" in this way, Aristotle says, is "as if someone
should make crooked the measuring stick he is about to use" (1354a25–
26). Here Aristotle takes his bearings in part by the practice of "well-
governed cities," which prohibit introducing in judicial proceedings any
matters extraneous to the case at hand, such as passionate appeals would
constitute: if all cities were so governed, the authors of technical treatises
"would have nothing whatever to say." "Correctly posited laws" should
define in judicial matters all that can be defined, thus leaving the fewest
possible things for the juror to decide or for the rhetorician to manipu-
late; the chief duty of the juror is to adjudicate questions of fact in individual cases that as such are beyond the foresight of every legislator. Least
of all should jurors be "instructed" by the litigants involved in a given case
(1354a31).

Aristotle is critical also of the emphasis these writers place on judicial rhetoric, to the neglect of political speechmaking, despite the fact
that "the same method" applies to both and that political speech is "less
pernicious" (1354b28) or indeed "nobler" and "more characteristic of
a citizen" than is the judicial, which is largely in the service of private
concerns (1354b22–26). The failings of "the writers," then, are not only
theoretical—their failure to understand the enthymeme—but moral or
political too. Hence Aristotle's defense of rhetoric, even before it inves-
tigates questions of method, takes the form of a defense of correct laws,
"the legislator," and a public spirited political discourse.

At this point Aristotle returns to discuss the technical core of
rhetoric—the modes of persuasion (*pisteis*)—but under that heading the

question of the relation of rhetoric to dialectic returns (1355a3–20). We learn now that it belongs to dialectic to observe what concerns every syllogism alike and hence also the rhetorical syllogism or enthymeme. Dialectic would thus seem to encompass rhetoric as the more comprehensive concern (consider 1356a30–31), and anyone competent to discover from what and how a syllogism (unmodified) comes to be would for that reason be especially skilled at the enthymeme, including, Aristotle notes, "the respects in which it differs from logical syllogisms" (1355a12–14, this being the sole mention of "logical syllogisms" in the *Rhetoric*). Aristotle develops the relation of, or difference between, the two arts, rhetoric and dialectic (logic), in a striking way. He suggests that anyone with the capacity to see what is true—presumably this is the province of dialectic or logic—can see also what resembles the truth—presumably the province of rhetoric. Is then rhetoric to be distinguished from dialectic because rhetoric is concerned only with what resembles the truth? Aristotle adds immediately, to his statement of the distinction between the truth and what merely resembles it, that human beings have a "natural competency [*pephukasin hikanōs*: 1355a16] when it comes to what is true, and for the most part they do hit upon the truth." Yet he stresses here only that someone able to aim or guess at (*stochastikōs*) the truth will for that reason be able also to aim or guess at "the generally accepted opinions" (*ta endoxa*). And these opinions are clearly inferior to the truth.

This is the first mention in the *Rhetoric* of the all-important *endoxa*. These are the generally accepted or acceptable opinions—opinions (*doxai*), one might say, that enjoy a good reputation (*doxa*)—which form the stuff of both dialectical and rhetorical syllogisms. Their range or variety is clear enough from their definition as "opinions that seem to be so to all or to most people or to the wise and, among these latter, either to all or to most of them or to those who are especially well-known and highly regarded [*endoxois*]" (*Topics* 100a30–b23; consider also 104a8–11). Aristotle's remarkably detailed listings in the *Rhetoric* of the various *endoxa* will remind us of this range: good reputation, for example, "is being supposed by all to be serious or to have the sort of thing that all—or the many or the good or the prudent—aim at" (1361a25–27). Similarly, "that which the prudent—or all people or the many or most people or the most excellent—would judge or have judged to be good or greater is necessarily so" (1364b11–14). But it is to say the least unclear whether the opinion of "the many" is always identical to that of "the prudent," for example, from whom they are distinguished. And in accord with this variety, Aristotle says that a mode of persuasion or proof in rhetoric is "a demonstration of a sort" (*apodeixis tis*: 1355a5) and that an enthymeme is a "rhetorical demonstration": *rhetorical* demonstration need not be demonstration, strictly speaking, at all.

Now that Aristotle has begun to define rhetoric and explained a reason or reasons for its questionable reputation, he turns to make, in four stages, his own case for its utility (1355a20–b2). First, "what is true and what is just" are naturally superior to (or stronger than) their opposites, but they can nonetheless go down in defeat, "and this is deserving of censure." It is the task of rhetoric properly conceived, then, to come to the assistance of truth and justice. The manner of that defense or something of its character is broached in Aristotle's second argument, for he now contends that, even if one makes a speech or argument that accords with "the most precise science," it would in the case of some people be "impossible" to persuade them (1355a24–29). To make use of some lines of Euripides that Aristotle will later quote (1397a17–19),

> But if in fact it is possible among mortals
> To make false pronouncements persuasively,
> You ought to believe the opposite, too,
> That mortals are often not persuaded by truths.

The very limits of science, or rather the limits of the capacities of some to grasp the teachings of science, mean that one must fashion "modes of persuasion and speeches" through what is "commonly available" or readily acceptable, as distinguished from the dictates of science: rhetoric must be able to persuade in the absence of teaching. This could mean, then, that the defense of the truth just mentioned might itself need to be more rhetorical than true in some cases. And if we accept the contention that rhetoric is itself a science, then it would include the precise knowledge of the limits of precise knowledge to bring about persuasion.

Aristotle also contends, third, that rhetoric is useful because we can learn by means of it to "persuade others of opposites"—that one and the same defendant is guilty *or* not guilty, for example. Aristotle adds, however, that this skill must be acquired, "not so that we may do both—for one must not persuade others of base [*phaula*] things—but so that it not escape our notice how the matter stands and how, when someone else uses arguments unjustly, we ourselves may be able to counter them" (1355a29–38). Even as he makes the case for rhetoric, then, Aristotle acknowledges its disturbing power. For to say that skilled rhetoricians can "persuade others of opposites" amounts to saying that they can make "the weaker argument the stronger," a claim that human beings were justly disgusted by when they heard the sophist Protagoras make it (1402a22–27; consider also, e.g., Aristophanes, *Clouds* 112–15 and Plato, *Apology of Socrates* 23d6–7). The problem with rhetoric is then not limited to the distortions imposed on it by "the technical writers," but inheres in the power of the art or capacity itself; in another context Aristotle speaks of those who are "most skilled in the art [of rhetoric] and most unjust" (1416b6–7). Yet, to repeat, we must never exercise that capacity to persuade others of opposites. Instead, an able defense of "what is true and what is better by nature" (1355a37) requires that one see the arguments against them leveled by others in order to parry them. Or, to return to the initial example of justice, Plato's *Republic* would not be the defense of justice that it is, were it not for the arguments of Thrasymachus—the rhetorician Thrasymachus. The very wish to defend "what is true and what is better by nature," or what is just, compels us to try to understand the truth ("how the matter stands") about them or it.

Aristotle now adds ("in addition to these considerations": 1355a38–b2) that rhetoric permits one to defend, not only justice or the truth, but oneself. For if it is a "shameful thing" not to be able to defend ourselves with our fists, is it not all the more shameful for us to be unable to do so with *logos*, with speech or reason, which is more one's own than is the body? In this way Aristotle takes up the question of the rhetorician's own good: rhetoric does redound to the benefit of the rhetorician—but only in a manner that permits one to avoid a shameful weakness or vulnerability, presumably in law courts and the like (consider Plato, *Gorgias* 486a4–d1, 508c4–d3, and 521c3–8).

To summarize, the art of rhetoric is useful because it is needed to defend what is true and what is better by nature as well as what is just—not even a precise science concerning these will suffice in all cases—against those who would advance what is the opposite of these; and rhetoric serves the noble purpose of self-defense in speech. Aristotle now adds, perhaps as a fifth consideration, that even if rhetoric may be misused, of what good thing is this not true—save for virtue itself (1355a38–b7)? Rhetoric, then, is a loaded gun that may be used well or badly, nobly or shamefully, virtuously or viciously. The "technical writers" have misused something that, it has to be said, readily lends itself to misuse. The worth of rhetoric depends on whether it, like "strength, health, wealth, [and] generalship," will be used justly: the just use of rhetoric is necessarily good. In this way Aristotle concludes his defense of rhetoric with an affirmation of the goodness of virtue in general and of justice in particular; the limits that the art of rhetoric comes up against in the promulgation of the truth are nonetheless compatible with its just practice.

As it seems to me, readers of the *Art of Rhetoric* must remember this injunction throughout, for the simple reason that it is easy to lose sight of it as the book proceeds. For example, Aristotle initially decries the manipulation of the anger, envy, or pity of the audience on the part of the technical writers, as we saw; but he repeatedly includes, in his own analysis of the passions, specific practical advice on how to rouse or quell a given passion—anger, envy, and pity included.[2] Aristotle also criticizes the same writers for their attention to the arrangement of the preface, narration, and each of the other parts of a speech, with a view to making the judge be "of a certain sort"—namely, favorable to the speaker and hence to his case. Yet in book 3 Aristotle, too, takes up the question of the arrangement of the parts of a speech, and he, too, is concerned with how one might make the judges be "of a certain sort" (compare 1354b16–20 with 3.13–19).

Toward the end of the first chapter, Aristotle restates rhetoric's kinship to dialectic and offers a description of the "task" of rhetoric, namely, "not to persuade but rather to see the persuasive points that are available in each case." He explains this by way of analogy to medicine, an analogy, however, whose precise application to rhetoric he does not supply. Just as it belongs to medicine not to produce health but rather to advance health to the extent possible in a noble manner (for not all patients can be restored to health), so it belongs to rhetoric—to do what precisely? The parallel to medicine, which after all *is* concerned in all cases to bring about the state as close as possible to health, seems imprecise: is it really the task of the art of rhetoric "not to persuade" but only to "see" what is persuasive in a given circumstance? Or is the task of rhetoric (as the example of medicine implies) also to bring that persuasion about to the extent possible, and in a noble manner? Aristotle here may be trying to

---

2 · Compare 1354a16–18 with 1380a2–4 (on anger); 1380b29–33 (on gentleness); 1382a16–20 (on friendly feeling and hatred); 1383a8–12 (on fear); 1385a34–b1 (on graciousness [*charis*]); 1387b16–20 (on pity); and 1388a25–29 (on envy). Consider also 2.1, end: it is essential to understand how the angry are disposed, and with whom, and at what sorts of things, "for if we should grasp one or two of these, but not all of them together, it would be impossible to foster anger in another, and similarly in the case of the other [passions]."

undermine the extravagant claims of some rhetoricians, Gorgias among them, to be able to convince any crowd of literally anything (consider, e.g., Plato, *Gorgias* 456a7–8 and 457a5–b1). This goes together with Aristotle's somewhat surprising stress on what one might call the theoretical character of rhetoric, for, to repeat, its task is to "see" or observe or contemplate the persuasive, not (necessarily) to effect it in a given case (consider also, e.g., *Topics* 149b25–27). And to observe what would be persuasive requires a sober assessment of the limits of such persuasion. Here we may recall Aristotle's criticism in the *Nicomachean Ethics* of the sophists, who are inclined to equate the political art with rhetoric or even to rank rhetoric above that art; as Aristotle puts it in the *Rhetoric*, "Rhetoric even slips in under [*hypoduetai*] the rubric of the political art [or science], as do those who lay claim to [a knowledge of rhetoric], partly through a lack of education, partly through boasting and other, characteristically human, causes" (1356a27–30; compare Plato, *Gorgias* 464c7–d1 [*hypodusa* and *hypedu*]). The sophists in particular betray a certain naïveté about the world, to the effect that everything in politics can be accomplished by speech or argument alone. "The many," counters Aristotle, "obey the governance of necessity more than of *logos*, and of punishments more than of what is noble" (*Nicomachean Ethics* 1180a4–5).

Aristotle also introduces the distinction in dialectic between a syllogism and a merely apparent syllogism—a logically flawed argument in the guise of a syllogism—just as in rhetoric the enthymeme must be distinguished from the apparent enthymeme (1355b15; 1356a35–b5). Moreover, as "the sophist" (1355b20) acts in accord not with the science of dialectic but rather with his own choice, and so (Aristotle implies) may use apparent syllogisms for his own ends, so one kind of rhetorician, without a name of his own but corresponding to the sophist, will act not in accord with the "science" of rhetoric but rather his own choice, and so (one assumes) will use what appear to be enthymemes but are not in fact. This suggestion depends on and to that extent emphasizes the parallelism between rhetoric and dialectic, but it seems liable to the following difficulty: since the persuasion that rhetoric observes is in principle distinguished from the persuasion peculiar to the result of teaching, why cannot many "apparent enthymemes"—that is, bad arguments—be at least as effective among some audiences as the enthymeme properly speaking? For the goal of rhetoric is not logical validity but persuasion. Hence it is but a "counterpart" of dialectic or, as Aristotle will soon say, it is an "offshoot" of analytics. Consider: "People also lend credence to something on account of *logoi*, when we establish what is true *or what appears to be*" (1356a19–20; emphasis added). And again: Since "what is persuasive is persuasive to someone, and either it immediately supplies in itself the stuff of persuasion and conviction [*piston*], or it does so *by being held* [*dokein*] *to establish something* through things of that sort" (1356b26–28; emphasis added). There are "modes of persuasion that arise through establishing something *or appearing* to establish something" (1356a35–36; emphasis added). And finally: "It is manifest also that it belongs to the same art [i.e., rhetoric] to see both what is persuasive *and what appears to be persuasive*" (1355b15–16; emphasis added). One can even grant, with Aristotle, that "what is true and what is better by nature are always more readily established by syllogistic reasoning and are more persuasive, to put it simply" (1355a37–38). But, in many circumstances, will not what *appears* to be persuasive for that very reason actually *be* persuasive?

Here we may cast a glance at the official treatment of the apparent enthymeme in 2.24. Aristotle lists there nine *topoi* from which one may form an apparent enthymeme; all such *topoi* are united in that they result in logically bad arguments. Here are some examples: the use of "therefore" (or the like) to convince an audience that a conclusion has been established when it has not been in fact; or saying that because we know the letters of the alphabet, we know all words, words being made up of nothing but letters; or that because someone is a dandy and goes about at night, he is an adulterer, since that is what adulterers do; or that since it is good to be able to live wherever you like, it is good to be an exile; or that since unlikely things are happening all the time, the unlikely is likely. That these make for bad arguments is indisputable; the only question is whether for that reason they also make for poor *pisteis*. As a theoretical matter, then, the distinction between apparent and real enthymemes makes sense. But as a practical matter? To be sure, the use of such arguments leaves the speaker open to attack from a competent speaker, and precisely *Rhetoric* 2.24 might help bring such speakers into being, since Aristotle not only lists the fallacies but explains them. Still, not all the *topoi* enumerated in the prior chapter devoted to the *topoi* of (genuine) enthymemes seem logically watertight (consider, e.g., 1400a35–b4), and there may even be some overlap between the two sets of *topoi*, valid and invalid, as we might call them.[3]

3 · On the last point, see the section entitled "On Distinguishing True and Apparent Enthymemes," in Larry Arnhart, *Aristotle on Political Reasoning* (Dekalb: Northern Illinois University Press, 1981), 154–55, with particular attention to the references in-

That we have not yet been given a complete account of rhetoric is made clear at the end of 1.1, where Aristotle announces the need to define rhetoric or its characteristic method "again, as if from the beginning." Aristotle's formal definition of rhetoric at the outset of 1.2 — he has yet to define it — is as follows: "Let rhetoric . . . be a capacity to observe [*theōrēsai*] what admits of being persuasive in each case, for this is the task of no other art" (1355b26–27), not excepting dialectic. Here again Aristotle underscores the "theoretical" character of rhetoric, despite the fact that he explicitly calls it, not a science, but a "capacity" (*dunamis*).[4] And the contrast he goes on to draw between rhetoric and "each of the other" arts indicates that those other arts are concerned with "teaching and persuading" about whatever subject matter underlies them: as we have already noted, and as Aristotle here confirms, rhetoric is essentially concerned with persuasion as distinguished from teaching. That Aristotle wishes to teach the art of rhetoric means that he must avail himself of an art different from rhetoric — which is not to deny that he also exercises something of the rhetorical art in so doing. The *Art of Rhetoric*, we can say provisionally, teaches a true *logos* about the capacity to supply oneself "methodically" with those *logoi* that are distinguished less by their truth than by their persuasive power before a particular audience. For example, "one must speak of whatever is honored among each [people] as though it were present to hand — for example, among Scythians or Laconians or philosophers" (1367b9–11). Speakers equipped with the art of rhetoric will necessarily take their bearings by the dominant opinions or prejudices of the audience to whom they address themselves, opinions that — with the possible exception of an audience of "philosophers" — may well be confused or self-contradictory. Yet rhetoric still deserves to be called an art insofar as it can understand that very necessity: trading in falsehoods, half-truths, and other irrationalities may in some circumstances be demanded by reason itself, and reason can guide the way to the best method for doing so.

Aristotle now turns from a general account of rhetoric to its "methodical" core, the modes of persuasion (*pisteis*), although his account of these

---

cluded in n. 25: Arnhart there lists the supposedly valid arguments in 2.23 that resemble invalid arguments in 2.24.

4 · Here W. Rhys Roberts notes that "*rhetorike* [i.e., the adjectival ending of the word] also implies *techne*; and so not *techne* but *dunamis* follows [in the text]. Rhetoric is both art and faculty." W. Rhys Roberts, "Notes on Aristotle's 'Rhetoric,'" *American Journal of Philology* 45.4 (1924): 357. One might add that Aristotle also refers here to "other arts," although that formulation can be ambiguous in Greek.

latter will prove to bear also on the former (1355b35–1358a33). The technical modes must first be distinguished from the non-technical ones, these latter being the givens in any particular (judicial) case that are not supplied by any art, but are constituted by such things as witness testimony, evidence gained by torture, and the relevant contracts. As Aristotle makes clear in his subsequent treatment of the non-technical modes of persuasion (1.15), the art of rhetoric can be employed here only by either augmenting or downplaying the importance of these givens: "If the contracts support one," for example, "then they are credible and authoritative, but if they redound to the benefit of the opponent, then they are the opposite" (1376a33–b2). Technical modes of persuasion, by contrast, are the preserve of those equipped with the requisite method, and so must be discovered by it. Here Aristotle sketches his famous threefold classification of the modes of persuasion: the speaker's character (*ēthos*), or rather the audience's perception of that character in and through the speech; the emotional disposition of the listeners or what they undergo (*pathos*) as a result of the speech; and the argument (*logos*) itself, "by establishing or appearing to establish something." Hence *ēthos*, *pathos*, and *logos* are the three technical "modes of persuasion" in rhetoric, and Aristotle will take up each in turn, in what constitutes the longest single section of the treatise: first *pathos* (2.1–11), then *ēthos* (2.12–17), and finally those general or common points belonging in principle to every rhetorical *logos* (2.18–26).

The fact that Aristotle counts the argument strictly or narrowly speaking as but one of three modes of persuasion is an indication already of the character of rhetorical, as distinguished from logical or apodeictic, proof—and it argues against the translation of *pistis* as "proof": the audience's conviction that the speaker is an honest fellow, for example, and the anger or pity such a speaker is able to arouse in his audience, are both effective means of bringing about *pistis*, the "conviction" or "trust," as distinguished from any (logical) "proof," that something is so (*pisteuein*).[5] Whereas the "technical writers" maintain that the manipulation of the passions of the audience is most important in a speech, Aristotle himself contends that the audience's perception of a speaker's character "wields pretty much the greatest authority, so to speak, when it comes to persuasion" (1356a10–13). But this means that neither "the writers" nor Aristotle

---

5 · For a detailed analysis of the manifold meanings of *pistis* in the *Rhetoric*, see William M. A. Grimaldi, *Studies in the Philosophy of Aristotle's "Rhetoric"* (Wiesbaden: Franz Steiner, 1972), 53–65.

regards the *logos* narrowly speaking as the most effective rhetorical means to persuade (consider also, e.g., 1366a8–12).

Even more important, perhaps, for our understanding of the character of rhetoric is the conclusion Aristotle here draws from his delineation of the three modes of persuasion. He now reveals that, in addition to being a "sort of offshoot" (*paraphues ti*: 1356a25) of dialectic, rhetoric is an offshoot also of "the concern with characters [*ta ēthē*], and this concern can be justly addressed as the political art [or science]." Rhetoric is connected to dialectic, to repeat, inasmuch as both serve to supply us with arguments that in principle concern any subject whatsoever. But only in principle. For much of rhetoric, we now see, is inextricably tied to the political art and to its necessary concern with character. Rhetoric "*seems* to be the capacity to observe what is persuasive concerning any given matter, *so to speak*" (1355b32–34; emphasis added). And, we can add, the two kinds of rhetoric that Aristotle has mentioned thus far, the judicial and public or deliberative, are obviously and emphatically political (consider also, e.g., 1391b17–19 and context).

Aristotle underscores the peculiar character of rhetoric in his later discussion of the five topics that anyone making a political speech before a deliberative body must know something about (1.4); and it is no accident that this discussion includes the reminder that "rhetoric is composed of the science of analytics, on the one hand, and of the political art concerned with characters, on the other" (1359b8–11). Here Aristotle is compelled to sketch these political subjects, even as he acknowledges that he must "leave to the political science their examination" (1359b16–18; 1360a37–38). For the more knowledgeable a rhetorician becomes about the specifics of politics, the more he becomes, not a rhetorician at all, but a statesman (*politikos*): the rhetorician as such will not know what the true statesman knows (recall 1359b12–16). Thus there is "no need" in a discussion of rhetoric to seek out a precise account of these political matters because "this does not belong to the rhetorical art but rather to an art marked by greater prudence and truth."[6] Rhetoric, then, is not distinguished by the prudence or truth that is its own. Here Aristotle adds: "As things stand, in fact, many more subjects of study have been

6 · Here Averroes identifies the art in question as philosophy: "It is the object of the art of philosophy, which is superior to this art [of rhetoric] in the formulation of concepts and conviction, and the premises used in it are more accurate than those used in this art [of rhetoric]." Averroes, *Commentaire moyen à la "Rhétorique,"* ed. and trans. Maroun Aouad (Paris: J. Vrin, 2002) 1.4.3 (= vol. 2, p. 32).

given to rhetoric than are properly its." He also revisits in this context his earlier comparison of dialectic and rhetoric to sophistry. According to that comparison, we recall, the dialectician but not the sophist is guided by the dictates of his art, just as one sort of rhetorician, but not his unnamed counterpart, is guided by the dictates of his art: as there is an artful rhetor comparable to the dialectician, so there is an unartful one comparable to the sophist (1355b18–20). Yet Aristotle now says that "in some respects [rhetoric] is similar to dialectics, but in others to sophistic arguments" (1359b11–12). To all appearances, then, Aristotle blurs the line he had drawn between the art of rhetoric and sophistry; it is to be noted that there is no name in existence for the "sophistic," as distinguished from the genuinely artful, rhetorician—we refer to both simply as "rhetoricians"—and Aristotle does not coin one. Does the distinction hold water? This passage prompted a leading modern student of the *Rhetoric* to say: "Certainly rhetoric is not like sophistic because it engages in deception. Rhetoric, like dialectic, studies apparent argumentation and apparent probabilities in order to discover where they are false, not in order to use them."[7] Yet Aristotle does not state such a limitation here. And why might not a skilled rhetorician use such fallacious or faulty arguments as he thinks will appear probable, or indeed true, in the eyes of his audience—provided that the cause he thus serves is a good or decent one?

It is hardly surprising that Aristotle now elaborates on the parallel between rhetoric and dialectic (1356a35–b26). He contends that, just as dialectic is concerned with the syllogism, the apparent syllogism, and induction, so rhetoric is concerned with the enthymeme, the apparent enthymeme, and the example. As for the last item in each list, induction and rhetorical arguments from example, on one occasion Aristotle describes them as being the same thing (consider 1356b9–10): "Establishing that something is so, by reference to many similar instances, is, in dialectic, induction and, in rhetoric, example" (1356b13–15). But it seems more accurate to say, as he also does, that an example is "*rhetorical* induction," that is, induction modified or qualified (1356b5). When Aristotle later takes up the example—which, together with the enthymeme, is one of the "common" modes of persuasion in rhetoric—he states that example is only "similar" to induction (1393a26). We soon learn that an example "is neither as part is to whole nor whole to part nor whole to

7 · William M. A. Grimaldi, *Aristotle, Rhetoric I: A Commentary* (New York: Fordham University Press, 1980), ad loc.

whole, but as part is to part, or similar to similar; whenever both things [being compared] fall under the same class, the one being more familiar than the other, this is an example" (1357b25–30). A case in point: since Peisistratus once requested a bodyguard and then became tyrant, and Theagenes once requested a bodyguard and then became tyrant, Diony-sius's present request for a bodyguard means that he, too, is about to be-come tyrant (1357b30–36). If inductive reasoning moves from particular to universal—in the *Topics* we are told that induction is "the passage from particulars to the universal" (105a13–14)—rhetorical induction or the ex-ample moves from particular(s) to particular. This is not to deny that rhe-torical arguments from example in fact "assume the universal" (see *Rheto-ric* 1402b16–18) and then reason syllogistically from it, without, however, making that universal explicit: all in positions of power who request a bodyguard are aiming at tyranny.

As for an enthymeme, if we grant that it is a rhetorical, as distinguished from a dialectical, syllogism, we cannot grasp the import of the adjective without first having a sense of the noun it means to modify: what then is a syllogism? In the *Topics*, the work devoted to the dialectical syllogism, Aristotle describes the syllogism in general as "an argument [*logos*] in which, certain things [i.e., premises] having been posited, something else other than those things necessarily results through [on account of] them" (*Topics* 100a25–27; consider also *Prior Analytics* 24b18–22): if we posit that all human beings are mortal and that Socrates is a human being, it follows because of those propositions that Socrates is mortal. In the cor-responding section of the *Rhetoric*, Aristotle says this about the syllogism: "Establishing that, certain things [i.e., premises] being the case, some-thing else results from those things because of them, either universally or for the most part, alongside those things by virtue of their being so— this in dialectic is called a syllogism, in rhetoric an enthymeme" (*Rhetoric* 1356b15–17). We note these differences between the two definitions: the statement in the *Topics* includes, the one in the *Rhetoric* excludes, "ne-cessity"; the propositions or premises are said to be "posited" (*tethentōn tinōn*) in the *Topics* but simply "are" (*tinōn ontōn*) in the *Rhetoric*;[8] and

---

8 · "The most natural interpretation of this is that . . . rhetorical argument is a matter of drawing inferences from the *facts* about something. Dialectical reasoning typically pro-ceeds from premises that are merely posited, for argument's sake or because they are acceptable to one's respondent. Rhetorical reasoning is more assertive: one's premises either state the facts of the case or at least they purport to do so." M. F. Burnyeat, "En-thymeme: Aristotle on the Logic of Persuasion," in *Aristotle's "Rhetoric": Philosophical*

only the *Rhetoric* emphasizes that the premises or conclusions in question may be only "for the most part so." Indeed, since rhetoric "is for the sake of a judgment" (1377b21), and we properly judge only matters of action that are up to us or within our power, rhetoric is principally concerned with things that are "for the most part so" or could in principle be other than they are, and so can be acted on by us; this concern for contingent things is reflected in both the premises and the conclusions of rhetorical argument. Rhetoric, then, is not fundamentally concerned with necessities, with what cannot be other than it is (consider 1357a22–24). If, as Aristotle indicates, nothing strictly prevents a rhetorical syllogism from being based on such necessities, "few" of its premises will have this character (1357a22): "The premises on the basis of which enthymemes are stated will, some of them, be necessary, but the greatest number of them will be only for the most part so" (1357a30–34).

To be more precise, all enthymemes are based on either "likelihoods" (or "probabilities": *eikota*)—hence what is only "for the most part so"—or "signs."[9] "Signs," in turn, may serve to link the particular to the universal or the universal to the particular: "The wise Socrates is just" may be taken as a sign that the wise as such are just, or "The wise are just" may be taken as a sign that Socrates, who is wise, is just. But the more important division within signs, implicit in the examples just given, is that between the "necessary" and the "non-necessary" signs (1357b3–5). The necessary sign constitutes "decisive evidence" (*tekmērion*) according to Aristotle, and so makes for an irrefutable argument: "He has a fever" is a necessary sign that the fellow is sick, and if the facts alleged are true (consider 1403a10–16), then the argument will be sound. As for "non-necessary signs," which, Aristotle says, do not have a name of their own, they may well make for persuasive arguments, but they cannot constitute an irrefutable argument. To take the assertion "Socrates is wise and just" as a sign that all the wise are just is refutable (even if true in the case of

---

Essays, ed. David J. Furley and Alexander Nehemas (Princeton: Princeton University Press, 1994), 18 (emphasis original).

9 · At 1402b12–14, Aristotle contends that enthymemes are stated on the basis of "four" things: likelihood, example, decisive evidence, and sign. He thus apparently adds "example." W. D. Ross argues that these four properly reduce to two, since elsewhere example "is made co-ordinate with enthymeme, and is said to be a rhetorical induction," just as "decisive evidence" is a subset of "sign." W. D. Ross, *Aristotle's Prior and Posterior Analytics* (Oxford: Clarendon Press, 1949), 499–500. See also, for a defense of Aristotle's consistency here, Grimaldi, *Studies,* 104–15.

Socrates): that Socrates was wise and just need not say anything about the justice of the wise as such (1357b10–14 and context).

Now, the two sources of "the greatest number" of enthymemes are, to repeat, likelihoods and non-necessary signs, but it is difficult to pinpoint the difference between these sources because both clearly deal with probable or contingent, rather than necessary, states of affairs. In the *Prior Analytics* Aristotle does indicate a distinction between them, to the effect that there may be a somewhat greater causal connection between a non-necessary sign and its signate than there is between a general likelihood— "Parents love their children"—and its specific manifestation—"Adam loves Cain":

> A likelihood and a sign are not the same thing: a likelihood is a premise generally accepted in the element of opinion [*endoxos*], for whatever people know as something that for the most part comes to be or does not come to be, or [for the most part] is or is not, is a "likelihood"—for example, that those who are envious feel hatred and that those who are loved feel friendly affection. But a sign wishes to be a demonstrative premise that is necessary or generally accepted in the element of opinion [*endoxos*]. For anything such that, when it is, another thing is, or when it has come into being the other has come into being before or after it, is a sign of the other's being or having come into being. An enthymeme is a syllogism based on likelihoods or signs. (*Prior Analytics* 70a3–9, reading the text of the principal MSS rather than Ross's emendation)

Still, one may wonder whether a non-necessary sign that "wishes" to be a demonstrative premise, but is an *endoxon* as distinguished from a necessity, differs all that much from a likelihood or probability.[10]

What, then, is an "enthymeme" understood as a syllogism of a sort (*sullogismos tis*)? The precise meaning of this term is surprisingly controversial, given its centrality to rhetoric, in part because Aristotle's explicit discussions of the enthymeme are brief and enigmatic. In fact, in the whole of the *Art of Rhetoric* Aristotle explicitly identifies only four enthymemes.[11] A leading scholar of Aristotle's logic goes so far as to contend that it is "impossible to extract" from the *Rhetoric*'s account of the

---

10 · See also Grimaldi, *Commentary*, on 1357a36.

11 · See Antoine Braet, "The Enthymeme in Aristotle's *Rhetoric*: From Argumentation Theory to Logic," *Informal Logic* 19.2–3 (1999): 104. The enthymemes in question are found at 1394a29–34, b4–6; 1399b15–17; and 1418b36–38.

enthymeme "a completely consistent theory of its nature."[12] We cannot do more than sketch a few, admittedly preliminary, considerations. To begin with, the term *enthymēma* (plural *enthymēmata*) was not invented by Aristotle. Its earliest appearance in the extant literature seems to be in Sophocles's *Oedipus at Colonus* (292). There the Chorus of Attic men responds to Oedipus's lengthy account of his plight, and of his innocence, by characterizing his heartfelt words as his *enthymēmata*, his reflections or thoughts that stem (as the etymology of the word suggests) from his heart or spirit, from his *thymos* (consider also *Oedipus at Colonus* 1199). In accord with this, the related verb (*enthymeisthai*) can mean "to take to heart" or "to ponder or reflect on" something. When, for example, captains approach Xenophon in the hope of persuading him to take on sole command of the army stranded in Asia Minor, three reflections or considerations—*enthymēmata*—come to his mind that incline him to accept the offer; but then again, when he reflects (*enthymoito*) on the uncertainty of the future and hence the risk of throwing away the reputation he has already earned, he is at a loss or perplexed (Xenophon, *Anabasis of Cyrus* 6.1.19–22; consider also *Cynegetikos* 13.9).[13]

If, then, Aristotle did not coin the term, he surely put it to new use. Let us take up just the first of the four arguments he identifies as enthymemes. Aristotle says that a "maxim" is in effect the conclusion of an enthymeme: a man who is by nature sensible should never have his children taught so as to be extraordinarily wise. This maxim or conclusion can be transformed into an enthymeme by supplying the reason for it: children rendered too wise will be made idle, and they will incur the ill-willed envy of their fellows (1394a29–34). The argument may be reconstructed about as follows: to be extraordinarily wise is to become idle oneself and envied by neighbors. To be idle and envied is bad. Therefore a father must never allow his children to be taught such that they become so wise. (Additional premises could of course be supplied.) This seems to comply well enough with the broad definition in the *Rhetoric* of the enthymeme ("establishing that, certain things being the case, something else results from those things because of them, either universally or for the most part, alongside

---

12 · Ross, *Aristotle's Prior and Posterior Analytics,* 499. Consider also: "The reader of Aristotle's *Rhetoric* will find no unambiguous statement defining the enthymeme." Lloyd F. Bitzer, "Aristotle's Enthymeme Revisited," *Quarterly Journal of Speech* 45.4 (1959): 399.
13 · For a helpful historical overview of the term "enthymeme," see Thomas M. Conley, "The Enthymeme in Perspective," *Quarterly Journal of Speech* 70.2 (1984): 168–87; consider also Grimaldi, *Studies,* 67–82.

those things by virtue of their being so"). But this is as much as to say that "enthymeme" here is a loose term indeed for an argument understood as a conclusion and a reason or reasons for it—one that cannot, in this case at least, be set out in properly syllogistic form.[14]

Here we may take up briefly the controversy as to whether an enthymeme as Aristotle understands it is necessarily an "incomplete syllogism."[15] The proposition has found both supporters (Cope)[16] and, more recently, critics. The clearest textual support in the *Rhetoric* for the contention is found in 1.2, where Aristotle notes that the "task" of rhetoric is performed "among the sorts of listeners who are unable to take a synoptic view of what proceeds through many stages or to calculate from afar" (1357a1–4). Accordingly, any syllogism that depends on some prior argumentation will be lengthy, if that dependence is spelled out, and so it will be "not easy to follow." The enthymeme, then, or the reasoning contained in it, should be above all easy to follow, and so "based on few things and often on fewer than those on which is based the first [or ordinary] syllogism" (1357a16–17; consider also the restatement of the point at 1395b24–26). If Dorieus has won an Olympic victory, there is no need to say that he won the contest in which the wreath is at stake: all know that the prize for Olympic victory is the wreath. Yet to say that the enthymeme may or even must omit unnecessary premises ("One must make enthymemes . . . as concise as possible": 1419a18–19) is not to say that it must omit premises or else cease to be an enthymeme. Moreover, *all* argument surely depends on prior awareness of (among other things) the terms at issue—that "all human beings are mortal" requires prior knowledge of the meaning of "human beings" and "mortality," for example. The question remains a controversial one, but the abbreviated or truncated character of the rhetorical syllogism does not seem essential to it, even if brevity is advisable in order to be persuasive.[17]

14 · It is "simply impossible to represent this argument as a syllogism" because "the children have to appear both as the subjects who earn hostility and as the subject of the verb 'to teach' inside the predicate of the maxim"—something that "syllogistic cannot represent." Burnyeat, "Enthymeme," 23–24. So also Braet, "Enthymeme in Aristotle's *Rhetoric*," 106.

15 · The phrase (*sullogismos atelēs*) stems from what is evidently an interpolation in the text of *Prior Analytics* 2.27 (70a10–11); Ross, for one, does not read it.

16 · See E. M. Cope, *An Introduction to Aristotle's "Rhetoric"* (London: Macmillan, 1867), 103 n. 1.

17 · The "fact that brevity is a virtue in enthymemes tells us nothing about the standards of validity to be expected of rhetorical speech, nor does Aristotle ever suggest

To judge from Aristotle's own words, as distinguished from the inge-
nious efforts of some scholars to clarify the enthymeme or the rhetorical
syllogism, the adjective "rhetorical" seems to imply or require a considerable relaxation in the structure of the "first syllogism" (1357a17), whether
it be in the number of premises involved, their completeness, or their
form. It is undeniable that Aristotle is more concerned here with the *content* of enthymemes—with their many topics, specific and common, that
may supply the stuff of rhetorical argumentation—than he is with setting forth any strict form to which it must adhere, and this stands to reason given his description of the audience at whom rhetorical argument
is directed. Indeed, it may be that the word *enthymēma* suggested itself
to Aristotle to describe the core of rhetorical argumentation because the
syllogism at work in rhetoric depends so much on the existing opinions,
the heartfelt convictions or prejudices, of the audience. And in contrast
to the practice of the dialectical syllogism, which requires in at least some
instances the active contributions of an interlocutor, the solitary rhetorician speaks to, but not with, a given audience or crowd. And yet that audience does participate in a kind of conversation with the skilled orator by
silently supplying, from their store of *endoxa* or of *enthymēmata* based on
those *endoxa*, the necessary premises that in the best case bring the "enthymeme" to its intended conclusion.

Aristotle brings 1.2 to a close by introducing "topics." All syllogisms,
both dialectical and rhetorical, are concerned with and based on "topics," be they "specific" or "common" topics. *Topos* means literally "place,"
and by extension the term came to signify a metaphorical place to look
for something or where it is to be found: a heading or classification containing (in the case at hand) rhetorical arguments of the same kind. "Specific topics" are derived from propositions or premises relating to each
class of thing or to a defined subject matter or science—to physics, ethics,
and the like. In strict parlance, then, the art of rhetoric is not concerned
with these specific topics,[18] at least not inasmuch as the concern for them
will propel the rhetorician "unawares [to] fashion a science different from
dialectic and rhetoric. For if he hits on its principles, it will no longer be a
matter of dialectic or rhetoric but rather that science whose principles he

---

that it does. A premise suppressed is still a premise of the argument." Burnyeat, "Enthymeme," 24.

18 · Grimaldi, *Commentary*, ad loc., here cites the remark of L. Spengel, editor of the
Teubner edition of the *Rhetoric*: "From Aristotle's theory nothing save *koinoi topoi*
[common topics] is proper to rhetoric."

has" (1358a25–26). Nonetheless, Aristotle will devote a good part of the *Rhetoric* to taking up what might be classified as specific topics, as exemplified by his account of the aforementioned five political subjects that any would-be advisor must know something about (1.4) and by his sketch of the kinds of regimes and what is advantageous to each (1.8). The peculiarly "in-between" character of rhetoric, between dialectics and politics, is evident here, for the more speakers avail themselves of specific facts relevant to the case or controversy before them, the more persuasive they are likely to be—and so the more they will depart from rhetoric understood as an art of speeches as such: "For the greater number of facts one has, the easier it is to establish something, and the closer they are to the matter at hand, the more immediately relevant and less general they will be"—and hence all the more persuasive (1396b9–11; consider also 1395b29–31).

By contrast, the common points (*ta koina*) belong in principle to every sort of speechmaking, and so to every kind of rhetoric: questions of what is possible and impossible, what did or did not happen, could or could not happen, will or will not be, and the greatness or smallness, importance or pettiness, of something (see 2.18, especially 1391b23–1392a1, noting *tōn koinōn* at 1391b28). Moreover, in 2.23, as part of the discussion of the mode of persuasion that is the *logos*, Aristotle will list twenty-eight "common topics," on the basis of which one may formulate arguments that at least in principle may be found in all three kinds of rhetoric.

Only in 1.3 does Aristotle explicitly identify these three: deliberative, judicial (or "forensic"), and epideictic (or "display," "ceremonial"). Deliberative rhetoric issues in speeches of exhortation or dissuasion, either to pursue or to shun a given course of action, and is most concerned with questions of some future good (advantage) and future harm (disadvantage). Judicial rhetoric issues in speeches of accusation or defense, deals with questions of justice and injustice, and is most concerned with the past: did the defendant commit an unjust act on the date in question? Epideictic rhetoric, finally, issues in speeches of blame or praise—a funeral oration, for example—and is most concerned with what is noble and base. And although epideictic speeches may deal with any time period, with past acts or future consequences, Aristotle contends that it deals mostly with the here and now.

This enumeration of the kinds of rhetoric is clearly meant by Aristotle to be exhaustive rather than exemplary. Yet he does note, in the chapter that effects the transition from the three kinds of rhetoric to the points common to rhetoric (2.18), that there can be a rhetoric used to exhort or dissuade a lone individual (consider 1391b8–17; see also 1358b9). This is as close as Aristotle comes to acknowledging in his *Art of Rhetoric* the possibility, taken up at length by Plato in the *Phaedrus*, of a strictly private, not to say "erotic," rhetoric. Given the overwhelmingly political character of the rhetoric of concern to Aristotle, this is not so surprising. Just as Plato speaks of erotic love where Aristotle prefers to speak of friendship, so Plato treats (also) erotic rhetoric where Aristotle prefers to treat only political rhetoric: the human peak that is essentially private, be it philosophy or love, is somewhat more difficult to glimpse in Aristotle than it is in Plato. Or, to put the same point another way, the dignity and gravity specific to political life are more in evidence in Aristotle than they are in Plato; it was Aristotle, not Plato, who discovered and defended "moral virtue," what Plato's Socrates would have called, or did call, "vulgar and political virtue" (Plato, *Phaedo* 82a11–b1).

As we have just noted, rhetoric appears eventually to be an "in-between" art, partaking of both the formality of analytics and the concrete specificity of politics. This is compatible with the thought that, according to Aristotle, a human being alone of the animals possesses speech or reason; and, as just such an animal possessed of speech, a human being is also the only political animal (consider *Politics* 1253a1–4 and 14–18). Yet one can put the "in-between" character of rhetoric another way: rhetoric partakes of neither the precision of dialectic ("analytics") nor the "prudence" (*phronēsis*) of political science. The key to the exercise of rhetoric, then, is less prudence—to take up the second consideration first—than the ability to guess at or hit on the governing opinions, the *endoxa*, of the crowd before whom one speaks (recall 1355a17–18; see also 1356b32–33); as Aristotle says in his praise of the use of maxims, which are effective "on account of the vulgarity of the listeners" (1395b1–2), one must "hazard a guess as to [or aim at: *stochadzesthai*] the character of the prior assumptions [the audience members] happen to have, and then speak accordingly about them in a universal way" (1395b10–11).

In accord with all of this, the "task of rhetoric is concerned with the sorts of things about which we deliberate"—for we deliberate in order to take some action in matters that are up to us—"and for which we do not possess *technai*"—for in that case we could listen to the advice of the skilled technician in question—"*and* among the sorts of listeners who are unable to take a synoptic view of what proceeds through many stages or to calculate from afar" (1357a1–4; emphasis added). Indeed, one must refrain from making arguments that depend on prior syllogisms, as we have

noted, for the results are "not easy to follow, on account of their length—
one supposes the judge to be a simple [*haplous*] fellow" (1357a10–12).
When Aristotle later repeats this advice to avoid lengthy and hence complicated arguments, he says: "The uneducated are more persuasive in
crowds than are the educated, just as the poets contend that the uneducated speak 'more musically' to a crowd than do the educated. For the
educated state general or universal points, whereas the uneducated speak
on the basis of the things they know and that are near to hand" (1395b26–
31). And from this Aristotle draws the following conclusion: "One should
speak, not on the basis of just any opinion held, but rather on the basis
of those opinions that have been marked off in some way, either by the
judges in question or by those whose authority they accept. And the fact
that this is the way it appears to be, either to everyone or to the greatest number, must be clear [to the speaker]" (1395b31–1396a2). Rhetoric
understood as an art includes the ability to speak "more musically" to a
given audience than do "the educated" in general, or, differently stated,
rhetoric includes the educated ability to imitate to the extent necessary
the musical speech of the uneducated.

  As for dialectic or the syllogistic analysis of generally accepted opinions, to turn now to the other of the two poles between which rhetoric
oscillates, Aristotle indicates in the *Topics* three uses of it: one's own intellectual training, in order to learn to see two sides of the same proposition; "engagement" or "converse" (*enteuxis*) with the many, which begins
from the opinions they hold and which may, on that basis, correct them
when they do not speak in a fine manner; and, finally, supplying the "principles" of the sciences, the foundational premises that make science possible (*Topics* 101a25–b3). Of these three purposes of dialectic, Aristotle in
the *Rhetoric* mentions (and with explicit reference to the *Topics*) only the
second or central one (compare *enteuxis* at *Rhetoric* 1355a29 with *enteuxeis*
at *Topics* 101a27). He does so, however, in the course of his contention
that even an argument based on "the most precise science," or a "teaching"
properly speaking, would fail to persuade some people (recall 1355a24–
29). Accordingly, Aristotle is mostly silent in the *Rhetoric* about attempting to correct the opinions of the many—as Socrates's practice of dialectic, for example, was famous or notorious for doing. Here we may note in
passing that Socrates's own practice of "dialectic" bears some resemblance
to the distinction between a dialectic that looks to correct the opinions
of others, on the one hand, and a rhetoric that looks only to persuade
them, on the other: depending on the nature of his interlocutors, Socrates

sought in conversation either to arrive at the truth of things on the basis of his interlocutor's own opinions or simply to foster agreement to a remarkable degree, without, however, leading the entire argument back to the hypothesis at issue (consider Xenophon, *Memorabilia* 4.6.13–15).

In any event, dialectic as Aristotle presents it includes among its concerns bringing such clarity and order to the *endoxa* of the many as is possible; rhetoric is concerned instead with wringing from those *endoxa* such persuasion as is possible in a given circumstance. Aristotle's opening assertion of the kinship between rhetoric and dialectic has in that context the effect of elevating rhetoric or of defending it; as he gradually details the character of rhetoric, however, we see more clearly that and why rhetoric cannot rise to the level of dialectic, and so is in that way only a "counterpart" to it.

ON THE THREE KINDS OF RHETORIC: DELIBERATIVE RHETORIC (1.4–8)

When Aristotle turns to take up each of the three kinds of rhetoric, he does so in an order slightly different from the one in which he had first mentioned them, namely, deliberative, judicial, and epideictic rhetoric (see 1358b7–8): deliberative rhetoric retains its primary rank in his subsequent analysis, but judicial is taken up last, with epideictic rhetoric rising to take its place (consider 1359a27–29 and 1.4–8 [deliberative], 1.9 [epideictic], and 1.10–15 [judicial]). Perhaps Aristotle acts in accord with his praise of deliberative rhetoric (1354b22–29), by treating it first, and with his criticism of the undue stress on judicial rhetoric characteristic of "the technical writers," by treating it last. At the same time, however, the undeniable importance of judicial matters is suggested by the fact that the rhetoric dealing with them receives the most extensive treatment here, epideictic rhetoric being taken up in a single chapter.[19] And if an enthymeme is the "body" of a mode of persuasion in rhetoric, "enthymemes," in turn, "are most suited to judicial speeches, for what has happened in the past, on account of its lack of clarity, especially admits of [arguments concerning] cause and demonstration" (1368a31–33; see also 1418a1–2). Thus the core of rhetoric as a technical matter is most at home in judicial rhetoric, even if the task of deliberative rhetoric is of greater dignity or worth. Ar-

19 · Consider also the beginning of 2.1, where Aristotle first mentions or alludes to all three kinds of rhetoric but proceeds to speak of only judicial and deliberative.

istotle's initial criticisms of "the technical writers," that they stress judicial rhetoric too much and have neglected the enthymeme, thus prove to be distinct, for to give due weight to the enthymeme will entail a certain emphasis on judicial rhetoric.

To turn, then, to deliberative rhetoric, it finds its proper place in a political assembly of some kind. Its general subject matter is all those good and bad things that may or may not come to be and whose beginning can be traced to us: just as we do not deliberate about what is either necessary or impossible, so we do not deliberate about contingent things over which we have no influence—over matters of chance, for example. The more specific subject matter of deliberative rhetoric is what is advantageous or disadvantageous in politics or to the community. Accordingly, Aristotle's treatment of deliberative rhetoric begins and ends with the most directly political discussions of the entire *Rhetoric*: the five political concerns that belong to political deliberation (revenues; war and peace; the guarding of the territory; imports and exports; and legislation: 1.4; compare Xenophon, *Memorabilia* 3.6.4–13); and the varieties of regimes (democracy; oligarchy; aristocracy; monarchy), together with what is advantageous to each (1.8). The most comprehensive concern that lies behind every political deliberation—surely far behind in most cases— proves to be nothing less than "happiness" (1.5). Accordingly, the speeches of exhortation and dissuasion in which deliberative rhetoric issues are ultimately concerned with happiness and more immediately with the things held either to foster or to impede it, things good or bad (1.6) and better or worse (1.7).

Aristotle's discussion of happiness, in the context of deliberative rhetoric, can serve to remind us that the *Rhetoric* deals in large measure with *endoxa* as distinguished from Aristotle's own judgments of things. For if one compares that discussion to the much longer and more nuanced treatments of happiness found in the first and last books of the *Nicomachean Ethics*, one sees how low the ceiling of the present discussion is. For example, although Aristotle does discuss good luck here as a component of happiness (1361b39–1362a12), he is silent about the grave problem that our exposedness to luck or fortune poses for our hope for happiness, a key theme of the *Ethics*.[20] Here Aristotle is content to speak "summarily," "simply," and "by way of a paradigm" about happiness (1360b6–8),

20 · Consider *Nicomachean Ethics* 1096a1–2, 1098a18–20, 1099a31–b8, 1100b1–12 and context, 1177b24–26, and 1178b33.

and he contends that a "precise account" concerning one of its parts is "not at all useful for what concerns us at present" (1361b34–35). Here Aristotle defines happiness as being one of a list of four possibilities—a faring well accompanied by virtue, *or* self-sufficiency, *or* an abundance of property, *or* the most pleasant and secure life—or again some combination of these. "For quite all agree that happiness is pretty much one or more of these things" (1360b17–18). Whereas in the *Ethics* we learn that happiness is "a certain activity of soul in accord with complete virtue" (1102a5–6), in the *Rhetoric* Aristotle does not explicitly mention the soul (or indeed "activity") in any of the proffered definitions; here "virtue" (of soul) is but one of the twelve "parts"[21] of happiness; and Aristotle expressly postpones the treatment of virtue until the discussion of praise and hence of epideictic rhetoric (1360b18–24, noting even here the absence of "soul"; 1362a12–14). In other words, virtue, to say nothing of contemplative virtue, gets short shrift in the official discussion of happiness in the *Rhetoric* (consider also 1362b5). This may be because "people hold that, of virtue, any amount whatever is sufficient, whereas when it comes to wealth and money and power and reputation and all such things, they seek a limitless excess" (*Politics* 1323a36–38). At any rate, the inadequacy from Aristotle's point of view of the *endoxa* concerning happiness implies that the understanding of the given end or principle that guides every political community is defective. And it falls to the skilled orator, not to elevate that understanding, but to make good use of it.

In the course of patiently recording these authoritative *endoxa*, Aristotle does bring to the reader's attention the limits of the discussion, in part by occasionally drawing near to them; in this respect Aristotle the teacher of rhetoric shows his perspective to be more comprehensive than that of the practicing rhetorician. To take a modest example first, Aristotle is sure to praise, in the account of wealth, the goodness of those "liberal" possessions that as such supply in themselves some enjoyment, as distinguished from any income to be derived from them (1361a16–17 as well as a8; 1367a27). More important, Aristotle makes plain that what a "nation and a city" regard as best "in common" may not be in every respect the same as what is or is held to be best for a "private person" (compare 1360b31 with b34 and 1361a1 with a5). In treating the latter,

21 · The twelve parts of happiness are (1) good birth, (2) abundance of friends, (3) fine friends, (4) wealth, (5) good children, (6) abundance of children, (7) a good old age, (8) the virtues of the body ("for example, health, beauty, strength, size, athletic power"), (9) reputation, (10) honor, (11) good luck, and (12) "virtue" (unmodified).

Aristotle brings out what the political opinions as recorded here omit altogether: that one must pay attention not only to the men but also to the women, to the virtue or excellence belonging to women as such (consider 1360b34–35 and b38; 1361a5–8). This attention Aristotle justifies, it is true, before the bar of political opinion or by recourse to a politically acceptable standard: "For all those whose affairs pertaining to women are in a poor condition, as is the case with the Lacedaemonians, are more or less half unhappy" (1361a9–12; consider *Politics* 1269b12–14 and context). There is a "natural" tendency for the political community to focus on the virtue—especially the courage or manliness (1362b32–33; 1364b20, 35–37; 1366b5–7 and 11–12)—of the males, above all with a view to warfare, and to educate or train them accordingly. From that point of view, moreover, "the beauty of someone in his bloom" (or prime) "relates to the exertions of war, and its being pleasant [to see] seems to go together with its being fearsome." And yet it is the pentathletes, among the youths, who are "most beautiful" inasmuch as they are "naturally fitted for bodily force together with speed," natural capacities that fall among the things "pleasant to see . . . just for the enjoyment of it" (compare 1361b11–13 with b7–11). Aristotle reminds or teaches us, in other words, that there is a superlative natural capacity whose beauty is not reducible to its utility in war.

This is not to deny, in fact it is to affirm, that the general tenor of the discussion of the good or advantageous here is utilitarian. Almost everything is judged by its contribution to one's own advantage, including the concern for honor (it is "pleasant and productive of many goods") and even friendship ("for a friend is both choiceworthy in himself and productive of many [goods]"; compare 1380b35–36). All that is choiceworthy is what is good or better or at any rate less bad for oneself, in the way that "intellect" or "prudence" or "intellect and prudence" would judge the matter (1362a23–26; 1363a16–17, b12–20; 1364b11–18). And when Aristotle turns from the goods that are "pretty much agreed on" to those that are "subject to dispute" (1362b28–30), the principal difference is that the latter goods are communal as distinguished from private; the pivot point is the assertion of the goodness of the just, "for it is something advantageous in common."

Aristotle now suggests that what is good is "the opposite of what is advantageous to enemies. For example, if our being cowards is especially advantageous to our enemies, it is clear that courage would be especially advantageous to the citizens. And in general, that which is the opposite of what our enemies wish for or delight in appears advantageous." People "choose to do ... [things] that are bad for their enemies and good for their friends" or things that will "delight friends or vex enemies." Here the judgment of the prudent—Athena, Theseus, "the goddesses" (Hera, Aphrodite, Athena), and Homer—competes with the judgment implied by the assertion that what "many people aim at" and "fight over" is by that very fact good, "for that which all people aim at was said to be the good, and 'many' people appears tantamount to 'all.'" As for those disputes about what constitutes the greater good or advantage (1.7), Aristotle combines the two standards of judgment or blurs them: "That which the prudent—or all people or the many or most people or the most excellent—would judge or have judged to be good or greater is necessarily so, either simply or insofar as they judged in accord with prudence" (1364b11–14).

The inquiry into the good or advantageous reaches its culmination in what Aristotle himself calls "the greatest and most authoritative consideration of quite all, with a view to being able to persuade and advise in a noble manner"—namely, understanding the variety of regimes and what appears advantageous to each (1.8). Here it is assumed that each regime does not look to the common good or to justice so understood—the terms appear nowhere in the chapter—but instead to what is advantageous to each regime, that is, to the advantage of the "authoritative body" (1365b27) that actually rules in each community: "Quite all are persuaded by what is advantageous, and that which preserves the regime is to its advantage." Perhaps it is for this reason that Aristotle declares at the end of this chapter that he has treated his subject adequately "to the extent commensurate with the present occasion": "what concerns [these matters] has been stated precisely in the *Politics*." And only in the *Politics* do we find Aristotle taking seriously the highest concern of the decent political community, that of justice or the common good, a good that certainly includes the concern for the preservation of the city or regime but goes beyond it, too, in the direction of something higher: the good life. Justice finds its fullest treatment here in the discussion of the rhetoric belonging to courtrooms, but for that the reader must first consider the intervening discussion of epideictic rhetoric.

EPIDEICTIC RHETORIC (1.9)

The adjective *epideictic*, related to the Greek verb meaning to "show," "set forth," or "display" (*epideiknumi*), is understandably translated by some as "ceremonial." Epideictic rhetoric belongs above all to those grand occasions when a community looks up in admiration of something or someone and wishes to give voice to that admiration. Strictly speaking, epideictic rhetoric has two concerns of equal weight according to Aristotle: praising the nobility characteristic of virtue and blaming the baseness characteristic of vice. Here, however, Aristotle focuses entirely on praise as distinguished from blame, which he leaves for the reader to deduce from his positive remarks (see the last sentence of 1.9). This choice means that the nobility belonging to virtue is front and center throughout the chapter.

Aristotle begins by reproducing the *endoxa* concerning the noble or beautiful (*to kalon*), and the bifurcation within those *endoxa* is striking: the noble is either "what is choiceworthy for its own sake, and praiseworthy accordingly" or "it is that which is good, it being pleasant because it is good" (consider also Plato, *Gorgias* 474d–475c). That the nobility attending virtue meets more the first criterion than the second is at least implied in Aristotle's immediately following observation: "So if this is the noble, virtue is necessarily noble, since virtue, being good, is praised." If there is something in which what is pleasant and good and noble all converge (consider *Nicomachean Ethics* 1099a24–25; compare a27–28), there is also something noble whose goodness is tied to praise, to the approval of others. To take an extreme example, whatever is peculiar to or characteristic of a given city will be noble, and "in Lacedaemon to have long hair is noble, for that is a sign of a free man, since it is not at all easy to perform a menial task with long hair" (1367a27–31; compare 1381a22–24). But people praise especially those who choose what seems noble as distinguished from the good or advantageous for themselves, let alone the pleasant. The classic embodiment of this choice is Achilles:

> Both those who praise and those who blame do not examine whether someone acted advantageously or harmfully, but they often praise him because, in slighting what was profitable for himself, he acted because it was noble to do so—for example, they praise Achilles because he came to the aid of his comrade Patroclus, knowing that he himself must die, when it was otherwise possible for him to live. To him, then, such a death was nobler, whereas continuing to live was advantageous. (1358b38–1359a6)

Accordingly, people regard as noble "those virtues characterized by the enjoyment they bring others, rather than oneself. Hence what is just, and justice [itself], are noble" (1367a18–19).

The fact that everyone, so to speak, praises the goodness of virtue is easy to understand on the basis of the premise that "virtue, as it seems [*dokei*], is a capacity to provide and protect good things, and a capacity to effect many great benefactions—even all benefactions pertaining to everything" (1366a36–b1). "Preeminence" in virtue consists in benefiting "everyone" (1367b6–7). We may praise virtue, then, because we appreciate the results of the virtues of others: we are benefited by them. According to this logic, "the greatest virtues are necessarily the ones of most use for others, if in fact virtue is a capacity for benefaction." Ranked first among the virtues so understood are justice and courage, on account of their utility to others in peace and in war, with liberality (generosity with money) following close behind (1366b5–7). The praise we offer to virtue or to the virtuous, through the practice of epideictic rhetoric, could well seem to be little more than an exhortation to others to benefit us.

  Without announcing it, however, Aristotle is also careful to reproduce the special character of nobility as it is seen or experienced, not by someone treated virtuously (i.e., advantageously), but by someone acting virtuously. Or, more precisely, Aristotle points to our admiration of those who nobly serve the good of another, even as we look upon such service as something other than its direct beneficiaries. For in this context he brings out repeatedly our admiration for virtue or nobility precisely because it demands, at a minimum, the neglect of one's own good, which is a difficult thing inasmuch as each of us seeks "happiness" and does all else for its sake (1362b10–12). Noble, then, are

> all those virtuous actions someone carries out not for his own sake. And all those things that are good unqualifiedly that someone does on behalf of the fatherland, while overlooking his own [good]. And the things good by nature, and which are good not for him himself, for [natural goods] of that sort would be for his own sake. . . . And all such deeds as are for the sake of others, since they are less for one's own sake. And all such actions as benefit others, but not oneself, and as benefit benefactors—for that is just. And beneficent deeds, for they do not pertain to oneself. (1366b36–1367a5)

The very nobility prized and praised by "everyone" seems to be of great goodness to others and of little or no goodness—indeed, of some badness—to the virtuous themselves. In faithfully reproducing the *endoxa* concerning virtue and nobility, Aristotle is compelled to present these as good for others because advantageous to them, including "the fatherland" (1366b37; consider also 1395a14); and he presents them as good for the virtuous themselves—because bad for them and hence noble and praiseworthy.

Aristotle then turns to offer practical advice in formulating a speech of praise, and he does so by addressing the reader in the second-person singular for the first time (1367b37). His advice, it has to be said, is not guided by the truth, by a frank assessment of the object of praise. The simpleton should be called "upstanding," for example; the angry and the manic, "frank"; the reckless, "courageous"; the spendthrift, "liberal." "For this will be the opinion of the many, and, at the same time, fallacious reasoning derives from the cause in question: if someone is apt to run risks where it is not necessary to do so, all the more would he be held to be such where it *is* noble to run them, and if someone is lavish with any chance persons, he will be such also with friends" (1367b3–6). Again, Aristotle advocates the use of "many kinds" of "amplification"—making the very most of some quality or attendant circumstance—and if the person in question leaves the speaker with mighty little to praise, then compare the fellow to someone whom it is easier to praise. If the fellow is of "good birth," then make something of that, on the grounds that "it is likely that good human beings arise from those who are good"—a proposition Aristotle himself will later deny (consider 1390b26–31).

Since 1.9 contains Aristotle's principal account of virtue in the *Rhetoric*, the differences between the *endoxa* concerning virtue and the presentation of virtue in the *Ethics* deserve mention. First and most obviously, Aristotle does not introduce here the crucial distinction between moral and contemplative virtue that determines the argument of the *Ethics*. In fact the term "moral virtue" appears just once in the *Rhetoric*, if I am not mistaken, and that only late in book 3 (1414a21); "contemplative virtue" is never mentioned. Accordingly, Aristotle enumerates nine parts of "virtue" (unmodified) and includes prudence and wisdom in the company of justice, courage, moderation, magnificence, greatness of soul, liberality, and gentleness (1366b1–3). He thus omits ambition or love of honor (*Ethics* 4.4) as well as the three "social virtues"—truthfulness, wittiness, and friendliness—that are least obviously political or subject to law (*Ethics* 4.6–8). Here virtue is said to be a "capacity" (*dunamis*), whereas in the *Ethics* it is explicitly said not to be one (1106a6–9) but rather a "characteristic" (*hexis*). And it cannot be said that courage ranks first or even second among the virtues in the *Ethics*, for we learn eventually that it, together with moderation, is the virtue of the non-rational part of the soul only and merely (see *Ethics* 3.10, beg.). Aristotle's definitions of justice, courage, and moderation in the *Rhetoric* all feature what "the law" (*nomos*) commands, whereas the *Ethics* stresses instead the guidance supplied by "reason," "correct reason" (consider, e.g., *Ethics* 1103b31–34); it is characteristic of a false sort of courage, for example, to take one's bearings by the penalties for cowardice inflicted by "the laws" (*Ethics* 1116a17–19).

Above all, Aristotle here emphasizes the benefits that accrue to others or to the community from virtuous deeds, as we have seen, whereas in the *Ethics* the end of virtue is "the noble" and nothing beyond it (consider, e.g., 1115b12–13): the moral virtues are meant to be choiceworthy in themselves or "for their own sakes" and hence not means to some other, supposedly higher end or greater good. The end of moral virtue is never said there to be the good of the fatherland, for example (consider *Ethics* 1169a20 and context). From this vantage point one can begin to glimpse the extraordinary task that Aristotle sets for himself in the *Ethics*. By teaching of "moral virtue," Aristotle means to bring as much clarity and orderliness to moral opinion as is possible within the political community; he means also to sketch a respectable vantage point within the community that permits or compels one to look up to something other than any community or its ends (consider, e.g., *Nicomachean Ethics* 1177b4–24 and *Politics* 1323b21–26).

JUDICIAL RHETORIC (1.10–15)

Aristotle's account of judicial rhetoric, and hence of accusation and defense, has three express aims: to make clear (1) the ends for the sake of which people commit injustice; (2) how they themselves are disposed when they do so; and (3) the sorts of people most likely to be the victims of injustice. The account proves to be organized as follows. After a preliminary definition of injustice that depends decisively on law, written and unwritten (1368b5–26), Aristotle inquires into the motives of the unjust—what it is they typically hope to gain or avoid by committing injustice (1.10–11)—together with a sketch of their characteristic state or disposition when they do commit it (1.12, up to 1372b23). He then brings to a close his stated program of inquiry by indicating who the typical victims of injustice are (1372b23–1373a37). He concludes: "These, then, are pretty much the states that those who commit injustice are in, and the sorts of injustices they commit, and against what sorts of people, and why" (1.12, end). Yet the section devoted to judicial rhetoric continues for three more chapters (1.13–15), and so it remains to be seen what contribution they make to the treatment as a whole.

Aristotle begins from a definition, not of justice, but of injustice, presumably because it is more pertinent to judicial rhetoric and may in any case be easier to identify (consider *Nicomachean Ethics* 1129a31 and context). Injustice is "doing harm voluntarily contrary to the law." Aristotle thus drops the ambiguity inherent in the terms "justice" and "injustice" that he makes so much of in the *Ethics*: as the "unjust" person may refer either to a lawbreaker or to someone eager for too much gain (or too little sacrifice), so the "just" person may refer either to someone obedient to law or to one who takes only his fair share of gain (or all his fair share of sacrifice) (*Ethics* 1129a25–b1). Here, by contrast, Aristotle takes his bearings exclusively by law. Yet "law" (*nomos*), too, turns out to be ambiguous. For it can mean either "particular law," which has been "written down, in accord with which people govern themselves," or "general [*koinos*] law," meaning "all those unwritten laws that seem to be agreed on by everyone": a shared sense of right and wrong not reducible to, and sometimes even in conflict with, particular (positive) law.

The more important and controversial idea here is surely that of the "general" law. For when Aristotle returns to law in 1.13, at the beginning of the section unanticipated by his opening programmatic statement, he adds not only that the particular law, too, can be unwritten, in the form of what one might call custom, but also that the general law "accords with nature" (1373b6). Aristotle thus seems to affirm the existence of what is in Greek philosophic thought a contradiction in terms: a convention (*nomos*) that is by nature (*physēi*). For example, in the *Ethics* Aristotle reports that "the noble things and the just things," which "admit of much dispute and variability," are as a result "held to exist by law [*nomos*] alone and not by nature" (1094b15–16); and although Aristotle contends that there is indeed something *just* by nature (*Ethics* 5.7), he does not entertain there the thought of a *law* by nature. For law is traceable to human making or opinion, and so is essentially changeable, whereas what is by nature is not due to human beings in the same way, and so enjoys a fixity the merely conventional cannot claim: fire by nature burns the same everywhere, in Greece and in Persia. And even here, in the *Rhetoric*, Aristotle immediately drops the *law* by nature in favor of the *just*, or he equates the two: "For there is something that all people divine, a *koinos* justice and injustice by nature, even if there is no community in relation to one another and no compact."

The striking looseness in Aristotle's terminology here continues in his elaboration, by way of three examples, of the law (or justice) by nature. First, according to Aristotle, Sophocles's Antigone contends that it is "a just thing" to bury her disgraced brother precisely because doing so is just "by nature." Second, Empedocles says that refraining from killing any animate being is not just among some people but unjust for others; rather, refraining from such killing is "lawful [*nomimon*] for all." And third, Alcidamas says (if the scholiast on this passage is to be believed): "Free did god send forth all; nature made no one a slave." A certain burial rite, then, the prohibition against killing, and the free nature of all human beings: these are the three examples Aristotle adduces of "the law that accords with nature."

All three prove much less than they might first appear to. For it is Aristotle, not Antigone, who speaks of what is just *by nature*. Antigone herself, while professing ignorance of precisely how extralegal justice appears, traces its ultimate source emphatically to gods—to Zeus and Dike in particular. About nature here she is perfectly silent (Sophocles, *Antigone* 450–60). Aristotle comes close to confirming this when, in 1.15, he gives another, and this time highly truncated, quotation from *Antigone*: "For these things, then, I was not, . . . of any man, going to." The original reads as follows: "For these things, I was not—because I feared the pride of any man—going to pay the penalty among the gods" (458). Thus Aristotle declines to quote Antigone's recourse to "the gods." The immediate source of Antigone's sense of obligation is surely the family, and however "complicated" her own may be, it has a root in nature; but she understands herself to be complying with a *divine* injunction that as such trumps the wish of any mortal, ruler or no. Antigone's self-understanding does not yet establish "the law that accords with nature." Similarly, Empedocles's apparently blanket prohibition against killing all animate things seems a bizarre example of "something that all people divine": neither brute nor human nature observes this *nomimon*. In his commentary on the passage, Averroes cites this as an example of precisely a particular, not a natural, law: "This is not obligatory either for all or by nature."[22] And as for the contention of Alcidamas, who speaks ambiguously of both god and na-

---

22 · Averroes, *Commentaire moyen à la "Rhétorique"* 1.13.2, end.

ture, Aristotle himself is willing to go on record as affirming the existence of the slave by nature (e.g., *Politics* 1254b16–20). Even the case against all slavery he reproduces does not mention a law that accords with nature. Aristotle, then, failed to see, as a law of nature divined by everyone, the prohibition against slavery.

It is surely wrong, on the basis of the *Rhetoric*, to credit Aristotle with founding the tradition of "natural law."[23] At most he gives voice to the thought that, generally speaking, human beings divine a sense of obligation—call it law, call it justice or right—that is not exhausted by this or that positive law: that we should be grateful to a benefactor, for example, even if ingratitude is not illegal (1374a23–24; compare Xenophon, *Education of Cyrus* 1.2.7). What is more, Aristotle manifestly introduces this thought or divination for rhetorical purposes, as becomes clearest in that section of 1.15 devoted to the "non-technical mode of proof" constituted by "laws" (1375a27–b26). For if the written law is against your case, then you should appeal to "the general law" and undermine the written law in any number of ways, flattery included: "the judge is like the assayer of silver in that he distinguishes the counterfeit justice from the true," and "it belongs to a better man to make use of and abide by the unwritten rather than the written laws" (1375b5–8). Then again, if the written law favors your side, contend instead that "there is no difference between a law's not having been set down and its not being used" or that "seeking to be wiser than the laws is just the thing that is prohibited in the laws that are praised" (1375b20–25). In other words, "the law that accords with nature" is of interest here inasmuch as it can be used to undo the force of a given written (or indeed unwritten) particular law that is damaging to one's case.

After his first definition of injustice, Aristotle inquires into the motives of the unjust, and he makes clear that this inquiry is meant to serve a practical purpose: "For it is clear that the accuser must examine how many and which of these things characterize the accused, things that all who commit injustice against their neighbors aim at, just as it is clear that he who is defending himself must examine which of these things, and how many of them, do *not* characterize him" (1368b29–32). Following Aristotle's lead, we may summarize his account of the motives of all people and hence also of the unjust as follows: "Quite all the things that people

23 · "Natural law becomes a philosophic theme for the first time in Stoicism." Leo Strauss, "On Natural Law," in *Studies in Platonic Political Philosophy* (Chicago: University of Chicago Press, 1983), 140.

do on their own account either are good or appear good, or are pleasant or appear pleasant" (1369b18–20; compare 1369a5–7). The pleasant and the good, then, be they real or merely apparent, have an unshakable hold on us, and our yearning for them in large measure determines our actions. Because Aristotle has already treated the good in the section devoted to deliberative rhetoric, as he notes, he turns instead to an account of pleasure as a motive (1.11); Aristotle thus acts on the supposition that the good is not pleasure, or he rejects in deed hedonism.

Aristotle states, immediately before turning to discuss pleasure, that the definitions he offers will be "sufficient" for the purpose "if they are in each case neither unclear nor [overly] precise [*akribeis*]" (1369b31–32; consider also, e.g., 1418a39–b1). Yet the account of pleasure in particular is not obviously limited to the demands of rhetoric in dealing with the motives of the unjust. For example: "Both learning and wondering are for the most part pleasant, for in wonder there is desire to learn such that the object of wonder is an object of desire, and in learning there is a coming into one's natural state" (1371a31–34). What Aristotle presents as serving a strictly practical (rhetorical) purpose, then, clear enough but far from exacting, oversteps that limit from time to time; the same will be true of his account of the passions, as we will see.

Aristotle posits the following as his "hypothesis" concerning pleasure: "Pleasure is a certain motion of the soul and a concentrated, perceptible settling into the soul's underlying natural condition, whereas pain is the opposite" (1369b33–35). In this way Aristotle stresses the role of nature in determining our pleasures, the natural pleasures being identified here with those stemming from the needs of the body (thirst, hunger, sex) and the senses of touch, smell, hearing, and sight (1370a20–25). But then again, complicated creatures that we are, our sources of pleasure can be altered by habituation, "for the habitual happens just as if it is already by nature: habit bears some similarity to nature, since what happens often is close to what happens always, and while nature is a matter of 'always,' habit is a matter of 'often'" (1370a7–9). Even those things marked by necessity and compulsion, which are by nature unpleasant, may become pleasant should we become habituated to them.

Now, this distinction, between pleasures traceable to nature and those traceable to habit, must be put together with the primacy of "desire" in us, to which Aristotle turns next, for "quite everything the desire for which is in us, is pleasant," desire being "a longing for the pleasant." The "non-rational" desires are here linked to the natural (i.e., bodily) pleasures, whereas the "rational desires" are not said to be natural. What then is their status or character? These rational desires are rational in the sense, and only in the sense, that they depend on *logos*, on "some supposition" we form (consider 1370a19–20), and they are produced in us by undergoing "some persuasion." "For people desire both to behold and to possess many things because of what they have heard and been persuaded of": "hearing" may give rise to natural pleasures (1370a24), but it is also key to the formation of our "rational" desires and hence to the pleasures that stem from their satisfaction. The import of this remark for rhetoric is clear enough, for it implies that rhetoric has the power to foster pleasure in the audience by means of persuasion; but the remark surely goes beyond rhetoric, since law or convention or custom, for example, may habituate us to derive pleasure even from its dictates or demands.

Pleasures, then, may arise on account of the nature of the body, on the one hand, and on account of the soul's openness to both habit and persuasive speech, on the other. Pleasures belong also to our peculiar ability to dwell in the past, the present, and the future, more or less simultaneously. Pleasure, that is, may be gained from an experience here and now; from recollection of the past—even recollection of things unpleasant in themselves, if we triumphed over them; and from hopes for the future. Among the sources of pleasure mentioned in this context is erotic love, which Aristotle presents as supplying present pleasure because we "take delight not only in the presence of the beloved but also in remembering him in his absence." Presumably that absence is only temporary. That Aristotle omits mention of the pleasures of love connected with the future, or with the awareness of the future, may be compensated for by his immediate recourse to the pleasures—surely the austere pleasures—of "mourning and lamentation": just as the (temporary) absence of the beloved furnishes pleasure, so even the (permanent) absence of the deceased affords pleasure, in remembering the sort of person he or she was. Both love and death, then, can be accompanied by pleasure, if also mixed with pain. Just as memories of past trials may be pleasant now, provided one was "saved" or preserved therefrom (1370b4), so the anticipation of even the distant future may be pleasant, provided we somehow believe or hope that we will be "saved" or preserved then too. Aristotle says in another context that whatever we conceive an erotic desire for is possible, on the grounds that "nobody loves or desires what is impossible"—to which he is compelled to add, "for the most part" (1392a23–25).

To return to the broader context of justice: if the unjust hope to at-

tain some pleasure or (other) good for themselves, or at least rid themselves of a greater ill, their victims are typically those from whom the
unjust expect to suffer less than they will be profited: those who are far
distant, the easygoing, those off their guard, the easily slandered, those in
the grip of shame, friends or the friendless. The precision and specificity
with which Aristotle speaks here suggests, at least, that he was remarkably open-minded in forming his circle of acquaintances or in the company he sometimes kept, for there are some things one cannot learn from
even the best books.

We have just seen that the three chapters forming a sort of appendix
to the treatment of justice proper (1.13–15) serve the purpose of clarifying
the character of law, written and unwritten, particular and general, and
of exemplifying the use in judicial rhetoric of "the law that accords with
nature." To these Aristotle adds an account of what it is to be treated unjustly (1373b27–38), which means that he turns or returns to looking at injustice from the victim's point of view. This gives way to an explanation of
the ambiguity of actions (1373b38–1374a18). Someone, that is, may well
concede that a given deed was done but deny that a legal charge properly
applies: "For example, someone did take something but did not steal it;
and he struck the first blow but acted without insolence; and he engaged
in intercourse but committed no adultery; or he stole but did not rob a
temple (for what was stolen did not belong to a god)" (1374a2–5). In the
contest between the two parties, accuser and accused, Aristotle in effect
counsels keeping a cool head: even striking another and taking something
in stealth need not by themselves constitute crimes (1374a13–17). This
thought leads to an account of the limits of law to delineate what is just
or unjust, for there may be a kind of justice that either transcends what the
particular written law can command—for example, to assist one's friends
or a benefactor—or is simply omitted from the law. These omissions may
be voluntary or involuntary on the part of legislators: involuntary when
the omission simply escapes their notice, voluntary when it is impossible
for the law to speak both universally and accurately but must instead rest
content with addressing what is only "for the most part so" (1374a25–31).

To remedy these two omissions or failings characteristic of particular law, Aristotle has recourse, not to natural law, but to "equity"
(1374a26–b23), a kind of justice beyond the particular law. If the letter
of the law says that striking another while wearing a ring is a graver crime
than simple assault, an equitable interpretation of the particular facts may

deny it (1374a35–b2). Not every "mistake" or error is an injustice, and "forgiveness" may well be called for: "Examine, not the law, but the legislator, and not the legislator's statement but his understanding, and not the action but the choice involved . . . and not the sort of person the fellow is now but the sort of person he always or for the most part was" (1374b10–16). Just as he does also in the *Ethics* (5.10), Aristotle here seeks to calm moral indignation by way of equity, by an appeal to a less narrow or crabbed sense of fairness: "It belongs to equity, too, to remember the good things one has undergone, rather than the bad. . . . And to be willing to have things decided by *logos* rather than by deed. And to be willing to proceed to arbitration rather than to a legal suit, for the arbitrator sees what is equitable, whereas the juror sees [only] the law, and the arbitrator was invented for this reason—so that equity would hold sway" (1374b16–22). Equity, one might say, wishes to fulfill the promise of every law and of all justice—that it be good for all those subject to it. As a measure of the distance between the ordinary *endoxa* and the spirit of equity, it is enough to compare what Aristotle says about the equitable person—that it belongs to him "to tolerate it when being treated unjustly" (1374b18)—with this: "Being avenged on one's enemies and not being reconciled with them [is noble], for payback is just and justice is noble, and it belongs to a courageous man not to get the worst of it, and victory and honor are among the noble things" (1367a20–22).

Of a piece with Aristotle's advice in the spirit of equity is his subsequent account (1.14) of the greater or lesser injustice. For there are two ways this may be judged: by recourse to the potential that lies within the perpetrator implied by his act; and by the actual harm he has done (1374b29–30). Judged from the harm done, then, stealing three consecrated half-obols from a temple is a small thing; judged from the potential to commit injustice the act implies, it is great. Yet Aristotle evinces a clear preference here for looking to the actual harm done. He thus tries to support a certain forgiveness, or he tries to dampen even the kind of anger likely to be roused by temple-robbing and the like (1374b25–29; recall 1374a4–5; also 1363b32). We conclude that an important purpose of the section constituted by 1.13–15 is to alter ordinary opinion, in part by appealing to thoughts—of the necessary limits of legal justice, for example, or of all law—that are easy to forget when in the grip of moral anger. This section, then, is one of the relatively rare places in the *Rhetoric* where Aristotle seeks not just to record ordinary opinion but to leaven it.

JUSTICE AND RHETORIC

If Aristotle's principal discussion of justice is to be found, reasonably enough, in his treatment of judicial rhetoric, justice or the concern for it nonetheless appears in many places throughout the *Rhetoric*. A somewhat more general look at justice is therefore warranted.

We have already seen Aristotle's contention that the power of rhetoric must be governed by something other and better than it: by love of the truth, for example, or concern for justice. In fact, as we have seen as well, the defense of justice itself is among the legitimate uses of rhetoric. That rhetoric is capable in principle of either defending or defeating the just cause ("persuading others of opposites") is an indication of a serious problem, and not only with rhetoric. Justice, that is, may be by nature "superior" (*kreittō*) to injustice, but it is not for that reason alone always "stronger" (*kreittō*) than injustice (1355a21 and context). Aristotle suggests that this difficulty, the possible weakness of justice in the world, must have its effect on the practice of a decent rhetoric. For, as he remarks in the course of his treatment of diction and delivery in book 3, a clever delivery can determine victory, not just in poetic contests, but in political ones too: style may well triumph over substance even where the stakes are high. Aristotle traces this regrettable fact first to "the depravity of the regimes" (1403b35). Indeed, a concern for such showy things is "vulgar" (1404a1). Yet he also defends his own treatment of rhetorical delivery and diction, on the grounds that "the whole matter of concern in rhetoric is related to opinion, [and] one should be concerned with [diction], not on the grounds that it is correct to do so, but on the grounds that it is necessary." Justice itself, it is true, deplores this state of affairs: "Justice, at any rate, seeks out nothing more, when it comes to the speech, than not causing [the listeners] pain or delight, for it is just to contend [against one's opponent] with the facts themselves, such that anything apart from the demonstration is superfluous." This high standard set by justice cannot always be complied with, however, for as a matter of fact diction "has great power . . . on account of the depravity of the listener" (1404a7–9). Accordingly, attention to the delivery of the speech "has some small *necessary* presence in all instruction, for speaking in this or that way does make some difference in making one's point clear" (1404a8–10; emphasis added).

What does this concession on Aristotle's part mean? It means that, in the case of precisely those speakers who wish to defend the just course, their strict adherence to the mode of speaking approved of by justice will lead them to fail too many times—a speech that refuses on principle to foster either pain or pleasure in the audience seems doomed to fail—and so the "necessary" concern for delivery and the like must take precedence over the procedure preferred by justice. Justice, in other words, must yield to a kind of necessity. It is therefore inadequate to say, as Aristotle had contended early on, that the just use of rhetoric is sufficient to assure that rhetoric will secure the greatest benefits and avoid doing the greatest harm (recall 1355b6–7 and context)—at least if we mean by "just use" compliance with the standard of conduct preferred by justice itself. Aristotle urges us here to comply instead with the harsh necessity according to which the defense of justice must sometimes set its course by the depths to which the unjust are willing to sink. Precisely the defense of justice may demand, for example, that the skilled rhetorician thwart the jury's anger that has been roused by a clever prosecutor against an innocent defendant, and that he do so by means of arguments that are more persuasive than true, that are craftily arranged, and that are movingly delivered. Aristotle is concerned to teach us, not only *that* this must be done but also, in outline at least, *how* it may be done. He therefore presupposes that his audience is decent or that their interest in rhetoric is not simply reducible to the desire to "get ahead" (consider the comparable case of the audience best suited to study politics: *Nicomachean Ethics* 1095a2–11 and 1179b29–31).

When we cast a somewhat broader glance at justice in the *Rhetoric*, we see that, in the context of an enumeration of the things held to be good, "happiness" is followed immediately by "the goods of the soul," the first of which is precisely "justice" (1362b12 and context). Justice, then, would seem to be an important example of "that which is choiceworthy for its own sake, and that for the sake of which we choose something other than it, and that which all things, or all things that have sense perception or intellect, aim at (or would aim at should they gain intellect)" (1362a21–24). Aristotle elaborates on this last point as follows: "All that intellect would give to each, and all that intellect does give to each individually—this is what is good for each; and that which, when it is present, renders each in a good condition and possessed of self-sufficiency" (1362a24–27). Justice, then, first appears in the *Rhetoric* as a good the intellect approves of because it is good for the just themselves. Surely this much is implied by the inclusion of justice among, and probably chief among, the "goods of the soul." And it is from this point of view, perhaps, that justice may be defined as "a virtue through which each attains the things that are one's own, and as the law [indicates], injustice being that through which one attains what belongs to others and not as the law indicates."

But when Aristotle returns to speak of virtue at greater length, in 1.9, and there again lists justice first among the parts of virtue (1366b1), he stresses instead the *endoxon* that "the greatest virtues are necessarily the ones of most use for others, if in fact virtue is a capacity for benefaction." Hence, as we have seen, people honor in time of war the courageous above all and, in peacetime too, those who are just: justice is praised because it is *the* inclination to benefit others. "The just," as Aristotle notes in another place, is held to be good because it is "something advantageous in common" (1362b28). So great is the inclination to see in justice the concern for the good of others or of the whole that, in his discussion of the "greater good" or "better," Aristotle gives this as an example of what is regarded as better—at least by the better sort of person: "It is better to suffer injustice than to inflict it, for this is what the more just person would choose" (1364b21–24). Aristotle thus reproduces the stand taken by Socrates in the *Gorgias*, to the amusement or bafflement of Callicles; and he equates "better" with "more just," as distinguished from the considerations that immediately surround justice in this context, namely, the more prudent (1364b11–18) and the more pleasant (1364b23–28). The just person, then, as distinguished from the pleasure-seeker and even the prudent, prefers to suffer than to do injustice because he looks in all things to the good of another, as distinguished from his own good, or at any rate he prefers suffering something bad himself, if he must, to harming another.

In the element of opinion, then, justice is, as a or the virtue of soul, one's own truest good; and it is the good of another, which may come at very great cost to oneself. In recording the *endoxa* concerning justice, Aristotle thus lays bare a typical confusion concerning its goodness: justice is at once the most excellent of the virtues, "neither the evening star nor the morning dawn being so wondrous" (*Nicomachean Ethics* 1129b28–29), and it is essentially the good of somebody else. One could attempt to reconcile these conflicting *endoxa* by contending that precisely the just concern for the good of others *is* one's own truest good or at least that such just concern issues from the state of soul best also for oneself. Hence the preference to suffer injustice over committing it could be explained on the grounds of the supreme goodness, for the just themselves, of possessing a just soul: to be willing to treat others unjustly amounts to a kind of cancer in one's own soul. But this does not solve the puzzle—it may post-pone solving the puzzle—of precisely whose good is primary.

Now, Aristotle is surely right to note that, in making (deliberative) speeches that involve justice, "one must grasp whether it is good or is not good on the basis of the attributes that belong to justice and to the good" (1396a31–33); to defend justice properly, we remember, one must come to know also the arguments against it (recall 1355a29–33). Aristotle's lengthy enumeration of the motives of the unjust (1.11–12), which supplies in out-line the stuff of every crime novel ever written or to be written, amounts to this: in attempting to commit injustice, the unjust believe that the greater good (understood not least as the greater pleasure) will be theirs. They therefore hold that successful or unpunished injustice is best, with only unsuccessful injustice, or justice avenged, being worse for them than having to stick, alas, to the just course. This implies that the perfect *repu-tation* for justice, combined with injustice in fact, would make for an en-viable life according to them.

No wonder, then, that some people are attracted to rhetoric's reputa-tion in certain circles as an all-powerful art capable of convincing any-one of anything—even, for example, that one is supremely just (consider 1372a11–12). And given the ordinary confusion about the goodness of justice, this sentiment, of the inherent badness of justice, is found not only in the criminal element. As Aristotle notes, "People assert that even justice is a small thing, because it is more choiceworthy to be held to be just than to be it—but not so in the case of being healthy." Human beings "do not praise the same things out in the open and behind closed doors, but in the open they praise the just and the noble things especially, while in private they want the advantageous things more" (1399a28–91). What we have called the problem of justice first appears in the *Rhetoric* as the fact that the just course may sometimes be defeated; it has now appeared as the opinion that the just course sometimes *deserves* to be defeated—that is, that it is sometimes bad. As Aristotle says in another context, it is held that "the just is not altogether good," for if that were the case "justly" would be the same as "well" or "advantageously," but instead, "as things stand, dying justly is not choiceworthy" (1397a20–23). Or, as he also notes as if in passing, no one will be indignant if someone is just or courageous, "for neither do people feel pity at the opposites of these" (1387a12–13): we do not pity the unjust in particular because we do not (consistently) believe that they are suffering something bad as a result of their injustice or that their injustice is inherently bad for them. On the contrary, we tend to become indignant at the unjust when they "get away with it," with something, that is, we regard as good for them.

Aristotle does not solve the problem of justice in the *Rhetoric*, but he is careful both to record it and to indicate its importance for persuasion: from the fact that (to repeat) people "do not praise the same things out in the open and behind closed doors, but in the open they praise the just and the noble things especially, while in private they want the advantageous things more," one should "draw from these [opposing views] the one or the other as a conclusion" (1399a28–32). Aristotle says of this "topic" alone that it "exercises a very great authority" in producing "paradoxes."

THE MODES OF PERSUASION: PASSIONS (2.1–11)

The first chapter of book 2 both summarizes part of the ground covered in book 1 and prepares for what is to come. The specific topics taken up in book 1—among them what is good or bad, noble or base, just or unjust— serve as the subject matter of enthymemes and the source material from which the rhetorician will fashion them, for "enthymemes are concerned with these matters and are based on them, as appropriate for each kind of speechmaking" (1377b19–20). With this much for now concerning the speech itself or the *logos* narrowly conceived (consider 2.18–26), Aristotle turns to the importance of the speaker's "establishing that he himself is a certain sort of person," on the one hand, and his "rendering the judge of a certain sort," on the other. In deliberative rhetoric especially, but secondarily in judicial too, it is of vital importance that the speaker appear to the audience to be of a certain sort—decent or credible, for example, or otherwise sympathetic; that the audience suppose him to be disposed toward them in a certain way—favorably; and that as a result "they themselves happen to be disposed in a certain way" toward him—also favorably.

All three goals involve altering the judgments or opinions of the audience. As for the perception of the speaker's decency or credibility, this depends on his appearing to be (1) prudent or knowledgeable, (2) virtuous, and (3) of goodwill (consider also Plato, *Gorgias* 486e5 and following). "It is necessarily the case, therefore, that he who seems to possess all three of these is credible in the eyes of his audience." This effect produced in the audience implies that, according to them, it is impossible for someone to be prudent, virtuous, and of goodwill and yet reserved with the truth or

indeed deceptive. But Socrates, for one, despite his being prudent, virtuous, and philanthropic, eventually became notorious for his "irony" or for
saying rather less than he thought (*Nicomachean Ethics* 1127b25–26), and
in general people "get angry at those who are ironic to them when they
are being serious" (*Rhetoric* 1379b31–32).

Aristotle turns next to consider, and at much greater length, the passions, that is, the things that the audience undergoes or suffers (*ta pathē*)
on account of the speech (2.1–11). Aristotle's account of the passions lies
at more or less the center of the *Art of Rhetoric* and is certainly central to
it. Commentators over the ages have understandably devoted much attention to the section, for it constitutes Aristotle's most extensive remarks
on the subject of the passions and is in any case extraordinarily rich, combining as it does a broad scope with eagle-eyed detail.[24] We cannot do
more than offer a brief overview of the section, followed by a closer account of the first passion he takes up, and the one to which he devotes
most attention: anger.

In *De anima*, Aristotle distinguishes between the approach to the
definition of the passions characteristic of a student of nature (*physikos*)
and that of a dialectician (*dialektikos*). The former will define anger, for
example, as "a boiling of the blood or heat around the heart," the latter
as "a longing to inflict pain in return"; the former thus "gives [as a defi-
nition] the material" involved, the latter "the form and the *logos*" (*De
anima* 403a29–b3). It is only to be expected, given rhetoric's status as a
counterpart to dialectic, that Aristotle proceeds here much more in the
spirit of the dialectician: the passions are "all those things on account of
which people, undergoing a change, differ in the judgments they make,
things that pain and pleasure accompany" (1378a20–23). Far from giving
a material cause or precondition of the experience of the passions, then,
Aristotle attempts to describe that experience in a suitably comprehensive way. A passion is such a thing that, when it befalls us, it alters our
judgment, and it is necessarily accompanied by pleasure or pain. Aristotle

---

24 · "Aristotle investigated the *pathe* [passions] in the second book of his *Rhetoric*. Contrary to the traditional orientation of the concept of rhetoric according to which it is
some kind of 'discipline,' Aristotle's *Rhetoric* must be understood as the first systematic
hermeneutic of the everydayness of being-with-one-another." Martin Heidegger, *Being and Time*, trans. Joan Stambaugh (Albany: SUNY Press, 2010), 130. Consider also
Heidegger's early lectures on the *Rhetoric* in Heidegger, *Basic Concepts of Aristotelian
Philosophy*, trans. Robert D. Metcalf and Mark B. Tanzer (Bloomington: Indiana University Press, 2009).

has already noted that jurors who feel friendly affection for an accused will judge the fellow's case very differently than will jurors who hate him (1377b31–1378a6).

The three examples of passions Aristotle then mentions are anger, pity, and fear. Taking anger as his example or guide, Aristotle notes the three things that must be determined about it and hence about all the passions: how the angry are disposed, with whom they are accustomed to being angry, and at what sorts of things. More striking is the reason Aristotle gives for being concerned with these: "If we should grasp one or two of these, but not all of them together, it would be impossible to foster anger in another, and similarly in the case of the other [passions]" (1378a25–27). In other words, Aristotle's extensive inquiry into the passions as they are experienced serves a practical purpose: we must know the phenomenon of anger, for example, so that we may foster it in others as necessary. In the case of eight of the passions, as we have already noted,[25] Aristotle explicitly draws attention to the utility for rhetoric of creating the passion in question. Still, just as in his treatment of pleasure, Aristotle will include observations that seem to outstrip any possible rhetorical use.

Although he does not analyze all of them, Aristotle speaks of sixteen passions in total, in the following order: anger (2.2) and gentleness (2.3); friendly feeling (*philia*) and enmity or hatred (2.4); fear and confidence (2.5); shame and shamelessness (2.6); graciousness (*charis*) and its lack or absence (2.7); pity (2.8) and righteous indignation (*nemesis*) (2.9); envy (2.10); emulation and contempt (2.11). Most, but not all, of the passions are paired with their opposite. Enmity and hatred are treated more or less synonymously (1381b37–1382a4) in opposition to friendly feeling (*philia*), and envy is first taken up, but then rejected, as the opposite of pity.

Aristotle does not tell us what principle, if any, guides his selection of the passions or his ordering of them. One may well wonder whether the presentation has an order (compare, e.g., 1363b6 and 1390b16). Anger and gentleness are taken up first and at greatest length; anger is mentioned also in the discussions of friendliness (1381b9), enmity and hatred (1382a2–15), fear (1382a33), confidence (1383b7–8), and pity (1385b30) (consider also 1392b21 and 1393a2). Aristotle thus gives anger a certain prominence, perhaps because it is a passion at once powerful, disruptive, and frequently encountered; it is also true that he devotes attention

---

25 · See n. 2 above and the references there.

to the ways to foster its opposite, gentleness (2.3). Pity and indignation (*nemesis*) are the only passions explicitly identified as belonging to a "fine [*chrēstos*] character" (1386b13). Pity is pain at the undeserved suffering of another, indignation pain at his undeserved prosperity, and hence a concern for justice lies at the heart of both passions (e.g., 1387b8). This is not to deny, however, that the pain involved in pity is inseparable from a concern for oneself—we pity only those whose sufferings we suppose might befall us too (1386a2–3)—or that *nemesis* can involve a judgment about one's own rank or merit in relation to another (consider 1385b13–16 and 1387b4–14). So it is that we "attribute the feeling of indignation even to the gods" (1386b15–16)—Nemesis *is* a goddess (Hesiod, *Theogony* 223)—but it cannot be said (and Aristotle does not say) that the immortal gods take pity on us: the immortals may well bring down a mortal who thinks himself something special, but they in their superiority to us cannot be moved to pity us, let alone envy us.[26] Emulation "both is a decent [*epieikes*] thing and belongs to decent people" (1388a33), for emulation prompts us to strive to better ourselves: we emulate someone when we see in him, whose nature is similar to ours, honorable goods we know we lack. Envy, by contrast, "is base and belongs to base people" (1388a34): the envious wish merely that the other fellow not have the goods in question, and they resent him accordingly (1388a29–b2). *Philia* and above all graciousness are clearly characteristic of a serious human being. If anger is roused in defense of oneself or one's own, a respectable thing within limits, *philia* is concerned with the good of another and for that other's sake, even if each friend is necessarily pleasing to the other. Graciousness (*charis*) goes still further in the same direction by performing a service "for someone in need and not in return for something nor so that the person performing the service may gain something for himself, but rather so that the other fellow may do so" (1385a17–19; consider, however, 1371b1–2). Still, Aristotle does not single out graciousness for explicit praise in the way that he does emulation, on the one hand, and pity and indignation, on the other.

With this much as an overview, let us turn to Aristotle's presentation of anger. It begins with a formal definition: "So let anger be a longing,

26 · "The old conception . . . of Nemesis, which made the divinity and its action in the world only a leveling power, dashing to pieces everything high and great—was confronted by Plato and Aristotle with the doctrine that God is not *envious*." G. W. F. Hegel, *Encyclopedia of the Philosophical Sciences*, §564 (see Hegel's *Philosophy of Mind*, trans. William Wallace [Cambridge: Clarendon Press, 1971]).

accompanied by pain, for manifest vengeance on account of a manifest slight that was carried out against oneself or those in one's circle, on the part of those for whom such a slight is inappropriate" (1378a31–33). Thus anger first appears to be a painful passion whose core is bound up with a sense of justice, or of justice violated, that as a result seeks "vengeance." The moral character of anger is underscored by the fact that the perceived harm may be done, not only to oneself, but also to someone in one's circle. If according to this definition anger would not be roused at the sight of the mistreatment of complete strangers—this might prompt pity, if we supposed the strangers to be somehow similar to us—neither is it restricted to concern for oneself alone. We are also always angry at an individual entity, at one person or one nation, for example, at this "Cleon" but not "human beings" as such (1378a34–35; also 1382a5). What is more, it turns out that the pain of anger, which is surely primary, is necessarily mixed with pleasure—"the pleasure," that is, "that stems from the hope of being avenged" (1378b3–9). More clearly than any of the other passions, anger is a mixed thing, keenly protective of both oneself and one's own, at once painful and pleasant.

Central to Aristotle's presentation of anger is "slighting," which he defines as "an actualization [*energeia*] of an opinion about something that appears to be worth nothing" (1378b10–11). Such slighting may take one of three forms: the expression of contempt; spitefulness—the inclination to impede the wish of another not to gain something oneself but to insure that the other fellow does not; or insolence (*hubris*)—"doing and saying such things as are a source of shame to the person suffering them, not so that some other advantage may accrue to the insolent person or because something happened to him, but so that he may gain pleasure thereby." Here Aristotle traces the anger of Achilles, surely the most famous anger in all literature, to his view that he had been treated insolently and hence slightingly by Agamemnon (see the quotations of the *Iliad* at 1378b31–33). Aristotle concludes: "It is manifest by now, on the basis of these points, how the angry themselves are disposed and at whom they are angry and for what sorts of reasons" (1379a9–10).

Yet Aristotle's exposition of anger continues. Without noting that he is introducing a new consideration, he adds that "if someone places a direct obstacle before another in anything—for example, before a thirsty man in drinking," then the fellow thus thwarted will become angry (1379a11–15). Just as anger is complex in that it is not simply painful but is also pleasant, so there are not one but two causes of anger, the first traceable (as in the present example) to frustrated desire, the second to a sense of undeserved slighting. In confirmation of this, Aristotle at one point speaks of "the anger connected to slights" (1379b11). Anger is the general heading under which falls that kind of moral anger, linked to manifest slights, that one might call, and Aristotle does call, "indignation" (not here *nemesis* but *aganakteō*: 1379a6; see also 1380b19, 1389a11, and 1411a11). It is true that Aristotle will soon return to "slighting" (1379a18 and following). As a result, the stress here is very much on the anger connected to slights. Surely this is the anger of most concern to the rhetorician, since it or the reaction to it could easily give rise to legal suits and hence require the exercise of judicial rhetoric, just as an assembly's moral anger, potential or actual, could be of great use to an orator. But insofar as Aristotle wishes to give a fuller picture of the thing, he also mentions anger understood as the result of frustrated desire, an anger sparked not so much by moral outrage, or by our concern for justice, as by our concern for the good.

We might note, finally, also a possible connection between the two kinds of anger. For it is pleasing to believe that we have, not merely the *wish* to satisfy our desires, but also the *right* to do so: in that case our poor and paltry and needy selves confront the world with a moral claim upon it. And the natural anger we feel at the frustration of our desires can thus be elevated into a blame of anything or anyone standing as an obstacle to that satisfaction. In this way the anger traceable to thwarted desire can easily give rise to moral indignation, as if the cosmos itself stood in support of our desires.

CHARACTER (2.12–17)

Aristotle turns next to considerations of "character," and he notes that a person's character relates to the following: passions; virtues and vices; ages or times of life; and instances of luck. But having treated to the extent that he will both the passions and the virtues, Aristotle focuses now on character especially as it relates to age—the young (2.12), the old (2.13), and those in their prime (2.14)—together with the effect on character of the goods of fortune or luck: good birth (2.15), wealth (2.16), and power (2.17). To protest that the treatment here of the characters of young, middle-aged, and old amounts to "stereotyping" is to miss the massive point, namely, that these are sketches meant to aid a speaker in addressing a group or crowd. In fact, after he has concluded his sketch of the two extremes of age, the young and the old, from which he easily deduces the traits of those in their prime (2.14), Aristotle says this: "As a result—since all people accept speeches spoken in a way that accords with their own character, and accept those who are like them—it is not unclear how, by employing speeches, both the speakers themselves and their speeches may appear to be of a given sort" (1390a25–28). That the statements here may not apply to literally everyone in the crowd does not negate their possible power or utility—after all, one need not persuade literally everyone. Readers must decide for themselves whether the traits Aristotle describes have a foundation in nature, and hence whether they accurately describe the young and the old as we encounter them still (consider, e.g., 1389a4–6).

At all events, to resist the utility of these general statements is to deprive oneself of the most charming and even the most beautiful passages of the *Rhetoric*. Of the twenty or so character traits that typify the young, almost all find their counterparts—or their opposites (1389b13–14)—in the elderly. Where the young love honor and victory far more than money, for example, the elderly have an illiberal attachment to money, "since property is one of the necessities and, at the same time, they know through experience that possessing it is difficult and losing it, easy" (compare 1389a14–16 with b27–29). The young choose what is noble over what is advantageous, "since they live more by their character than by calculation, and calculation aims at the advantageous, virtue at the noble" (1389a35–36). The elderly, by contrast, "live more than they should with a view to advantage, rather than what is noble, because they are self-lovers: the advantageous is what is good for oneself, whereas the noble is what is good simply" (1389b36–1390a1). The young are fond of their "comrades" or pals and are disinclined to form friendships with an eye to their utility; the elderly "do not have intense feelings of friendly affection" because "experience" has taught them to be distrustful; the young have not yet been so taught.

The young and the elderly do share one quality, a propensity for pitying others. But the young are given to pitying as a result of their fondness for human beings as such, supposing as they do that "all are fine people" because the young "take their measure of their neighbors by their own lack of vice, such that they suppose their neighbors to be suffering undeservedly" (1389b8–10). The elderly, by contrast, pity others because they have a keen sense of their own weakness: "They suppose that any and all sufferings are just around the corner for them" (1390a21–22). The elderly "live more by memory than by hope, for what remains of life for them is small, what has gone by, vast; and hope belongs to the future, memory to things past" (1390a6–9). The young are hopeful because, "like those who are drunk," they are "by nature hot-blooded" and have yet to suffer much failure. "In fact they live for the most part on hope, since hope belongs to the future, memory to times gone by, and for the young the future is vast, the past brief. On the first day, so to speak, one can remember nothing, but hope for anything" (1389a21–25).

Aristotle devotes three chapters to the effect on one's character of the goods of fortune or chance (*tychē*: 2.15–17). It should be noted, first, that Aristotle does attribute such precious goods as a fine family or lineage, political power, and wealth to chance and not to a god or "daemon" (see 1399b22): such goods are meaningless as markers of a divine or cosmic favor. Even the undeniable involvement of "nature" in one's lineage means little, since such goods of nature are distributed as if by chance over time: a family may give rise to "extraordinary men" for a while, only to "deteriorate" once again, the better natures in fact tending to give way to "crazier characters," "stable ones" to "stupidity and sluggishness"—as the case of Socrates's offspring shows (1390b25–31).

Aristotle thus cannot be accused of being blind to the limits of an aristocracy rooted in the "best" families. And if nature as it is expressed in lineages cannot well ground an aristocracy, still less can wealth: the wealthy are "given to self-indulgence and pretentiousness, being self-indulgent on account of luxury and the open display of their prosperity, pretentious and vulgar because they all are accustomed to spending their time concerned with what is loved and admired by them, and because they suppose that others strive after the very things they themselves do" (1391a3–7). The character trait of the wealthy man, in short, is that of a "happy fool" (1391a14). And yet, because judging true human excellence is difficult, wealth tends to become the de facto measure of it. As we learn in this context, even the wise poet Simonides held that it is better to be wealthy than wise, since he saw the wise coming to the doors of the wealthy but not the other way round—and, as the context of this remark shows, he lived what he taught (1391a8–12). For his part, Socrates declined to visit the ruler Archelaus on the grounds that it would be insolent of him to be treated well by Archelaus when he himself would be unable to return the favor (1398a24–26). To a remarkable degree, Socrates declined to curry favor with any ruler, democratic or tyrannical, although (as we will soon be reminded) it proved to be a democracy that killed him.

Aristotle concludes his treatment of character and luck by noting the one very good trait that attends luck: the fortunate "are god-loving [or dear to gods: *philotheoi*] and stand in a certain relation to the divine, believing in it on account of the good things that have arisen from chance" (1391b1–4). What Aristotle here attributes to chance, then, the fortunate themselves attribute to the divine, for theirs is so uncanny a circumstance that they cannot regard its cause as something indifferent to them. Aristotle thus implies that it is the fortunate, as distinguished from the unfortunate (see 1391b5–7), who turn most readily to the divine to understand their lot. Good luck breeds belief because we are inclined to endow our good fortune with a moral significance — a sign of the approbation of the gods, which would confirm that we deserve what we have and have what we deserve. But why might not wretched misfortune, too, prompt us to seek out the divine and even to believe all the more fervently in it? Aristotle does not say.

According to what he does say elsewhere in the *Rhetoric*, we infer that this might occur only if the unfortunate were still able to succumb to fear, for the reason that fear presupposes a measure of hope: beyond the reach of both fear and hope are "those who have already suffered what they hold to be all manner of terrible things, and so have grown coldly indifferent to the future, like those in the course of being cudgeled to death." Instead, "some hope of salvation must endure" for one still to fear its loss (1383a3–6). Those who are not altogether without hope, then, who can still tremble in fear, may well turn to the gods in moments of crisis (consider Thucydides, *War of the Peloponnesians and Athenians* 7.71.3). This is especially so in the case of those who regard themselves as the victims of injustice or who see their present plight as the result of another's injustice, for in these cases they may feel not only hope but even confidence: "anger inspires confidence, and it is not committing injustice but rather suffering it that is productive of anger; and the divine is thought to come to the assistance of the victims of injustice" (consider, e.g., Thucydides 1.86.4–5). This requires, of course, that their "affairs pertaining to gods [be] in a fine state, as regards signs and oracles and the rest" (1383b5–6). If the divine aids the unjust and we have been treated unjustly, and anger fills our hearts as a result, we will enjoy a certain confidence that the unjust will pay for what they have done to us: we live in hope. If all this is so, then faith in just gods would serve as the root of the hope in question. Or is the moral hope for the vindication of justice the truly primary thing, recourse to the divine subsequent, as an evidently necessary means to make the world right again? In this case, the status of that hope, whether intensified or lessened or done away with altogether, would presumably have its corresponding effects also on one's recourse to the divine.

THE *LOGOS*: RHETORIC, PHILOSOPHY, AND THE POLITICAL COMMUNITY (2.18–26)

In the long and complex section that brings book 2 to a close, Aristotle returns to focus on the *logos*, on the speech itself. One could say, of course, that everything in the *Art of Rhetoric* bears on the *logos*. But whereas in book 1 Aristotle had taken up those "specific topics" that are or are derived from subject matters of the three kinds of rhetoric, he is now concerned with what is "common" (*koina*) to all the kinds of rhetoric. These are, first, the subject matters or categories common to all speeches regardless of particular subject (2.19): what is possible and impossible; what has or has not happened; what will happen; and (treated very briefly) what is of great or small, or greater or lesser, importance. Aristotle then considers in more detail than before the two "common modes of persuasion" belonging to rhetoric, namely, the example (rhetorical induction) and the enthymeme (rhetorical syllogism) (2.20). As for the "maxim," or a judgment pertaining to action expressed in universal terms, it is properly classified as a part of the enthymeme because it is in effect the conclusion of an enthymeme stated without the premises leading to it (2.21). Noteworthy here is Aristotle's delineation of the varieties of arguments from example, characterized by whether the examples are based on historical fact or are made up, and, if they are made up, whether they feature a comparison of one's own devising or a fable. Aristotle also expands his account of the enthymeme by noting its two kinds (1396b22–26), those that either establish a point or refute one (for the latter, see 2.25). But the longest section here is devoted to setting out twenty-eight topics common to the enthymeme, an impressive catalogue of the kinds of argument that can in principle be deployed in any situation demanding rhetoric, whether that argument establishes a point of one's own or demolishes an opponent's. This is followed by the nine common topics characteristic of the apparent enthymeme.

These, then, are the primary concerns of the section as a whole. Despite some difficulties in interpreting the section caused by Aristotle's use of historical events and literary texts now lost to us, his exposition of the *topoi* is generally clear. Less clear, perhaps, is Aristotle's presentation of the tension between the political community and wisdom or philosophy that gradually emerges through the organization of his argument here, together with his choice of subject, example, and quotation. It is in the light of that tension, moreover, that one can begin to glimpse the possibility of another and higher rhetoric, one in the service of wisdom or in defense of philosophy. We can only indicate some of the pointers Aristotle gives along the way, beginning from the most salient parts of those chapters (2.19–21) that precede the turn to the *topoi*.

In his discussion of the possible and impossible (2.19), Aristotle speaks of sciences and the arts, and he contends that it is possible for that of which there is a science or an art to come into being (1392a25–26). This implies, reasonably enough, that there can be no knowledge or art of things that cannot come to be (and hence that do not exist or have never existed). His examples in this section include the natural (health and sickness, a boy and a man), the artificial (a house, a shoe, a ship or trireme), and the scientific or mathematical (diameter, double, and half). He speaks explicitly of nature twice (1392a24 and b4). The account of whether or not something has happened relies somewhat more on nature (1392b15–16, 26, 28) as well as on (non-human) "necessity" (1392b31; compare the remark of Agathon quoted at 1392b9 as well as 1392a27–28). Here Aristotle speaks twice of the necessary relation of thunder and lightning. More interesting still is the case of the future, for deliberative rhetoric is concerned chiefly with future events (recall 1358b13–15), and the future happens to be of special interest also to the art of prophecy or divination (consider, e.g., Thucydides 2.8.2, 2.21.3, 5.103). Here Aristotle speaks of the motives governing human beings; of the natural world—if it is overcast, it is likely to rain; and of art—if there is a foundation, there will be a house too. It hardly needs to be said that thunder and lightning are treated here as natural phenomena,[27] and the rain is not "the rain from heaven" or from Zeus.[28] As Aristotle will say later on, "The cause and that of which it is the cause go together, and there is nothing without a cause" (1400a30–31). Although Aristotle is confined in this context to speaking mostly of what is "likely" (*eikos*) to happen or what will "for the most part" be so (1392b25 and 22; compare 1392b31), he does nothing to encourage recourse to divination and the like (consider, e.g., Thucydides 7.50.4). Yet the admitted difficulty of knowing what will be, together with the gravity of what may

---

27 · Consider Thucydides 6.70.1 and 7.79.3; and Xenophon, *Apology of Socrates to the Jury* 12.

28 · See, e.g., Thucydides 2.77.6; Aristophanes, *Clouds* 369–76 and context.

be at stake in a city's deliberations, means that an opening for divination remains, as is suggested, perhaps, in these well-worn maxims: "A single bird-omen is best: to defend the fatherland" and "Impartial is Enyalus," god of war (1395a13–15).

In his analysis of the example as one of the "common modes of persuasion" (2.20), Aristotle notes that examples conveying a comparison—the present case X is just like Y—are "characteristic of Socratic speeches," the first mention of Socrates in a section that proves to feature a cluster of references to him. And Aristotle gives this example of a Socratic comparison:

> Those who hold office ought not to be chosen by lot, for maintaining that is similar to somebody's saying that one should appoint as athletes, not those who are capable of competing, but those whom the lot determines, or that one should appoint by lot anyone at all among the sailors to pilot the ship, on the grounds that the one on whom the lot falls, but not the person possessed of the requisite knowledge, must pilot. (1393b4–8)

In this tough rebuke of democratic practice, Socrates implies that sound governance requires the union of capacity or power, as in the athlete, with the requisite knowledge, as in the pilot (consider also Xenophon, *Memorabilia* 1.2.9). But these qualities are ones that the lot, the selection of citizens at random, cannot guarantee. Aristotle thus chooses as an example of a Socratic comparison one that makes plain how much Socrates was at odds with the very principle of democracy; and the vividness of the argument raises a question, at least, about its (or his) prudence. If it is easy, as Socrates used to say, to praise Athenians among Athenians (1367b8–9)—Aristotle cites this to support the thought that one must know one's audience and cater to them—Socrates himself seemed quite willing to criticize Athenians among Athenians.

In turning to "maxims" (2.21), Aristotle develops some verses of Euripides, that friend of Socrates,[29] according to which no man who is sensible ought to have his children educated, at least not to be "extraordinarily wise" (*perissōs ... sophous*: 1394a29–30; see also 1399a9–15). Such wisdom will render them "idle" and make them the target of their neighbors' "ill-willed envy" (as we saw in the discussion of the enthymeme above). This suggests that wisdom is regarded as something simultaneously bad and good, or that popular opinion is either confused about it or divided over

---

29 · Aristophanes, *Frogs* 1491–99; Diogenes Laertius 2.18.

it. We recall that Aristotle had recorded this *endoxon* in his discussion of pleasure: "And since ruling is very pleasant, it is pleasant also to be held to be wise, for being prudent is the mark of a ruler, and wisdom is knowledge of many wondrous things" (1371b26–28). "Wisdom" here is largely conflated with "prudence" and is respectable insofar as it is useful in gaining a most pleasing political goal. In accord with this, perhaps, Aristotle had noted that "wisdom" especially can elicit the envy of others (1378b30–31). But this is also to say that a "wisdom" not reducible to a good popularly approved of runs the risk of seeming to be a dubious thing, useless at best and pernicious at worst—if, for example, it inquires into matters too great or awesome for human beings, into "the things aloft" and the things "beneath the earth." One of the highly regarded maxims that Aristotle quotes in this context runs as follows: "One who is mortal must think of mortal things / it is not for the mortal to think of immortal things" (1394b24–25). What Aristotle himself made of this injunction to abstain from thinking about gods and the like, or about immortal necessity, is clear from the culminating section of the *Nicomachean Ethics*: "So if the intellect is something divine in comparison to the human being, the life in accord with this intellect would also be divine in comparison to the human life. But one ought not—as some recommend—to think only about human things because one is a human being, nor only about mortal things because one is mortal, but rather to make oneself immortal, insofar as possible" (1177b31–1178a2).

We turn now to Aristotle's account of the common topics belonging to all of rhetoric (2.22–23). Interwoven throughout this section are repeated references to the problem of justice, as we have called it;[30] to the gods and piety (or impiety);[31] and to wisdom in general and the philosophers in particular.[32] Justice, piety, and philosophy: Socrates the philosopher was found to be unjust by a jury of his fellow citizens because he did not believe in the city's gods and because he as a result corrupted the young. One might even say that Socrates's life culminated in a famous or notorious example of rhetoric, judicial rhetoric more precisely—his defense speech (*apologia*) before a jury. Further, if we assume that Socrates

30 · 1397a20–23; 1398a29–32; 1399a20–25 and a28–32.
31 · 1397b12–13; 1398a15–17, b24; 1398b32–1399a1; 1399a6–9, a20–25, b6–8.
32 · 1397b23–25; 1398a24–28, b9–19, 21; 1399b9–11. The chapter refers to philosophers, sophists, the wise, and Theodectes, Euripides, Sophocles, Aristippus, Plato, Xenophanes, Anaxagoras, and of course Socrates—four times explicitly (consider n. 33 below) and once by way of unattributed (but obvious) quotation: 1398a15–17.

wished to secure his own acquittal by means of that speech, we are forced
to judge his use of rhetoric on that occasion a terrible failure, since he
managed to secure thereby only his own execution. As it seems to me, the
fate of Socrates lies behind the whole of this section of the *Rhetoric* and
gives it both a unity and a gravity it would otherwise lack. For the legal execution of Socrates is indicative of the fundamental tension between philosophy and the political community, between the philosopher's ceaseless
search for the truth about the most important things and the community's necessary reliance on *endoxa* that cannot finally be questioned, let
alone openly rejected. Hence the trial of Socrates really is the trial of philosophy in the court of popular opinion: "You are going to judge, not
about Socrates, but about a mode of living—whether one ought to philosophize" (1399b9–11).[33]

In his general account of the enthymeme (2.22) that precedes the turn
to the *topoi*, Aristotle stresses again the limits of the enthymeme, that it
must not be too long or too complicated, for example (1395b20–1396a3;
recall 1357a1–23). It is also here that he notes the disadvantage of the educated, in contrast to the uneducated, in speaking to a crowd: as the poets
say—Euripides among them—the uneducated speak "more musically"
to a crowd than do the educated (1395b26–31). And near the beginning
of his treatment of the *topoi*, Aristotle quotes lines (again from Euripides)
we had occasion to cite early on:

> But if in fact it is possible among mortals
> To make false pronouncements persuasively,
> You ought to believe the opposite, too,
> That mortals are often not persuaded by truths. (1397a17–19)

Aristotle thus begins the inquiry into the *topoi* with a strong statement of
the fact that we mortals can be as unmoved by the truth as we are moved
by falsehood (or lies: *pseudē*).

Immediately thereafter we learn, in a discussion of grammatical inflection, of the view that "the just is not altogether good" (1397a21). Hence
the problem of justice is raised again. This is soon followed by the thought
that, "if not even the gods know all things, much less could human beings" (1397b12–13). On the one hand, this is a statement of the superiority
of gods to humans in precisely knowledge; on the other hand, it is a state-

33 · The modern editors read here "Isocrates" for "Socrates," on the basis of a similar
remark in Isocrates's *Antidosis* 173–75, but this seems to me insufficient warrant to depart from the reading of all the MSS.

ment also of the grave limit that marks even the gods. If Socrates himself held that the gods know all things (Xenophon, *Memorabilia* 1.1.20), this is only to set him further apart from orthodoxy. The next example of the same *topos* at issue here (of "the more and the less") involves striking one's father or "father-beating": so little did Socrates countenance the law or custom, so consistently did he follow the premise that knowledge is the only reasonable title to rule, in the manner of a ship's pilot, that he thought sensible sons could in principle rule over their foolish fathers—and hence beat them if need be (consider Aristophanes, *Clouds* 1321–1439; on philosophy in its relation to law, consider the remark of Alcidamas: 1406b11–12). We are relieved to learn, then, in the next *topos*, of this argument: "If none of the others who possess a technical craft are base [*phauloi*], then neither are philosophers; and if generals are not base because they are often condemned to death, then neither are sophists" (1397b23–25).

It was of course something other than the philosophers' possession of an art that got them, or at any rate Socrates, "condemned to death." In explaining the topic based on definition, Aristotle paraphrases Socrates's cross-examination of his accuser Meletus concerning the meaning of the *daemonion*, that idiosyncratic voice that Socrates claimed came to him and him alone: "Is it a god or the work of a god? Yet whoever supposes that it is a work of a god must necessarily suppose also that gods exist" (1398a15–17; compare Plato, *Apology of Socrates* 26a8–28a1). Aristotle thus puts on the table the popular suspicion that a philosopher is heterodox at best and an "atheist" at worst (Plato, *Apology of Socrates* 26c3). (At one point Aristotle himself mentions the possibility of a speech blaming a god [1396a24 and context]; he limits himself in the immediate sequel to explaining how to give a speech in praise of a demigod [1396a25 and 1396b12–20].) Accordingly, Theodectes in his *Socrates* was compelled to ask: "In what temple did he act impiously? Who among the gods believed in by the city has he not honored?" (1399a7–9). The context of these remarks is lost, but they remind us of Xenophon's attempt to free his teacher from the charge of impiety, an attempt that looked only to Socrates's public speeches or deeds rather than to his "silent deliberations" (compare Xenophon, *Memorabilia* 1.1.20 with 1.1.19).

It is true that Aristotle will develop at some length the thought that, as the rhetorician Alcidamas put it, "all honor the wise" (1398b10). The list of wise honorees is striking. First are Archilochus, Homer, Sappho, Chilon, Pythagoras, and Anaxagoras, all thinkers whose wisdom seems to have taken the "musical" form, pleasing to many, of poetry—pleasing even (in the case of Chilon) to the Lacedaemonians, who are "least of all fond of speech or reason [*philologoi*]" (1398b14). In fact all are said to have been honored, despite a drawback in almost every case (the exception being Pythagoras). To this list Aristotle adds three more honorees: the Athenians became prosperous as a result of the laws of Solon, the Lacedaemonians as a result of the laws of Lycurgus, and "at Thebes, as soon as the leaders in the city became philosophers, the city prospered" (1398b16–19). Solon was the statesman-poet (1375b32) who brought about democratic reforms at Athens, and Lycurgus is said to have brought the divine laws of Apollo to Sparta (Plato, *Laws* 624a1–5): neither clearly qualifies as a philosopher strictly speaking. As for Thebes, better known for its horsemanship than its intellectual attainments,[34] we have no record of these philosopher-statesmen; Epaminondas and Pelopidas do not obviously constitute exceptions to this, and neither does Philolaus, according to Aristotle's account of him (*Politics* 1274a31–b5). In any event, Alcidamas's statement taken at face value suggests a perfect harmony between philosophy and politics or between wisdom and the community: if only all cities were, like Thebes, ruled by philosopher-kings! The statement proves rather less. But even if we accept Alcidamas's contention without hesitation, this serves only to raise the question of what made Socrates so irksome to his fellow citizens. Not quite "all" honor (all) the wise.

The beginnings of an answer may be suggested in the next *topos*, pertaining to judgment. It can be useful, Aristotle says, to oppose a given judgment by recourse to the contrary judgment of "all," or, failing that, "at least the greatest number—or the wise, either all or the greatest number of them—or the good." Only here in the *Rhetoric* does Aristotle include, in his survey of opinion holders, the wise (compare 1361a25–27 and 1364b11–14); he also gives three examples of those whose opinions "it is not noble to oppose": the gods, one's father, and teachers. But what if one's teachers, or rather "the wise," oppose the judgment of the gods or one's father? We also learn here of a Spartan, Agesipolis, who consulted first Zeus, through the oracle at Olympia, and then, as a sort of test of him, Apollo, through the oracle at Delphi, "on the grounds that it would be a shameful thing [for Apollo] to contradict him." It is impious indeed to test an oracle, especially if doing so means (as in this case) pitting god against god and hence father against son. This reference to the con-

34 · Consider Plato, *Meno* 70a, *Hippias Major* 284a, and *Laws* 625d.

sultation of the oracle at Delphi may remind us of the fateful question that Chaerephon one day put to that same oracle, as to whether anyone was wiser than Socrates. In Plato's *Apology*, Socrates presents his incredulity at the response of the god (that "no one is wiser" than Socrates), and he makes clear his initial thought or reaction: he must set out to "refute" the god (20c1 and context), as in fact he did set out to do.

In the final reference of concern to us in this context, Aristotle reports, as a further example of the *topos* concerning judgment, the following rebuke of Aristippus, student of Socrates, which he leveled against Plato: Aristippus was of the view that Plato "spoke in too definitive [*epangeltikōteron*] a way: 'But our comrade,' he said, 'was not at all like this'—meaning Socrates" (1398b29–31). To judge from Xenophon's portrait of him, Aristippus was not the most impressive fellow in Socrates's circle (*Memorabilia* 2.1.1–34 and 3.8.1–7). Here he seems not to have wondered whether Plato had good reason to pronounce a definitive doctrine—of the eternal and unchanging Ideas, for example—whereas Socrates apparently did no such thing. This remark by itself surely supplies too little material from which to deduce Plato's understanding of the necessities, political and philosophic, that guided his unrivaled rhetoric in defense of philosophy understood as a way of life. On the one hand, Plato presents Socrates as the philosopher of ignorance; Socrates knew that he knew nothing, or at any rate he did not claim to know things that he did not know, the opposite of being "definitive" or doctrinaire or dogmatic. At his trial, for example, Socrates claimed not to know anything "noble and good" (*Apology of Socrates* 21d3–5). Such was his "human wisdom." But wisdom of this kind is corrosive of the *endoxa* that every healthy community needs in order to thrive; such wisdom runs the risk, if publicized, of undermining the community's definitive answers to the questions of what is true and good, noble and just. Accordingly, and on the other hand, Plato also presents Socrates as knowing that perfect knowledge (of the Ideas) *is* possible, if not in this embodied life, then in the next, disembodied one, where the eternal soul may commune with the eternal Ideas. Plato also, of course, portrays Socrates as a dauntless man of principle who died a hero's death akin to that of Achilles (*Apology of Socrates* 28c2–d5)—a portrait whose effect on the reputation of philosophy over the millennia it would be hard to overstate. Aristotle, for his part, keeps much closer in his political philosophy to the perspective of serious (*spoudaioi*) human beings in their communal concerns. In the *Rhetoric*, as we have seen, he takes pains to record and even to defer to the very *endoxa* that Socrates made it his mission to interrogate. This procedure seems to have given Aristotle a freedom from espousing such high-flown "metaphysical" doctrines as the Ideas, for example, and it even permitted or required him, as confirmation in his political writings of his commonsensical sobriety, to criticize them (*Nicomachean Ethics* 1.6).

NOTES ON BOOK 3

As we stated at the outset, the final book of the *Art of Rhetoric* falls into two main parts: the first devoted to "diction" (*lexis*), or questions pertaining to the selection of words and phrases appropriate to one's task (3.1–12); the second devoted to the proper arrangement of the parts necessary to a speech (3.13–19). To this we can now add that Aristotle also speaks briefly, in the first part of book 3, of "delivery," that is, "how one ought to use [one's voice] relative to each passion (that is, when to use a loud voice and when a quiet and when a middling one), and how to use different tones (that is, high-pitched and deep and middling), and what rhythms relate to each" (1403b27–31). It was among actors who recite or perform poetry that delivery first became a subject of study, whereas in rhetoric, "an art about these things has not yet been composed"— although Thrasymachus has dealt with the question "to a small extent" (1403b35 and 1404a13–15). It is here (as we noted before) that Aristotle deplores the "vulgar," if nonetheless "necessary," attention to such matters. The fact that sustained interest in matters of delivery and diction had its roots in poetry should in no way be thought to permit the rhetorician to mimic the poetic: "The diction involved in speech and that involved in poetry are different" (1404a28). In fact, even the poets, led by Euripides (1404b25), have begun to imitate the diction characteristic of conversation, and it would be ridiculous for the rhetorician to be more poetic than the poets.

Aristotle contends that the virtue or excellence of diction consists in clarity (1404b1–2 and 37; 1406a34–35). This means, for example, that one must use words in their prevailing sense, so that audiences immediately grasp their import, just as one must use dialect or unusual terms, compound words, and made-up words only sparingly—when one is speaking in a particularly passionate or emphatic way (see 1408b10–20). One must also speak correctly, observing basic rules of grammar (3.5). Metaphors are especially important to rhetoric because they can convey "clarity, pleasure, and the foreign" (1405a8–9). For metaphors can make a point with particular vividness, conjuring up an image in the mind's eye of the listener, and metaphors can even effect a kind of learning in the audience that is pleasing to them (1410b13–16). Yet metaphors must be appropriate to the subject matter, neither too trivial nor highfalutin or far-fetched—this last being one of the four causes of "corny" expressions or expressions that fall flat (3.3). Epithets, too, can be effective, whether they bring out what is better or shameful in a given circumstance: one and the same man may be addressed as either "father-avenger" or "mother-killer" (1405b21–23). In all cases, "clarify by means of metaphor and epithets, while guarding against the poetic" (1407b31–32). A good speech, moreover, must have a certain rhythm to it, imitative of conversation (1408b33), but never an actual meter, "for in that case it will be a poem" (1408b30–31). Jokes or puns, hyperbole, asyndeton, and similes, too, may be used, albeit with due caution.

Aristotle's many strictures here, which we need not detail, amount to this: the skilled rhetor will employ a deceptively artless artfulness that as such will conceal from the audience the fact that what appears altogether natural and even conversational is actually the product of careful planning and technical prowess. Properly composed, the speech will have something novel or foreign to it, yet that too will go unnoticed as such, even as it works its effect. To obtrude one's artfulness is to raise suspicions in the audience, just as if you were "hatching a plot" (1404b18–21), and so draws one's good character into question. Just as the skilled actor will disappear into his role, as it were, and so appear to be anything other than an actor (1404b22–25), so the skilled rhetorician will appear to be something other than a skilled rhetorician—as a passionate advocate, for example, a sober statesman, or an innocent victim.

We may treat the parts of a speech briefly (3.13–19). According to Aristotle the most necessary parts of any speech are the statement of the subject matter and the "demonstration" or "mode of persuasion" pertaining to it (3.13)—in other words, the point the speech seeks to make, and then the making of it. Beyond that, there may be a preface (3.14) at the very beginning and an epilogue (3.19) at the very end, the better in the former case to thwart an opponent's preceding attack, and in the latter to drive home one's point a final time. Narration (3.16) belongs especially to judicial rhetoric—a prosecutor's recitation of the most relevant facts of a case—but it has its place in epideictic rhetoric too, although there it will be set out in parts rather than all at once. In deliberative rhetoric, by contrast, one cannot, strictly speaking, narrate the future; at best or most, a narration of past events may help shape present deliberations about what will be.

Here we might note that, no matter how comprehensive and detailed a *technē* may be, there can be no substitute for the judgment of the orator on the spot; it necessarily falls to the speaker to apply Aristotle's many general rules or suggestions to the situation at hand. Consider: "And as for those circumstances that arise on the spot, one must search out the relevant premises in the same manner, by looking not to indefinite propositions but rather to the facts at hand pertaining to the subject matter of the speech and specifying the greatest number of points that are as close as possible to that subject" (1396b6–9). Aristotle can instruct us as to the necessity of this "searching out"; he cannot be at our side to aid us in a particular search. Again, Aristotle rejects as "laughable" the present-day contention that narration in judicial speeches should be quick: "Just as a fellow said to the baker, who asked whether he should knead the dough hard or softly, 'What's that? Is it impossible to do it well?'—the case is similar here too: one must not narrate at length, just as one must not state prefaces at length either, or modes of persuasion. For doing so well does not consist in doing it either quickly or concisely, but in due measure" (1416b29–35). This ability to apply general rule to particular circumstance surely involves prudence or practical judgment. It may even involve "philosophy," for "it belongs to a shrewd person to contemplate that which is similar even in things that are far apart, just as Archytas said that an arbitrator and an altar are the same thing, for with both the victim of injustice seeks refuge" (1412a11–14).

Aristotle's final chapter here (3.19) deals with the epilogue and its special functions. He notes that, for the end of a *logos*, the absence of connecting particles, or asyndeton, is fitting. And, living what he teaches, Aristotle concludes the *Art of Rhetoric* with the following: "I have spoken; you have heard; grasp it; judge."

⊙   ⊙   ⊙

It is safe to assume that, for so long as human beings have gathered together in communities, they have tried to persuade their fellows by means of speech or argument—to recommend, to praise, to condemn. In other words, human beings have long engaged in a kind of rhetoric. It hardly needs to be said, then, that Aristotle's treatise did not found the practice of rhetoric. It did not found even the art of rhetoric, for Aristotle's references to Corax, Alcidamas, Thrasymachus, Callippus, Pamphilius, and

Gorgias, among others, make plain that *rhetorikē* was very much alive before he began to write or lecture. Yet he held that art to be defective as he found it, and his act of writing the *Art of Rhetoric* constitutes an intervention in the practice of rhetoric and, by extension, in political life.

Aristotle means, first, to defend rhetoric as something crucial to the conduct of a decent deliberative politics: rhetoric is a counterpart of the science of dialectic; it deserves to be called an art and hence involves real knowledge; and it fulfills functions at once necessary and noble by helping us give voice to our concern for what is good and bad, just and unjust, noble and base. Aristotle also confronts the fact that rhetoric permits its skilled practitioners to persuade others without, strictly speaking, teaching them anything, and so it may well be more "effective" than decent. Aristotle deplores the unjust use of rhetoric, as we have seen, which means that he does not deny the possibility of it. Instead, he exhorts students of rhetoric to employ well or justly the very skills his treatise seeks to refine. Those who are more impressed by the technical refinement than the moral exhortation could, it is true, use the *Art of Rhetoric* to foment in an audience anger or fear, for example, for their own illicit purposes. But there will be rhetoric with or without Aristotle's intervention, just as there will always be those who prefer their own good to the common good; and Aristotle does what he can not only to make rhetoric more deserving of the title of "art" but also to yoke its practice to decent ends.

Beyond that, Aristotle's inquiry into rhetoric may serve as a means for some, especially the politically ambitious, to become more reflective about their own strivings and doings. Those whose ambitions lead them to a serious interest in rhetoric may be led by it, in turn, to a study of the *Ethics* and *Politics* (1356a22–23; 1366a21–22),[35] to the *Topics* and *Analytics* (1355a28 and context; 1356b9), and to the *Poetics* (1371b33–1372a2). Both in itself and as a point of entry, then, the *Art of Rhetoric* is an important part of Aristotle's unsurpassed attempt to understand those strange beings who, alone among the animals, are equipped with speech or reason.

---

35 · Consider also: "It is clear as a result that, for legislation, accounts of traveling the earth are useful—for in these it is possible to grasp the laws [or customs] of nations— and for instances of political advice, the inquiries of those who write about human actions are useful. But quite all of these are the task of politics, not of rhetoric. Such, then, are the most important matters of which someone who is going to give advice must have a grasp" (1360a33–b2).

GLOSSARY

A

ACCEPTED OPINIONS, GENERALLY ACCEPTED OPINIONS (*endoxa*): These opinions supply the stuff that constitutes the subject matter of all rhetorical argumentation. The orator, then, proceeds not from axioms or first principles, but from the opinions that predominate in a given audience.

ACCUSATION (*katēgoria*): Generally a legal term indicating a formal charge against someone. Accusatory speeches are one of the two principal concerns of judicial rhetoric, the other being defense speeches. See also *slander*.

ACTIVITY, ACTUALITY (*energeia, energein*): A technical term in the philosophy of Aristotle meaning the realization of a potential or power or capacity (*dunamis*). Also, in the *Rhetoric*, what can be conveyed by an effective metaphor: a state of realized activity that is brought before the mind's eye of the listener.

ADVICE, DELIBERATION, ADVISE (*sumbolē, sumbouleuein*): Giving advice in a political assembly is the chief concern of deliberative (*sumbouletikē*) rhetoric; the connection between "advice" (*sumbolē*) and "deliberation" (*boulēsis*) can sometimes be difficult to convey in translation. "Advisory rhetoric" is another possible translation.

AMPLIFICATION (*auxēsis, auxanein*): Together with "downplaying," one of a pair of rhetorical devices intended to sway an audience, in this case to make as much as possible of a fact or circumstance favorable to one's argument, or to stress the importance or gravity of a given matter. See 2.26.

ANGER, IMPULSE (*orgē, orgizein*): The first of the passions discussed by Aristotle, anger is a painful passion, mixed with the pleasure of the thought of vengeance, in response to a perceived slight against oneself or someone in one's circle, on the part of someone for whom such slighting is judged inappropriate. See 2.2.

APPARENT ENTHYMEME (*enthumēma phainomenon*): Just as Aristotle distinguishes between a syllogism and a merely apparent syllogism, so he distinguishes between a rhetorical syllogism, or enthymeme, and a merely apparent one. Aristotle details nine topics characteristic of apparent enthymemes in 2.24.

ARGUMENT, SPEECH, REASON, WORD, DEFINITION, FABLE (*logos*): A term that cannot be captured by a single English equivalent, *logos* means in the first place "human speech" and then also "an argument." The *logos*, in the sense of the argument contained in the speech, is one of the three "modes of persuasion" available to the orator, the other two being character (*ēthos*) and passion (*pathos*). Consider 2.18–26.

ARRANGEMENT (*taxis*): In the context of rhetoric, the term refers to the best or most effective placement of the various parts of the speech. Aristotle devotes the last section of the text, 3.13–19, to questions pertaining to arrangement.

ART, TECHNICAL SKILL (*technē*): Less "art" in the sense of "fine art" than any craft or body of "technical" knowledge that may be used to produce an artifact—for example, tables, shoes, and ships, and hence the "art" of carpentry, shoemaking, and shipbuilding. The title of the present work indicates that rhetoric deserves to be understood as an art and hence a body of knowledge.

B

BLAME (*psogos*): One of the two principal concerns of epideictic rhetoric (1.9), which issues in speeches of either praise (of someone's nobility) or blame (of someone's baseness).

C

CAPACITY: See *power*.

CHARACTER (*ēthos, ēthikos*): One's moral character as revealed above all in the actions one chooses to undertake. The art of rhetoric is much concerned with conveying to an audience a sense of the speaker's (good) character. Hence one of the necessary substantive concerns of rhetoric is *ta ēthika*—"ethics" in the sense of the concern for or study of character.

CHOICE (*proairesis, proaireisthai, proaireton*): Aristotle's account of choice is an important part of his complex argument concerning the voluntary and the involuntary in the *Nicomachean Ethics* (3.2); here Aristotle stresses that a speech ought to convey a sense of the speaker's choices in a given case and therewith of his character.

COMMON TOPICS: The "common" topics are to be distinguished from the specific or particular ones taken up in 1.4–18; the common topics include the twenty-eight listed and discussed in 2.22–23 and are meant to be used to generate arguments regardless of specific subject matter.

COMPARISON (*parabolē, paraballein*): In his discussion of the use of examples, Aristotle notes that some examples the speaker may make up, by way of comparing the present case to some other: that the present case X is just like Y. "Comparison," Aristotle suggests, "is characteristic of Socratic speeches" (see 2.20).

CONCLUSION (*sumperasma*): The thought that follows, necessarily or for the most part, from the preceding premises posited by the speaker.

CONTEMPT (*kataphronēsis, kataphronein*): One of the three sources of "slighting" according to Aristotle, which in turn gives rise to the important passion of anger; see 2.2.

CREDENCE, CREDIBLE (*pistis, pisteuein*): The state of mind induced in one who has been persuaded of something, without, however, having been taught anything, strictly speaking; to find something credible or to give credence to something. See also *mode of persuasion*.

D

DECISIVE EVIDENCE (*tekmērion, tekmeriōdēs*): Of the two kinds of "signs" on which enthymemes may be based, "necessary signs" constitute "decisive evidence," and so make for an irrefutable argument (assuming that the facts adduced are true): "he has a fever" is a necessary sign, and so constitutes decisive evidence that "he is sick."

DEFENSE, DEFENSE SPEECH (*apologia, apologeisthai*): One of the two principal concerns of judicial rhetoric, the other being, of course, speeches of accusation. Socrates's "apology"—his defense speech—ranks among the most famous such speeches, and Aristotle will allude to and even quote from that speech.

DELIBERATION (*bouleuein*): The process of weighing different plans in the realm of things that are up to us or in our control and subject to action. Deliberative rhetoric (*sumbouleutikē*) means to influence the result of deliberation. See also *advice*.

DELIBERATIVE RHETORIC (*sumbouleutikē*): One of the three kinds of rhetoric according to Aristotle. It means to guide the progress, and so alter the result of, deliberations in any public assembly. See also *advice*.

DELIVERY, ACTING (*hupokrisis, hupokrinesthai, hupokritēs, hypokritikos*): In book 3 Aristotle notes that the concern for delivery and diction first arose in poetry, or more precisely in the concern of actors to perform poetry. It made its way from there to public speaking, a tendency Aristotle seeks to limit.

DEMAGOGUE, PUBLIC SPEAKING (*dēmēgoria, dēmagōgos, dēmēgorein, dēmēgorikos*): Although the term can have a pejorative connotation, in both Greek and English, Aristotle also uses it as equivalent to public speaking, that is, addressing the *demos* or people.

DEMONSTRATION (*apodeixis, apodeiknunai, apodeiktikos*): Although "demonstration" can refer to a deduction that produces knowledge in the strict sense (*epistēmē*), Aristotle claims no more for rhetoric than that it as a rule produces only rhetorical demonstration, i.e., an indication sufficient to produce persuasion or conviction in a given audience.

DESIRE (*epithumia, epithumein*): A species of *orexis* or the longing in the soul, and so the origin of action.

DIALECTIC (*dialektikē*): Related to the verb meaning simply "to converse" (*dialeges-thai*) "dialectic" can also be used to describe Socrates's characteristic analysis of the guiding opinions, or *endoxa*, of his interlocutors. In the *Rhetoric*, Aristotle begins by showing the (limited) kinship between dialectic and rhetoric or between the dialectical syllogism and the rhetorical syllogism: if one of the purposes of the former is to correct the opinions of the many, where they fail to speak finely, the purpose of the latter is to bring about persuasion.

DICTION, PHRASING (*lexis*): While regretting the necessity to do so, Aristotle devotes the first part of book 3 to a discussion of "diction," that is, the selection of the best word or phrase to bring clarity to one's speech.

DISSUASION (*apotropē, apotrepein*): Since deliberative rhetoric seeks to influence the course of public or political deliberations, the orator must master techniques of dissuasion, that is, the discouragement of a given course or policy. See also *exhortation*.

DOWNPLAYING (*meioun*): The twin of amplification, downplaying is useful in slighting those facts of a given case or circumstance that go against the argument one wishes to make. See 2.26.

E

EMULATION (*zēlos*): The passion that prompts us to better ourselves, when we see another, similar to us by nature, possessed of honorable goods we lack. Aristotle praises emulation as belonging to decent human beings. See 2.11.

ENTHYMEME (*enthumēma*): Despite the fact that the enthymeme is the "body" or core of the mode of persuasion in rhetoric, just what it is remains a matter of some scholarly controversy. Aristotle defines it as follows: "Establishing that, certain things being the case, something else results from those things because of them, either universally or for the most part, alongside those things by virtue of their being so—this in dialectic is called a syllogism, in rhetoric an enthymeme."

ENVY (*phthonos*): A perturbing pain caused by a peer's faring well. The envious resent that the other fellow has certain honored or honorable goods, not so that the envious person himself may gain something but because another has done so. A "base" passion according to Aristotle. See 2.10.

EPIDEICTIC RHETORIC: Related to the verb meaning "to show," "set forth," or "display," epideictic rhetoric offers speech of praise and blame: praise of what is noble, blame of what is base. See 1.9.

EPILOGUE (*epilogos*): The final part of a speech that (as its name suggests) follows, or comes at the end, of the *logos* proper.

EXAMPLE (*paradeigma*): One of the two "common modes of persuasion," together with enthymeme. An example in rhetoric reasons from particular instance to (similar) particular.

EXHORTATION (*protropē*): Deliberative rhetoric issues in exhortation when it urges the audience to adopt a certain course of action, as distinguished from dissuading it.

F

FRIENDLY AFFECTION, FRIENDSHIP (*philia, philein*): Here treated chiefly as a passion (2.4) as distinguished from (if of course closely related to) the phenomenon of friendship, which is the subject of two books of the *Nicomachean Ethics* (8–9). *Philia* in the *Rhetoric* is defined as wishing for someone the things one supposes to be good, for that person's sake and not one's own, and being apt to bring these goods about to the extent possible.

G

GENTLE, GENTLENESS (*praos, praotēs*): The opposite of the passion of anger, the "settling down and quieting of anger." See 2.3.

GRACIOUSNESS, GRATITUDE, FAVOR, DELIGHT (*charis, charizesthai*): A term difficult to capture in English, *charis* refers first to the disposition to benefit another without thought for oneself, a kind of graciousness or gracious generosity, but then also the feeling characteristic of one who has been so treated: gratitude. See 2.7.

H

HAPPINESS (*eudaimonia, eudaimonein, eudaimōn, eudaimonikos*): Since all deliberative rhetoric aims at encouraging courses of action that secure what is good or avoid what is bad, Aristotle takes up happiness, the greatest good, in the context of deliberative rhetoric. Here happiness is said to be one of four things or some combination thereof: a faring well accompanied by virtue, *or* self-sufficiency, *or* an abundance of property, *or* the most pleasant and secure life. See 1.5.

I

INDIGNATION (*nemesis, nemesan, nemesēton, nemesētikoi*): A passion belonging to a "fine" character, indignation or righteous resentment is directed at those who fair well undeservedly. As Aristotle notes, even the gods are said to feel this passion, and so to bring low those mortals who are riding high undeservedly. See 2.9.

INDUCTION (*epagōgē*): As the example is in rhetoric, so induction is in dialectic: the process of drawing a conclusion from some number of particular, comparable instances of something. Contrasted with deductive or syllogistic reasoning.

INSOLENCE (*hubris, hubrizein, hubristēs*): Doing and saying such things as are a source of shame to the person suffering them, not so that some other advantage may accrue to the insolent person or because something unjust happened to him, but so that he may gain pleasure thereby. One of the three causes of "slighting" and hence of anger.

J

JUDICIAL RHETORIC (*dikanikē, dikanikos*): That branch of rhetoric devoted to speechmaking in a courtroom or other judicial setting. Judicial rhetoric issues in speeches of either defense (*apologia*) or accusation (*katēgoria*). See 1.10–15.

JUROR (*dikastēs*): There is no distinction in Greek between "judge" and "juror" in a legal context: the assembled jurors acted as the judge, as in the trial of Socrates.

L

LAW, CUSTOM (*nomos*): The term suggests in general the opinion of the authoritative element of a community, as to the way things ought to be; this opinion may be written down, as a "law," or may take the form of an unwritten "custom." In the philosophy of Aristotle, the key alternative to *nomos* is what is according to nature and hence is not dependent on human opinion. See 1.13 for Aristotle's controversial account of "the law that accords with nature," or natural law.

LIBERALITY (*eleutheriotēs, eleutherios*): The virtue of soul characteristic of a free (*eleutherios*) human being. In Aristotle, the moral virtue of liberality has to do with money: being free of a slavish attachment to money in particular, the liberal person will spend the right amounts on the right things and for the right reasons.

LIKELIHOOD, LIKELY (*eikos*): A term frequently used in ordinary speech simply to express what may well (but need not) happen; "likelihoods" (*eikota*) are also one of the two sources of enthymemes, the other being "signs."

M

MAXIM (*gnomē*): A universal judgment concerning matters subject to human action. Aristotle discusses maxims, which are considered under the rubric of the enthymeme, in 2.21. One example of a maxim is the following: "Foolish is he who, having killed the father, leaves the sons untouched."

METAPHOR (*metaphora, metapherein*): A particularly effective device in rhetorical speeches, metaphors assert that one thing is another—Achilles is a lion (see 3.4, beg.)—and so help bring to the mind's eye of the audience a vivid image. See 3.2.

MODE OF PERSUASION (*pistis*): Sometimes translated as "proof," a *pistis* is that which brings the audience to the conviction that something is so. Aristotle contends that there are three such modes of persuasion in rhetoric that are "technical" in the sense that they are the product of the art: the speaker's (good) character; the passion of the audience; the characteristics of the speech itself. Non-technical modes of persuasion are all those givens of a case the rhetorician must simply make the best of, including contracts, witness testimony, and testimony gained by torture.

N

NECESSARY SIGN: One of the two sources of enthymemes, together with likelihoods, signs may be either "necessary" or non-necessary, for which Aristotle says there is no particular name. Necessary signs amount to "decisive evidence" that something is so. For example, "he has a fever" is a necessary sign that the fellow is sick, and so constitutes decisive evidence and makes for an irrefutable syllogism. See 1.2.

NOBLE, BEAUTIFUL (*kalos*): The Greek term requires at least three English words to capture its sense: that which is physically "beautiful"; that which is beautiful in a moral sense, i.e., "noble"; and that which is in general "fine." Aristotle's discussion of what is or is held to be noble is found chiefly in his discussion of epideictic rhetoric: 1.9.

O

OPINION, REPUTATION (*doxa, doxazein*): One's notion or judgment of something that does not, however, rise to the level of knowledge; hence the common rendering of the term is "opinion," which is often equivalent to mere conjecture. Aristotle's typical procedure in examining a controversial or puzzling point is to begin from what is "held to be" (*dokein*) the case, i.e., from opinion. The term may also refer to the opinion others have of someone, and hence refers to reputation. See also *accepted opinions* (*endoxa*).

P

PAIN (*lupē, lupein, lupēros*): Aristotle's account of pain (and pleasure) is central to his understanding of moral virtue, in the *Ethics*, and, in the *Rhetoric*, to that mode of persuasion that is the passions, the passions the skilled orator will induce in his audience.

PASSION, EMOTION, EXPERIENCE (*pathos, pathētikon*): Related to the verb meaning "to suffer" or "undergo," a passion is in the simplest sense what one experiences or undergoes, good or bad. In the *Rhetoric*, passions are defined as "all those things on account of which people, undergoing a change, differ in the judgments they make, things that pain and pleasure accompany." See 2.1–11.

PERSUASION (*peithein, peithesthai, pithanos, pithanoun*): The end or goal of the art of rhetoric as defined by Aristotle is to observe what can be persuasive in any given circumstance or case.

PITY (*eleos, eleein, eleeina, eleētikon*): Aristotle defines pity as a certain sort of pain at what is manifestly bad, as well as destructive or painful, and that befalls someone who does not deserve it. But—Aristotle adds—we can feel such pity only if we can imagine that we ourselves might one day suffer such a thing ourselves. Hence the gods cannot pity mortals, for the distance between them is too great. See 2.8.

PLEASURE (*hēdonē, hēdesthai, hēdus*): Together with pain, pleasure is a crucial determinant of human action and hence crucial to Aristotle's account of moral virtue and vice. The rhetorician's ability to foster pain and pleasure in an audience—in the form of anger, for example, or friendly affection—is key to persuasion.

POWER, CAPACITY, POTENTIALITY (*dunamis*): A broad term in the philosophy of Aristotle, *dunamis* can refer to power in a general sense, to political power in particular, and to the potential of something, a potential that may be realized or brought into a state of actualization (*energeia*). In 2.17, Aristotle discusses power, understood as political power and as a gift of fortune or luck.

PRAISE (*epainos, epainein, epaineton*): One of the two concerns of epideictic rhetoric, since the speeches that issue from it take the form of either praise (of what is noble) or blame (of what is shameful or ignoble).

PREFACE (*prooimion, prooimiazesthai*): One of the two absolutely necessary parts of a rhetorical speech, the preface or proem tells the audience of the purpose of the speech or the point it wishes to convince them of. For a detailed discussion of its proper functions, see 3.14.

PROOF (*pistis*): See *mode of persuasion*.

PRUDENCE (*phronēsis, phronein, phronimos*): Although in the *Nicomachean Ethics* (book 6) prudence is an intellectual virtue that is inextricably linked to moral virtue, here in the discussion of rhetoric, prudence or practical judgment does not appear to be of much importance; at one point Aristotle notes that the art of rhetoric, being bound up with *endoxa* or opinions, is not especially marked by prudence or truth. Perhaps most striking for its relative absence in the *Art of Rhetoric*.

R

REFLECT ON, OBSERVE, CONTEMPLATE, THEORIZE, CONTEMPLATION (*theōrein, theōria*): Meaning in the first place simply "to look on" or "observe something," the term came to mean "theorize" or "contemplate," an activity that looks to no other end outside itself and may be contrasted with action (*praxis*) or activity (*energeia*). Aristotle here defines the art of rhetoric as the "capacity to observe [*theōrēsai*] what admits of being persuasive in each case." In the *Ethics*, he distinguishes moral virtue from theoretical or contemplative virtue.

REFUTATION (*elenchos, elenktikos*): Enthymemes, or the rhetorical syllogism, can either establish a point of one's own or "refute" that of an opponent. In 2.25 Aristotle takes up two forms of refutation, "counter-syllogism" and "objection." The counter-syllogism will take advantage of the fact that the opponent's enthymeme is based on *endoxa,* and *endoxa* often contradict one another. It remains, then, to point out some such contradiction in the opponent's argument, and so to refute it.

REGIME (*politeia*): Traditionally translated as "constitution," a community's *politeia,* be it written or unwritten, answers the question of who rules, and on the basis of what understanding of merit or desert. Aristotle's principal discussion in the *Rhetoric* of the regime, or regime types, is found in his account of deliberative rhetoric: 1.8.

RHETORIC (*rhētorikē, rhetorikos*): An art that conveys to its possessor the capacity to observe or contemplate what admits of being persuasive in any given case. Rhetoric bears some connection to dialectic, in that both are in principle concerned with speeches as such and no particular subject matter, but then again rhetoric is necessarily also concerned with politics, that is, with matters pertaining to character ("ethics") and with judicial matters.

S

SCIENCE, KNOWLEDGE, UNDERSTANDING (*epistēmē, epistasthai, epistēton*): Knowledge in the strict sense, science. On a couple of occasions Aristotle does refer to rhetoric as a science, but for the most part he is content to call it either a *dunamis* (capacity or power) or an art.

SIGN (*sēmeion, sēmainein*): Together with likelihoods, signs are the principal source of enthymemes, be they "necessary signs" or "non-necessary signs," the former but not the latter making for an irrefutable argument.

SLANDER (*diabolē*): Meaning principally a false or malicious accusation and hence also slander, the term can suggest also a legal charge that is not necessarily false. Aristotle's principal account of slander and how either to promote or to thwart it is found at 3.15. See also *accusation.*

SLIGHTING (*oligōria, oligōrein*): In his account of anger (2.2), Aristotle stresses that kind of anger whose source is "slighting," that is, the actualization of one's opinion that someone or something is worth nothing. Aristotle indicates that there are three kinds of slighting: contempt, spitefulness, and insolence (or hubris).

SPECIFIC TOPICS: In contrast to the "common topics" that belong in principle to all the kinds of speechmaking, the specific topics are those derived from the subject matters peculiar to the three kinds of rhetoric, judicial, deliberative, and epideictic: what is just and unjust, good and bad, noble and base. See 1.4–15.

SPITEFULNESS: One of the three causes of "slighting" and hence of anger, spitefulness is the inclination to impede the wish of another not to gain something oneself but to insure that the other fellow does not. See 2.2.

SYLLOGISM: Aristotle defines the syllogism, or the principal means of deductive reasoning, as follows: "Establishing that, certain [premises] being the case, something else results from those [premises] because of them, either universally or for the most part, alongside those premises by virtue of their being so—this in dialectic is called a syllogism, in rhetoric an enthymeme" (1356b15–17).

T

TOPIC (*topos, topikos*): Meaning, literally, "place," *topos* came by extension to signify a metaphorical place to look for something, or where it is to be found: a heading or classification containing (in the case at hand) rhetorical arguments of the same kind. See also *common topics* and *specific topics*.

TORTURE (*basanos*): The evidence gained by torture (often of slaves) falls in the category of "non-technical means of persuasion" or proof, i.e., the givens of a judicial case that as such are not the product of the rhetorician's art. Aristotle is critical of such torture and of the reliability of the evidence gained thereby. See 1.15.

V

VICE (*kakia*): Literally, "badness," the root of the word being the opposite of "good" (*agathos*). Epideictic rhetoric, insofar as it seeks to blame, is concerned with vice.

VIRTUE (*aretē*): The excellence specific to something that both permits it to do its characteristic work well and the state of excellence thus implied. A virtuous or excellent eye will be both healthy and able to see well. Virtue is the concern of epideictic rhetoric, which seeks to praise the nobility that attends virtue especially.

W

WICKEDNESS (*mochthēria, mochthēros*): Although the term may mean simply a "bad state" or "defective condition" of a thing or person, it almost always amounts to a harsh moral condemnation.

WITNESS (*martus, marturein, marturia*): Evidence presented by a witness at trial is one of the kinds of "non-technical modes of persuasion" according to Aristotle. That is, the rhetorician will simply be presented with witness testimony, and although the art of rhetoric may be exercised in trying either to augment or to diminish its importance, the art does not by itself determine that testimony. See 1.15.

KEY GREEK TERMS

adikia: injustice
agathos: good
aisthēsis: perception
aitia: cause, responsibility
andreia: courage
apodeixis: demonstration
apologia: defense, defense speech
archē: beginning, principle; rule, empire
aretē: virtue
auxēsi: amplification

bouleuein: deliberation, to deliberate

charis: graciousness, gracious favor; gratitude

deilia: cowardice
dēmēgoria: demagoguery, public speaking
diabolē: slander; suspicion; legal charge
dialektikē, dialektikos: dialectic, dialectical
dikaiosunē: justice
dikanikē: judicial art; judicial rhetoric; judicial
dikastērion: courtroom
dikastēs: juror, judge
doxa: opinion, reputation
dunamis: power, capacity, potentiality

eikōn: simile, likeness
eikos: likelihood

ekklēsia: assembly
elenchus: refutation
eleos: pity
eleutheriotēs: liberality
endoxa: accepted opinions, generally held opinions
enthumēma: enthymeme
enthumēma phainomenon: apparent enthymeme
epagōgē: induction
epainos: praise
epēreasmos: spitefulness
epideiktikos: epideictic
epilogos: epilogue
epistēmē: science, knowledge
epithumia: desire
erōs: love, erotic love
ēthos, ēthikos: character
eudaimonia: happiness

gnomē: maxim

hēdonē: pleasure
hexis: characteristic, fixed state, established condition, [moral] habit
hoi polloi: the many
hubris: insolence
huperbolē: hyperbole, excess
hupokrisis: delivery, acting

kakia: vice, badness

kalos: noble, beautiful

kataphronēsis: contempt

katēgoria: accusation

koinos: community; common, general, shared

krisis: judgment

lexis: diction, phrasing

logos: speech, argument, reason, word, definition; fable

lupē: pain

martus: witness

meioun: downplaying

metron: meter, measure, verse

mochthēria: wickedness

nemesis: indignation

nomos: law, custom

ochlos: crowd, mob

oligōria: slighting

orgē: anger

paradeigma: example, paradigm

paralogos, paralogismos, paralogizesthai: fallacy, false reasoning

pathos: passion, emotion, experience

peithein: to persuade

phantasia: imagination

philia: friendship, friendly affection

phobos: fear

phronēsis: prudence

phthonos: envy

pisteis: modes of persuasion

pistis: mode of persuasion; credence, credible

politēs: citizen

praos, praotēs: gentle, gentleness

proairesis: choice

prooimion: preface

prosthesis: proposition

protasis: premise

protropē: exhortation

psogos: blame

rhetor: orator, rhetorician

rhētorikē: rhetoric

sēmeion: sign

sophia: wisdom

sōphrosunē: moderation

sullogismos: syllogism

sumbolē, sumbouleuein, sumboulos: advice

sumperasma: conclusion

technē: art, technical skill

tekmērion: decisive evidence

telos: end, goal

tharros: confidence

thumos: spiritedness, spirited anger

timōria: vengeance, penalty

topos: topic

zēlos: emulation

AUTHORS AND WORKS CITED

References are to the standard Bekker page numbers in the margin of the translation. Since the line numbers following the letters are keyed to the Greek text, they indicate only the approximate position in the translation.

For brevity's sake, 54a–99b = 1354–1399b; and 00a–20b = 1400a–1420b.

PROPER NAMES

References are to the standard Bekker page numbers in the margin of the translation. Since the line numbers following the letters are keyed to the Greek text, they indicate only the approximate position in the translation.

For brevity's sake, 54a–99b = 1354–1399b; and 00a–20b = 1400a–1420b.

GENERAL INDEX

References are to the standard Bekker page numbers in the margin of the translation. Since the line numbers following the letters are keyed to the Greek text, they indicate only the approximate position in the translation. **Boldface** numerals indicate books of the *Art of Rhetoric*. (+) indicates that a word appears more than once in the context. Occasionally the demands of translation require that a word be repeated in English that does not appear in the Greek or, therefore, in the index.

For brevity's sake, 54a–99b = 1354–1399b; and 00a–20b = 1400a–1420b.

accepted opinion, generally held opinion (*endoxa*): **1.** 55a17; 56b32; 57a10, 13; **2.** 02a34

accusation (*katēgoria, katēgorein, katēgoros*): **1.** 54a6; 58b11, 16; 59a18; 64a19; 68b1, 29; 74b26; 75a26; **2.** 77b17; 85b5; 91b33; 96a22, 23+; 98a10, 11; 99a12; 00a2, 9, 32; 00b9; 01b7; 02b26, 27; **3.** 14b3; 15a29; 16a29, 33, 34; 18a30

activity, actuality (*energeia, energein*): **1.** 61a24; **2.** 78b10; **3.** 10b36; 11b26, 28+; 12a3; 12b32

adjudicate, to speak in a courtroom (*dikazein, dikazesthai, dikologia, dikologein*): **1.** 54b1, 26, 29; 55a20; 58b15, 26, 31; 59a14; 68a21; 75b17; 77a25; 77b10; **2.** 00a19; **3.** 18a21

admiration, wonder (*thaumazein, thaumaston, thaumastēs*): **1.** 63a34; 71a22, 23, 31+, 33; 71b11, 28; 73a16; **2.** 79b25; 81a28, 29; 81b11, 14; 84a27+, 28, 29; 84b12, 37; 88b20; 91a6; **3.** 04b11, 12; 15b2, 15

adornment, ornamentation (*kosmos, kosmein*): **3.** 04a34; 04b7; 05a14; 08a14; 15b38

advantage (*sumpherein, sumpheros*): **1.** 54b4, 9; 58b22; 59a1, 6; 60a21, 31; 62a18+; 62b28, 31+; 63b5, 7, 24; 65b24, 25, 26; 66a7, 18; 69b8+, 10, 28, 29; 75b3, 13; 76a15; 76b29; **2.** 83a24; 89a34, 39; 89b1, 36+; 90a17; 90b1; 96a30; 99a30; **3.** 17a36

advice (*sumbolē, sumbouleuein, sumboulos*): **1.** 54b31; 58b8, 9, 14, 22, 23, 33, 34; 59a14, 28, 31, 34, 37; 59b19, 24, 33; 60a36, 38; 62a17; 65b23; 67b36, 37; 76a4; **2.** 77b21, 25, 30; 78a10, 14; 85a5; 91b25, 32; 96a7, 25, 30; 99b31; 00a36; 00b7; **3.** 14b4, 35; 15a1; 17b16; 18a30; 18b7

amplification (*auxēsis, auxanein, auxētikos*): **1.** 59b26; 68a10, 22, 23, 27; 76a34; 76b7, 34; 77b11; **2.** 82b19; 91b32; 92a4; 93a15; 01b5, 6; 03a17+; **3.** 04b16; 08a3; 11b12; 13b34; 14a5; 14b10; 15b37; 17b32; 19b12, 20, 22, 23

02a18; **3.** 16b19; 17a28, 34; 17b17, 34;
19a26

chance, luck (*tuchē, tuchanein*): **1.** 59a35;
60b29; 61b29, 31, 39+; 62a6; 66a31;
67b6, 24; 68a15; 68b34, 37; 69a6,
32, 35; 69b4; 72b17; **2.** 85b2; 86a6, 9;
88b28, 32; 89a1; 90b14; 91b4

character (*ēthos, ēthikos*): **1.** 56a2, 5, 13,
23, 26; 58a19; 59b10; 66a10, 12+,
15, 26; 69a18, 29; 72b8; 76a25, 28;
2. 84a7; 86a25; 86b11, 13, 33; 88b31;
89a3, 35; 89b12, 14; 90a17, 18, 26, 29;
90b15, 16, 29, 32; 91a14, 21+; 91b2, 5,
6, 21, 22, 27; 95a21, 25; 95b13; 96b33;
3. 08a11, 25, 31; 13b10, 31; 14a21; 17a15,
17+, 21; 18a15, 16, 18, 38, 39; 18b24

characteristic, fixed state, established
condition (*hexis*): **1.** 54a7; 62b13;
67b32; 69a8, 17, 20; 71a27; **2.** 86a25;
87b26; 88b31, 34; 96b34; **3.** 08a27+

choice (*proairesis, proaireisthai, proaireton*): **1.** 55b18+; 63a19, 30, 35; 66a15;
67b22+; 68b11, 12, 13; 72b36; 73b36,
37; 74a11, 13; 74b14; **2.** 82a19, 35;
82b1; 88b35; 95a27; 95b14, 16; 00b2;
3. 07a32; 17a17+, 24; 18a16

citizen (*politēs*): **1.** 60a16; 62b33; 71a11;
2. 84a11; 98b13; 99b2; **3.** 03b35; 04b9;
10a13

city (*polis*): **1.** 54a19; 59b24, 26, 34, 37;
60a12, 20; 60b31, 35; **2.** 88b8; **3.** 11b10

clarity (*saphēs, saphēnizein*): **3.** 04b2, 6,
36; 05a8; 06a35; 14a23

class, genus (*genos*): **1.** 55b8, 34; 57a26;
58a33; 58b7; 60b38; 63a29; **2.** 77b20;
78b35; 82a6; 86a25; 87a20; 87b25;
90b22, 25, 28; 91b23; 92a33; 92b2;
93a24; **3.** 07b1, 7; 08a27; 10b15; 13b3;
14a29; 15b29

comedy (*kōmōdia, kōmōdopoios*):
2. 84b10; **3.** 06b7; 08a14; 15a21

community, common, general, shared
(*koinos, koinōnia, koinōnein, koinōnos,
koinōnikos*): **1.** 54b29; 55a27; 58a12,

28, 32; 61a1, 9; 62b4; 68b7, 8; 72a16;
73b4, 6, 7, 8, 19+, 20, 34; 75a28, 32;
76b25; **2.** 91b28; 92a2, 4; 93a22, 23;
95a11, 12; 95b30; 96b11, 12; 99b12;
01a20, 21; **3.** 10b30; 14a28; 15a25

compacts (*sunthēkē*): **1.** 60a15; 73b8;
75a24; 76a33+; 76b6+; **3.** 11b16

comparison (*parabolē, paraballein*):
1. 68a25; **2.** 93a29; 93b3; 94a5;
3. 13b14; 19b35; 20a4

compulsion, force (*bia, biaios*): **1.** 61b9,
10; 68b35, 37; 69a6; 69b5; 70a9, 13;
77b5; **2.** 84a21

conclusion (*sumperasma*): **2.** 94a27;
94b29; 01a3; **3.** 19a8, 25, 36; 19b1

confidence (*tharros, tharrein, tharraleos*):
2. 81b33; 83a14, 15, 16, 19, 25, 31; 83b7;
85b30; 89a27, 29; 90a31

contempt (*kataphronēsis, kataphronein,
kataphronētikon*): **1.** 71a15; **2.** 78b14,
15, 16; 79a33; 79b6, 8, 31, 33; 80a20,
27; 81b20; 84a29; 84b23; 88b22+, 23,
25; 90b19

courage (*andreia, andreios*): **1.** 61a4;
62b12, 33; 64b20, 35, 36, 37; 66b1,
5, 11, 29, 30; 67a21; 67b2; **2.** 81a21;
85b30; 87a11, 29; 88b16; 89a26; 90b3,
4, 5; 00a28; **3.** 16b23; 18a37

courtroom (*dikastērion*): **1.** 75a13; 76a9;
3. 10a17; 16a32

cowardice, coward (*deilia, deilos*):
1. 62b32; 68b18; **2.** 82b5; 85b27;
89b29; 90b6

crowd, mob (*ochlos, sundromē*): **2.** 95b28;
3. 11a29; 14a9

danger, risk (*kindunos, kinduneuein,
sunkindineuein*): **1.** 66b12; 67b4;
68b18, 19; 71b11; 75b28; 76a12; 77a14;
2. 82a32; 82b5; 83a30; 85a24, 25;
95a13; **3.** 11b5, 9

death (*thanatos, thanousthai, apoth-
nēskein*): **1.** 59a4, 5; **2.** 80b14; 82a26;
86a7, 20; 97a22; 97b9+, 24; 98b28

superiority, excess (*huperechein*):
1. 61b18; 62b1; 63b8, 11, 20, 21, 33, 34;
64a27; 64b32; 65a11; 71b1; 2. 78b28,
29; 79a1; 79b1; 83a35; 88a4, 12
syllogism (*sullogismos, sullogizesthai*):
1. 55a8+, 14, 30, 34; 55b6, 16, 17;
56a22; 56b1+, 2, 4, 8, 34; 57a8, 9,
16, 17, 23, 28; 57b24; 58a4, 11, 15,
19; 59a9, 10; 62b30; 68b2; 71b9;
2. 94a26, 28; 95b22, 23; 96a4; 96b1,
26; 98a27; 00b29, 34, 37; 01a2, 9;
02a4, 33; 02b18; 03a23, 33; 3. 10a21;
18a11; 18b3; 19a23

thought, understanding (*dianoia*):
1. 66b20; 74b12; 77b6; 2. 78b8;
03a36; 3. 04a19; 09b8; 10b26, 27;
15a13; 17a23
time (*chronos, chronizein*): 1. 54b2;
58b13; 63a24; 64b32; 65a20; 68a13;
71a29, 31; 2. 79a25; 80b5, 6; 82a7;
88a6; 90b27; 97b27; 00a16; 02b37
topic (*topos, topikos*): 1. 55a28; 56b12;
58a12, 14, 29, 30, 32; 60a8, 11; 61a33;
62a13; 65a20; 72a32; 73a32; 76a32;
2. 80b31; 88a6; 95b21; 96b4, 21, 22,
30+; 97a2, 3, 7; 98a28; 99a6, 15, 19,
32; 00a4; 00b15, 37; 01a33; 02a33, 35;
03a18, 19, 24, 32; 3. 03b15; 16a6, 13;
19a24; 19b18, 24, 27
torture (*basanos*): 1. 55b37; 75a25;
76b31+
tragedy (*tragōdia, tragikē, tragikos*):
3. 03b22, 24; 04a29; 06b8, 16;
15a18
trial, penalty (*dikē*): 1. 58b10, 33; 59a29;
72a7+, 33; 73a8; 74b20, 32, 33;
2. 77b22, 26, 31; 80a14; 3. 14a10;
18b7
truth (*alētheia, alētheuein, alēthēs,
alēthinos*): 1. 54b10; 55a14, 16, 17, 18,
21, 37; 56a19; 59b5, 7; 64b9; 65b1, 6,
15; 71a10, 14; 74b1; 75b3, 6; 77a2, 4,
5; 2. 81b21; 84a33; 84b24, 26; 87a26;

90a33; 95a30; 98a33; 02a26; 02b23; 3.
08a21; 12a21; 19b2, 14
tyranny (*turannis, turannein*): 1. 57b31,
33, 36; 66a2, 6; 72b2

unjust (*adikos*): 1. 54a29; 55b3, 7; 58b25,
26, 36; 59a21; 66b3; 68b16, 22; 69a16,
27; 73b3, 8, 28; 74a10, 18; 76a15;
2. 81a25; 82a23, 35; 86b14; 87b8;
96a30; 96b33; 99a22, 24; 02a2;
03a22; 3. 16a8; 16b7; 17a9, 11
urbane (*asteios*): 3. 10b7, 16; 11b21; 12a18,
22; 12b2, 3, 27, 28, 30; 13a18
utility (*chrēsimos*): 1. 55a20; 55b5; 60a17;
61a16; 65b8; 66b4

vengeance, penalty (*timōria, timōrein,
timōrētikos*): 1. 63a26; 67a20; 68b21;
69b12, 13; 70b13, 29, 31; 72b1, 4, 27;
74b31; 2. 78a31; 78b2+; 80b7, 16, 23;
86b29; 01a10, 38
vice (*kakia*): 1. 64a32, 34; 66a23; 66b22;
68b14; 74a22; 2. 83b19; 84a8, 15;
88b34; 3. 17a5
virtue (*aretē*): 1. 55b5; 56a23; 60b14,
21, 23, 36; 61a3, 5, 7; 61b3, 18, 21, 29,
33; 62a12; 62b2, 13, 15, 18; 64a31,
34; 66a23, 28, 35+, 36; 66b1, 3+,
20, 22; 67b26, 27; 68b25; 74a21;
77a18; 2. 78a9, 17; 78b35; 81a27;
82a35; 87a11; 88b11, 34; 89a36; 90a18;
90b22; 3. 04b2, 37; 14a21, 22; 14b34;
17a3
voluntary (*hekōn, hekousios*): 1. 68b6, 9,
11; 69b21+; 73b28, 29, 32, 35; 74a28;
76b12; 77b4; 2. 80a9; 84a20; 00b1

war (*polemos, polemein, polemikos, po-
lemios*): 1. 59b21, 33, 36, 37, 39; 60a1,
4, 36; 61b12; 66b6; 72b10; 74a6;
2. 79a19, 20; 82b14; 83b2; 96a8, 11
wealth, money (*ploutos, ploutein, plou-
sios*): 1. 55b6; 59b29; 60b20, 26;
61a12, 23, 25, 31; 62b18; 65b10, 15;